LIBRARY OF NEW TESTAMENT STUDIES

672

Formerly the Journal for the Study of the New Testament Supplement series

Editor
Chris Keith

Editorial Board
Dale C. Allison, Lynn H. Cohick, R. Alan Culpepper, Craig A. Evans, Jennifer Eyl, Robert Fowler, Simon J. Gathercole, Juan Hernández Jr., John S. Kloppenborg, Michael Labahn, Matthew V. Novenson, Love L. Sechrest, Robert Wall, Catrin H. Williams, Brittany E. Wilson

Luke in His Own Words

A Study of the Language of Luke–Acts in Greek

Jenny Read-Heimerdinger

LONDON • NEW YORK • OXFORD • NEW DELHI • SYDNEY

T&T CLARK
Bloomsbury Publishing Plc
50 Bedford Square, London, WC1B 3DP, UK
1385 Broadway, New York, NY 10018, USA
29 Earlsfort Terrace, Dublin 2, Ireland

BLOOMSBURY, T&T CLARK and the T&T Clark logo are trademarks of
Bloomsbury Publishing Plc

First published in Great Britain 2022
Paperback edition published 2024

Copyright © Jenny Read-Heimerdinger, 2022

Jenny Read-Heimerdinger has asserted her right under the Copyright, Designs and
Patents Act, 1988, to be identified as Author of this work.

For legal purposes the Acknowledgements on p. vii constitute an extension
of this copyright page.

All rights reserved. No part of this publication may be reproduced or transmitted
in any form or by any means, electronic or mechanical, including photocopying,
recording, or any information storage or retrieval system, without prior permission
in writing from the publishers.

Bloomsbury Publishing Plc does not have any control over, or responsibility for,
any third-party websites referred to or in this book. All internet addresses given in
this book were correct at the time of going to press. The author and publisher regret
any inconvenience caused if addresses have changed or sites have ceased to exist,
but can accept no responsibility for any such changes.

A catalogue record for this book is available from the British Library.

Library of Congress Cataloging-in-Publication Data

Names: Read-Heimerdinger, Jenny, author.
Title: Luke in his own words : a study of the language of Luke–Acts in Greek / by Jenny
Read-Heimerdinger.
Description: London ; New York : T&T Clark, 2022. | Series: The library of New Testament
studies, 2513-8790 ; 672 | Includes bibliographical references and index. |
Summary: "An analysis of linguistic features of Luke's writing, applying tools of discourse
analysis and taking account of variant readings among early manuscripts"–
Provided by publisher.
Identifiers: LCCN 2021060454 (print) | LCCN 2021060455 (ebook) |
ISBN 9780567692986 (hb) | ISBN 9780567706683 (paperback) |
ISBN 9780567692993 (epdf) | ISBN 9780567692979 (epub)
Subjects: LCSH: Bible. Luke–Manuscripts. | Bible. Acts–Manuscripts. | Manuscripts, Greek.
| Bible. Luke–Language, style. | Bible. Acts–Language, style. Classification: LCC BS2589.
A22 R43 2022 (print) | LCC BS2589.A22 (ebook) | DDC 226.4—dc23/eng/20220201
LC record available at https://lccn.loc.gov/2021060454
LC ebook record available at https://lccn.loc.gov/2021060455

ISBN: HB: 978-0-5676-9298-6
PB: 978-0-5677-0668-3
ePDF: 978-0-5676-9299-3
ePUB: 978-0-5676-9297-9

Series: Library of New Testament Studies, volume 672
ISSN 2513-8790

Typeset by RefineCatch Limited, Bungay, Suffolk

To find out more about our authors and books visit www.bloomsbury.com
and sign up for our newsletters.

Contents

Preface		vi
Acknowledgements		vii
Abbreviations		viii
1	Introduction	1
2	The article before proper names	21
3	Sentence connectives	49
4	Word order	93
5	Expressions for the Holy Spirit	135
6	The tracking of participants	159
7	Parallel terms	177
8	The structure of Luke's books	207
9	Conclusion	231
Bibliography		237
Index of scriptural references		245

Preface

This book gathers together some of the linguistic studies that I have published over the past decades, investigating the Greek of Luke's work that has been handed down in two volumes, the first known as a Gospel and the second as the Acts of the Apostles. Most of the studies presented here originally concentrated on the book of Acts. To some degree, they have now been developed to incorporate further consideration of the Gospel. They have also been re-formatted so as to give a uniform presentation, and much of the introductory material that was presented at the start of each of the original publications has been gathered together in Chapter 1 to avoid repetition.

In bringing the previously published studies into one volume, my aim is to allow interaction between them and to use them to identify features of Luke's writing that characterize him as a writer and as a New Testament author. While any writing necessarily involves content, the concern here is less on what Luke wrote as how he wrote it. Thus, his work is approached with a curiosity to find out features of his Greek, to see how he intervened as a narrator, to observe how he expressed his relationship with his characters and his addressee. Of course, language is a vehicle to communicate a message, but as much as possible, I have sought to allow the words and their forms to speak for themselves, without calling on my presuppositions about their meaning. This is the thought behind the title, *Luke in His Own Words*. Exegetical discussion is nonetheless brought into play, drawing notably on research carried out in collaboration with Josep Rius-Camps and it may be helpful to look at relevant passages of our publications for understanding some of the linguistic discussion, especially for interpretation that depends on unfamiliar manuscripts. Reference to our exegetical work is therefore given at the start of each chapter.

Beyond the technical matters, my interest in Luke's language is that it leads to getting to know Luke himself, as a narrator and as an investigator of the events and characters he writes about. At the centre of his work is the person he addresses his writing to, Theophilus. I have also written about these things and hope to bring together studies that I have made of them in a second volume, entitled *Being Theophilus*.

In the present volume, along the way I raise questions about the text that is used to read Luke's work. It is a well-known fact that the text of his writings has been transmitted in two main forms, and that there are witnesses to both, not only among the earliest manuscripts in Greek but also in the early versions and the writings of the Church Fathers. This knowledge, however, is frequently accompanied by generalized notions, which obscure the true picture of the manuscript tradition of Luke–Acts. By presenting factual information, the studies of this volume seek to counter some of the popular ideas about the state of Luke's work and the prejudices concerning the relative value of the manuscripts, and to offer ways of opening up new avenues of research – or at the very least, some alleyways to explore.

Jenny Read-Heimerdinger
4 October 2021

Acknowledgements

Work that has been previously published elsewhere is reproduced in the current volume, after some revision and updating. The material is included here with kind permission from the original publisher. Introductory material that is repeated in more than one original publication has been gathered in Chapter 1, Introduction.

The Bezan Text of Acts: A Contribution of Discourse Analysis to Textual Criticism. JSNTSup. 236. Sheffield: Sheffield Academic Press, 2002: for **Chapters 1, 3, 4, 5, 7.I**

'The Function of the Article with Proper Names: The New Testament Book of Acts as a Case Study'. In *The Article in Post-Classical Greek*, edited by D. King, 153–85. Dallas: SIL International: for **Chapter 2**

'The Tracking of Participants with the Third Person Pronoun: A Study of the Text of Acts'. *Revista Catalana de Teologia* 31 (2006): 439–55: for **Chapter 6**

'Luke's Use of ὡς and ὡσεί: Comparison and Correspondence as a Means to Convey his Message'. In *Grammatica Intellectio Scripturae: Saggi filologici di Greco biblioc in onore di padre Lino Cignelli, OFM*, edited by R. Pierri, 251–74. Studium Biblicum Franciscanum, Analecta 68. Jerusalem: Franciscan Printing Press, 2006: for **Chapter 7.III**

'Discourse Analysis of the Book of Acts'. In *Discourse Analysis of the New Testament Writings*, edited by Todd A. Scacewater, 159–92. Dallas: Fontes Press, 2020: for **Chapter 1.III; Chapter 8.1-V**

The task of bringing these articles together and re-fashioning them into a cohesive volume has been made all the lighter and more enjoyable thanks to the encouragement of students and colleagues, especially those of the community of St Pere de Reixac in Catalunya, Spain, and the post-doctoral study group (John's Gospel) at the Institut Catholique in Toulouse, France.

Abbreviations

AJP	*American Journal of Philology*
ANRW	*Aufstieg und Niedergang der römischen Welt*
B-A-G	Bauer, W. *A Greek-English Lexicon of the New Testament and Other Early Christian Literature*, translated and edited by W. F. Arndt and F. W. Gingrich. Chicago: Chicago University Press, 1957.
Bib.	*Biblica*
CP	*Classical Philology*
CUP	*Cambridge University Press*
ETR	*Etudes théologiques et religieuses*
FilNeo	*Filologia Neotestamentaria*
JBL	*Journal of Biblical Literature*
JSNTSup	*Journal for the Study of the New Testament Supplement Series*
JSNT	*Journal for the Study of the New Testament*
JSOT	*Journal for the Study of the Old Testament*
JTS	*Journal of Theological Studies*
LNTS	Library of New Testament Studies
NovT	*Novum Testamentum*
NTS	*New Testament Studies*
SAP	Sheffield Academic Press
WUNT	Wissenschaftliche Untersuchungen zum Neuen Testament

Manuscripts and editions

MS(S)	manuscript(s)
א01	Codex Sinaiticus
B03	Codex Vaticanus
D05	Codex Bezae
MT	Massoretic text
NT	New Testament
N-A[28]	Aland, B., K. Aland, J. Karavidopoulos, C. M. Martini and B. M. Metzger (eds). 28th edn. *Novum Testamentum Graece*. Stuttgart: Deutsche Bibelgesellschaft, 2013
UBS[5]	Aland, B., K. Aland, J. Karavidopoulos, C. M. Martini and B. M. Metzger (eds). *The Greek New Testament*, 5th edn. Stuttgart: Deutsche Bibelgesellschaft/United Bible Societies, 2014.
LXX	Septuagint: Rahlfs, A. (ed.). *Septuaginta*. 8th edn. 2 vols. Stuttgart: Württembergische Bibelanstalt, 1965.

Grammatical and text-critical terms

acc.	accusative
dat.	dative
gen.	genitive
inf.	infinitive
lac.	*lacuna*
om.	omit
part.	participle
prep.	preposition
pro.	pronoun
vb	finite verb
vl.	variant reading (*varia lectio*; plural *vll.*)

1

Introduction

I. Background to the studies

Before setting out the technical aspects of the studies in this book, it may be helpful for readers to know how the research that led up to them came about.

My initiation into New Testament Greek happened in much the same way as for most students of the New Testament wanting to read its text in the original. I followed a crash course using a basic manual – only, while mastering the basics, I found out to my consternation that we do not have 'the original'. Being reassured, however, that we do have a critical edition[1] which reconstitutes the original with an acceptable degree of reliability, the next step was to undertake a course in textual criticism to learn how to use it. My teacher was Christian-Bernard Amphoux, at the Facultés Catholiques in Lyons, France. There was nothing basic about his course, though plenty of 'crashing' as seminar after seminar brought new discoveries and realizations that challenged my presuppositions about the New Testament writings and the certainty of their attestation. Amphoux, like many scholars in France and more generally beyond the Anglo-Germanic sphere, was – and still is – convinced that there are authentic readings in the witnesses to the NT text that have been traditionally disregarded by the editors of the Greek NT since at least the end of the nineteenth century, and he encouraged us as students to explore some disputed passages. Although Amphoux's interest lies principally in the variety of the attestation to the rejected variants,[2] in working on an assignment to investigate the 'long' text of Acts 8.37–39 I found other evidence that suggested his openness was justified, namely the Jewish nature of the longer material.[3]

---

[1] Barbara and Kurt Aland et al., eds., *Novum Testamentum Graece*, 28th edn (N-A²⁸; Deutsche Bibelgesellschaft, 2013). The same text, with a different apparatus that aims to serve translators primarily, is reproduced in *The Greek New Testament*, 5th edn. (UBS⁵; Deutsche Bibelgesellschaft/ United Bible Societies, 2014).
[2] See e.g. Christian-Bernard Amphoux, 'Le dernier repas de Jésus. Lc 22, 15–20 et par', *ETR* 56 (1981): 449–54; 'Les manuscrits du Nouveau Testament: du Livre à la Parole, *ETR* 67 (1992): 345–57; 'L'édition savante ancienne des Evangiles', *Résurrection. Revue de doctrine et d'actualité chrétiennes*, 40 (1992): 13–21.
[3] Originally published in French (Jenny (Read-)Heimerdinger, 'La foi de l'eunuque éthiopien: le problème textuel d'Actes 8/37', *ETR* 63 (1988): 521–8), my research was later translated into English: Jenny Read-Heimerdinger, 'Acts 8:37: A Textual and Exegetical Study', *The Bulletin of the Institute for Reformation Biblical Studies* 2 (1991): 8–13.

The principal manuscript (MS) in Greek that differs extensively from the text adopted for the current edition is Codex Bezae (D05); in fact, it is the only MS in Greek of any length that has a consistently variant text (reason no. 1 for doubting its authenticity – why would its text not have been better preserved if it represented anything like the original? hypothesis to follow, Chapter 9). To be precise, in its present state D05 only has the four Gospels (in the order Matthew, John, Luke and Mark) and Acts; any other books that it once contained were bound in 66 pages between Mark and Acts.[4] It is known as the chief representative of the 'Western' text (reason no. 2 for doubting its authenticity – surely it is safer to trust the majority of scholars who believe that it is a secondary text,[5] preferring the more familiar 'Alexandrian' text? see §II.1 below on this assumption). Despite its missing pages (including those with Acts 8.37–39), the fact that D05 was the only Greek MS of any length that was different from the critical edition spurred me on to investigating it in detail. I selected the book of Acts as a sample, mainly because it is the form of that book that is reputed to be the most odd in D05 (reason no. 3 for doubting its authenticity – odd must mean a later scribe had intervened, mustn't it? 'oddness' is what this book challenges) and set about noting every variant compared with the main representative of the Alexandrian text, Codex Vaticanus, B03.

This was in the days when we worked with paper and coloured pencils, and the results are much easier to see than on a computer screen, where it is doubtful that I would have noticed what my annotations were showing. Having a visual representation of the two MSS, with copies of their pages spread across the floor, I could see that the majority of differences affected apparently insignificant features of language: the choice of conjunctions, the presence of the article, word order, synonyms, the choice or use of prepositions, use of pronouns. An overview of quantity and types of variation is set out below (§IV). These were all matters that the basic NT Greek textbook had told me were a matter of 'style', with little if any bearing on meaning. Consequently, textual critics tend to attribute them to scribal habit, local custom or, notably in the case of D05, scribal fantasy or carelessness. In that case, except for the material in one MS that was absent from the other, there was little of interest in the variation between them.

Following on from my learning of the basics of NT Greek and how to use a critical edition, now came a third step. Since the late 1960s, Bible translators had been applying the tools of a developing linguistic approach, 'discourse analysis', to understanding how language operates not just on the level of the sentence within a text but also on the level of the text beyond the sentence (see §III.2 below). While traditional manuals of NT Greek explain components of the language work at sentence-level, translators were exploring how the authors of the NT writings communicated their message by means of features of Greek that operated between sentences, holding the writing together and expressing the author's purpose in a way that a native speaker would use and respond

---

[4] For a thorough examination of the external features of Codex Bezae, see David C. Parker, *Codex Bezae: An Early Christian Manuscript* (Cambridge: CUP, 1994).

[5] David Parker makes the laconic comment: 'There are, and long have been, scholars who maintain that Codex Bezae provides the authentic text. They have always been in a minority', 'Codex Bezae', in *Cambridge University Library. The Great Collections*, ed. Peter Fox (Cambridge: CUP, 1998), 42.

to instinctively. These features were not matters of style but involved principles specific to Greek that needed to be recognized for effective translation into other languages, which in turn operate with their own distinctive principles. A pioneer who applied an approach of discourse analysis to the Greek NT text is Stephen Levinsohn, working with Wycliffe Bible Translators.[6] At the same time that I was busy identifying the variants of Acts, I had the good fortune to be taught by him as part of a course on biblical interpretation.

And so it was that I discovered that the list of linguistic items that I had classified as characteristically affected by variation (§III.1 below) were precisely features that were of interest to linguists working with discourse analysis. In other words, what looked at first sight like inconsequential differences between the language of B03 and D05 were, on the contrary, highly likely to be significant. Rather than simply arising through scribal habit or whim or carelessness, they potentially reflected different ways of communicating the story of Acts, different perspectives on the events, different relationships with the characters and with the addressee. This is what I set out to investigate. In so doing, I found that the language of the variant readings of D05 most often corresponds to the language of the text that is common to B03 and D05; in other words, the linguistic patterns in D05 are the same as those found in passages of Acts without variants – they are equally 'Lukan'. Rather than reflecting the language of a later scribe or a succession of them, they reflected a different perspective on the story of Acts, using consistent language throughout. The chapters of this book present the results of some of that research on Acts, incorporating further study of Luke's language in his Gospel.

At the same time as analysing the language, I was examining the content of material in D05 that is missing from B03, and finding increasing evidence of reference to Jewish tradition, sometimes scriptural but more frequently oral, confirming my initial findings of Jewish material in Acts 8.37–39 that is missing from the familiar Greek text. The two strands, linguistic and exegetical, were presented together in a PhD thesis in 1994; the linguistic component was later published,[7] leaving the analysis of Jewish material to be more fully developed.

At that point, I thought I was the only person alive who, because of the particular combination in Codex Bezae of typically Lukan language with references to Jewish tradition, believed that its text was closer to what Luke wrote than the more familiar text of the critical edition.[8] Then came a chance encounter. With their shared interest in Codex Bezae, in 1994 Christian Amphoux and David Parker jointly organized a

---

[6] He has published a manual corresponding to an expanded version of the MA course he gave at London Bible College, 1983–85, see Stephen H. Levinsohn, *Discourse Features of New Testament Greek: A Coursebook on the Information Structure of New Testament Greek*, 2nd edn (1992; Dallas: Summer Institute of Linguistics, 2000).

[7] Jenny Read-Heimerdinger, *The Bezan Text of Acts: A Contribution of Discourse Analysis to Textual Criticism*, JSNTSup 236 (Sheffield Academic Press, 2002).

[8] There had been some noteworthy predecessors earlier in the twentieth century, such as A. C. Clark in 1918 and B. H. Streeter in 1933. For discussion of the history of attitudes to the 'Western' text in general, see William A. Strange, *The Problem of the Text of Acts* (SNTS Monograph Series 71; Cambridge: CUP, 1992), 1–34.

colloquium in France to celebrate the MS – the one being what the meeting's president referred to as an 'amant' and the other an 'ami' of Codex Bezae.[9] Another 'amant' was a participant from Catalunya in northern Spain, Josep Rius-Camps. Having worked independently on the Bezan text of Luke's Gospel and Acts for many years he, too, thought he was the only person alive who believed that Codex Bezae was closer to what Luke wrote than the usual text of both books. He, however, had come to the conclusion from another direction to me, for the ground for his judgement was the critical attitude of the Bezan narrator towards the Christian protagonists, including (nay, principally) Peter and Paul. Less than a hostile opponent but more of a sympathetic observer, the Luke of this text draws Theophilus' attention to the difficulties that the apostles experienced as they struggled to understand the radical nature of Jesus' teaching in the light of their Jewish upbringing and expectations.

Thus, between us we had three reasons for believing that the traditionally low opinion of the Bezan text of Acts was in need of rethinking: the language, the references to Jewish tradition and the critical portrayal of the apostles. In due course, we produced an exegetical commentary comparing the message communicated by Acts in D05 with that derived from the Alexandrian text.[10] Where there are references in the chapters that follow here to what Codex Bezae says in contrast to the more familiar text, the reasoning behind the comments can be consulted in the respective volumes of that commentary. As for the Gospel, we worked through features of its text in D05 in producing an edition of it together with Acts, accompanied by exegetical notes and a parallel English translation.[11]

II. The text of Luke and Acts

II.1 Attestation

For all that the matter of textual variants is one that both NT linguists and exegetes tend to shy away from, there is an inherent and inevitable connection between the disciplines of linguistics and textual criticism: for any analysis of the language of a book, it is clearly essential to know what the text actually says. The difficulty regarding the text of Luke's Gospel, and even more so of the book of Acts, is that there is a high degree of uncertainty as to what the author wrote. For many practical purposes, the edition of the Greek New Testament generally serves well enough as a reference tool, based as it is on a consideration of a range of early witnesses by an international committee of expert textual critics. The published text represents what, in their

---

[9] The proceedings of the colloquium were edited by David C. Parker and Christian-Bernard Amphoux in *Codex Bezae: Studies from the Lunel Colloquium, June 1994* (Leiden: Brill, 1996).

[10] Josep Rius-Camps and Jenny Read-Heimerdinger, *The Message of Acts in Codex Bezae: A Comparison with the Alexandrian Tradition*, 4 vols (JSNTSup 257/LNTS 302, 365, 415; London: T&T Clark, 2004–09).

[11] Jenny Read-Heimerdinger and Josep Rius-Camps, *Luke's Demonstration to Theophilus: The Gospel and Acts of the Apostles according to Codex Bezae* (English expanded edn. London: Bloomsbury, 2013).

Introduction 5

judgement, is at least the earliest retrievable form of the text if not the original form, with a small selection of variant readings noted in the critical apparatus.[12]

While Luke probably wrote his two volumes some time in the last quarter of the first century CE,[13] for the next two centuries the evidence for them in Greek is limited to Patristic citations and fragmentary copies on fragile papyrus. The first complete copies, necessary for an extended study of the text, are uncials dating from the middle of the fourth century onwards. Among those, the one most represented in the successive editions of the Greek New Testament in use since the early twentieth century is Codex Vaticanus, B03.[14] Dating from *c.* 350 CE, its text is attested by earlier papyri and authors from the late second century onwards; it is also widely supported by another uncial from the same time, Codex Sinaiticus, ℵ01. Both are taken as representatives of the Alexandrian tradition, accepted by the majority of New Testament textual critics as the 'best' MSS available. The MS with the text of Acts that is most different from that of B03 is a bilingual Greek-Latin MS, Codex Bezae, D05,[15] dated to around 400 CE.[16] Its text of Luke's Gospel has also some striking variant readings, though the extent of its differences with the Alexandrian text is not usually recognized as widely as it is for Acts (see §IV below).

A chief reason for textual critics to reject D05 as a reliable witness to the original text of Luke's writings is its frequent disagreement with the preferred text. Notwithstanding the circularity of this argument, it is a prized one because other factors seem to confirm it. Thus, there is little extant evidence of support for D05 in Greek. An additional factor is that many of its variant readings are difficult to make sense of, or appear as simply the colourful modifications of a fanciful scribe.[17] Its text is by and large regarded as the result of emendation carried out by a succession of

---

[12] For a fuller account of the extent and complexity of the variation, the *editio critica maior* may be consulted. For Luke's Gospel, see *The Gospel According to St. Luke*. 2 parts, ed. The American and British Committees of the International Greek New Testament Project (Oxford: Clarendon Press, 1984, 1987). For Acts, see *Novum Testamentum Graecum: Editio Critica Maior*, volume 3: *Die Apostelgeschichte/The Acts of the Apostles*; 3 parts, ed. Holger Strutwolf, Georg Gäbel, Annette Hüffmeier, Gerd Mink, and Klaus Wachtel (Stuttgart: Deutsche Bibelgesellschaft, 2017).

[13] Discussion about the date of Acts in particular has been recently reinstated by the publication by Karl Leslie Armstrong, *Dating Acts in its Jewish and Greco-Roman Contexts* (LNTS 637; London: T&T Clark, 2021). Although he advocates a date before the Jewish attack on Jerusalem, the dating of Luke's writing has little bearing on the linguistic analysis of the studies presented here.

[14] The MS can be consulted online at http://digi.vatlib.it/view/MSS_Vat.gr.1209?sid=1f2e1a937299b864df0f51ecb184c2ac.

[15] The text of Acts in D05 is unfortunately not complete, with lacunae as follows: 8.28b–10.14a; 22.10b–20a; 22.29a–28.31. Any references to passages within these pages will be indicated as missing (*lac.*) in D05.

[16] Retrieved in Lyons, France, by the French Protestant leader Théodore de Bèze in 1562, the MS was given to Cambridge University Library in 1581. The association of its text with Lyons may date from at least the second century; see Louis Holtz, 'L'écriture latine du Codex Bezae,' in *Codex Bezae: Studies from the Lunel Colloquium, June 1994*, ed. David C. Parker and Christian-Bernard Amphoux, 14–55 (Leiden: Brill, 1996). A digital copy of D05 is available online: http://cudl.lib.cam.ac.uk/view/MS-NN-00002-00041/1).

[17] Comments to this effect are found throughout the commentary on the text of N-A[27], compiled by Bruce M. Metzger, *A Textual Commentary on the Greek New Testament*, 2nd edn (1975; Stuttgart: Deutsche Bibelgesellschaft, 1994), a volume that informs much of the textual discussion found in commentaries on Luke and Acts.

somewhat capricious scribes who, careless of the authority of the original text, supposedly modified and expanded it to make it more colourful and to bring it into line with their own later, Gentile, church context.

There is, in contrast, widespread support for its text among all the earliest translations (versions) into all the languages around the Mediterranean (Latin, Syriac, Coptic, Middle Egyptian, Aramaic), before the translations were standardized around the fourth century. Furthermore, the citations of Luke's writings by Church Fathers from the time of Irenaeus towards the end of the second century show that several of them used a text similar to the one transmitted by D05. On top of that, fresh archaeological discoveries over recent decades have brought to light early papyri fragments as well as new early versions that show that the readings of Luke–Acts in Codex Bezae were known well before the date of the MS.[18] All of this goes to underline that the date of a MS is not the same as the date of the text it transmits.

If the text of Codex Bezae represents a late revision, the attestation of the versions, the patristic citations and the growing number of discoveries are all awkward and puzzling pieces to fit into the jigsaw. It is hoped that the linguistic analyses presented here will help to show that by moving some other pieces into their right place, the awkward ones can be fitted in so as to create a more complete and accurate picture, as suggested in Chapter 9.

II.2 The 'Western' text

In order to bring some clarity into the thinking about Codex Bezae, it is important to clear up a misconception that concerns the grouping of the witnesses of Luke–Acts. It is customary to think of the ancient witnesses to Luke's writings as falling into two main families, the Alexandrian text and the Western text, with a third, the Byzantine, usually seen as a combination of readings from both.[19] The reason for using the label 'Western' was because it was thought in the eighteenth century to have originated in the Western Roman Empire; despite the discovery of MSS in the east, the label has stuck. The outstanding problem that needs to be recognized is not with the geographical inaccuracy but with the very grouping.

---

[18] Important recent discoveries of MSS of Acts that attest otherwise singular readings from Codex Bezae include the Middle Egyptian version (mae or G^{67}), containing Acts 1–15; the Syro-Palestinian (Aramaic) fragment (sy^{pal} or sy^{msK}), attesting a few verses of Acts 10; and the Greek papyrus P^{127} (c. 400), with portions of Acts 10–16. Greek MSS that support the Bezan readings of Acts at each place of variation are documented in Rius-Camps & Read-Heimerdinger, *The Message of Acts*. The support among the papyri, whose fragmentary state allows only for localized comparisons, has been analysed systematically in Jenny Read-Heimerdinger and Josep Rius-Camps, 'Tracing the Readings of Codex Bezae in the Papyri of Acts', in *Reading New Testament Papyri in Context. Lire les papyrus du Nouveau Testament dans leur context*, ed. Claire Clivaz and J. Zumstein, 307–38 (Leuven: Peeters, 2011). See also R. Swanson, *New Testament Greek Manuscripts: Variant Readings Arranged in Horizontal Lines Against Codex Vaticanus. Luke* (Carol Stream, Ill.:Tyndale House Publishers, 1995); *The Acts of the Apostles* (Sheffield: SAP, 1998).

[19] There are scholars who challenge this evaluation of the Byzantine text; see Maurice A. Robinson, *New Testament Textual Criticism: The Case for Byzantine Priority*, accessible at http://rosetta.reltech.org/TC/v06/Robinson2001.html (last accessed 4/01/21).

Whilst the grouping into families corresponds broadly to some aspects of the situation, it masks the fact that among the witnesses of each group there are significant variant readings. This is true to some extent of the Alexandrian MSS of Luke–Acts which, despite agreement most of the time, differ in some of the details. It is especially true of the so-called 'Western' witnesses, whose chief point of agreement is that they differ from the Alexandrian text![20] Furthermore, since many of the MSS that display a 'Western' text are translations, what may have been the points of agreement or difference in their exemplars are obscured by translation. The variety among the witnesses in each group means that global comparisons between the two main traditions are likely to produce misleading results; a comparison of actual representatives of the two groups allows more accurate conclusions to be drawn, which can be developed for the examination of other MSS or versions.

In the studies presented here, D05 is compared primarily with B03 because they are generally the most far apart for Luke's writings. The attestation of ℵ01 is also noted, particularly where there is disagreement with B03.

II.3 Luke as author

The writings selected for these studies have been traditionally ascribed since at least the end of the second century to a certain 'Luke', as the author of what became the third Gospel in the NT canon as well as the book eventually placed after the four Gospels. The first book presents Jesus as a master with disciples who, in the second volume, seek to put his teaching into action. The action of Acts takes place over a period of time following the end of the Gospel; some of the locations (Jerusalem and Judaea) and characters (notably Jesus, Peter and the apostles) appear in both books, though new locations and new characters are quickly introduced in Acts as the story develops. It is possible that the two books were initially intended as two volumes of a single work and not just because they are addressed to the same person, Theophilus.[21] Internal evidence in Codex Bezae that the author intended them to be part of the same work includes the way in which the second book critically evaluates its characters and their actions against the model set out in the first one. The analysis of language features of the two books can be an important contribution to establishing whether they have a common authorship, not by looking at the style, which may indeed vary given the distinct nature of the books' content, but by comparing the patterns in the use of linguistic devices. If Acts was intended to be a sequel to the Gospel as two parts of a unified work, it is not possible to say when they became separated, for there is no evidence of Acts being in circulation before the time of Irenaeus, who knows and refers to it extensively.[22]

---

[20] In introducing the *editio critica maior* of Acts, Klaus Wachtel as one of the editors is clear in his conclusion that the 'Western' text 'should not be called a text at all', *Editio Critica Maior*, vol. 1; 3.

[21] That the same author wrote both the Gospel and Acts, or that the two books are intended to be linked, is a matter of ongoing scholarly dispute. With regard to the text of Codex Bezae, the connections between the two books are clearer and stronger than in other MSS; see Read-Heimerdinger & Rius-Camps, *Demonstration*, xv-xvii.

[22] The attestation of the Luke's Gospel and Acts is explored by Andrew Gregory, *The Reception of Luke and Acts in the Period Before Irenaeus: Looking for Luke in the Second Century* (WUNT II/169; Tübingen: Mohr Siebeck, 2003).

As to who Luke was, these studies use the name for convenience but make no assumptions as to whether he was a Gentile, from Syrian Antioch, a doctor, or the *Loukas* mentioned by Paul in his letters (Col. 4.14; 2 Tim. 4.11; Phil. 24). He will be referred to as 'he', as will his addressee, Theophilus; they may also be referred to as 'speaker' and 'hearer' as terms used in discourse analysis (see §III.2 below). In view of the consistently Jewish viewpoint that analysis of Luke's Gospel and Acts in D05 tends to reveal, expressed as it is through an intricate system of allusions to Jewish traditions and ways of thinking, the natural conclusion is that the writer and addressee of that text were both Jews. Indeed, my own motivation to study the language of Luke in more detail was initially prompted not by the linguistic variation among the MSS but by the nature of numerous readings in D05 material absent from the Alexandrian text that I identified as sophisticated allusions to Jewish traditions presented, moreover, from an inner Jewish perspective.[23] The issues of interpretation that this material raises will be left to one side while focusing on Luke's language, with the intention of looking at them in a following volume of exegetical articles, *Being Theophilus*.

III. Linguistic analysis

III.1 Nature of variation

In comparing the language of Codex Bezae with that of Codex Sinaiticus and Codex Vaticanus, the first task was to look at the variant readings that involved differences, whether lexical or syntactical or of word order and regardless of how important they appeared *prima facie* to be.[24] The principal categories that emerged are set out in Table 1.1.

Table 1.1 Linguistic categories of variant readings between D05 and ℵ01/B03

Syntactical	connectives
	article before proper names
	use of noun/pronoun to refer to participants (tracking)
	prepositions
	speech introducers (dative or preposition πρός)
	participle versus finite verb
	word order within a) noun phrases b) verbal clauses c) sentences
Lexical	synonyms
	spelling
	divine titles

---

[23] I have set out the justification for identifying the Jewish context of Bezan readings in Acts, supported by further extensive evidence in the Bezan form of Luke's Gospel, in Rius-Camps & Read-Heimerdinger, *The Message of Acts*.

[24] The N-A[28] critical apparatus avowedly presents a selection of the variant readings that the committee considered to be 'the most important', though exactly what were the criteria for 'importance' is not explicit (N-A[28], 'Introduction', 55).

Variants involving the above items may indeed be noted in a critical apparatus and discussed by textual scholars (even if by no means systematically), but such variables are generally viewed as features of style or scribal habit; the critic's decision to select a reading as the most likely to be authentic is generally guided by what is judged to be an author's usual practice, on the basis of statistical frequency. As a result, the printed text represents a mixture of MSS; it is 'eclectic'.[25]

III.2 Discourse analysis

It is striking that the list of features that emerges from an examination of variants between D05 and ℵ01/B03 includes many aspects of Greek that linguists adopting the approach known as 'discourse analysis' had identified as early as the 1960s as playing a role in conveying meaning rather than expressing personal style.[26] That is, they attribute to them an objective value rather than a subjective one, one that is peculiar to the language and accessible primarily to a native speaker. They view them as much a part of the grammar of Greek as the features of a traditional grammar handbook, with the difference that whereas grammar in the familiar sense tends to consider the way a language functions within a sentence, these more recently identified features operate on a level beyond the sentence and even depend on pragmatic factors outside the verbal communication (the 'discourse') itself. Thus, they link the parts of a discourse with each other and bind it together as a whole; they give it structure; they relate the discourse to the context in which it takes place; they are a means to present a story or argument from the recipient's point of view, and to connect the author (the 'speaker') with the one being addressed (the 'hearer'), in such a way that the communication is truly bi-directional even if the addressee never makes an utterance. It is important to note that, despite some shared concerns, discourse analysis is not a method of literary criticism, nor is it one possible, optional approach to a text among others that will eventually go out of fashion as it is replaced by another new discovery.

Being familiar with such a set of linguistic features clearly has implications for textual criticism. Textual criticism (and much exegesis for that matter) typically has tended to think of scribes as copying their texts in isolation, adapting them in the process to suit their own understanding, preferences and customs. A discourse analysis approach to language breaks down this notion, viewing MSS as creations of both the scribe and the people for whom the text is being copied, so that the early scribe is truly an editor more than a simple copyist. In the first centuries of the Church, when texts would frequently be copied in order to be transmitted to another community, the location, the identity and nature of the intended recipient community will inevitably

---

[25] That, at least, is the theory, even if in reality the text currently printed largely reflects the editors' prejudgements in favour of the Alexandrian MSS, with B03 usually given preference in Luke–Acts where ℵ01 differs from it.
[26] Notable among the early linguists working on the biblical text and using discourse analysis as a tool to aid translation were Kenneth L. Pike, *Language in Relation to a Unified Theory of the Structure of Human Behavior* (1967; repr. The Hague: Mouton, 2015); J. E. Grimes, *The Thread of Discourse* (The Hague: Mouton, 1975).

have influenced the ways in which the copyist felt the need to make modifications. It is a poor storyteller who does not alter the tale when retelling it to a new audience: leaving out information that would only make sense to previous recipients who had first-hand knowledge of the setting and characters of the story, articulating the narrative so that its purpose was clearer to an audience more distant in time and space, adding in explanations, or changing the vocabulary to suit the speech of the new hearers. The editing of texts to adapt it to a new audience was not to disrespect the earlier form but, on the contrary, was entirely in keeping with the Jewish view of Scripture as the living voice of a living God: updating it was a way to honour his word so that it was intelligible to those who received it in changed circumstances.

From a theoretical point of view, there is a variety of different schools and methods among discourse analysts, which sometimes focus specifically on one aspect more than others. I propose here to avoid the theoretical discussions, which can be as complex and abstract as in any other branch of linguistics,[27] in order to show the practical consequences of the approach. There are in any case certain interests and features that characterize all schools of discourse analysis. It will be useful to set out some concepts that will recur throughout the studies in this volume:

- Language in use: discourse analysis considers language that actually exists, rather than elucidating or imposing theoretical rules on what might be said; from this perspective, there is no 'correct' or 'incorrect' Greek, but rather whatever a speaker uses is treated as legitimate within the circumstances in which he or she speaks.
- Languages in their own right: it is recognized that each language has not only its own grammar but also its own inherent way of organizing speech. In consequence, it cannot be assumed that what is true of one language is true of another. In the case of NT narrative, for example, this applies even to the way that a story is told, how the climax of the story is indicated, how resolution to the plot is brought about.
- Language as communication: the overall purpose of language as a vehicle of communication is an irresistible truth to which discourse analysts are very sensitive, in comparison with non-discourse oriented linguistics which may view language more as a system in isolation. It is taken as a given that a 'speaker' who wishes to communicate (as opposed to set up barriers) will constantly, and instinctively, be monitoring the understanding of the one they are addressing, the 'hearer'.
- Choice implies meaning: this is a fundamental notion guiding those discourse analysts who pay meticulous attention to linguistic detail.[28] Much of what traditionally has been seen simply as a matter of style or rhetoric, such as choosing a different construction or a synonym, for example, is understood as involving a difference in meaning.

---

[27] For a survey of contemporary approaches to NT Greek linguistics, including a variety of forms of discourse analysis, see David Alan Black and Benjamin L. Merkle, eds, *Linguistics and New Testament Greek* (Grand Rapids, Mich.: Baker Academic, 2020).

[28] See Benjamin Merkle, 'Where do we Go from Here?', in *Linguistics and New Testament Greek*, ed. Black & Merkle, 249.

- Marked and unmarked: usage by any particular author that is normal, not intended to create a special effect, is identified as their 'default' or unmarked usage. Where patterns are disrupted for any reason, such as to underline something, that usage is said to be 'marked'.
- Frequency of occurrence: discourse analysis shows that frequency of occurrence is an irrelevant factor in establishing what an author's default usage is, because the circumstances of a given communication may require the language to be heavily emphatic, for example. Equally, then, frequency is not a useful criterion for assessing the authenticity of a MS.
- Narrative: Luke wrote his two books as continuous narrative text, with passages in direct speech set within it. For the purposes of discourse analysis, speeches are viewed as unified chunks within the narrative, which have their own speaker and hearer and also their own inner structure.
- Context: utterances are not viewed in isolation but as belonging to a wider unit of communication, the 'discourse'. In order to grasp their intended meaning, account must be taken of the fact that any given discourse is produced as an act of communication within a certain context. On the one hand, this means the textual context, the surrounding discourse with its internal features of structure and form (sometimes referred to as the 'co-text'). On the other, it means the real-life context, the surrounding circumstances, the people involved in the communication, the thought processes, social conventions, and so on; in this sense, it belongs to the domain of pragmatics. The tools of discourse analysis cannot, of themselves, identify the context, but rather they are applied in taking account of what is known of the context through studies in other disciplines.
- Stylistics: for all that discourse analysis pays detailed attention to an individual's way of using language, it views its concerns as distinct from 'style', which would be an matter of aesthetics or literary criticism or even rhetoric.[29] The principles that discourse analysis elucidates are not an optional extra that can be ignored, rather they are as fundamental to a language as the rules governing morphology and syntax.

This review of commonly found characteristics of discourse analysis as a linguistic approach illustrates how, in comparison with traditional grammar, it comes to be referred to as 'deep grammar', as opposed to the 'surface grammar' of the more familiar approach.

It should not be thought that discourse analysis envisages the discourse features of a language as consciously acquired. On the contrary, their acquisition by the native speaker is regarded as being as natural and thorough as that of any features of surface grammar. The difficulty for the New Testament analyst is that there are no native speakers to consult in order to test or refine conclusions, which is nevertheless partially offset by the number of Greek MSS available as well as a range of authors from different linguistic backgrounds. The implication of the absence of native speakers is, however, that some of the conclusions proposed in the studies of the present book are tentative, and invite further research.

---

[29] Rhetorical criticism and discourse analysis can, and should, successfully complement each other; see Jenny Read-Heimerdinger, 'The Interface between Rhetorical Analysis and Discourse Analysis', in *Studi del Terzo Convegno RBS*, ed. R. Meynet and J. Oniszczuk, 325–46 (Rome: G&B Press, 2015).

As indicated above, discourse analysis views language as 'language in use', which means that the purpose of the discourse is understood to play a crucial role in the shaping of it. There is then an inevitable difficulty that arises for us as readers today, in that we know very little indeed of the circumstances in which Luke wrote his work. Furthermore, anything we know about the original author and about the addressee, and of the relationship between them, has to be deduced from the text.[30] All these elements are bound to the context of the time when Luke's work was written, embedded as it was in Judaism alongside other cultures that are unfamiliar to us today. At a distance of 2000 years, and belonging to a considerably different social – and, dare I say, religious – context, we are confronted with a significant difficulty in retrieving that earlier context and there is the danger of imposing on the text not only our own context but also our preconceived ideas about what the text means.

In sum, the application of discourse analysis to an ancient text certainly provides greater access to it than is otherwise possible, but it is nevertheless important to keep an open mind and honestly acknowledge that whatever we say about a biblical text has to be viewed with some element of caution.

III.3 Why use manuscripts?

With its interest in linguistic features that characterise so much of the variation between MSS of Luke's writings, discourse analysis becomes a tool for navigating a way among the variants which, given their interconnectedness, have to be considered collectively rather than as a string of independent variants such as can be gleaned from a selective critical apparatus. The counter point to this is that analysis of the language of a text should ideally work from MSS if the results are going to be precise. Working from an edition of the Greek NT that presents an eclectic text, reconstructed without recourse to discourse analysis and according to the editors' understanding of variant readings as reflections of scribes' personal preferences or errors, means that to some extent the results will be skewed.[31] MSS have the additional advantage of increasing the data available for studying the Greek of a NT book, in providing examples of language that speakers actually used. As long as it is borne in mind that whatever is used is legitimate, at least for one speaker and in all likelihood their hearer, too, then MSS are a rich source of linguistic information.[32]

---

[30] In view of the consistently Jewish viewpoint that analysis of Luke–Acts in D05 tends to reveal, expressed as it is through an intricate system of allusions to Jewish traditions and ways of thinking, the natural conclusion is that the addressee of that text was a Jew, too; and the only known Jew with the name Theophilus in the first century is the High Priest of 37–42 CE, third son of Annas, brother-in-law of Caiaphas (Tal Ilan, *Lexicon of Jewish Names in Late Antiquity:* Part I: *Palestine 330 BCE –200 CE* (TSAJ 91; Mohr Siebeck, 2002).

[31] I have considered the shortcomings of working from an eclectic text of Acts in Jenny Read-Heimerdinger, 'Eclecticism and the Book of Acts', in *Texts and Traditions. Essays in Honour of J. K. Elliott*, ed. Peter Doble and J. Kloha, 71–92 (Leiden: Brill, 2014).

[32] Micheál Palmer discusses the problems of collecting data for analysis of NT Greek and the formulating of hypotheses based on limited information in 'How do We Know a Phrase is a Phrase? A Plea for Procedural Clarity in the Application of Linguistics to Biblical Greek', in *Biblical Greek Language and Linguistics*, ed. Stanley E. Porter and D. A. Carson, 159–69 (LNTS; London: Bloomsbury Publishing, 1993).

It may be thought that given the accessibility of many NT MSS in electronic format, it is no longer necessary to work with individual hard copies. Certainly, it is true that digital copies both enhance the ease with which MSS can be consulted and also facilitate collaboration among researchers.[33] There are, however, dangers at the point when research is carried out solely by electronic means insofar as this depends on prior editing, programming or analysis, because it can result in perpetuating underlying faults.[34] Whatever the obvious usefulness of being able to access MSS in digital format, there is an inestimable value in seeing a single MS visually as continuous text rather than as a string of variants when undertaking linguistic analysis.

IV. Quantity and types of manuscript variation

While the work of determining which text of Luke's work corresponds most closely to the original version is a long and complex matter involving a careful and thorough examination of the contents of the MSS, specific information concerning the quantity and the nature of the variation can be offered relatively easily and with some precision. The aim of this section is to set out an accurate overview of variation, and to establish thereby a basis for a more detailed analysis of specific features. The book of Acts will be examined here first, followed by an analysis of the variation in Luke's Gospel, which has been examined in less detail but an overview nonetheless provides useful comparable information.

For the purpose of the comparative analysis of Luke's writings presented here, Codex Vaticanus (B03) has been taken as the representative of the Alexandrian tradition. The variant readings were considered in three different ways. First, they were taken *en masse* and counted in the two MSS overall. This gives a general idea of the size of the difference between the MSS. In a second step, the global number of variants was broken down into different types of variation which are numerically compared among themselves. This allows the initial picture to be refined and more detail to be filled in. For Acts only, a final step was to compare the amount and distribution of variant readings in the narrative portions of the text with those in direct speech in order to see if the two kinds of discourse are affected differently by variation.

---

[33] These issues are considered by Claire Clivaz and G. V. Allen (ed.), *Ancient Manuscripts and Virtual Research Environements*, Classics@ 18 (2021), available at https://classics-at.chs.harvard.edu/volume/classics18-ancient-manuscripts-and-virtual-research-environments/ (last accessed 3/10/2021).

[34] This is potentially a problem with the web-based tool OpenText, designed to provide annotated Greek texts and tools with which to analyse them; see Catherine Smith and Matthew Brook O'Donnell, 'Computer-Aided Linguistic Analysis for a Single Manuscript Witness: Preparing to Map the OpenText.org Annotation, in *The Language and Literature of the New Testament Essays in Honor of Stanley E. Porter's 60th Birthday*. ed. Lois K. Fuller Dow, Craig A. Evans, Andrew W. Pitts, 106–37 (Leiden: Brill, 2017). The authors explain how Porter had initially wanted to use single MSS for the NT, but difficulties with accessing electronic copies led him to use the N-A text instead, which then needs to be compared with the *editio critica maior* for variant readings.

IV.1 Categories of variation

Within the total amount of variation, four categories can be identified that serve to provide a clearer and more nuanced comparison of the two texts. Although for practical purposes the categories take D05 as their starting point, that is a pragmatic decision and is not intended to be a statement about the primary or secondary nature of one text or the other. The four categories are:[35]

1. additional – material present in D05, absent in B03
2. omitted – material absent in D05, present in B03
3. alternative – same material in both MSS but in a different form
4. word order – same words in both MSS but in a different order

The first category of variants represents material (which can be anything from a definite article to several verses) that is found in D05 but not in B03. The second category consists of material found in B03 but not in D05, so creating a category the reverse of the first. The third category is more diverse for it groups together words, phrases or sentences that are present in both texts but not in an identical form. The difference may be lexical (synonyms are used) or grammatical (e.g. tense or number varies) or syntactical (the sentence is constructed differently). The only variation in this category that was disregarded when it came to the actual count of words was spelling differences that are purely orthographical and can have no possible effect on the meaning of the word. These include changes of vowel/diphthongs and single/double consonants, which may reflect regional or historical differences of pronunciation.[36] They do not include the variation in the spelling of the city of Jerusalem, since the difference in that instance is more than one of pronunciation, involving a choice between a Hellenistic and a Hebrew-derived form.[37] Occasionally, it is the alternative syntax that produces a different number of words (e.g. πρὸς αὐτόν/αὐτῷ). In such cases, the additional words

---

[35] M. Wilcox, 'Luke and the Bezan Text of Acts', in *Les Actes des Apôtres: tradition, rédaction, théologie*, ed. J. Kremer, 447–55 (Gembloux: Leuven University Press, 1979), also identifies four categories: a) additions b) omissions c) substitutions d) alterations to sense, whereby word order changes are included in c) or d). The problem with Wilcox's final category is that it is often not apparent which variants do or do not affect the meaning until the whole passage in which they are found is analysed both linguistically and exegetically, and even then, some of the decisions are necessarily tentative. The desire in adopting the categories for the present study was to be both factual and objective.

[36] J. H. Moulton, *A Grammar of New Testament Greek*, vol. 2 (Edinburgh: T&T Clark, 1929), 40–6, gives a summary of the shifts which occurred in pronunciation in the first centuries CE. He essentially finds that there was a great deal of fluidity and that the situation varied very much according to locality as much as to social class, the same class adopting different standards at different periods. His conclusion is that 'A history of Greek pronunciation in the Hellenistic period is greatly needed, showing both when and where the various developments first appeared... Such a history would have an important bearing on textual questions' (46). Although among the MSS generally there is a great deal of variation and inconsistency, a fair degree of regularity can be observed within the text of Acts in D05 itself regarding such things as ε for ει, υ for οι, ν for νν. Given the unusual extent of consistency, a history of pronunciation could potentially be of value for determining with some precision the date of the Bezan text.

[37] On the spelling of Jerusalem, see Read-Heimerdinger, *Bezan Text*, 311–44; see also a condensed account in Rius-Camps & Read-Heimerdinger, *The Message of Acts*, IV, 6–8.

are only counted in Category 3 (alternative material), but they are not included in the count of words in Categories 1 or 2 because they do not properly constitute supplementary material.

The final category is specific to variation in word order, where identical words are used but in a different order. Where alternative words (Category 3) are found in a different place in the sentence (Category 4), such words are counted for both categories, unless the change in the position of the words is due to a grammatical constraint (e.g. καί occupies first place in a clause, whereas the alternative conjunction δέ cannot do so).

IV.2. The book of Acts

In the first instance, the two MSS were compared and every difference between them noted.[38] It is unfortunate that the lacunae in the Bezan text at 8.29—10.14; 21.2–10, 16–18; 22.10–20, 22.29—28.31 mean that the analysis has to be restricted to something less than the entire book of Acts but in the absence of a complete Greek witness to the 'Western' text, there is no way to avoid this shortcoming. The number of words in D05 was counted, as was also the number of words which varied from the readings of B03.[39] The total number of words affected by variation is found to be over three and a half thousand (see Table 1.2). The exact figure needs to be compared with the number of words in the book overall to see what proportion of the whole it represents (excluding the lacunose portions in D05), as set out in Table 1.2.

These global results already shed light on the nature of the differences between the Alexandrian and the 'Western' traditions. The two texts are often referred to as the 'short text' and the 'long text', as if the greater length of the 'Western' text were the most remarkable feature that distinguished it from the Alexandrian text. This idea is

Table 1.2 Proportion of Acts affected by variation

	D05	B03
Total number of words	13,904	13,036
% of text affected by variation	28%	26%

---

[38] The text used for Codex Bezae was the transcription by F. H. Scrivener, *Bezae Codex Cantabrigiensis* (1864; repr. Pittsburgh, Penn.: Pickwick Press, 1978). It was checked against the online transcription at https://cudl.lib.cam.ac.uk/view/MS-NN-00002-00041/1 (last accessed 28/09/2021). A facsimile transcription of Codex Vaticanus is available online at https://digi.vatlib.it/view/MSS_Vat.gr.1209 (last accessed 20/07/21); or in a more readable transcription at http://www.truebiblecode.com/codexvaticanus.html (last accessed 20/09/21). The text of Codex Vaticanus is available in J.H. Ropes, *The Text of Acts*, vol. 3 of *The Beginnings of Christianity*, ed. F. J. Foakes-Jackson and K. Lake, London: Macmillan, 1926. Eberhardt Nestle's collation of Codex Bezae against Tischendorf's edition of the Greek New Testament, *Novi Testamenti Graeci. Supplementum editionibus de Gerbhardt Tischendorfianis. Codicis Cantabrigiensis Collatio* (Leipzig: Tauchnitz, 1896) is a valuable aid for checking variant readings.

[39] Similar numerical results would have been produced if Codex Sinaiticus (א01) had been used instead. B03 agrees with D05 against א01 at 103 places for Acts, whereas א01 agrees with D05 against B03 at 114 places. The majority of these disagreements between א01 and B03 occur within the category referred to here as 'alternative material'.

bolstered by figures given by F. G. Kenyon who compared the text of Westcott and Hort (Alexandrian) with that of A. C. Clark (Western) and found the latter to be 8.5% longer. Kenyon's figure has generously been rounded up to 10% in more recent publications, such as Metzger's *Textual Commentary* which accompanies the UBS edition of the Greek New Testament.[40] However, when an actual count of words in the two texts is made, it turns out that the overall difference in the length is 868 words. When this figure is expressed as a percentage of the shorter of the two texts, the D05 text of Acts is seen to be 6.6% longer than that of B03.

Although discussion of the text of Acts typically focuses on the relative length of the different forms, there are in fact other types of variation than those of addition/omission that are just as numerous. In other words, the difference in length is only one aspect of a more complex state of affairs and the use of the terms 'longer' and 'shorter' to describe the two texts is somewhat misleading, although it may be convenient when referring to specific units of variation. The existence of further categories of variation tends to tell a somewhat different story about the state of the text of Acts from that traditionally presented. Table 1.3 shows the amount of variation for each category in the extant text of D05 compared with the corresponding text of B03.

The highest percentage of variation is accounted for by additional words in D05. It is interesting to note, however, that the amount of variation brought about by alternative forms is almost as high. Furthermore, words omitted by the Bezan text represent a considerable proportion of variation, demonstrating that the portrayal of D05 as essentially an expanded text is somewhat simplistic. Word order variation is comparatively small but the reasons for its occurrence need to be carefully studied and form the topic of Chapter 4 in this volume.

Following the global comparison, the distribution of variation across the chapters of the book of Acts was analysed. It was found that the highest figures correspond to the accounts of the journeys of Paul in Acts 14–19, but also that narrative portions are affected significantly more by variation than are passages in direct speech, except for the speeches of Paul.[41] Indeed, the speeches in which Paul is involved, either as the

Table 1.3 Distribution of categories of variation in Acts

	Additional	Alternative	Omitted	Word order	Total
Variant words in D05	1448	1352	579	263	3642
% of total variant words	39.7	37.1	16	7.2	100

[40] Metzger, *A Textual Commentary*, 260, where reference is made to Kenyon's calculations. In contrast, Strange, *The Problem of the Text of Acts*, 213, makes a more rigorous comparison between the MS traditions by setting the number of words in D05 (which he counts as 14,062 rather than our 13,904) against the number of words in the N-A[26] text as the Alexandrian base (mostly a combination of ℵ01 and B03), given as 13,236. On Strange's figures, the difference in length is 6.24%, which again is considerably less than Metzger's 10%. Larry Hurtado, in contrast, aims way higher when he cites 14% in a blog post, without supporting evidence (https://larryhurtado.wordpress.com/2017/12/23/editio-ctitica-maior-acts-volumes/ – last accessed 22/07/2021).

[41] For a detailed breakdown of the figures for comparison of the variation by chapter, and also by narrative versus direct speech, see Read-Heimerdinger, *The Bezan Text*, 5–21.

speaker or as addressee, show considerably more variation than those involving other characters in the first half of the book.

Overall, the greater proportion of additional material in D05 is found in the narrative text. In contrast, there is a higher proportion of alternative material in the speeches. The proportion of variant readings represented by omitted material and word order variation is likewise higher in the speeches than in the narrative sections of the text. Within the narrative text, it can be observed that variation is often concentrated in the introduction to new episodes or in the transitions between episodes, which transmit the narrator's comments and evaluation. Variation at these points is frequently complex and is of such a nature as to suggest differences in the way that the purpose of each text is viewed.

IV.3 The Gospel of Luke

The proportion of Gospel text affected by variation is similar to what has been seen for Acts, for approximately one quarter of the overall number of words are variant. The difference in length between the two texts of B03 and D05 being only 59 words, with D05 the shorter (19,435 : 19,494), the percentage of variation is close to 26% in both cases.

The distribution of variation in the Gospel, on the other hand, is strikingly different from that seen in Acts, as Table 1.4 demonstrates.

Across the four categories, the variation is much more evenly distributed in the Gospel than in Acts. The closeness in length between the two texts is accounted for by the fact that there are almost as many words present in D05 but absent in B03 (additional) as the other way round (omitted). While the so-called 'non-Western interpolations' account for a small part of the material 'omitted' in some seven verses of Luke 22 and 24 in D05,[42] there is considerably more material absent from D05 in other chapters.

The high proportion of word order variation (26.2%) is particularly remarkable in comparison with the relatively small proportion in Acts (7.2%, cf. Table 2). In order to understand the reasons for so many differences between the two texts, detailed analysis is needed, seeking to ascertain the nature of the changes and identify reasons for them. A study of the Gospel variation would necessarily involve a thorough consideration of Synoptic parallels, for it is possible that differences arise because of harmonisation with other Gospels, That said, passages that are unique to Luke are not significantly less

Table 1.4 Distribution of categories of variation in Luke's Gospel

	Additional	Alternative	Omitted	Word order	Total
Variant words in D05	1,105	1,593	1,144	1,365	5,197
% of variant words	21.2	30.6	22	26.2	100

[42] Luke 22.19b–20; 24.3b, 6a, 12, 36b, 40, 51b and 52a.

affected by variation than those with parallels that could have influenced one text or the other. Caution must be exercised, in any case, in assuming inter-Gospel influence, for examination of alleged parallels in Matthew's Gospel has shown that this is far less extensive than the impression given by the critical apparatus of the edited Greek NT.[43]

IV. 4 Conclusions on the textual situation

The analyses reproduced here of the variation between the Luke's text in D05 and B03 as representatives of the 'Western' and Alexandrian texts, respectively, make available precise information that facilitates an accurate comparison of the two principal texts of the Gospel and Acts. The advantage of taking actual MSS rather than 'texts' (such as Alexandrian or 'Western') that are themselves subject to variation among their witnesses is that no hypothetical presuppositions about the grouping of MSS or about recensions need to be called upon. At the same time, it is wise to acknowledge that there are certain limitations to the uses to which the information can be put. While overviews of the quantity of variation are useful for obtaining a general idea, statistics and summaries can only tell part of the story. The actual content of the variant readings needs to be examined in order to understand the reasons for their existence. In this initial survey, little attempt has been made to interpret the significance of the figures. Interpretation of the patterns and the fluctuations that emerge necessarily depends on a thorough examination of variation in specific passages, an exercise that requires the perspective and purpose of the respective texts to be carefully acknowledged. These are factors that will be given consideration in the chapters of this volume as the language of the MSS is examined.

V. Methodology

In the chapters that follow, the linguistic topics that have been identified as recurringly subject to variation among the MSS (§III.1 above) are taken in turn: sentence connectives, the use of the article, word order, expressions to refer to the Holy Spirit, the use of pronouns to refer to participants; finally, aspects of the previous chapters are applied to an analysis of the structure of Luke's two books. It will be seen that there is often interaction between the various features explored, indicated by cross-references. The overall aim is to elucidate the principles governing Luke's usage and to evaluate variant readings. A concluding chapter draws together the findings and proposes ways to advance discussion about Luke's language.

The topics are each considered in two stages: first, in the text common to B03 and D05, and secondly in the material that is variant, noting differences with ℵ01 and

---

[43] The extent of Gospel harmonization, notably on the part of D05, implied by the number of indications given in the N-A[28] apparatus has been analysed by Laurent Pinchard, 'The Greek Text of the Gospel of Matthew: A Renewed Text-Critical Approach with a Focus on the Issue of Harmonisations in Codex Bezae,' (unpublished PhD diss., University of Wales Trinity Saint David, Lampeter, 2015). He found that many of the alleged parallels in D05 do not, in fact, reproduce the text of other Gospels and that a number of instances of close reproduction of a parallel Gospel text exist in B03 that are not noted in the N-A[28] apparatus.

including material that is present in only one of the MSS. Patterns in the shared text are noted, and then those of the variant text are compared with the ones previously identified. When citing from a MS, words that vary in one of the other witnesses will be shown as follows:

- words present in one MS and absent in the other are underlined with a solid line
- the absence in the corresponding passage of the other MS is shown with an arrow ↑
- synonymous material (whether grammatical or syntactical) is indicated with a dotted line
- [square brackets] indicate variation in word order

The topics are looked at from a discourse analysis perspective: what are the default patterns and what do the marked forms communicate? what does Luke's usage reflect about his purpose? how does that differ according to the perspective of the two textual forms? By paying attention to the resemblance of the linguistic patterns in the variant readings to those established in the shared text, some conclusions about the language of the respective MSS can be drawn. Although it will not be possible to state definitively that the same author was responsible for the common text as well as the text of one MS or the other, the range of topics examined should yield sufficient information for determining their respective distance from the common text.

2

The article before proper names[1]

I. Introduction

I.1 A complex picture

The fluctuation in the presence of the article with definite nouns is an issue noted in grammar books of NT Greek as one that is particularly intriguing.[2] Many of the rules that have been discerned for its use only work so far before they seem to be contradicted by an example that does not follow them.[3] Part of the reason for the complexity surrounding its use is that, for all that the article is often referred to as 'the definite article', its presence before a noun does not necessarily denote definiteness from every point of view, just as its absence does not always signify indefiniteness.[4] To add to the confusion, even when the noun it precedes *is* a particular one, the same particular noun may well be found in an adjacent clause without the article. Another problem is that although the use of the article can sometimes be explained on the grounds that the referent of a noun is known, the omission of the article cannot by any means be taken

---

[1] The material in this chapter was first published as Jenny Read-Heimerdinger, 'The Function of the Article with Proper Names: The New Testament Book of Acts as a Case Study', in *The Article in Post-Classical Greek*, ed. D. King, 153–85 (Dallas: SIL International, 2019). Some of the preliminary material on textual matters has been included in Chapter 1, §II.

[2] It led one author to comment, 'The development of the Greek article is one of the most interesting things in human speech' (A. T. Robertson, *A Grammar of the Greek New Testament in the Light of Historical Research*, 4th edn (1914; Nashville, Tenn: Broadman, 1934), 754; he devotes a section to the topic, *ibid.* 754–96. For a recent collection of studies that examines the question of the article in *koine* Greek, see D. King (ed.), *The Article in Post-Classical Greek* (Dallas: SIL International, 2019), where this current chapter was originally published.

[3] That the use of the article in Greek is not a straightforward matter can be seen from the discussions on the subject in the various New Testament Greek grammar books, among which may be cited: Friedrich W. Blass, Albert Debrunner and Friedrich Rehkopf, *Grammatik des neutestamentlichen Griechisch*, 15th edn (1896; Göttingen: Vandenhoeck & Ruprecht, 1979), §252–62, esp. 261; Stanley E. Porter, *Idioms of New Testament Greek* (Biblical Languages: Greek 2. Sheffield: JSOT Press, 1992),103–14; Nigel Turner, *A Grammar of New Testament Greek*. vol. III, *Syntax* (Edinburgh: T&T Clark, 1963), 172–84; Daniel B. Wallace, *Greek Grammar beyond the Basics* (Grand Rapids, Mich.: Zondervan Publishing House, 1996), 206–90; G. B. Winer, *A Treatise on the Grammar of New Testament Greek* (trans. W. F. Moulton, 1882; repr. Eugene, Ore.: Wipf and Stock 2001), 131–75.

[4] What constitutes definiteness and how it is communicated are themselves subjects of debate. In linguistic investigation, the concept is usually seen as needing to be discussed in terms of the notions of identifiability and accessibility. For a detailed study of the topic, see Christopher Lyons, *Definiteness* (Cambridge: CUP, 1999).

as necessarily signalling that the referent is unknown. This is notably the case with the article that is found before proper nouns, a characteristic use of the article in Greek that illustrates how different its function is compared with its role in English.

The diversity in the use of the article before proper nouns by NT writers is made more complex by the existence of a large number of variant readings among the Greek MSS. Variation has tended to be dismissed by textual critics as arising from the personal style or custom of the scribe, reflecting the notion that there are no particular rules for the inclusion of the article. The absence of clear rules makes it difficult, if not impossible, to decide which reading is authentic at places of divergence; the common answer is to adopt an eclectic approach, whereby the non-variant text is examined to see whether the article is more often used than not with a given noun and variant readings are evaluated in the light of the results.

The approach of discourse analysis indicates that where there are no explanations for linguistic variation at the level of the sentence grammar, there may well be at the level above the sentence; and pragmatic factors outside the text itself may be playing a role, too. This will be seen to be the case, for example, with the choice of sentence connectives (Chapter 3) or word order (Chapter 4), two other issues widely affected by apparent inconsistency on the part of Greek authors as well as later copyists, which are only partially accounted for by traditional grammars. And indeed, detailed study of Greek texts on their own terms, applying the perspectives and insights of discourse analysis, does bring to light specific principles in the use of the article with nouns and accounts for the variation in its use.

My investigation into the use of the article in Luke's writing has focused on Acts, and on its presence with proper nouns, which are by their nature definite and particular, thus avoiding the uncertainty of interpretation with common nouns that are capable of being used indefinitely. The names of persons were considered in a first study carried out in collaboration with Stephen Levinsohn (1991),[5] followed later by a consideration of the names of places in a contribution to a Festschrift for Levinsohn (2011).[6] The analysis below incorporates material from the earlier investigations, developing some of the examples, summarising the findings, and modifying them on occasion.

I.2 Data for the study

The book of Acts is especially appropriate for a systematic linguistic survey of the use of the article with proper names because of its extensive narrative with a carefully

---

[5] Jenny (Read-)Heimerdinger and Stephen H. Levinsohn, 'The Use of the Definite Article before Names of People in the Greek Text of Acts with Particular Reference to Codex Bezae', *Filologia Neotestamentaria* 5 (1992): 15–44. The study was adapted in Jenny Read-Heimerdinger, *The Bezan Text of Acts: A Contribution of Discourse Analysis to Textual Criticism*. JSNTSup 236 (Sheffield: Sheffield Academic Press, 2002), 116–44; and developed further to include common nouns in Stephen H. Levinsohn, *Discourse Features of New Testament Greek*. 2nd edn (Dallas: Summer Institute of Linguistics, 2000), 150–62.

[6] Jenny Read-Heimerdinger, 'The Use of the Article before Names of Places: Patterns of Use in the Book of Acts', in *Discourse Studies and Biblical Interpretation: A Festschrift in Honor of Stephen H. Levinsohn*, ed. Steven E. Runge, 371–402 (Bellingham, Wash.: Lexham Press, 2011).

developed sequence of actions, involving a wide range of participants, several of them reappearing in more than one scene, and covering a wide geographical area where many place names occur, again often on more than one occasion. The names of both the characters and the places are examined here exhaustively, taking into account the narrative setting and interaction with other characters. Consideration is also given to the metanarrative circumstances of Luke as author and his addressee ('speaker' and 'hearer'), though the absence of verifiable external information renders this aspect somewhat open to question; furthermore, the speaker and hearer are subject to change with successive copyings of the manuscript, the more so the greater the distance between the time and place of the author and his intended audience on the one hand, and the date and place of the copy, on the other.

For this examination of the use of article in Acts, two of the early Greek MSS that are most different from each other have been selected for comparison, Codex Bezae (D05) and Codex Vaticanus (B03); occasional places of discrepancy with Codex Sinaiticus, ℵ01, will be pointed out. As discussed in the Chapter 1, §II, while B03 together with ℵ01 are the Alexandrian MSS on which the edition of the Greek NT has been based since the end of the nineteenth century, D05 is generally marginalized in the study of Acts because many of its readings are hard to make sense of and/or are not found in any other early Greek MSS. The difficulty of its readings and their singularity, however, are two considerations that do not impinge on the matter of the article. What is important, in contrast, is the evidence that can be retrieved from the numerous allusions to Jewish traditions in Bezan Acts of the narrator's close familiarity with the Jewish context of the events, since this is a significant pragmatic factor that serves as an indication of the perspective from which the characters and places are being viewed.[7] The text of the Alexandrian MSS reflect, by comparison, a more distant perspective and display less evidence of first-hand knowledge of the Jewish context of the story it tells. A further distinguishing feature of the Bezan text, which is relevant to a study of the article with names of persons in particular, is the narrator's critical appraisal of the Jesus-believer protagonists. Whereas in the Alexandrian text the characters are presented as heroes who unerringly enact the plan of God for the foundation and growth of the Church (certainly, that is how the text of Acts has all but universally been interpreted over the centuries), the narrator of the Bezan text presents a more nuanced account in which the Church's leaders make mistakes and sometimes fail to understand the divine plan correctly. While this narratorial stance, like the Jewish perspective, is identified by reading the D05 narrative of Acts as a continuous whole and not specifically by applying discourse analysis to its language, they both are relevant when considering variant readings concerning the article.[8]

---

[7] The evidence for the Jewish context is explored throughout Josep Rius-Camps and Jenny Read-Heimerdinger, *The Message of Acts in Codex Bezae: A Comparison with the Alexandrian Tradition*. 4 vols, JSNTSup 257/LNTS 302, 365, 415 (London: T&T Clark, 2004–09). See also Jenny Read-Heimerdinger, 'The Apostles in the Bezan Text of Acts', in *Apostelgeschichte als Kirchengeschichte*, ed. T. Nicklas and M. Tilly, 263–80 (BZNW 122; Berlin & New York: Walter de Gruyter, 2003). The general failure of textual critics to notice the Jewish context of readings of Codex Bezae in Acts has meant that the text has continued to be dismissed as a late scribal revision.

[8] Discussion of the relevance of the article to specific passages can be found in Rius-Camps & Read-Heimerdinger, *The Message of Acts*.

Thus, while from a simple statistical count the pattern of presence and absence of the article in D05 is different from that found in B03, discourse analysis shows that frequency of occurrence is an irrelevant factor in assessing the authenticity of a manuscript or even the date of its text. The differences between the two texts do, however, provide useful sets of comparable of data: alongside the agreement concerning the article with proper names in the majority of readings, which allows the principles governing its use to be teased out, a high proportion of variant readings serve as material to refine the observations made on the basis of the common text.

In view of the lacunae in D05 (8.28b—10.14a; 22.10b–20a; 22.29a—28.31), only names that occur up to end of D05 are included in this comparison with B03; however, further mentions of those names that arise where D05 is missing may be referred to. Where citations are given in the discussion, the variants will be identified according to the usual categories as follows: material read by only one of the MSS is underlined with a solid line; an arrow is placed at the corresponding place in the text of the other manuscript to indicate an absence; lexical or grammatical variation is shown by a dotted underline; words that vary in order are placed in square brackets.

II. Names of Persons

II.1 Statement of the problem

The only rule for the use of the article with names of persons that emerges from the NT Greek grammars, and about which there is some consensus of opinion, is that names of persons are not usually preceded by the article (in other words, reference to them is anarthrous); but the article may be used (reference is arthrous) if the person has already been introduced by name before (anaphoric reference).[9] The grammars note, however, that there is a great number of unaccountable deviations from this rule. Different authors appear to adopt different practices and even two works by the same author do not necessarily conform to the same pattern, if indeed a pattern can be recognized. And then there is the complication of manuscript variation.

Several studies of the article in variant readings have been made by textual critics. For example, with regard to Peter in Acts, Elliott concludes that it is not at all clear how the article was used in the original text although there would be reason to prefer generally the arthrous reading in cases of variant readings because it seems to him that the custom of Luke was to prefer to use the article before his name.[10] Boismard and Lamouille, looking specifically at the book of Acts, believe that the linguistic origin of the name is responsible for the variation: that the original text read the article before

---

[9] Porter (*Idioms of New Testament Greek*, 107) notes: 'Proper names often do not appear with the article.... But in some contexts a name has the article', and he includes anaphoric reference as one of those contexts. Winer, for his part, declares that 'The use of the article with names of persons can hardly be reduced to any rule' (*A Treatise*, 140 §6).

[10] J. K. Elliott, 'Κηφᾶς: Σίμων Πέτρος: ὁ Πέτρος: An Examination of New Testament Usage', *NovT* 14 (1972): 241–56. See also Elliott, 'The Text of Acts in the Light of Two Recent Studies,' *NTS* 34 (1988): 250–8 (255–6).

names of Greek origin but not before those of Semitic origin, successive scribes making their corrections according to their own linguistic background.[11] These conclusions will be challenged by the results of the examination of the article carried out here.

II.2 The emergence of principles

In attempting to obtain a clearer picture, every occurrence of the names of persons in Acts was studied exhaustively (leaving aside those arising only in the portions of text missing from D05). The movement of the characters was noted as they move in and out of the story of Acts and the interaction between the characters was considered. Likewise, the opinion or the prior knowledge that hearers of the narrative could be expected to have had of the people in the story was taken into account. These factors are relevant because, as discourse analysis studies acknowledge, a narrative is not told simply through the eyes of the narrator but rather the speaker constantly takes account of the point of view of the audience as well as the internal perspectives of characters within the story.

Luke's non-variant text where both MSS agree on the presence or absence of the article (the 'common text') was examined first to provide a baseline against which to evaluate variant readings, which in turn can be used to refine the initial deductions. The principle that emerges from this study is that the default way of referring to people by name is with the article. By 'default' is meant that this is the practice a speaker would normally adopt in mentioning a person by name, unless there were special circumstances that called for the article to be omitted. Specifically, when a name is anarthrous it is because the participant is highlighted as prominent in one way or another at that point in the discourse. In other words, the pattern of use that emerges in Luke's writing is that inclusion of the article before a name is neutral, whereas omitting the article is a device of markedness, its function being to draw that person to the attention of the hearer at that particular point in the narrative.[12]

It is helpful to think of a narrative as a play being acted out on a stage. As characters move on and off the stage, take centre stage or wait in the wings, for example, the significance of their presence changes. At times, they are established figures on stage, whereas at others they play a particular role on which the dramatist wishes to focus attention, which may be done with the use of a spotlight. Clearly, in some instances the choice to focus on a character at a given point is open to interpretation, and what the

---

[11] M.-E. Boismard and A. Lamouille, *Le texte occidental des Actes des Apôtres: Reconstitution et réhabilitation*. 2 vols (Paris: Éditions Recherche sur les Civilisations, 1984), I, 110.

[12] The same pattern has been identified for the language of Plato, see David Sansone, 'Towards a New Doctrine of the Article: Some Observations on the Definite Article in Plato', *Classical Philology* 88 (1993): 191–205. Cf. the conclusion of the classical grammarian Basil Gildersleeve, who concluded that the article was not generally used with proper names in classical Greek: 'Proper names being in their nature particular do not require the explicit article, and when the article is used with them, it retains much of its original demonstrative force' (Basil L. Gildersleeve, *Syntax of Classical Greek from Homer to Demosthenes*. 2 vols (New York: American Book Company, 1900–11), II, §514). See further Gildersleeve, *Syntax*, II, §547–61, as well as specific essays: 'On the Article with Proper Names', *American Journal of Philology* 11 (1890): 483–7; 'Problems in Greek Syntax: II. The Article', *American Journal of Philology* 23 (1902): 1–27.

playwright had in mind may be viewed differently by subsequent directors, which they are at liberty to express in their staging of the play. Such freedom can frequently be seen as the cause of variation involving the presence of the article before names in Acts, where Luke is the playwright and the editors and/or copyists are later directors.

The following analysis classifies the circumstances that call for spotlighting of a character and presents some of the occurrences of variation.

II.3 First entry of participants

II.3.i First entry in the book

As noted in §II.1, handbooks of NT grammar generally agree that the first mention of a person by name is anarthrous, and the principle as stated above provides a reason for this to be so. When a participant is first introduced into a story, the author almost always spotlights their initial appearance as they take their place on stage, as a way of ensuring that their presence is clearly registered by the audience. The linguistic device for switching on the spotlight is to omit the article before the name of the person. Subsequently, once the participant has entered the story, he or she can be referred to as a known factor, and the article is therefore retained.

A high level of consistency is seen in the omission of the article when a character is mentioned for the first time in the book of Acts, as there are no variant readings in this respect. Whether the name is mentioned alone (e.g. Jesus, 1.1; Matthias, 1.23; Pilate, 3.13; Silas, 15.22) or introduced with an expression such as εἷς/τις ὀνόματι (e.g. Agabus, 11.28, Timothy, 16.1), or a title such as 'king' (Herod, 12.1), the reference is anarthrous. The only apparent exception to this pattern is the first mention of Peter by name at 1.13. Here, the article is included and, indeed, embraces the other ten names of the list of apostles who are presented as a unified group (see §II.6.i below). The article can be accounted for by the previous introduction of 'the apostles' at 1.2; its presence does, nevertheless, imply that Peter was already identified and acknowledged by Luke's addressee as the leader of the group.

The pattern of anarthrous first mention followed by arthrous anaphoric mentions in the book of Acts is illustrated by the references to Simon Magus in Acts 8 (8.9 anarthrous, cf. 8.13, 18, 24 arthrous) or to Gallio in Acts 18 (18.12 anarthrous, cf. 18.14, 17 arthrous). The procedure is similar to the slight emphasis given in spoken English to the name of a person who is being referred to for the first time in a story, an emphasis that is normally absent on subsequent mentions of the name.

II.3.ii First entry within a speech

An important consideration to bear in mind is that portions of speech within a narrative operate as independent units, with their own speaker and audience who are distinct from the narrator and the narrator's addressee. It is not uncommon for a person to be referred to in speech who has already been established in the section of the narrative within which the speech occurs. However, when the speaker mentions that person by name for the first time the article is omitted. This is to be expected for, as far as the speaker and his or her own hearers are concerned, a true 'first mention' is made. This is seen in the common text at 10.22 (the men from Caesarea speaking of Cornelius to Peter); 12.11 (Peter speaking of Herod to himself); 15.26, 27 (the Jerusalem apostles and elders speaking of Barnabas and Paul, Judas and Silas in their letter to the Gentile brethren); 19.38 (the Ephesian clerk speaking of Demetrius to the crowd).

On two occasions, the article is omitted in the Bezan text, not in direct but in indirect speech at 12.14b and 21.29. The variant reading seems to arise because the two texts are looking at the person mentioned from different points of view. At 12.14b, it is the narrator who relates that the servant girl, Rhoda, announces to the church praying in Mary's house in Jerusalem that Peter is at the door. From the point of view of Rhoda and the church, this is a first mention, which accounts for the omission of the article in D05. At the same time, from the point of view of the narrator of Acts as he speaks to his audience, this is an anaphoric reference that justifies the article in the B03 text. Similarly, at 21.29, there is ambiguity: the narrator explains that some Jewish opponents were attacking Paul because it was supposed that he had taken a Gentile into the Temple. According to B03, the supposition is attributed to the attackers: ὃν ἐνόμιζον ὅτι εἰς τὸ ἱερὸν εἰσήγαγεν ὁ Παῦλος, and Paul is viewed from the point of view of the narrator for whom Paul is well-established as the focal character of the story at this point. D05 presents the situation differently, attributing the supposition to Paul's companions, the 'we-group', through whose eyes Paul is seen for the first time in the present context and the name is anarthrous: ὃν ἐνομίσαμεν ὅτι εἰς τὸ ἱερὸν εἰσήγαγεν ↑ Παῦλος.

II.3.iii First entry from the point of view of another character

The shift in perspective just observed arises because the characters in the story of Acts not only present themselves to the hearer or reader of the story; they also interact with each other; they speak with, listen to, confront, follow one another, especially in the case of the secondary characters as they meet the Christian leaders. And when some points of meeting are referred to for the first time, Luke marks this initial encounter by the omission of the article before the name of the person who is the object of the meeting, even if he or she is already an active participant in the scene. It is as if that person were being seen from the point of view of the other character and not of the ones telling or listening to the story. The point is illustrated by 3.3 (the lame man sees Peter and John); 13.7 (the proconsul calls Barnabas and Saul); 14.11 (the crowds in Lystra see the healing carried out by Paul). The D05 narrator of Acts is especially sensitive to the internal point of view of the characters and the article is omitted on numerous additional occasions as a variant reading, where this more intimate perspective accounts for the highlighting of a character. See, for instance, 8.6D05 (the crowds were attentive to what Philip said); 13.50D05 (Jewish opponents persecuted Paul and Barnabas in Antioch of Pisidia); 16.14D05 (Lydia was attentive to what Paul said); 17.15D05 (Silas and Timothy receive a command from Paul); 20.9D05 (Eutyches listened to Paul's lecturing).

II.4 Re-entry of participants

A modified type of 'first entry' is seen when, following a character's first introduction on the stage, the character leaves the stage to wait in the wings until he or she reappears in a new scene. Thus, at the start of a new episode, the reference is sometimes anarthrous – Philip, 6.5; cf. 8.5, 12, 13, 26; Aquila and Priscilla, 18.18, cf. 18.26. Following the initial anarthrous introduction in a new episode, subsequent mentions are arthrous unless other factors intervene (see §II.5 below). These anarthrous references at the beginning of a new incident can be explained by the fact that the participant has been inactive or off-stage since the last mention and is now being reintroduced as a salient participant.

When certain other characters, in contrast, reappear in a new scene the article is maintained. In these cases, the character in question is a major participant whose presence was, as it were, always active even though they were not visible. Thus, in the first part of Acts, the name of Jesus is typically arthrous, though less so in א01/B03;[13] Peter is often arthrous at the start of new scenes throughout the first five chapters, as is Paul, too, throughout the second part of the book. There are not a few variant readings in this respect (for example, the name of Peter at 1.15 is arthrous in D05, but not B03; at 5.3, it is the B03 text that is arthrous). It seems that when Luke holds major characters as active over a long stretch of narrative, this gives rise to varying views among successive editors and copyists as to their status at specific points in the developing narrative. This is not, however the same as saying that it is a matter of authorial style, as if the decision to use the article were dictated by an inherent personal tendency – on the contrary, the choice to use the article or not reflects how the author/editor/copyist perceives the role of the participant at a given point in a story; it depends on his or her understanding of the unfolding of the story and the prominence of the characters at the point at which they are mentioned by name.

II.5 Participants on stage

In the circumstances presented above, the omission of the article before the name of a participant functions as a device to draw the attention of the audience to that character. At their point of entry into the narrative or into the consciousness of the audience, Luke's characters acquire a natural prominence that causes them to stand out temporarily from any other character.

During the course of a narrative, too, once a participant is established on stage within an episode, Luke may omit the article again on grounds that derive from the principle of salience, as characters need to be distinguished from other characters, or even other possible participants. In these instances, the anarthrous reference is seemingly a way of marking the named character as salient at that point. Various circumstances can be identified that call for the absence of the article to focus the spotlight on a character after the first mention. These can be grouped according to the categories of i) selection; ii) contrast; iii) switch of focus; iv) highlighting a speech.

---

[13] Anarthrous *vll* for the name of Jesus are found at 1.14 (א01) and 1.16 (א01/B03).

II.5.i Selection

When more than one participant is introduced at the outset of a story and comment then made concerning only one of those initially named, Luke omits the article before the second mention to indicate that that particular participant is salient at that point. The following examples show how this works:

- Matthias is introduced into the account of events at 1.23 together with Joseph, both being candidates to replace Judas. The two names are anarthrous at this first mention, as would be expected. When lots are cast and the lot falls on Matthias (1.26), the name is still without the article because here 'Matthias' is the one of the pair who is selected and there is a special focus on him.
- Stephen is mentioned for the first time in Acts at 6.5 at the head of the list of the seven Hellenists, without the article. Then, at 6.8, he is singled out for specific mention as he takes on a specific role. Even though the reference is anaphoric, it is anarthrous because Stephen becomes salient at this point when he becomes the focus of interest in the story of the Jerusalem church.
- John, first mentioned at 13.5, is singled out from the rest of Paul's company at 13.13b as doing something different because he alone goes back to Jerusalem.

II.5.ii Contrast

When there is contrast, explicit or implicit, Luke omits the article. The second part of Acts from chapter 13 to the end of the book, in which Paul is the main protagonist, is characterized by many examples of such omission (see, for example, 17.6, where an angry mob look for Paul and Silas but, not finding them, seize Jason instead). There are many variants, sometimes because a person is mentioned in one text but not in the other (e.g. Judas and Silas at 15.34, 35D05; Apollos at 19.1B03); elsewhere, it is D05 that displays a consistent tendency to highlight contrast – to be precise, contrast between Paul and other characters (e.g. Timothy and Silas are set against Paul, 18.5D05; the chiliarch's acquisition of Roman citizenship is contrasted with that of Paul, 22.28D05; see also on 15.36–40 below).

II.5.iii Switch of focus

Once a character is established in an episode Luke usually retains the article, as was seen above (§§II.3.i, ii). When, however, attention is transferred from one established participant or group of participants to another within an episode and this switch of focus needs to be emphasized, the new participants are reintroduced without the article. In this way, they re-emerge as salient. This is the case at such places as: 8.1, switch from Stephen back to Saul, already introduced at 7.58; 12.19, switch from Peter back to Herod, already named at 12.1; 12.25, switch from Herod back to Barnabas and Saul, already introduced at 11.30.

Among the MSS, once again there is variation on this point, for example at 12.6. Throughout Acts 12, attention moves back and forth between Herod and the threat of danger on the one hand, and Peter and his miraculous escape on the other; in D05 at

12.6, the omission of the article before Herod marks his plan to have Peter accused by the people in Jerusalem as particularly salient.

Likewise at 15.35; 16.18, 25 and 19.30 the article is omitted before Paul (and Barnabas or Silas) in the B03 text as the story turns from a temporary focus on secondary characters to the activities of the main protagonists. D05, on the other hand, would seem to consider that they do not need to be given renewed prominence (by omitting the article) as their story is picked up; they have always been 'front of stage' and the article is retained.[14]

The episode relating the separation of Barnabas from Paul illustrates the function of the omission of the article both to highlight contrast and to switch attention between characters:

Ref. D05	B03
15.36 Μετὰ δέ τινας ἡμέρας [εἶπεν <u>ὁ</u> Παῦλος πρὸς Βαρναβᾶν],'Ἐπιστρέψαντες δὴ ἐπισκεψώμεθα τοὺς ἀδελφοὺς <u>τοὺς</u> κατὰ *πᾶσαν πόλιν* ἐν <u>οἷς</u> κατηγγείλαμεν τὸν λόγον τοῦ κυρίου, πῶς ἔχουσιν.	Μετὰ δέ τινας ἡμέρας [εἶπεν πρὸς Βαρναβᾶν ↑ Παῦλος],'Ἐπιστρέψαντες δὴ ἐπισκεψώμεθα τοὺς ἀδελφοὺς ↑ κατὰ *πόλιν πᾶσαν* ἐν <u>αἷς</u> κατηγγείλαμεν τὸν λόγον τοῦ κυρίου, πῶς ἔχουσιν.
15.37 Βαρναβᾶς δὲ ἐβουλεύετο συνπαραλαβεῖν ↑ Ἰωάννην τὸν ἐπικαλούμενον Μᾶρκον.	Βαρναβᾶς δὲ ἐβούλετο συμπαραλαβεῖν <u>καὶ τὸν</u> Ἰωάννην τὸν καλούμενον Μᾶρκον.
15.38 Παῦλος δὲ οὐκ ἐβούλετο λέγων τὸν ἀποστήσαντα ἀπ' αὐτῶν ἀπὸ Παμφυλίας καὶ μὴ συνελθόντα ↑ εἰς τὸ ἔργον [τοῦτον μὴ εἶναι σὺν αὐτοῖς].	Παῦλος δὲ ἠξίου τὸν ἀποστάντα ἀπ' αὐτῶν ἀπὸ Παμφυλίας καὶ μὴ συνελθόντα <u>αὐτοῖς</u> εἰς τὸ ἔργον [μὴ συμπαραλαμβάνειν τοῦτον].
15.39 ἐγένετο δὲ παροξυσμὸς ὥστε ἀποχωρισθῆναι αὐτοὺς ἀπ' ἀλλήλων, <u>τότε</u> ↑ Βαρναβᾶς παραλαβὼν τὸν Μᾶρκον ἔπλευσεν εἰς Κύπρον.	ἐγένετο δὲ παροξυσμὸς ὥστε ἀποχωρισθῆναι αὐτοὺς ἀπ' ἀλλήλων, <u>τόν</u> τε Βαρναβᾶν παραλαβόντα τὸν Μᾶρκον ἐκπλεῦσαι εἰς Κύπρον.
15.40 Παῦλος δὲ ἐπιδεξάμενος Σιλᾶν ἐξῆλθεν παραδοθεὶς τῇ χάριτι ↑ κυρίου ἀπὸ τῶν ἀδελφῶν.	Παῦλος δὲ ἐπιλεξάμενος Σιλᾶν ἐξῆλθεν παραδοθεὶς τῇ χάριτι <u>τοῦ</u> κυρίου ὑπὸ τῶν ἀδελφῶν.
15.41 διήρχετο δὲ τὴν Συρίαν καὶ τὴν Κιλικίαν ἐπιστηρίζων τὰς ἐκκλησίας.	διήρχετο δὲ τὴν Συρίαν καὶ τὴν Κιλικίαν ἐπιστηρίζων τὰς ἐκκλησίας.

In the B03 text, particular attention is drawn to Paul, both by the omission of the article and also by the clause-final position, the position of natural prominence for a clausal constituent.[15] On both counts, D05 treats Paul as the established main character, as he proposes to Barnabas (anarthrous, setting him up as distinct from Paul; cf. 15.35 where they are presented as a unit, especially with the single article in D05) to go and

---

[14] When Paul is acting in unison with another participant, one article before the first named functions for the pair as a whole; see §II.2.3 below).

[15] See Steven Runge, *Discourse Grammar of the Greek New Testament: A Practical Introduction for Teaching and Exegesis* (Peabody, Mass; Hendrickson Publishers, 2010), 185–9. It is not surprising that the omission of the article should often be observed to be operating in conjunction with other features, notably word order, as a combined means to indicate the important information of a sentence, where 'important' naturally means 'important for the speaker in terms of his or her communication goal' and not in any absolute sense.

visit the cities they had previously evangelized. The independence of Barnabas in relation to Paul is then maintained as his wish (B03) or decision (D05) to take John-Mark is presented – the reference is treated as anaphoric in B03 even though the last mention was several episodes earlier (cf. 13.13), but his name is underlined by the omission of the article in the D05 text, as an indication that the choice was not necessarily the expected one.[16] Disagreement between Paul and Barnabas develops as Paul is set in contrast to Barnabas with the omission of the article as his name is mentioned 15.38. The conflict (nothing less than a παροξυσμός) is maintained with the omission of the article before Barnabas' name in 15.39, and again before Paul's in 15.40. Silas is likewise anarthrous, not because of conflict but because Paul's decision to choose him as his companion has not been anticipated and because Silas stands in contrast to John-Mark.

II.5.iv Clauses introducing speech

There is a tendency for the article to be omitted before proper names in clauses that introduce speech, though this is less pronounced in the Bezan text and there is too much variation between the MSS for Luke's own practice to be identified. The omission arises especially when Peter or Paul either initiate a conversation or make a key speech of proclamation, encouragement or warning even though they are already established in the scene (e.g. 10.34, Peter to the household of Cornelius; 11.4, Peter to the Jerusalem brethren; 17.22B03, Paul in the Areopagus; 19.4B03, Paul to the disciples in Ephesus). Sometimes, the speaker is singled out from other participants as he is about to speak (1.15B03, Peter from among the other apostles; 2.38; 4.8; 5.29B03; 8.20), or there is a switch of focus from a minor participant back to Peter or Paul as he speaks (16.28B03, from the jailor to Paul as he addresses the jailor for the first time). In these instances, it is not so much the speaker himself who is the focus of attention, but rather his function as the proclaimer of a key message.

II.6 Technical reasons

Three further technical factors influence Luke's choice of the article before proper names.

II.6.i Two or more names

When two or more names mentioned together are joined with καί, and the first has the article, the second (or any subsequent) name does not take the article if the pair or group are viewed as acting in harmony: 1.13 (Peter and the other named apostles); 4.13 (Peter and John); 13.2 (Barnabas and Saul); 15.22 B03 (Paul and Barnabas – both names are anarthrous in D05). There are a further eight such instances in Codex Bezae

---

[16] Barnabas' choice of John-Mark is discussed in Rius-Camps & Read-Heimerdinger, *The Message of Acts*, IV 237–9.

(3.11; 13.43, 46; 15.2a, b; 16.19, 29; 17.15), where the B03 text reads the article before both names, apparently reflecting the importance that Paul acquired as a character distinct from his co-workers. In material that is omitted by the Alexandrian text, it is apparent that the Bezan narrator does not view him with the same degree of approval and often purposefully points out his weaknesses.

II.6.ii Stereotyped phrases

In stereotyped phrases that include a reference to a named person, the reference is anarthrous without variants whether the person has already been mentioned in the story or not. This is notably so for the repeated occurrences of τὸ βάπτισμα Ἰωάννου, 'the baptism of John' at 1.22; 18.25; 19.3; and τὸ ὄνομα Ἰησοῦ, 'the name of Jesus' at 2.38; 3.6; 4.10; 16.18.

II.6.iii Dependent genitive

A final issue concerns a name in the genitive, dependent on an articular phrase. The article is retained before the person's name, without variant readings in the MSS studied, whenever the reference to the person is anaphoric (e.g. 12.7, 14; 20.37; 21.11). When the article is omitted, the reference is either a set phrase like 'the name of Jesus' or a first mention. In other words, the presence or absence of the article with such dependent genitives is not determined by the syntax. The principle is clearly illustrated in Acts 10 where, at 10.17, (διερωτήσαντες) τὴν οἰκίαν τοῦ Σίμωνος, 'the house of Simon', is an anaphoric reference (cf. 9.43, D05 *lac.*) and as such Simon is prefaced by the article; however, at 10.32, we see ἐν οἰκίᾳ Σίμωνος, quoting the earlier conversation of 10.3–6, where it is a first mention in direct speech, and the name Simon is therefore anarthrous.

It is worth noting that grammatical case does not, in general, affect the use of the article before names of persons, despite apparent statistical evidence to the contrary. For example, a numerical count shows that a high proportion of names in the nominative case are anarthrous – that is not because of the case but because the subject of a sentence is frequently salient.

II.7 Conclusion on the use of the article with names of persons

In summary, it may be observed that first mentions of a person by name are anarthrous, with practically no variation within or between the MSS. Secondly, reference to named persons is anarthrous when attention is being drawn to their presence or to their actions at that particular point in the text. This factor, described here as salience, is determined by several aspects, all of which are characterised by a fair amount of variation both within and between the MSS. There are, finally, technical reasons for anarthrous reference to named persons that tend to apply with a high degree of consistency. In the absence of any of these three factors, the article is used to refer to persons by name.

The identification of the main principle of saliency tallies with the result of a study regarding ordinary nouns in classical Greek. There, too, salience has been recognized as the overall factor that lies behind the omission of the article before a noun where it would normally be expected. Thus, in his study of the use of the article in Plato, Sansone concludes that the 'definite article tends to be more at home with topic than with focus'.[17] This will be a feature of the use of the article to take into account in considering names of places in the next section.

III. Names of places

III.1 Statement of the problem

Like names of persons, place names also fall into the category of nouns that have a sole, identifiable referent. To use the classification proposed by Porter, place names are identifiable as 'particular'.[18] In fact, they are even more particular than names of persons since there is rarely more than one referent designated by any given geographical name, unlike the many people called Mary, Peter or Jesus, for example. The aim of this part of the study is to see if the pattern that has been established with respect to the use of the article with names of persons also applies to the place names. The book of Acts is again a most useful source of data, because both the narrative and the speeches within it abound in references to geographical locations of many kinds, whether associated with the land or the sea: countries, regions, cities, mountains, islands, seas.

Treatment of the article with geographical names in the standard Greek grammars suggests that, as with names of persons, there are no real rules. Blass–Debrunner–Rehkopf, for example, present a list of observations, noting the 'frequent', 'many' or 'occasional' occurrences of the presence or the absence of the article with certain names or categories but without explanation; Robertson speaks of 'obscurity and uncertainty'.[19] Other works make no distinction between proper names of people and proper names of places, any 'clear and consistent principles' being in any case rated as undetectable.[20] Gildersleeve identifies the general 'rule' that the article is present with geographical names, while noting that exceptions occur chiefly in enumerations, conjoined nouns functioning as a unity and the predicate.[21] It is telling that, commenting on Gildersleeve's analysis of the spectrum of classical works, Robertson notes that usage of article with place names 'greatly varies among Greek writers'.[22] Winer, for his part, gives the impression that apart from a regular tendency for the first mention of a name to be anarthrous, the presence or absence of the article depends on the nature of the place (e.g. country versus cities) or on the grammatical context (e.g. after prepositions, or in oblique cases) or on the author.[23]

---

[17] Sansone, 'Towards a New Doctrine', 199.
[18] Porter, *Idioms of New Testament Greek*, 313.
[19] Blass, Debrunner & Rehkopf, *Grammatik des neutestamentlichen Griechisch*, §261; Robertson, *A Grammar of the Greek New Testament*, 1397.
[20] E.g. Wallace, *Greek Grammar beyond the Basics*, 245–7.
[21] Gildersleeve, *Syntax*, II, §568, 603 and 666 respectively.
[22] Robertson, *Grammar*, 759.
[23] Winer, *A Treatise*, 139–40.

The situation in the grammar books is thus not a little confused, despite some extensive and detailed analysis and a genuine search for general principles. It lends itself to the conclusion that the choice to use the article or not is 'as much a question of style as of grammar'.[24] Taking into account the additional variation found in the different MSS, only occasionally if ever mentioned in the NT grammar books, it would be an easy step to assume that scribal custom should also figure in the list of factors determining the use of the article.[25]

In view of the principles that were able to be identified with respect to personal names using the tools of discourse analysis, there is reason, however, to have some optimism about recognizing the linguistic factors influencing a speaker's choice to use the article with geographical names. In order to reach a full and complete explanation, a range of texts and authors would need to be examined in detail, elucidating patterns and testing the principles that evolve in a variety of situations. This study of Luke's practice with geographical names in the book of Acts is presented as one small part of that examination, in the hope that it can contribute to a wider and more complete study of the question that will achieve the all-important goal of 'explanatory adequacy'.[26]

III.2 Emergence of a principle

The following analysis tends to confirm that salience is the key factor affecting the use of the article. With all of the different types of places, the default usage is to include the article with geographical names, and omission of the article is a way of marking the place out as of particular significance. Unlike names of persons, however, the first mention of the name of a place is not marked in this way, except for cities (and island-cities) which are generally anarthrous at their point of introduction into the narrative.

In the following analysis, names of places will be examined according to the nature of the place: countries, regions, islands, mountains and cities.

III.3 Countries

Among the places mentioned in Acts, only a few can be classified as countries because of the changing nature of their boundaries and identity as they were absorbed by foreign powers, notably the Roman Empire by the time of the events recorded in Acts. Areas that had been made into Roman provinces are dealt with under the next section §III.4.[27]

---

[24] Sansone, 'Towards a New Doctrine', 204, referring to the work of Gildersleeve.
[25] Sansone does draw attention to the existence of variant readings concerning the presence of the article in the text of Plato and the need to take account of it in establishing patterns of use ('Towards a New Doctrine', 202).
[26] Wallace, *Beyond the Basics*, 246, citing Chomsky.
[27] Israel is not included in this study because whenever it is mentioned in Acts (× 10), the name refers to Israel as a people or ethnic identity rather than a geographic location. It may be noted, however, that while the majority of references to Israel are anarthrous, all of them arise in a fixed expression such as 'the people/house/sons of Israel'. On the two occasions when the article is present (4.8; 5.31), the mention occurs in a phrase that is not stereotypical.

III.3.i Egypt

This is the most frequently mentioned country, principally in the speech of Stephen in Acts 7. The name first occurs before that speech, at the head of the list of countries (regions) cited as being represented in Jerusalem at Pentecost (2.9), and thereafter is mentioned 11 times (+ 1 B03; + 1 D05) by Stephen. On all save two occasions the name is anarthrous, even when it occurs twice in successive sentences (e.g. 7.10a b, 34a b).

At 7.11, the article is used where Egypt is mentioned in conjunction with Canaan, as famine came ἐφ' ὅλης τῆς Αἰγύπτου καὶ Χανάαν. The name of Egypt has just occurred in the previous sentence in a salient reference to Moses being appointed the governor of the country; when the country is mentioned again in 7.11 it is a true anaphoric reference with no need to highlight its salience. The article is then found at 7.36B03 with some support:[28] ἐν τῇ Αἰγύπτῳ, where Egypt is mentioned as a place in conjunction with the Red Sea and the desert where miracles were performed. The similarity of the uncials Γ and Τ could have led to confusion with ἐν γῇ Ἰγύπτῳ of D05 and other MSS, but even if the article is secondary from a linguistic point of view that does not make it an 'error' or even a scribal preference. On the contrary, the arthrous reference could be the default form, altered by the fixed nature of the phrase ἐν γῇ... (cf. comments on Midia, below).

When the article is omitted, the country is always salient for one reason or another. For example, at 7.12, Jacob is said to have heard at the time of the famine that there was corn in Egypt, where the country is seen as being of particular importance from his point of view in comparing it with Canaan. At 7.15, Egypt occurs in a sentence full of weighty significance: καὶ κατέβη Ἰακὼβ εἰς Αἴγυπτον,[29] a statement that is central to Stephen's argument in his speech. The omission of the article before Egypt tallies with the anarthrous, though anaphoric, mention by Jacob and combines with the asyndetic introduction to the sentence to highlight the statement in a powerful way. The omission of the article in other references to Egypt can be justified similarly, as a device used to draw attention to the name for one reason or another.

III.3.ii Other Mesopotamian countries

Stephen mentions several countries in his speech as he reviews the history of Israel. As indicated in the paragraph above, Canaan is mentioned anarthrously once (7.11), where it is associated with Egypt. Midian is named without the article (7.29), in the phrase ἐν γῇ Μαδιάμ, which is typically anarthrous.[30] Finally, the name of Babylon occurs (7.43) in an adapted quotation from Amos, where the reference is highlighted as the destination corresponding to Israel's punishment: μετοικιῶ ὑμᾶς ἐπέκεινα Βαβυλῶνος.[31]

---

[28] The reading of the article is supported by C04 36 453 *pc*. Other MSS read ἐν γῇ Αἰγύπτῳ (Αἰγύπτου D05 *et al*).

[29] B03 alone omits the mention of Egypt in this sentence.

[30] Cf. Lk. 2.4D05: Ἀνέβη δὲ καὶ Ἰωσὴφ ἀπὸ τῆς Γαλιλαίας ἐκ πόλεως Ναζαρὲθ εἰς γῆν Ἰούδα (εἰς τὴν Ἰουδαίαν, B03).

[31] At 7.43, D05 reads ἐπὶ τὰ μέρη Βαβυλῶνος, a chorographic genitive, which Gildersleeve observes to be usually anarthrous (*Syntax*, 2:§552).

III.3.iii Greece

The country is named as such only at 20.2, where Paul is said to go there (ἦλθεν εἰς τὴν Ἑλλάδα, 20.2). Although the reference is not strictly anaphoric, it corresponds to the decision earlier attributed to Paul at 19.21 to go 'Achaia' (see §III.4.viii below), and so the information is not especially salient. Anaphora, however, is probably not the factor that accounts for the retention of the article with Ἑλλάς, for comparison with the one other country mentioned in Acts, *Italy*, shows that the article is present at both isolated references: at 18.2, Aquila is said to have recently come (to Corinth) from Italy, which is of only indirect relevance to the narrative and plays no further role; at 27.6, the centurion found a boat for Paul to travel with as it was going to Italy, the country that had long been presented as his final destination, hitherto referred to by the capital of Rome.

In sum, as far as countries are concerned, it can be deduced that the use of the article is the default way of referring to them. Omission of the article occurs either in a fixed expression (ἐν γῇ...) or, more usually, as a means to highlight the country, but this is not a device used for the first occurrences of the name, unlike the pattern observed with names of persons (see §II.1 above).

III.4 Regions

For ease of classification, the names of regions are discussed according to the section of the Acts narrative with which they are particularly associated.

III.4.i Judaea

This area, seen in Acts as the homeland of the Jews, is of crucial significance for the first part of the book of Acts since the action is centred there for the first five chapters. All the references are arthrous irrespective of the criterion of first mention, except for a variant anarthrous reading at 10.37D05. Here, Peter is seen, exceptionally, to be addressing an audience of Gentiles to whom he mentions Judaea as the region where Jesus had been active among the Jewish people. The absence of the article in the Bezan text seems to reflect Peter's awareness of the viewpoint of his audience, for whom Judaea is country not theirs but it is the country of the Jews (cf. 10.39), and he will go on in the next sentence to contrast it with Galilee (arthrous). The sensitivity of the writer of Acts, especially the Bezan narrator, to the viewpoints of different characters was already noted with reference to the names of persons in §II above.

One other variant reading involving the article with Judaea is found at 8.1, where D05 has an anarthrous reference: πάντες δὲ διεσπάρησαν κατὰ τὰς χώρας τῆς (om. D05) Ἰουδαίας καὶ Σαμαρείας. Since the one other reference to the two regions is arthrous with one article serving the two names (see 1.8), and since there is no obvious cause for the narrator to highlight the names at 8.1, the D05 reading could be interpreted as an example of what Gildersleeve calls the 'chorographic genitive'.[32] The perspective

---

[32] See previous note.

of discourse analysis, however, prompts the consideration that the narrator has a reason for highlighting the reference to Judaea and Samaria at this point, at least in D05. The text of 8.1 goes on to specify that πάντες does not include the apostles for they were *not* dispersed (πλὴν τῶν ἀποστόλων), and at that point an additional clause is read by D05: <u>οἳ ἔμειναν ἐν Ἰερουσαλήμ</u>. This comment carries a great deal of weight in the Bezan text, where the narrator uses the dual spelling of the city of Jerusalem to evaluate the spiritual progress of the characters, reserving the Hebrew-derived spelling to refer to the seat of Judaism as opposed to the geographical city.[33] Thus, the disciples of Hierosoluma (ἐν Ἰεροσολύμοις, 8.1b) were driven out of Judaea and Samaria by the persecution, but the apostles remained in Jerusalem (<u>ἐν Ἰερουσαλήμ</u>, 8.1c) under the protection of the Jewish authorities, as will emerge in due course.[34] On this reading, the contrast between the apostles, who had been commanded by Jesus precisely to go to all of Judea and Samaria (ἐν πάσῃ τῇ Ἰουδαίᾳ καὶ Σαμαρείᾳ, 1.8) and the Hellenist disciples who in fact do go there, is stark, and may be the explanation for the omission of the article before the regions on this occasion in the Bezan text.

At 2.9, Judaea is mentioned in a list of nine regions and countries from where people were present at Pentecost:

οἱ κατοικοῦντες τὴν Μεσοποταμίαν Ἰουδαίαν <u>τε</u> (om. D05) καὶ Καππαδοκίαν Πόντον καὶ τὴν Ἀσίαν Φρυγίαν <u>τε</u> (om. D05) καὶ Παμφυλίαν, Αἴγυπτον <u>τε</u> (om. B03) καὶ τὰ μέρη τῆς Λιβύης τῆς κατὰ Κυρήνην...

The article is found before Mesopotamia, before Asia and before Libya. The reason for its presence with certain names and not others may depend on the particular way the countries are grouped. The first three, which include Judaea, may be considered to form an initial grouping (especially with the linking τε), for which a single article suffices (as discussed in §II.6.i above). Mesopotamia is arthrous on its single other appearance (7.2). Asia itself will be considered separately below, but meanwhile it may be observed that both Phrygia and Pamphilia could be being viewed as belonging to the larger land mass of Asia. As for Libya, the article in the phrase τὰ μέρη... is not surprising given that the area is specifically qualified as τῆς κατὰ Κυρήνην. There remains Pontus as the only name without an article that is not accounted for by any of the explanations presented so far and, in this sense, it is indeed, something of an anomaly.

III.4.ii Samaria and Galilee

These two names are always arthrous, sometimes by virtue of their being linked to one or two other regions of which the first named bears the article (but note the D05 variant at 8.1, on which see above in this section; and 15.3, where many MSS including D05 repeat the article before Samaria – διήρχοντο τήν τε Φοινίκην καὶ <u>τὴν</u> Σαμάρειαν, thus treating the two regions as distinct).

---

[33] See Read-Heimerdinger, *The Bezan Text*, 275–344. See also Rius-Camps & Read-Heimerdinger, *The Message of Acts*, IV, 6–8.
[34] See Rius-Camps & Read-Heimerdinger, *The Message of Acts*, II, 117–20.

The places beyond the ancient territory of Israel take on a greater importance after Acts 8 once the Church moves out beyond the boundaries of Judaea and Samaria, and especially once the believers begin to proclaim the gospel to the Gentiles from Acts 10 onwards. Most locations are associated with the travels of Paul, though they are often already mentioned before he becomes an active participant in the narrative.

III.4.iii Asia

The Roman province of Asia Minor is mentioned nine times (+ 1 B03; + 1 B03 [D05 lac]; + 2 D05). After first appearing in the list of 2.9 (on which see §III.4.ii above) it is next named at 6.9. The name is usually arthrous, even when the country is referred to for the first time in the context. The article is also retained when the region is set in contrast to Jerusalem at 19.1D05:

Ref. D05	B03
19.1 ↑ Θέλοντος δὲ τοῦ Παύλου κατὰ τὴν ἰδίαν βουλὴν πορεύεσθαι εἰς Ἱεροσόλυμα εἶπεν αὐτῷ τὸ πνεῦμα ὑποστρέφειν εἰς τὴν Ἀσίαν διελθὼν δὲ τὰ ἀνωτερικὰ μέρη ἔρχεται εἰς Ἔφεσον	↑ Ἐγένετο δὲ ἐν τῷ τὸν Ἀπολλῶ εἶναι ἐν Κορίνθῳ ↑ Παῦλον ↑ διελθόντα ↑ τὰ ἀνωτερικὰ μέρη ἐλθεῖν εἰς Ἔφεσον

Although the mention of Asia in the D05 reading is particularly salient – indeed, critical information in terms of the Bezan narrator's portrayal of Paul as someone whose own plans are not endorsed by the Holy Spirit – Paul had already indicated when he was last in Asia that he would return (18.21). Thus, Asia represents the direction both expected and intended for Paul and, as will be seen with reference to Syria and Macedonia at 20.3 (see §§III.4.vii+viii below), this factor apparently plays a part in the retention of the article before names of places.

The three anarthrous references to Asia stand out as exceptional, though none is a firm reading. At 6.9, it is a question of people who began to argue with Stephen, people who were from Cilicia and from Asia (D05 omits this mention of Asia). Neither region has the article. It could be that the narrator is highlighting Cilicia as being of special importance, for this is the province from which Paul originated, and his later role in the story concerning Stephen (see 7.58; 8.1) suggests he would have been among those Jews from Cilicia disputing with Stephen. Asia, too, will later emerge as the place from which the fiercest Jewish opponents of Paul as a Jesus-believer came (τὴν Ἀσίαν, 21.27); pointing out their presence here anticipates the part they will continue to play in opposing the attitudes of Jewish Jesus-believers to the Temple. For the unexpected absence of the article before Cilicia and Asia at 6.9 to have such a highlighting function, it may be supposed that the addressee of the narrative would have had some prior knowledge of this aspect of the conflict between believers and non-believers.[35]

---

[35] This point is of particular relevance for the addressee of the Bezan text for whom there is strong evidence of a Jewish, non-Christian, origin. See Chapter 1, §II.3.

At 19.26, 27, the references to Asia made by Demetrius in his address to the Ephesian craftsmen could be seen as salient according to the articulation of the narrative. At 19.26, he speaks of the harm caused by Paul not only in Ephesus but also in the whole of Asia, where an adverbial καί in D05 underlines the spread of the damage: οὐ μόνον Ἐφέσου ἀλλὰ <u>καὶ</u> σχεδὸν πάσης (τῆςB03) Ἀσίας. When Demetrius then goes on (18.27) to praise the goddess Artemis who is worshipped throughout Asia and the inhabited world, B03 (but not ℵ01) omits the article before both places: ἣν ὅλη ἡ (om. B03) Ἀσία καὶ ἡ (om. B03) οἰκουμένη σέβεται. The first omission could have arisen through homoioteleuton (ΟΛΗΗΑCΙΑ) and the second then could be a means to balance the two phrases. Alternatively, both omissions by B03 of ἡ in this sentence could be a way of highlighting the wide extent of the worship of the goddess of Ephesus.

III.4.iv Cilicia

The Roman province is always arthrous after the mention at 6.9 analysed above. When it is named together with Syria at 15.23, the single article groups the two regions together. The joint reference to Syria and Cilicia occurs again at 15.41, where B03 (not ℵ01) maintains a single article, whereas D05 repeat the article before Cilicia, thus indicating that it is being viewed as distinct from Syria. At the one further occurrence of Cilica at 23.34 (D05 *lac.*) the mention of the province provides important and new information about the origin of Paul to the governor Felix, from whose perspective Cilicia is named. This could be the factor that accounts for the omission of the article.

III.4.v Phoenicia

This region is introduced into the narrative of Acts at 11.19 as the first-named in a group of places (Phoenicia, Cyprus and Antioch) outside Jewish territory, which the Jesus-believers ventured to. As such, the name is in no way anticipated and is of particular significance for the account of the spread of the gospel (note the preposition ἕως which, in itself, highlights the places named). At 21.2, Phoenicia is again anarthrous, being the destination of the ship Paul and his companions were fortunate enough to find. In that sense, the place is not an expected or anticipated destination, but is implicitly singled out from among other potential landing places along the Syrian coast.

The one remaining reference to Phoenicia at 15.3 is arthrous – in this instance, the region is named together with Samaria as places Paul and Barnabas travelled through on their way from Antioch to Jerusalem. Insofar as these regions lie on the path of the itinerary between the two cities, that they are cited as places where the travellers met with other believers occasions no surprise.

III.4.vi Pamphylia, Pisidia, Lycaonia

The region of Pamphylia was discussed above with reference to the list of 2.9, where it was suggested that the absence of the article could be due to its being considered as a part of the larger area of Asia. It is then mentioned again (13.13) as the area of the mainland at which Paul and his companions arrived on leaving Cyprus, with particular reference to the town of Perga, εἰς Πέργην τῆς Παμφυλίας. Here, it is Perga that is in focus, Pamphylia being the region that serves to identify it. In that respect, the reference is similar to that of 27.5, where it is a question of crossing the 'open sea off Cilicia and Pamphylia' (τὸ πέλαγος τὸ κατὰ τὴν Κιλικίαν καὶ Παμφυλίαν), where the one article serves to group together the two regions as one (cf. §II.6.i above).

At the one remaining occurrence of Pamphylia (14.24), the article is present in B03 but not in D05. The region is mentioned in the course of the description of the return journey of Paul and Barnabas from Pisidia to Syrian Antioch (14.23–26), when they retrace the steps of their outward journey. Luke has the travellers go through the region of Pisidia and on to Pamphylia, where they stop in the town of Perga. B03 has the article for both regions, unlike D05 which only has the article for Pisidia:

Ref. D05	B03
14.24 διελθόντες δὲ τὴν Πισιδίαν ἦλθαν εἰς ↑ Παμφυλίαν,	καὶ διελθόντες τὴν Πισιδίαν ἦλθον εἰς τὴν Παμφυλίαν,
14.25 καὶ λαλήσαντες ἐν Πέργῃ τὸν λόγον κατέβησαν εἰς Ἀττάλειαν κἀκεῖθεν ἀπέπλευσαν εἰς Ἀντιόχειαν...	καὶ λαλήσαντες ἐν Πέργῃ τὸν λόγον κατέβησαν εἰς Ἀττάλειαν κἀκεῖθεν ἀπέπλευσαν εἰς Ἀντιόχειαν...

That Pisidia should be arthrous can be explained by the geographical situation, for the last town the pair stopped in, Antioch, belonged to the province of Pisidia (cf. 13.14).[36] In this case, it is entirely in keeping with the trajectory that Luke is describing for the article to be then omitted before Pamphylia, if it were being mentioned as a new place that he wished to underline. In other words, after finishing their business in the church there, they travelled through the province not as a new place but as one in which they were already present. Arriving in Pamphylia, on the other hand, is a new stage where a significant stop is made in Perga to 'speak the word' for the first time in the town (cf. 13.13). B03 links the account of the return journey to the previous narrative with καί and has the article before Pamphylia, in keeping with the fact that the region was an inevitable stage in their journey as Paul and Barnabas headed towards the seaport. D05, on the other hand, marks the development at 14.24 with the connective δέ and presents Pamphylia anarthrously. If absence of the article is to be taken as a marker of salience, as the analysis of this section so far has been suggesting, it causes the province to be highlighted, seemingly marking thus the action of speaking in its capital, Perga.

Lycaonia is also mentioned in the context of the travels of Paul and Barnabas in the same area, as they moved on to cities in the province on leaving Iconium after their initial visit there (14.6). It is the only reference to the region and the name is arthrous without variant.

---

[36] At 13.14, most MSS read with D05, παρεγένοντο εἰς Ἀντιόχειαν τῆς Πισιδίας, where the article serves to define which Antioch is meant; other MSS including B03 read παρεγένοντο εἰς Ἀντιόχειαν τὴν Πισιδίαν.

III.4.vii Syria

The first of the five references to the province of Syria belongs to the address of the letter from the Jerusalem leaders to the churches of Antioch, Cilicia and Syria (15.23), where the names of both regions are arthrous, being covered by the one article at the head of the list (see §II.6.i above): οἱ πρεσβύτεροι ἀδελφοὶ τοῖς κατὰ τὴν Ἀντιόχειαν καὶ Συρίαν καὶ Κιλικίαν ἀδελφοῖς. The defining function of the place names accounts for the article. When the names are repeated by the narrator as he reports that the letter was delivered to the named regions (15.41), the names are again arthrous, the intention being fulfilled: διήρχετο δὲ τὴν Συρίαν καὶ (τὴν D05) Κιλικίαν. On the repetition of the article before Cilicia in D05 see §III.4.iv above).

Syria as the intended destination likewise accounts for the article before the name at 18.18 and 20.3B03. In both cases, it is a matter of Paul returning by sea, from Corinth and Greece respectively, to the place of his mission's origin: ἐξέπλει/ἀνάγεσθαι εἰς τὴν Συρίαν, Syria being the general area that was essentially his familiar base. 20.3 presents, however, a telling variant reading, for D05's reference to Syria is anarthrous in the midst of considerable divergence between its text and that of B03:

Ref. D05	B03
20.3 ποιήσας δὲ μῆνας τρεῖς καὶ γενηθείσης [αὐτῷ ἐπιβουλῆς] ὑπὸ τῶν Ἰουδαίων ἠθέλησεν, ἀναχθῆναι εἰς ↑ Συρίαν. εἶπεν δὲ τὸ πνεῦμα αὐτῷ ↑ ὑποστρέφειν διὰ τῆς Μακεδονίας. 20.4 ↑ Μέλλοντος οὖν ἐξιέναι αὐτοῦ μέχρι τῆς Ἀσίας Σώπατρος, κτλ...	ποιήσας τε μῆνας τρεῖς ↑ γενομένης [ἐπιβουλῆς αὐτῷ] ὑπὸ τῶν Ἰουδαίων μέλλοντι ἀνάγεσθαι εἰς τὴν Συρίαν ἐγένετο ↑ γνώμης τοῦ ὑποστρέφειν διὰ ↑ Μακεδονίας. ↑ συνείπετο δὲ αὐτῷ. ↑ Σώπατρος, κτλ.

There is here an instance where the variation in the use of the article reflects a difference in the narrative purpose. According to the articulation of the familiar B03 text, there is nothing surprising or exceptional about Paul's intention to go to Syria; it is Macedonia (anarthrous) that is unexpected, a change of itinerary forced on him by the plot. In D05, on the other hand, his decision to go to Syria was only prompted by the plot of the Jews – nothing more is said about the plot or why it caused Paul to turn back to Syria when, to all intents and purposes, he was already on his way to Rome.[37] The mention of Syria is, in consequence, very much contrary to expectation, although to recognize this requires an appreciation of the wider narrative beyond this local variation. The unexpected nature of the destination of Syria at this point in the Bezan text justifies the absence of the article. In this text, it is the Spirit who tells Paul to go back through (arthrous) Macedonia, as a place that he had already been directed to (cf. 16.6–10) and that would put him back on the route to Rome.

---

[37] The Bezan presentation of Paul's struggle to resist the divine plan for him to go to Rome until he had taken the collection of the Gentiles to the Temple in Jerusalem is explored in detail in Rius-Camps & Read-Heimerdinger, *The Message of Acts*, IV, see esp. Excursus 3, 168–70.

The extensive account of the sea-voyage from Greece to Syria finally reaches its conclusion at 21.3b (D05 *lac.*). The article at this mention could be expected since this is the destination that has been in view throughout the journey. The explanation for its absence is not obvious, though within the perspective of the Bezan version of the narrative so far a comparison could be being made with Cyprus (21.3a) which, the narrator makes a point of noting, was not visited, the implication being that it ought to have been.[38] This example of the principles directing the use of the article with place names illustrates the importance of taking account of the message that the narrator wishes to communicate, which is not always possible to do with certainty in the absence of firm knowledge about the circumstances of the writing and the identity of the intended addressee.

III.4.viii *Macedonia*

This region is a place of key importance for Paul's travels, as was seen above in the D05 reading of 20.3. It represents an obligatory stage on the itinerary between the home province of Syria and the divinely appointed final destination of Rome. It is introduced into the narrative at the point when Paul was first called to take the step of moving away from his familiar territory to proclaim the gospel there: in 16.9–12 it is mentioned three times, the first anarthrously as an unexpected destination that had not figured in Paul's plan hitherto, and thereafter arthrously.

Macedonia becomes topical again when Paul, in Ephesus, planned to revisit places where he was intending to take up the collection from the Gentiles in order to deliver it to Jerusalem. Thus, at 19.21, Macedonia is named along with Achaia, the latter having been mentioned several times in Acts 18 as the province in which the city of Corinth, the centre of action, was situated (18.2D05,12,27) – all three references to Achaia are arthrous by virtue of their association with the prior mention of Corinth. D05 reads the article before both Macedonia and Achaia at 19.21, so treating them as distinct, but in B03 one article groups them together. This accounts for the anarthrous reference to Macedonia in the following sentence (19.22B03), when it is singled out as the country to which Paul sent Timothy and Erastus ahead of him. In contrast, D05 retains the article, simply picking up the reference to Macedonia from the previous sentence, as the first place Paul planned to travel to.

In the event, Paul's departure is delayed by trouble in Ephesus, and attention is focused strongly on his activity there in countering the opposition as well as in talking with the disciples. When, then, he finally did get away, there is a marked switch of focus from Ephesus to Macedonia so that even though it had been anticipated as the next stopping place, it is introduced anarthrously as a new area of activity (20.1). The painful nature of Paul's separation from the Ephesian community is highlighted in the Bezan text of this verse:

---

[38] See Rius-Camps & Read-Heimerdinger, *The Message of Acts*, IV, 149–50.

Ref. D05	B03
20.1 Μετὰ δὲ τὸ παύσασθαι τὸν θόρυβον <u>προσκαλησάμενος</u> ↑ Παῦλος τοὺς μαθητὰς καὶ <u>πολλὰ παρακελεύσας, ἀποσπασάμενος</u> ἐξῆλθεν ↑ εἰς Μακεδονίαν.	Μετὰ δὲ τὸ παύσασθαι τὸν θόρυβον <u>μεταπεμψάμενος ὁ</u> Παῦλος τοὺς μαθητὰς καὶ ↑ <u>παρακαλέσας, ἀσπασάμενος</u> ἐξῆλθεν <u>πορεύεσθαι</u> εἰς Μακεδονίαν.

Paul's involvement in Ephesus is underlined as attention switches from the riot in the city back to Paul (anarthrous Παῦλος in D05), and his close ties with the disciples are brought into focus, especially in D05 with the lexical choice of προσκαλησάμενος ... παρακελεύσας ... ἀποσπασάμενος, the inclusion of πολλά and finally the absence of the infinitive πορεύεσθαι. The insistence on the separation seems to be what justifies the omission of the article before the new destination, Macedonia. This analysis is intimately linked to a recognition of the accentuated interest in the difficulties posed by the Ephesians to Paul's plan for the Gentile collection, as expressed by the Bezan narrator throughout these episodes of Acts.

The mention of Macedonia at 20.3 and the variant reading involving the use of the article are discussed in relation to Syria above (§III.4.vii).

III.4.ix Mysia, Bythinia, Thessaly

Towards the beginning of the second phase of Paul's mission, a number of regions are mentioned that Paul and Silas either passed through or attempted to go to. Following the intervention of the Holy Spirit to stop them from speaking the word in Asia (arthrous,16.6), they arrived at the border of Mysia (arthrous, 16.7a) to the north-west of Asia from where they wanted to go east into Bithynia (arthrous Bithynia, anarthrous D05, 16.7b) but being prevented they headed south through Mysia (arthrous, 16.8a) to Troas (16.8b). The consistently arthrous references confirm what has been seen so far, that when regions are not particularly salient, especially if they lie on the route of an itinerary, the article is retained. The variant reading concerning Bithynia illustrates this. It would be a possible, expected step to go from Mysia to neighbouring Bithynia; indeed, B03 says that Paul and Silas attempted to go there: <u>ἐπείραζον</u> εἰς <u>τὴν</u> Βιθυνίαν πορευθῆναι. The Bezan text presents the direction as a wish rather than an actual attempt: <u>ἤθελαν</u> εἰς ↑ Βιθυνίαν πορευθῆναι. Given the sustained reference in the Bezan text to Paul's tactics of avoiding Rome until he had accomplished plans of his own and given the three successive measures of divine intervention in the episode of 16.5–10 to keep him moving towards Rome, Paul's desire to turn east instead of west at the border of Mysia is a significant narratorial comment on his resistance to God's leading.

In the Bezan text, an additional intervention is recorded to prevent Paul from going to a region that would take him away from Rome. As he headed towards Athens to escape from the threats to his life in Berea, it is reported that he sailed past Thessaly: παρῆλθεν τὴν Θεσσαλίαν, 17.15D05, since he was not permitted to evangelize there. The name is arthrous, Thessaly being a region he would necessarily pass through and one that remains in the background of the narrative.

To summarize the pattern that can be detected regarding the use of the article with regions, it may be noted that the default use is the arthrous name, just as it is with names of countries. The name is anarthrous when the place is being highlighted as particularly salient. However, it is important to note that recognizing the reason for an author's drawing attention to the place depends on understanding the author's purpose and message more generally.

III.5 Islands

Several islands are mentioned in the course of Paul's final journey to Jerusalem. Cos and Rhodes (21.1), are arthrous in B03, as is Crete during Paul's sea voyage to Rome (27.7, 12, 21, D05 *lac.*). In D05, however, Cos and Rhodes are anarthrous which could mean that the names are viewed as cities rather than islands, since cities are typically anarthrous at the first mention (see §III.7 below) and there is no apparent reason in the narrative for highlighting the islands. This possibility is supported by the references to the islands of Chios and Samos (20.15), also names of cities doubling for names of islands, and anarthrous in Acts without variant. It can thus be concluded that islands are generally referred to with the article, even at the first or an isolated mention, but that where its name is shared with the name of the city found on the island this may cause the article to be omitted.

III.5.i Cyprus

The island stands out for the amount of variation concerning the use of the article, both in the firm text and among the two MSS B03 and D05. Its introduction into the narrative at 11.19 has been mentioned above with reference to Phoenicia, where the name is anarthrous, apparently because of its narrative importance. The island readily acquires symbolic significance at 13.4, as the first place across the sea to which the gospel was taken by Barnabas and Paul, and as such the omission of the article is a means to draw attention to this information. The next mention of Cyprus at 15.39 alludes back to this event, when Barnabas chooses to return there after his separation from Paul (see §II.5.iii above).

The use of the article at the other two references to Cyprus in Acts demonstrates the highlighting purpose of its omission, even though the symbolic significance of the island is still relevant with the arthrous name. Luke's comment on Cyprus at 21.3 (D05 *lac.*) has been noted above in connection with Syria, which is negatively highlighted (anarthrous) as Paul's goal in preference over and against (arthrous) Cyprus. Finally, as Paul eventually sets off to Rome his ship sails under the protection of the lee of Cyprus, reflecting the protection of the Roman guard on his mission to the Gentiles.

III.6 Mountains

The only mountain mentioned in Acts is Sinai (7.30, 38), prefixed each time with the arthrous noun ὄρος.

III.7 Cities

When a city is mentioned for the first time it is almost always anarthrous, and at subsequent mentions within the same episode the article is then frequently present (e.g. Damascus in 9.2 (D05 *lac.*), cf. 9.3 (D05 *lac.*); Paphos in 13.6, cf. 13.13; Perga in 13.13, cf. 13.14; Athens in 17.15, cf. 17.16 and 18.1; Miletus in 20.15,27. From this it may be concluded that the article is present by default and that its omission reflects the salience of a town when it is mentioned for the first time. In that respect, the pattern of the article with the names of cities is similar to that noted with the names of persons. There are, however, several exceptions where the first mention (in the book or in an episode) is arthrous. And there are many more references that are anarthrous although anaphoric. On top of all that, there are numerous variant readings.[39] In order to justify each reading, it would be necessary to ascertain the intention of the narrator at each point and to examine how that corresponds to the articulation of the narrative in the distinct texts of the MSS. That represents a separate study in itself, such is the importance that Luke assigns to certain geographical locations. Some analysis, however, is possible here and serves to shed light on the question.

In the case of isolated arthrous references (Amphipolis, 17.1; Assos, 20.13) it is difficult to justify the presence of the article without comparison to references in other literature.[40] Where place names are introduced arthrously and occur later anarthrously, the contextual situation may help to account for the presence of the article on the first occasion. For example, Rome is first mentioned (18.2) where the narrator presents Aquila and his wife as having recently left Italy because of the emperor's edict for all Jews to leave Rome. In this context, Rome is anticipated by the prior mention of Italy of which it is the capital. It may also be presumed that the addressee of Acts, being a contemporary of these events, would have already been familiar with them and the mention of Rome would be expected. The next reference to Rome is made by Paul in direct speech (19.21) as he told the Ephesians that he knew that after his visit to Jerusalem he had to go to Rome: Μετὰ τὸ γενέσθαι με ἐκεῖ δεῖ με καὶ Ῥώμην ἰδεῖν, which is the first time he had made any mention of Rome to anyone. At the third and final mention of Rome, when Paul eventually arrives there (οὕτως εἰς τὴν Ῥώμην ἤλθαμεν, 28.14, D05 *lac.*), B03 reads the article as may be expected since it is his long-anticipated destination; MSS that omit the article[41] highlight, just as does the position of the name before the verb, the importance of the city in the context of Paul finally reaching his goal.

The place name that occurs most frequently in Acts is Jerusalem (× 47 D05; × 41 B03), with its dual spelling used to designate either the geographical location (Ἱεροσόλυμα) or the seat of Judaism (Ἱερουσαλήμ).[42] Both forms are always anarthrous with one exception (5.28), where the Hebrew-derived spelling is found without variant as the president of the Sanhedrin accuses the apostles of having contravened their

---

[39] The full list of cities can be found in the appendix to Read-Heimerdinger, 'The Use of the Article before Names of Places', 403–12.
[40] On Amphipolis, see discussion of the context of 17.1 in Chapter 3, §III.2.i.
[41] For the full list of witnesses, see Rius-Camps & Read-Heimerdinger, *The Message of Acts*, IV, 400.
[42] For an analysis of Luke's spelling of Jerusalem, see Read-Heimerdinger, *The Bezan Text*, 311–44.

orders not to teach about Jesus in the Temple (cf. 4.18), and thereby to have 'filled Jerusalem' with their teaching: πεπληρώκατε τὴν Ἰερουσαλὴμ τῆς διδαχῆς ὑμῶν. In this situation, the reference is to the immediate and specific environment of the holy city in which the Sanhedrin meeting is taking place.

Comparison with the words of Gamaliel as he addresses the Sanhedrin in similar circumstances is instructive, as he speaks of everyone living in Jerusalem (πᾶσιν τοῖς κατοικοῦσιν Ἰερουσαλήμ, 5.28) having heard about the apostles' healing activity, but there it is the people who are in focus rather than the city. On one other occasion, Jerusalem is mentioned in a similar context to that of 5.28, where the chiliarch was informed that 'all of Jerusalem is in confusion' (21.31, ὅλη συγχύννεται Ἰερουσαλήμ) but this reference is indirect, made anonymously via the narrator.

III.8 Conclusions on names of places

It has been contended by present-day scholars who are native Greek speakers that *koine* Greek is closer to modern Greek than is often supposed, that the development of the language was such that once *koine* usage had been established it then changed relatively little.[43] That being so, it is of interest to know the practice in modern Greek regarding the article with geographical names. Discussion with a contemporary speaker reveals that Greek today always has the article with names of places (towns, islands, countries and so on), unless the sentence wants to give some kind of emphasis.[44] The following sentences illustrate the point:

> 'Here is [arthrous] Athens' compared with, '[arthrous] Patra is nice, but it is not like [anarthrous] Athens'.

This present-day practice tends to suggest that the presence of the article with names of places could have been the expected usage even in NT Greek, and that anarthrous names were not the rule, which is in line with the findings of the present study.

It is at odds, on the other hand, with Gildersleeve's observations concerning classical Greek. On particular categories of places, he observes that Asia is always arthrous though other names of countries vary; postpositive, partitive and chorographic genitives are generally articular; towns/cities are generally anarthrous though the more notable regularly take the article. He suggests that names that are substantivized adjectives (frequently ending in -ια) are more likely to be arthrous.[45]

---

[43] See notably Chrys Caragounis, *The Development of Greek and the New Testament. Morphology, Syntax, Phonology, and Textual Transmission* (Grand Rapids: Baker Academic, 2006).

[44] Personal communication with Andreas Andreopoulos, Senior Lecturer in Orthodox Christianity, University of Winchester, UK. He reports that omission of the article is sometimes perceived by present-day Greeks as a sign of laziness in oral discourse. So, although in the question 'Do you live in Athens' the city is often anarthrous, it would be considered more 'correct' to use the article. Caragounis (*The Development of Greek*) makes no specific mention of geographical names in his extensive investigation.

[45] This claim is also made by Blass, Debrunner & Rehkopf (*Grammatik*) but is dismissed by Hemer as 'misconceived,' see Colin J. Hemer, *The Book of Acts in the Setting of Hellenistic History*, ed. Conrad H. Gempf (Tübingen: J. C. B. Mohr, 1989), 243.

At the heart of the difference between the present findings and the observations of grammarians such as Gildersleeve is the factor of frequency. What a discourse analysis approach demonstrates is that frequency as such is not relevant for ascertaining default usage. Because the principal effect of marked usage is emphasis, it may well happen that in a given text place names are particularly highlighted because they have a rhetorical function. Thus, where place names in a narrative such as Acts are used as indicators of the inner development of characters or themes, which the geographical journeys are seen as mirroring, the article before the names is liable to be more often omitted than in a text where the places are mentioned for the purpose of simply transmitting factual information.

IV. General conclusions on the use of the article with proper names

This study has been focused on the use of the article with names of people and names of places in Acts, which by their very nature provide workable sets of comparable data because they both reflect the function of the article to designate entities that are 'uniquely identifiable'.[46] In examining the patterns of usage in a narrative text, it has been found that common to the two sets, the principal factor affecting the choice to use the article or not is salience. Luke's default usage is to include the article with names of people and names of places; when it is omitted, it is because he (or some later editor/copyist) wishes to mark out a participant or a place as particularly significant at that point.

Within this context, the role of the named person or place in what is being related is of crucial importance. The use of the article before plays an important role in determining the status of the noun and tracking it within the course of a narrative. This is true, on the one hand, of the function of the character or location within the unfolding story; on the other, it also true of their function in connection with the purpose of Luke and the message to be communicated. In other words, marking a name as salient is not a matter of absolute or objective reality but of the perspective and intention of the speaker. To a meaningful extent, the speaker plays a part in the choice to use the article or not, and in that sense the article with proper names can be likened to verbal aspect, whereby the choice of one 'tense' in preference to another depends on how the speaker views the situation or wants to present it to the audience.

What is more, in order to communicate effectively, the speaker must also take into account the prior knowledge and understanding of the hearer. Thus, pragmatic factors play a key part in the choice to use or omit the article before proper names. Far from being a simple grammatical component in the language, the article serves to articulate the story on a deeper level and to give coherence as well as cohesion to the discourse, with a much broader scope than the immediate sentence in which the name is found. Grammatical context is, indeed, rarely relevant, though some few exceptions were noted in relation to names of people.

---

[46] Levinsohn, *Discourse Features*, 133.

The patterns elucidated in this exploration of the article in a *koine* Greek narrative are not 'rules' in the sense traditionally associated with languages, where there is one correct form and others that are incorrect. Rather they are principles, which a speaker can make use of in order to express the relative saliency of a participant or location in the story at a given point. They are not rules that have to be followed in order to conform to grammatical accuracy, but they are a device that reflects the flexibility of the language to adapt to situational aspects of the discourse as well as the nature of the discourse itself.

Given this inherent flexibility in the use of the article with proper names, variant readings in successive renderings of a narrative are a valuable source of information that provides data for comparison and for furthering the analysis. The examination presented here demonstrates the importance of reading variants in their context, of both the immediate passage and the wider discourse. This means that assessing them cannot be done effectively on a piecemeal basis but must take account of the perspective and purpose of the overall text. The findings suggest that the numerous variant readings among the early NT MSS of Acts that affect the article with proper names should be ascribed not to scribal habit but to the changing narratorial intentions, which may vary from one copying to another, and to the different audiences for whom the copies were intended. The article with proper names is part of the storyteller's collection of tools that serve to enhance the articulation of the story and to adapt it to the people listening to it.

3

Sentence connectives[1]

I. Introduction

I.1 The function of sentence connectives

This linguistic study will examine how Luke joins sentences together to construct a continuous narrative in the book of Acts, using links referred to here as 'connectives'. By 'sentence' is meant a finite verb and any associated subordinate clauses or phrases.[2] With their function of linking sentences, connectives belong to the class of conjunctions but they are distinct from other conjunctions in that they are only used to connect main clauses, not to link subordinate to main clauses. In NT Greek, and specifically in Luke's writings, most connectives are one word (e.g. δέ, καί) or occasionally two (μὲν οὖν). Sometimes, the function of a connective is served by a demonstrative pronoun (e.g. τούτον); occasionally, a relative pronoun is used, which in English would normally introduce a subordinate clause. When there is no kind of connecting word (asyndeton) but sentences are simply placed one following the other instead, this is sufficiently exceptional for it to be viewed as a distinctive type of connecting device.

Unlike in English, for example, where it is common to make no explicit connection between sentences, in ancient Greek it is far more usual to make clear the connection. Several factors render this necessary: early MSS were written entirely in capital letters, with no spacing between the letters, let alone between words or sentences, and no punctuation. Rudimentary punctuation together with occasional markers to indicate breaks in the text, such as indentation or blank spaces, were introduced gradually over the centuries but at the time when Luke was writing they were rare. They became more common and more developed with the use of cursive writing and minuscules after the ninth century but even then, spacing between words in written Greek was not used systematically. So connectives function as signs of

---

[1] This investigation into Luke's use of sentence connectives was initially published in Jenny Read-Heimerdinger, *The Bezan Text of Acts: A Contribution of Discourse Analysis to Textual Criticism* (JSNTSup. 236; Sheffield: SAP, 2002), Chapter 7, 202–53. The introductory material has been developed for the current chapter.

[2] For this definition of a sentence, see Stephen H. Levinsohn, *Textual Connections in Acts* (Atlanta, Ga.: Scholars Press, 1987), xviii.

punctuation in place of capital letters, commas, semi-colons, full-stops, paragraph breaks and so on.

From a discourse point of view, connectives serve to indicate the relationship of a sentence with what has gone before, and even to anticipate what will follow. Research on Greek sentence connections from this perspective has enabled the function of the various means of linking sentences to be defined with some precision and the differences between them to be clarified.[3] In a general way, the results show that while the connecting words serve to distinguish between simple differences of meaning, e.g. consequence or chronological sequence, in addition they indicate at a deeper level how the sentences fit into the wider narrative: whether they occur at a boundary between chunks of text, for example, or whether they are closely associated with other sentences within a chunk of text. In other words, they have quite distinct functions that go beyond an expression of style. For reasons that are not yet altogether understood, it is clear that the patterns of connectives vary to some extent among the books of the New Testament. Individual authors tend to use the range of connectives in their own, self-consistent ways, suggesting that there was variation in usage in different places or at different times. Consequently, what is said about the patterns in the use of connectives in Acts has to be modified when applied to the Gospels of Matthew or Mark, and especially John; even Luke's, too, though to a lesser degree, which is surprising given the many indications that the Gospel is the work of the same author as the book of Acts.[4] Analysis of the way Luke uses connectives in his Gospel will not be included in the present study, though some attention is paid to this topic later, in Chapter 8, §VI.

The connectives are, as it were, the joints and hinges of a text that hold a story together and allow it to be articulated not just between sentences but between sections of the discourse.[5] In this way, they play an important part in building the structure of a text. Alongside other aspects of language, notably word order which is the topic of Chapter 4, they are vital clues to understanding how a writer has chosen to organize a text. In particular, for narratives such as the Gospels and Acts, connectives indicate how the writing is structured into a hierarchy parts, grouping sentences together in units from the lowest level to the highest. More will be said about connectives in looking at narrative structure in Chapter 8, where the association of connectives with word order will be considered.

---

[3] With reference specifically to Acts, see Levinsohn, *Textual Connections*; see also his *Discourse Features of New Testament Greek*, 2nd edn (Dallas: Summer Institute of Linguistics, 2000), 83–161, where he extends his analysis to other New Testament writings. Levinsohn's work on connectives in Acts was reviewed, and largely confirmed, by the study in my *Bezan Text of Acts*.

[4] The unexpected differences in Luke's usage between his two volumes is examined by Randall Buth, 'Evaluating Luke's Unnatural Greek: A Look at his Connectives', in *Discourse Studies and Biblical Interpretation: A Festschrift in Honor of Stephen H. Levinsohn*, ed. Steven E. Runge, 335-69 (Bellingham, Wash.: Lexham Press, 2011).

[5] The function of connectives in the NT more generally is examined in Steven E. Runge, *Discourse Grammar of the Greek New Testament: A Practical Introduction for Teaching and Exegesis* (Peabody, Mass.: Hendrickson Publishers, 2010), 17–57.

I.2 Sentence connectives in Acts

The following sentence connectives are found in Acts, listed here in order of frequency (others, such as ἀλλά or ὡς, are not included in this list, being conjunctions to introduce clauses that are dependent on another):

καί
δέ
τε
τότε
μέν
μὲν οὖν
γάρ
asyndeton
demonstrative pronoun
relative pronoun

I.3 The problem of variant readings

In seeking to determine in what ways Luke uses the connectives, there is an immediate difficulty that lies in the uncertainty of his text. Linguistic analysis of connectives in the Greek NT is almost always restricted to the text of the current eclectic edition, which has been reconstructed without the insights of discourse analysis. It comes as no surprise that there exists a great deal of variation in the choice of connectives throughout the MSS of Luke–Acts, not least among the ones selected for study here, Codex Sinaiticus (ℵ01), Codex Vaticanus (B03) and Codex Bezae (D05). The most frequent pairs of alternatives are δέ/τε and δέ/καί. Variant readings are also associated with τότε, οὖν, μέν, μὲν οὖν , γάρ, the relative pronoun and asyndeton. Variation, of course, exists, too, between the Greek MSS and the versions, but the versions do not provide a reliable point of comparison in this matter for, given the evidence for Greek connectives expressing ideas beyond straightforward ones of meaning, it is rare to find a strict correspondence for any given connective between Greek and a translation language.

Differences among the MSS relating to sentence linking have often been ignored, perhaps because their importance has not been apparent from the treatment of them in the grammars of NT Greek, or because variants have been treated as evidence of stylistic preference or foreign (notably Semitic) influence. While not ruling out the influence of an author/scribe's habits altogether, the patterns in the use of connectives that are emerging from the studies of discourse analysts provide valuable indications that there are linguistic reasons for divergence among the MSS.

An examination of all the variant readings involving a connective would be a vast enterprise, so numerous are they. The task is made the more complex by the fact that many of the instances of divergence do not represent isolated variation but are rather part of a wider variation unit; they not infrequently reveal an underlying difference in the way the writer perceives the articulation of the story – how episodes relate to each other, who the main character is at any given time and what is the relative significance of his or her actions. As a result, an exhaustive analysis of the variant readings necessitates a thorough exegetical examination of the surrounding text.[6] In order to limit the size of the study here, examination is made only of Luke's second volume, Acts, with examples taken principally from narrative portions of text but complemented with some from speeches where further examples are useful to fill out the picture. As explained in Chapter 1, §III.2, passages in direct speech constitute discrete segments of discourse, with their own internal structure, which Luke crafts to suit both the speaker and the occasion; as such, they demand separate study, which can be carried out on the basis of the patterns of use identified in the Acts narrative. These could also be compared with patterns found in Luke's Gospel.

The presentation of the more frequent connectives δέ, καί and τε is limited here to a summary of the conclusions reached in the survey of the connectives in Acts by Levinsohn.[7] More detailed attention is paid to the pattern of variant readings and especially some characteristic uses of καί in the D05 text. The major part of the chapter will concentrate on an analysis of the less frequent connectives τότε, οὖν, μέν, μὲν οὖν, γάρ and asyndeton. The conclusions reached by Levinsohn regarding the purpose of these connectives will be taken as a starting point and refined or modified according to the findings contributed by a consideration of the variant readings.

In the following analysis, the method will be look first at the patterns of use of each connective in turn. In the first place, the connective is considered in the text that is firm, i.e. common to ℵ01, B03 and D05 without variant, summarizing the characteristics identified by Levinsohn. The next step is to examine the variant readings between ℵ01, B03 and D05, and to note patterns that can be observed, as well as any impact that the readings may have on the meaning of the text. In the citations of the variant readings, words that are present in only one of the texts is underlined with a solid line; lexical or grammatical alternative material is underlined with a dotted line; brackets [...] are used to indicate variation in word order.

II. δέ, καί and τε

II.1 In the common text

The summary that follows of the use of δέ, καί and τε in the common text of Acts is of a somewhat general nature. The remarks here apply specifically to Acts although initial explorations have shown them to be also generally true of certain other NT narrative texts including Luke's Gospel.

---

[6] Attention is paid to exegetical matters in Josep Rius-Camps and Jenny Read-Heimerdinger, *The Message of Acts in Codex Bezae: A Comparison with the Alexandrian Tradition*. 4 vols (JSNTSup 257/ LNTS 302, 365, 415; London: T&T Clark, 2004–09). Discussion of the relevance of connectives to the meaning of specific passages can be found in those volumes.

[7] Levinsohn, *Textual Connections*; see also his *Discourse Features*.

II.1.i δέ

Stories do not usually progress by means of a string of single sentences; instead, they advance by 'chunks' made up of groups of sentences. Each chunk causes the story to move on and its onset can be recognized by the existence of some new and distinctive information that occurs in the form of a change. This is frequently a change in the time or setting of the story, or a change in the topic. At such points in Acts, δέ is used. If the information in a sentence is seen (by the narrator, that is) as contributing to moving the story on, then δέ is used. It is important to understand that the choice to see information as marking a change is entirely the view of the narrator. It is dependent on the speaker's perspective in the way that verbal aspect is; that is, it is not an objective fact, but a subjective choice on the part of the narrator.

δέ is almost always found marking the boundary between units of narrative but it can also occur within a unit when an element signals an internal development of an incident. As such, δέ reflects something of the narrator's purpose as he tells his story. It indicates what he considers to be the elements that move the story on. It is found typically to introduce alternating speakers in a dialogue in direct speech. Another use for δέ, reflecting its force of discontinuity, is to indicate a parenthetical aside, notably a background comment that provides information relevant for something coming up in the following narrative. The function of δέ to introduce an aside overlaps with that of γάρ; however, an aside introduced with γάρ is of a different nature, as discussed in §IV below.

Given this range of uses, although δέ is often said in elementary grammars to imply contrast of some kind, for the most part that would be too strong a meaning to attach to it.[8] It is more accurate to think of δέ as expressing the general notion of discontinuity.

II.1.ii καί

καί contrasts with δέ in that it links elements that do not constitute new developments. If δέ separates sentences by signalling something new, καί groups together sentences that are considered as belonging to the same unit of development. They concern the

καί	δέ

Figure 1 A comparison of καί and δέ as sentence connectives.

---

[8] Daniel Wallace, *Greek Grammar beyond the Basics* (Grand Rapids, Mich.: Zondervan Publishing House, 1996), lists several categories of logical relationships between ideas, saying that it is the context that determines which one is active at any point (670–4). While this is true, it invariably leads to a circle of interpretation for the grounds for deciding which category is appropriate generally depend on prior exegetical presuppositions.

same topic, even though the grammatical subject may well change from one sentence to the next. The two connectives δέ and καί have been compared to ways of joining lengths of rope: δέ ties together the ropes of the narrative with knots whereas καί joins them by splicing the topes together. As any fisherman will report, while splicing gives a less visible join that a knot, it is extremely strong, and this is the effect of καί, which is not found in Acts as a link between units but occurs within a unit joining contiguous elements with one another. The elements are thus presented as being of equal importance, on an equal footing. Figure 1 illustrates the distinction between the two conjunctions when they function as connectives to join sentences.

II.1.iii τε

τε can be likened to καί rather than to δέ. It also conjoins sentences within the same unit of development rather than across the boundaries. It is, however, a stronger connective than καί and, in contrast to καί, τε sometimes connects elements that are of unequal importance; alternatively, the elements that it connects may have a close affinity with each other because they are very similar. τε can be used to introduce an additional statement about the event that has just been mentioned (and can be translated in such cases by 'moreover', or 'and finally'), or to connect similar events to the same basic subject.

The resemblance between δέ and τε is a phonological one and not a grammatical one. The characteristic function of τε in Acts is a useful criterion when evaluating variant readings of δέ and τε because τε will be rarely appropriate at the same place as δέ.

II.2 Variant readings

The following figures show the number of instances of variation involving δέ, τε and καί in the narrative portions of Acts (א01 and B03 are treated as one although there are, in fact, some differences – see on τε, §II.2.ii below).

D05	א01 or B03	Number of *vll*
καί	δέ	25
δέ	καί	8
καί	τε	7
τε	καί	0
δέ	τε	25
τε	δέ	10

II.2.i καί

In addition to the large number of readings of καί in D05 as an alternative to δέ or τε, there are several instances of καί in error: at the start of a line where there is a verb beginning with κ (4.15; 20.16), or in confusion with διά (4.2; 13.17).

It is tempting in view of the prevalence of καί as a connective in the Bezan text to speak of a 'scribal preference' for καί. However, detailed exegetical analysis of the places where καί is read as a variant reading shows that the Bezan reading reflects a particular perception of the narrative development and is justifiable from the context. A telling example is found at 1.7, where Jesus speaks in response to the question of the apostles:

Ref.	D05	ℵ01/B03
1.5	Ἰωάννης μὲν ἐβάπτισεν ὕδατι, ὑμεῖς δὲ ἐν πνεύματι [βαπτισθήσεσθε ἁγίῳ] <u>καὶ ὃ μέλλετε λαμβάνειν</u> οὐ μετὰ πολλὰς ταύτας ἡμέρας <u>ἕως τῆς πεντηκοστῆς.</u>	Ἰωάννης μὲν ἐβάπτισεν ὕδατι, ὑμεῖς δὲ ἐν πνεύματι [βαπτισθήσεσθε ἁγίῳ] ↑ οὐ μετὰ πολλὰς ταύτας ἡμέρας ↑.
1.6	Οἱ μὲν οὖν συνελθόντες <u>ἐπηρώτων</u> αὐτὸν λέγοντες· κύριε, εἰ ἐν τῷ χρόνῳ τούτῳ <u>ἀποκαταστάνεις εἰς</u> τὴν βασιλείαν <u>τοῦ</u> Ἰσραήλ…;	Οἱ μὲν οὖν συνελθόντες <u>ἠρώτων</u> αὐτὸν λέγοντες· κύριε, εἰ ἐν τῷ χρόνῳ τούτῳ <u>ἀποκαθιστάνεις</u> ↑ τὴν βασιλείαν <u>τῷ</u> Ἰσραήλ;
1.7	<u>καὶ</u> εἶπεν πρὸς αὐτούς· οὐχ ὑμῶν ἐστιν γνῶναι…	εἶπεν <u>δὲ</u> (om. B03) πρὸς αὐτούς· οὐχ ὑμῶν ἐστιν γνῶναι…

According to the text of ℵ01/B03, when Jesus told the apostles that they were going to be baptized with the Holy Spirit after not many days, they asked him if that would be the time when he would restore the kingdom to Israel, and Jesus' response is introduced in ℵ01 with the connective δέ, in line with Luke's usual practice in reporting a question-answer exchange.[9] The apostles' question according to D05 is a different one: they start to ask if the time when they will be baptized with the Holy Spirit would be the time when Jesus would restore into the kingdom of Israel… but they do not get to finish their question, for Jesus interrupts before they state what it is they are waiting for. The connective καί appropriately marks his response as not answering the question but rather cutting across it. The omission of any connecting word in B03, an unusual example of asyndeton discussed in §VI below, also suggests something unusual about Jesus' response. The amount of subtle textual variation in 1.6–7 indicates that there was more than a little uncertainty about this final exchange between Jesus and the apostles.

In the additional D05 material (that is, absent from ℵ01/B03), καί is indeed extremely common but its use is in keeping with the nature of the supplementary comments (for example, a second piece of information is given of an equivalent status to what has been said already, at e.g. 7.24,26; 12.10,17; 14.7; 22.9, all D05). Although καί dominates the peculiarly D05 material, other connectives are used as appropriate, as will be seen in the analysis of the less frequent connectives in the later sections of this chapter.

καί is twice found in addition to δέ (18.4D05; 21.40D05), which may look like the clumsiness of a scribe who, in altering the conjunction from δέ to καί, forgot to delete δέ but this is a construction which there is good reason to consider as correct Greek. Indeed, when the sentence connective in the two instances cited is taken as being δέ, καί at the beginning of the sentence has the adverbial function of emphasizing the verb

---

[9] Levinsohn, *Discourse Features*, 218.

it precedes. The emphatic nature of καί is especially striking at 18.4. At this point, when the narrator describes how Paul began to regularly lecture in the synagogue in Corinth, the D05 text is considerably fuller than the other text:

Ref.	D05	ℵ01/B03
18.4	<u>εἰσπορευόμενος</u> δὲ [<u>εἰς τὴν συναγωγὴν</u> κατὰ πᾶν σάββατον διελέγετο] <u>καὶ ἐντιθεὶς τὸ ὄνομα τοῦ κυρίου Ἰησοῦ</u> <u>καὶ</u> ἔπειθεν <u>δὲ</u> <u>οὐ μόνον</u> Ἰουδαίους <u>ἀλλὰ</u> καὶ Ἕλληνας	↑ [διελέγετο δὲ ἐν τῇ συναγωγῇ κατὰ πᾶν σάββατον] ↑ ↑ ἔπειθέν τε ↑ Ἰουδαίους ↑ καὶ Ἕλληνας

At the start of lines 3 and 4, D05 reads a καί absent from ℵ01/B03. At line 3, καί introduces an additional participial clause which is then followed by another καί preceding a finite verb, followed by δέ. The practice of inserting καί before the main verb of a sentence after a participial construction is a frequent peculiarity of the D05 text and is discussed in detail in the next paragraph. Certainly, if the two occurrences of καί in this verse are read as conjunctions, it looks as if the last clause has a redundant δέ. However, if δέ is taken as the proper and intended link between the sentences (signalling a new development in the story), then this allows both occurrences of καί to be construed as emphatic adverbs and not as conjunctions at all. In this case, καί in line 4 is the start of a new sentence and the verse in D05 translates (word for word) as:

> Going into the synagogue every sabbath he lectured, even introducing the name of the Lord Jesus. Yes, and (καὶ … δέ) he persuaded not only Jews but also Greeks.

The emphatic function of καί here is entirely in accordance with the heavy emphasis of the D05 text overall: the detail that Paul went into the synagogue, the specification that he talked about the Lord Jesus, the insistence that it was not only Jews but also Greeks who were persuaded by his teaching.

Seeing how καί serves to highlight the finite verb in 18.4 can help to understand the use of καί to introduce the main verb after a participle, a practice noted above as occurring repeatedly in D05. The complete list of occurrences in D05 is as follows: 2.1; 3.4; 4.3; 5.21; 7.4a,b; 8.2; 10.27; 12.16; 13.7,29; 14.6,14; 16.17; 17.1; 18.7; 20.10; 22.28 (and cf. 17.13 ὡς δέ + subord. verb + καί + main verb).

καί is generally regarded in this unusual construction as a conjunction and as such an apparently superfluous one. It has been explained both as a Semitism and as an attempt to rewrite the text in a vernacular style.[10] Whatever has prompted it, the important factor from a discourse analysis point of view is the circumstances in which it occurs, for there exist many other places where a finite verb follows a participle

---

[10] See David C. Parker, *Codex Bezae: An Early Christian Manuscript and its Text* (Cambridge, UK: CUP, 1992), 255–6. Cf. J. H. Ropes, *The Text of Acts*, vol. 3 of *The Beginnings of Christianity*, ed. F. J. Foakes-Jackson and K. Lake (London: Macmillan, 1926), 10; and B. M. Metzger, *A Textual Commentary on the Greek New Testament* (London/New York: United Bible Societies, 1975), 250.

without any intervening καί in D05. An examination of all the above references shows that each one occurs at a point of particular narrative drama, whether in the story of Acts or in the events related by a participant in direct speech. Some arise at the mention of a major event: Pentecost (2.1); the journey of Abraham to what will become known as Israel (7.4a,b); the burial of Jesus (13.29, in Paul's speech). Others are found in association with a dramatic incident in the lives of the participants, either at the outset, as in the arrest of the apostles (4.3), or more often at the crux of the story: the amazement of the church when Peter appears at Mary's house in Jerusalem (12.16); the horrified reaction of Barnabas and Paul when they are hailed as gods (14.14); the rupture with the Jewish community as Paul takes up residence in the home of a Gentile (18.7); the suspense when Paul takes up Eutyches alive (20.10). Several times, καί is found between a participle and a finite verb at the point of a specially significant encounter: Peter and John, and the lame man (3.1, the first miracle); Barnabas and Saul, and Sergius Paulus (13.7, S/Paul's first opportunity to evangelize); Paul and 'us', and the woman with the spirit of divination (16.17, pagan recognition of the spiritual identity of Paul and those with him).

The nature of the examples cited above suggests that καί preceding the main verb and following a participle operates with the purpose of drawing attention to the action of the main verb of the sentence. This is seen clearly at 10.27 where Peter goes into Cornelius' house and finds many people waiting to listen to him. In the non-Bezan text, the drama at that point (maybe consisting of Peter's surprise) is signalled by the use of the historic present: εἰσῆλθων καὶ εὑρίσκει συνεληλυθότας πολλούς, 'he went in and he finds many people gathered'; D05 uses καί between a participle and the finite verb, further intensified by τε: καὶ εἰσελθὼν τε καὶ εὗρεν σθνεληλυθότας πολλούς, 'and moreover (τε) having gone in, he even (καί) found many people gathered'.

The emphatic function of καί when linking participles and finite verbs sheds a certain light on to its occurrence at 17.1D05 where, at first sight, there does not seem to be any need for emphasis:

Ref.	D05	ℵ01/B03
17.1	διοδεύσαντες δὲ τὴν Ἀμφίπολιν καὶ [κατῆλθον εἰς ↑ Ἀπολλωνίδα] κακεῖθεν εἰς Θεσσαλονίκην ὅπου ἦν συναγωγὴ τῶν Ἰουδαίων	διοδεύσαντες δὲ τὴν Ἀμφίπολιν καὶ [↑ τὴν Ἀπολλωνίαν ἦλθον] ↑ εἰς Θεσσαλονίκην ὅπου ἦν συναγωγὴ τῶν Ἰουδαίων

The ℵ01/B03 text accords less importance to the stages of Paul and Silas' journey than D05. Although it is not immediately apparent that the itinerary of Paul and Silas is of particular dramatic importance, nevertheless, according to the above analysis of the D05 construction, καί preceding the main verb κατῆλθον and following the participle διοδεύσαντες, indicates that there is something quite remarkable about their movements. The clue to their significance lies in the reason given for their eventually stopping their journey in Thessalonica: ὅπου ἦν συναγωγὴ τῶν Ἰουδαίων, 'since there was a synagogue of the Jews'. Apollonia was their first goal (compare 'they went down' to Apollonia with 'they travelled through' Amphipolis), but presumably because Paul and Silas did not find there the synagogue they were looking for, they went on to Thessalonica. D05 overall is highly critical of Paul's strategy of seeking out synagogues in which to preach, a plan of action from which the narrator distances himself. Despite the problems created by Paul's last attempt to preach in the synagogue in Antioch of Pisidia (14.1), he and Silas are still determined to make this their primary objective. καί placed before the verb κατῆλθον is a way of underscoring the deliberate course of action that they were pursuing in going to Apollonia; attention is drawn to this town by the absence of the article in contrast to the presence of the article with Amphipolis (see Chapter 2, §III.7). In the context of the critical attitude of D05, it is also a signal that there was something very surprising about it. It anticipates the uproar that ensues not only in Thessalonica but also in Beroea (17.6–14, where the turmoil is accentuated in D05, cf. §III.3.i below).

That καί has the role of highlighting the action of the finite verb when it is placed between a preceding participle and the finite verb is confirmed by the fact that many times in immediately subsequent clauses that also contain a participle followed by a finite verb, no intervening καί arises. Examples can be seen at 4.4; 5.21; 12.17; 16.18,19 among other places. It does not follow, of course, that the only verbs in Acts that the writer wishes to highlight are those preceded by a participle and καί, for he employs a diversity of other ways to draw attention to the actions of his characters.

At the places where D05 reads καί between a participle and the main verb of the sentence, the text of ℵ01/B03 (indeed, the other MSS in general) reads one of several alternative wordings: either καί is omitted, or the participle is expressed by a finite verb, or (only at 17.1) the verb following καί is omitted. The systematic avoidance of the construction outside D05, without communicating the emphasis in another way, suggests that other editors/scribes were not familiar with it and did not understand its purpose if they found it in an earlier text.

It emerges from the above analysis that when καί occurs after a participle and before a following finite verb it does not have the function of a conjunction but of an adverb, whose role is to present the action of the main verb as one of dramatic importance.

II.2.ii τε

It can be seen from the table at the beginning of this section that τε occurs with much greater frequency in ℵ01 or B03 than in D05. In fact, Codex Sinaiticus and Codex Vaticanus are often divided in their choice of τε or καί/δέ. The distribution of τε, δέ and καί where there is disagreement between ℵ01/B03 is as follows:

καί	δέ	τε	Number of vll
B03/D05		ℵ01	1
	B03	ℵ01/D05	2
	ℵ01/D05	B03	3
	B03/D05	ℵ01	2

In *koine* Greek, the use of the particle τε declined as part of the trend towards simplification, but it appears to have been revived as an Atticism.[11] This development in the language may account for a proportion of the readings of τε in Acts. Others could have arisen because of phonological confusion and indeed, examination of the occurrences of τε as a variant reading shows that its use cannot always be justified from the context (e.g. 12.8 ℵ01).

III. τότε

In the NT, τότε is found both as an adverb and as a conjunction, in contrast to its use in classical Greek solely as an adverb of time. In the Gospel of Matthew, both uses are common whereas in Mark and John it is only used as an adverb; in Luke's Gospel, it occurs in narrative text occasionally as a conjunction but mainly as an adverb. In Acts, where again τότε is only found in narrative, there is yet another picture, for in the firm text τότε is only found as a conjunction; on the two occasions that it occurs as an adverb in the MSS that concern this study, there are variant readings. In point of fact, the distinction between τότε as an adverb and as a conjunction is not always obvious, for even τότε as an adverb can contribute to sentence linking; consequently, both types of occurrences of τότε in Acts will need to be considered to be sure that all aspects of the question have been looked at.

Within Acts, there is a high degree of variation concerning the use of τότε, with D05 reading 28 occurrences in the extant chapters against 15 in the same material in ℵ01 and B03. In seeking to circumscribe the force of τότε, it will be interesting to consider possible factors to which the increased frequency of τότε in D05 can be attributed, and how far, if at all, the variation can be ascribed to the interference of scribal habits.

III.1 The meaning of τότε in the common text

III.1.i As a conjunction

There are 10 examples common to both texts where τότε is used as a conjunction:

1.12; 4.8; 5.26; 7.4; 8.17; 10.48b; 13.3; 15.22; 21.26, 33

Levinsohn defines two purposes of τότε as a conjunction.[12] The first is to link two units of narrative that belong to the same episode; there is continuity of time and of some other feature such as the same topic or main character, but coupled with an aspect of discontinuity such as partial change in the people present or the topic. The second purpose is to introduce the concluding unit of narrative that represents the goal or outcome of an episode.

This definition is somewhat broader than the one Levinsohn gave in an earlier work[13] where it was suggested that τότε always meant 'forthwith' or 'thereupon', and

---

[11] Nigel Turner, *A Grammar of New Testament Greek*, vol. III, *Syntax* (Edinburgh: T&T Clark, 1963), 338.
[12] Levinsohn, *Discourse Features*, 50.
[13] Levinsohn, *Textual Connections*, 151–3.

always implied change of subject of the main verb. Certainly in Acts, when τότε indicates continuity of time, the second event takes place without any further impediment or deliberation (or is presented as such by the narrator; what happened in real life is not the issue). It is also true that after τότε in Acts there is almost always a change of subject from that of the previous clause. This phenomenon can usually be explained by the fact that when the concluding unit of an episode is introduced by τότε, it is equally a response to a previous speech or actions made by another participant, a response that finally ties up or rounds off the episode.

In τότε then, there can be the notion of time ('then', in English) and there can also be the notion of response ('and so', in English). As introducing a response, however, τότε always operates within the same story or episode (linking what Levinsohn terms 'low-level narrative units'), unlike δέ which can introduce a response that forms a new episode. When looking at the examples of τότε in Acts, there are thus four features to be aware of. The first condition is always true and occurs in the presence of one or more of the others:

- the clauses it links are situated within the same episode
- the second action may take place 'forthwith'
- the second action may be a response
- the second action may conclude an episode

III.1.ii *As an adverb*

τότε as an adverb means 'at that time'. There are no examples in the firm text of adverbial use in Acts. However, there are three variant occurrences of τότε as an adverb, studied in §III.3 below.

III.2 Occurrences of τότε as a variant reading

In addition to the ten references in the common text listed above, there are seventeen further occurrences of τότε in the text of D05 and two more in that of ℵ01/B03. Among the variant readings, one of the D05 readings is an adverb as is also one of the ℵ01/B03 readings; additionally, there is one occurrence of τότε at 6.11, which is an adverb in D05 but a conjunction in ℵ01/B03. In the analysis that follows, the supplementary occurrences of τότε as a conjunction will first be examined, grouping them according to the connective that they stand as an alternative to. Secondly, the instances of τότε as an adverb, including 6.11D05, will be examined.

III.2.i *τότε as an alternative to δέ*

Variant readings arise at nine places:

ℵ01/B03: 10.46b; 13.12; 21.13
D05: 2.37; 5.19; 10.21,48a; 19.15; 22.27

At some of these places, τότε is a straightforward alternative to δέ, whereas at others more extensive variation is involved. The variant readings will be examined in the order in which they occur in the text.

2.37 ℵ01/B03 links the end of Peter's speech and the reaction of those hearing it with δέ, so starting a new narrative unit of development, which leads into their question, 'What shall we do …?'. D05 introduces the response to Peter's speech with τότε, so tying the reaction more closely to the speech, firstly as following without any deliberation or discussion, and secondly as part of the same episode rather than the start of a new development. The importance of this close linking is that in D05 the reaction is, in fact, carefully presented as a dual response by means of two supplementary phrases following τότε: on the one hand, πάντες οἱ συνελθόντες καὶ ἀκούσαντες were troubled in their hearts; and on the other hand, a group among them, τινες ἐξ αὐτῶν, went on to ask what they should do. Without going into the significance of the distinction here, it is sufficient to note that the Bezan text draws attention to two separate responses to Peter's speech.

5.19 A series of additional comments in the Bezan text of this passage (5.18, 21, 22) reveals a greater interest in the sequence of events concerning the imprisonment of the apostles by the Jewish authorities. In 5.18D05, a statement marks the finality of the action of the Jewish authorities in that, once the apostles were securely in prison, they all went back to their homes, καὶ ἐπορεύθη εἰς ἕκατος εἰς τὰ ἴδια. τότε in the next sentence in the Greek page of D05[14] introduces the immediate response of God to counter the evil intention, so thwarting the plan of the authorities instantly. As soon as the Jewish leaders put the apostles in prison and abandon them for the night, God intervenes. In this way, D05 stresses the difference between the treatment of the apostles by the Jewish authorities who are the new oppressors of the People of God, and the providential care of God for them.

10.21 The sentence describes Peter's response to the Spirit's command to go down from the roof to the men who had come for him. τότε reinforces the notion of response and indicates that Peter obeyed without delay; it is entirely appropriate in the context of Peter's readiness to accept a new teaching. The conjunction gives a cohesion to the episode, further strengthened in D05 by the use of the article before Peter, which has the effect of underscoring the anaphoricity of the reference (cf. Chapter 2, §II.3). The second τότε as an alternative to οὖν at 10.23D05, again with ὁ Πέτορς, adds yet another element to the overall picture of Peter's willingness to respond to the instructions he has just received (cf. §III.2.iv below).

10.46b The Alexandrian text uses τότε here to present Peter's response to the falling of the Holy Spirit on the Gentiles in Caesarea. That it is a response is made clear by the choice of verb as well as the conjunction in ℵ01/B03: τότε ἀπεκρίθη Πέτρος, rather than εἶπεν δὲ ὁ Πέτρος in D05. The absence of the article before Peter in ℵ01/B03 further indicates a switch of focus from the circumcision party as they observed the Gentiles (10.45), back to Peter as he makes a key proclamation (cf. Chapter 2, §II.5.iv). The Bezan text, with the article maintained, considers Peter to be always in focus and his comments to be a prelude to the critical response that is held over to 10.48.

---

[14] The Latin page d5 has *vero*, generally translating δέ, as found in most of the Greek MSS.

10.48a τότε in D05 introduces Peter's unhesitating action in response to his own deliberations: τότε προσέταξεν αὐτοὺς [βαπτισθῆναι...], 'Then he ordered them to be baptized...'. The baptism leads into the concluding sentence of the epsiode, introduced by τότε in both texts, which records the Gentiles urging Peter to stay a little longer. There are thus two consecutive τότε clauses in D05, a feature unique in Acts although there are other examples of τότε occuring in close proximity, particularly in D05 (cf. 10.21, 23D05; 10.46, 48b ℵ01/B03; 22.27, 29D05).

13.12 τότε is read by the Alexandrian text which records that when the proconsul in Paphos saw what happened to the magician Elymas, his faith followed forthwith: τότε ἰδὼν ὁ ἀνθύπατος τὸ γεγονὸς ἐπίστευσεν. D05 has good reason not to use τότε, for it reads a supplementary comment: when the proconsul saw what had happened, 'he marvelled and believed in God', ἐθαύμασεν καὶ ἐπίστευσεν τῷ θεῷ. There is no cause for underlining that the marvelling took place without delay nor was it in itself a conclusive response and δέ is therefore the appropriate conjunction.

19.15 τότε follows directly in D05 from the considerably fuller D05 text of the previous verse. As the story of the sons of Sceva is told in the short text, there is a number of incongruities in the account. D05 contains several variant readings at the beginning of the story and in 19.14 specifies a particular incident, not mentioned by the other text, in which the exorcists attempt to cast out the evil spirit from a demonized man. When they have given the command, the evil spirit responds with a question followed by violent action. The D05 sentence begins appropriately enough with τότε: the spirit immediately dominates the situation by challenging the exorcists and attacking the men so that the exorcism comes to a rapid end.

There is nonetheless a difficulty with the text of D05 at this point. In the original hand, two main verbs follow without a conjunction: τότε ἀπεκρίθη τὸ πνεῦμα τὸ πονηρὸν εἶπεν αὐτοῖς..., 'Then the evil spirit answered; he said to them...'. Corrector D has modified the line by adding καί before the second verb. This then creates a construction after τότε that exists nowhere else in Acts, of τότε – main verb – subject – καί – main verb. At every other place where there are two verbs following τότε, the first is always a participle (5.26; 7.4; 10.21D05, 23D05; 13.30ℵ/B03, 12ℵ01/B03; 16.22D05; 19.9D05; 21.33; 22.27D05).

21.13 The reading of τότε in ℵ01/B03 is comparable to 10.46b in the same text (see above) with wording that is similar: ℵ01/B03 τότε ἀπεκρίθη ↑ ὁ Παῦλος (D05: εἶπεν δὲ πρὸς ἡμᾶς ὁ Παῦλος). The situation which Paul addresses is the pleading of the 'we'-group and the residents of Caesarea that he should not go to Jerusalem in view of the prophecy just given by Agabus that he would be taken prisoner there. In the Alexandrian text, Paul responds without any further deliberation to the group as a whole, rebuking them for their tears and entreaties; τότε is justified by the nature of the response. His response appears to be conclusive in so far as it leads the group to resign themselves to the will of God. According to D05, Paul addresses the 'we'-group alone, and the focus in this as well as the following verse of D05 is on the resistance of Paul to the Holy Spirit. His response is not at all conclusive, for the 'we'-group do not accept his argument but instead trust among themselves that the will of God will be done.

22.27 This verse provides a final example of a straightforward τότε/δέ alternative with no other variation involved. It is the Bezan text that reads τότε to introduce the response of the tribune to the information brought to him that Paul was a Roman citizen. τότε is appropriate in view of the tribune's anxiety to verify the information. The conjunction further adds cohesion to the narrative of the episode because of its retrospective nature, linking what has just happened to the following conversation. Elements of the centurion's report in the previous verse 22.26D05 also serve to strengthen the cohesion of the narrative in this episode: τοῦτο, referring back to Paul's comments; the repetition of Paul's words, ὅτι Ῥωμαῖον ἑαυτὸν λέγει; the 3rd person pronoun αὐτῷ to specify the tribune; the opening word of his report, ὅρα, inviting the tribune to reconsider the action that he had ordered (cf. 22.24). Further discussion of this passage appears at §III.2.iv below.

III.2.ii *τότε as an alternative to καί*

Two variant readings are found:

D05: 16.22; 18.17b

16.22 D05 has τότε where all the other Greek MSS (and almost all the versions) read καί. There is a number of other differences in the first part of the verse that account for the different conjunctions used:

Ref. D05	ℵ01/B03
16.22 καὶ <u>πολὺς</u> [ὄχλος <u>συνεπέστησαν</u>] κατ' αὐτῶν <u>κράζοντες</u>. <u>τότε</u> οἱ στρατηγοὶ περιρήξαντες αὐτῶν τὰ ἱμάτια ἐκέλευον ῥαβδίζειν	καὶ [συνεπέστη ὁ ὄχλος] κατ' αὐτῶν ↑ καὶ οἱ στρατηγοὶ περιρήξαντες αὐτῶν τὰ ἱμάτια ἐκέλευον ῥαβδίζειν

In the non-Bezan text, when the owners of the girl with the spirit of divination complain about Paul and Silas to the magistrates, a crowd joins in attacking them and the magistrates have the offenders stripped and flogged. The two sets of actions, linked by καί, are presented as parallel and not interdependent. In comparison, the Bezan text firstly heightens the importance of the crowd who side with the accusers and secondly, it presents the magistrates as responding to the situation as a whole. This effect is achieved by the combination of details in 16.22D05, which function together:

- the crowd is large πολύς
- ὄχλος is placed before the verb in a position of prominence
- the verb συνεπέστησαν is plural, portraying the crowd as many people rather than as a single mass
- the people shout out κράζοντες
- τότε introduces the action of the magistrates as a response to both the complaints of the owners and the agitation of the crowd.

The influence of the crowd is referred to again in the Bezan text by the magistrates at the end of the episode, confirming their significance in the scene at 16.22: <u>μήποτε πάλιν συστραφῶσιν ἡμῖν</u>, 'lest they assemble us again, shouting against you' (16.39D05).

18.17b The context is important for the reading of τότε in this verse in D05 but this unfortunately is not without problems of interpretation. The Jews in Corinth had complained to Gallio the proconsul about the teaching of Paul but Gallio had refused to intervene on the grounds that it was an internal Jewish affair and he dismisses them. In the Alexandrian text, what happens next is that all (πάντες) turn against the ruler of the synagogue, Sosthenes (18.17a) and (καί) Gallio takes no notice of the attack (18.17b). According to D05, it was all the Greeks (πάντες οἱ Ἕλληνες) who took away (ἀπολαβόμενοι) Sosthenes, in response to which (τότε) Gallio took no notice. The difficulty for interpreting the text is knowing who is meant by both 'all' and 'the Greeks', and also understanding why they took the ruler of the synagogue. There is further difficulty with the reading of D05 in that the text of the Greek page of the codex is almost erased:

T............................ΩΓΑΛΛΙΩ............EN

The reconstruction that best fits the few letters that remain visible is: τότε προσεποιεῖτο ὁ Γαλλίων αὐτὸν μὴ ἰδεῖν, 'Then Gallio pretended not to see him', corresponding to the Latin page d5: *tunc Gallio fingebat eum non videre*. ℵ01/B03 present the response of Gallio differently: καὶ οὐδὲν τούτων τῷ Γαλλίωνι ἔμελεν, 'and nothing of this mattered to Gallio'. Although τότε is read by no other Greek MS, in so far as the passage can be properly understood, the D05 reading is justified. τότε introduces a response that entails a switch of subject from the previous clause and that concludes the episode concerning the accusations of Paul by the Jews. The comment about Gallio's attitude rounds off the story as attention subsequently switches back in 18.18 to Paul as fore-fronted subject. τότε is thus appropriate and fulfils the usual conditions for its presence. In contrast, καί simply conjoins the two sentences and states Gallio's attitude without drawing attention to it as a response.

III.2.iii τότε as an alternative to τε

This variant is found at one place:[15]

15.39 As the narrative relates the consequences of the disagreement between Paul and Barnabas over John-Mark's presence with them on their second journey, the Alexandrian text presents two results expressed each by an accusative-infinitive construction after ὥστε: the result was that they separated from each other and that, in addition, Barnabas sailed away to Cyprus taking Mark with him (τόν τε Βαρναβᾶν παραλαβόντα τὸν Μᾶρκον ἐκπλεῦσαι εἰς Κύπρον). In contrast to the usual interpretation of this incident, the way the story is told in D05 invites criticism of Paul, and approval of Barnabas who is seen as the one who comprehends the scope of the gospel message with greater clarity. His departure to Cyprus with Mark is his own response to the disagreement (as opposed to a simple consequence), a response that concludes this episode: τότε ↑ Βαρναβᾶς παραλαβὼν τὸν Μᾶρκον ἔπλευσεν εἰς Κύπρον, 'Then Barnabas took Mark and sailed away to Cyprus'. τότε stands in place of

---

[15] At 7.26, τότε in Stephen's speech according to D05 appears to be written in error. The sentence in all other Greek MSS begins: τῇ τε ἐπιούσῃ ἡμέρᾳ. The omission of the necessary article in D05 makes it look as though τότε is the result of a confusion with τῇ τε (in uncial script, where words are not separated, there is only one letter difference between TOTE and THTE).

τόν τε, and the differences in the construction of the rest of the sentence confirm that the variant is not an instance of scribal error.

III.2.iv τότε *as an alternative to* οὖν

D05 has this variant reading twice:

D05: 10.23; 22.29

At both these places, most MSS have οὖν whereas D05 reads τότε with support almost entirely from the versions. The function of οὖν in the narrative sections of Acts is discussed in detail in §IV.1 of this chapter. In summary, as most grammars agree, οὖν indicates a consequential relationship between two sentences or, more specifically, 'the second event is the result of the first and conforms with its demands and expectations'. To some extent, therefore, there is an overlap with the function of τότε which also signals a retrospective relationship with the previous sentence and introduces a response to it. The difference seems to be that whereas the event introduced by οὖν follows naturally from the previous one, the event presented with τότε is by no means the expected one but depends on a personal response.

10.23 The text of this verse varies not only in the choice of conjunction but in a number of other respects, too, as Peter takes the men sent by Cornelius into his house:

D05 τότε εἰσαγαγὼν ὁ Πέτρος [ἐξένισεν αὐτούς]
ℵ01/B03 εἰσκαλεσάμενος οὖν ↑ [αὐτοὺς ἐξένισεν]

(The Latin page of Codex Bezae reads a combination of both Greek readings, *tunc ergo*.) In the Alexandrian version, οὖν suggests that Peter called the men inside and put them up because that is what the situation demanded. On the face of it, it might well seem the natural thing to do: the men have been sent to fetch him (10.5-9, D05 *lac.*) and they are not going to set off back to Caesarea until the following day (10.23b). However, in the context of Peter's earlier attitude to Gentiles and in view of the very recent nature of the new teaching he has received on the status of the Gentiles in the eyes of God, his response is not so natural. The Bezan wording indicates that there is something quite remarkable about Peter's readiness to receive then. He is mentioned by name, although there can be no ambiguity, which has the effect of maintaining Peter as the main centre of attention; he acts forthwith, τότε; and he leads the men inside, εἰσαγαγών, a verb that elsewhere in Luke indicates a determined strength of purpose (cf. Lk. 22.54; Acts 21.28).

22.29 The text of D05 is unfortunately missing after the first line of 22.29, where the reaction of Paul's interrogators on learning of his Roman citizenship is described, so there is only limited evidence to explain the D05 preference for τότε rather than εὐθέως οὖν of ℵ01/B03. From what has been noted so far about the meaning of the two conjunctions, it can be said that the former (D05) reading views the withdrawal of the interrogators as an immediate response to the tribunal's conversation with the prisoner, whereas the latter (ℵ01/B03) reading sees it as conforming to the demands and implications of the conversation.

The difference inherent in the connectives is backed up by an underlying difference in the way in which the story is told in the two texts at this point in the narrative. In the exchange between the tribune and Paul, a series of variants combine to make the D05 account less 'matter of fact' and to give more depth to the character of the tribune (cf. comments on the texture of 22.26–27 in §III.2.i above). In particular, when Paul counters the tribune's claim to have paid for his Roman citizenship with a large sum of money (even more emphatically stated in 22.28D05: ἐγὼ οἶδα πόσου κεφαλαίου) with the statement that he was born a Roman citizen, there is a contrast indicated in D05 by the omission of the article before Paul (cf. Chapter 2, §II.5.ii). In the text of א01/B03, there is less of a case for indicating contrast because the tribune had never really been brought into focus. What is more, in the א01/B03 text Paul has remained very much the sole centre of attention, being mentioned by name in the course of the episode overall an additional twice compared with the D05 text (21.37; 22.25). This difference between the two texts may account, in part at least, for the different conjunctions at the beginning of the next sentence, 22.29. In cinematographic terms, the Alexandrian text shows the exchange between Paul and the tribune in a long shot as part of the dealings of the Roman authorities with Paul. The telling of the exchange in that text brings out the general implications of the political 'faux pas', that is, the immediate withdrawal of those about to examine Paul. In the Bezan text, the camera zooms in on the tribune as he talks to Paul, displaying more of a personal interest in him. The withdrawal of the interrogators is therefore certainly a response to that conversation but not a natural consequence in so far as the Bezan text views the report of the conversation itself as having a greater narrative purpose than that of simply accounting for their action.

III.2.v τότε as an additional reading in D05

There are four such additional readings:

D05: 2.14; 18.5; 19.9b, 21

2.14 τότε is read by D05 in front of the sentence as it stands elsewhere in the Greek MSS: τότε σταθεὶς δὲ ὁ Πέτρος … ἐπῆρεν τὴν φωνὴν αὐτοῦ, 'Having then stood up, Peter … lifted his voice'. The use of τότε places δέ in third position in the sentence but this is not unknown among the NT writings. τότε introduces the reply of Peter to the questioning and taunts of the crowds, a response made without intervening deliberation. A similar formula introduces the speech of Peter at 4.8 (both texts), and also that of Paul at 27.21א01/B03 (D05 *lac.*). It is interesting to compare the word order in these three examples. 2.14D05 and 27.21 have τότε σταθεὶς ὁ Πέτρος/Παῦλος, that is, present participle–article–name. The article is used with the name because the person has been established as the central character in the narrative at that point (cf. Chapter 2, §II.3). At 4.8, however, the Jewish authorities address their question to the apostles as a whole and it is Peter who is detached from the group to give an answer; the singling out is marked by the omission of the article: Τότε Πέτρος πλησθεὶς πνεύματος ἁγίου εἶπεν πρὸς αὐτούς…. The salience of Peter at this point is further indicated by the position of the name immediately after τότε, before the participle.

19.9b The Greek page of Codex Bezae has two separate sentences in this verse (and appears to stand alone in doing so). The first sentence, describing the resistance to Paul of some of the people in the synagogue in Ephesus, is linked to the previous context by μὲν οὖν which is examined in detail in §IV.3.i of this chapter. It is seen there that μέν is prospective and in this case looks ahead to Paul's withdrawal from the synagogue with the disciples, in response to the criticisms. His response is introduced by τότε.

The Alexandrian text has the first sentence as a subordinate clause of time (ὡς δέ), dependent on the main verb ἀφώρισεν, 'he took (the disciples) away'. The overall effect of the Bezan text when compared with the Alexandrian MSS at this point is to heighten the conflict between the Jews and Paul: the latter is mentioned by name at two additional places in 19.8-9D05 and his moving out of the synagogue is not just 'when' some people criticised the teaching, it is 'in response' to their speaking ill of it 'to the Gentiles': τότε ἀποστὰς ὁ Παῦλος ἀπ' αὐτῶν ἀφώρισεν τοὺς μαθητάς.

19.21 Following the incident with the Jewish exorcists and the subsequent renunciation by many new converts of their previous occult practices, Paul decides to make his way back to Jerusalem. Here, the Alexandrian text (supported by all the other MSS except D05) begins a new episode, with a subordinate time clause. There are other differences in D05 in the previous sentence:

Ref.	D05	ℵ01/B03
19.20	Οὕτως κατὰ κράτος [ἐνίσχυσεν καὶ ἡ πίστις τοῦ θεοῦ]· ηὔξανεν καὶ ἐπλήθυνε.	Οὕτως κατὰ κράτος [τοῦ κυρίου ↑ ὁ λόγος] ηὔξανεν καὶ ἴσχυεν.
19.21	↑ Τότε ↑ [↑ Παῦλος ἔθετο] ἐν τῷ πνεύματι...	Ὡς δὲ ἐπληρώθη ταῦτα [ἔθετο ὁ Παῦλος] ἐν τῷ πνεύματι...

19.20 in both texts represents a statement summarizing the growth of the church in Ephesus. D05 specifies that it was faith in God, rather than the word, that was growing and it includes an unusual instance of asyndeton before the final pair of verbs. In the following verse in the Alexandrian text, Paul's plan to go to Jerusalem is presented as the start of a new episode following the summary statement, even though the action proper does not begin until 19.23. D05 does not read the subordinate clause of the ℵ01/B03 text but introduces Paul's decision to go to Jerusalem with τότε, placing the named anarthrous subject before the verb. Paul's response is thus highlighted by several devices. The reason for this lies in the negative appraisal by the Bezan narrator of Paul's insistence on going to Jerusalem. He had come to Ephesus because the Spirit had told him to return to Asia when he himself had wanted to go to Jerusalem some time earlier (19.1D05). Now that his mission to the Gentiles has met with considerable success, he is even more determined to go to Jerusalem and he will resist the various means the Spirit will use to dissuade him (20.3-4D05; 21.10-15). According to D05, the next episode will begin at 19.23.

III.3 τότε **as an adverb**

On four occasions, τότε is read as an adverb in one text but not the other:

D05: 6.11; 11.26; 18.5; ℵ01/B03: 17.14

6.11 Whereas τότε serves as a conjunction in ℵ01/B03, it has the function of an adverb in D05:

Ref.	D05	ℵ01/B03
6.10	... οὐκ ἴσχυον ἀντιστῆναι τῇ σοφίᾳ <u>τῇ οὔσῃ ἐν αὐτῷ</u> καὶ τῷ πνεύματι <u>τῷ ἁγίῳ</u> ᾧ ἐλάλει <u>διὰ τὸ ἐλέγχεσθαι αὐτοὺς ἐπ᾽ αὐτοῦ μετὰ πάσης παρρησίας.</u>	... οὐκ ἴσχυον ἀντιστῆναι τῇ σοφίᾳ ↑ καὶ τῷ πνεύματι ↑ ᾧ ἐλάλει ↑ ↑
6.11	<u>μὴ δυνάμενοι οὖν ἀντοφθαλμεῖν τῇ ἀληθείᾳ</u> τότε ὑπέβαλον ἄνδρας ...	↑ τότε ὑπέβαλον ἄνδρας ...

D05 has a considerably longer account of the response of Stephen's opponents, with the sentence of 6.10 linked to the next in 6.11 with the conjunction is οὖν; τότε then has the function of an adverb of time.

11.26 τότε is found in a passage of D05 which, although differing considerably in the wording, has a similar meaning to that of the ℵ01/B03 text:

Ref.	D05	ℵ01/B03
11.26	καὶ <u>τότε</u> <u>πρῶτον</u> <u>ἐχρημάτισεν</u> ἐν Ἀντιοχείᾳ <u>οἱ μαθηταὶ χριστιανοί</u>	χρηματίσαι τε ↑ <u>πρώτως</u> ἐν Ἀντιοχείᾳ <u>τοὺς μαθητὰς Χριστιανούς</u>

τότε follows the conjunction καί as an adverb, together with another adverb πρῶτον, with the resultant meaning 'and then for the first time'.

17.14 It is ℵ01/B03 that read τότε as an adverb following εὐθέως δέ in a sentence that describes the immediate action taken by the brethren to protect Paul when Jews from Thessalonica came to stir up trouble in Beroea. The account of Paul's preaching in Beroea and its consequences is fuller in D05 and the reaction of the brethren is introduced with μὲν οὖν (Greek side only; the Latin page has *statimque*). This variant is dealt with in more detail in §IV.3.i below.

18.5 τότε in D05 has been corrected by a later hand to ὅ τε, which is the reading of ℵ01/B03:

Ref.	D05	ℵ01/B03
18.5	<u>παρεγένοντο</u> δὲ ἀπὸ τῆς Μακεδονίας <u>τότε</u> Σιλᾶς καὶ Τιμόθεος· συνείχετο τῷ λόγῳ ↑ Παῦλος διαμαρτυρόμενος τοῖς Ἰουδαίοις ...	Ὡς δὲ κατῆλθον ἀπὸ τῆς Μακεδονίας <u>ὅ τε</u> Σιλᾶς καὶ ὁ Τιμόθεος, συνείχετο τῷ λόγῳ <u>ὁ</u> Παῦλος διαμαρτυρόμενος τοῖς Ἰουδαίοις ...

ℵ01/B03 read a subordinate time clause in place of the aorist verb παρεγένοντο, so making one sentence out of D05's three sense lines and Paul is clearly the subject of the imperfect main verb συνείχετο. In D05, συνείχετο begins a new sentence without a connective, of which Paul is the subject. The sequence of tenses, aorist followed by imperfect, indicates a close time connection between the two sentences; the adverb τότε reinforces the time connection, and the relationship between the sentences is also strengthened by the asyndeton, drawing attention to the incongruity of Paul's activity among the Jews at the point when Silas and Timothy joined him in Corinth; indeed, the verb παραγένοντο carries the sense of arriving into the presence of Paul, joining him, rather than simply arriving.

III.4 Conclusions on the use of τότε

Where τότε occurs as a variant reading in either the Alexandrian text or the Bezan text, it is justified by the context in which it is found. Overall, neither the use nor the non-use of τότε can be satisfactorily ascribed to the whim or personal style of a scribe or editor. At a discourse level, it can be seen to communicate a way of perceiving how the story fits together. Its use in the MSS under consideration fulfils the conditions that have been deduced from previous examinations of τότε in Acts: it introduces a sentence that is part of the same episode as that which has gone before, and that takes place either next in time or as a response to what has happened, often in drawing an episode to a close. Sometimes, τότε is used because one text brings out a particular relationship between sentences that the other text either ignores or replaces with a different sentence relationship. At other times, τότε arises in the presence of other variation that precludes its use in the other text. Its frequent use as a conjunction in D05 tends to make of this text a writing that is more cohesive and more concerned with the way events are linked together; τότε does not acquire this function in isolation but rather in conjunction with other cohesive devices. The use of τότε to pinpoint responses and draw attention to concluding events is in keeping with the overall purpose of D05 whose narrator, rather than producing a straightforward historical account, comments on the events related and evaluates them for the benefit of the recipients.

IV. οὖν, μέν, μὲν οὖν

There is a sufficient number of variant readings involving οὖν, μέν and μὲν οὖν to warrant a close examination of their occurrence in the MSS with which this present study is concerned (א01, B03 and D05). Sometimes, they arise in an additional clause that is not read by all three MSS. At other times, an alternative structure or conjunction (principally δέ or τότε) is read by one or two of the MSS. When attention is paid to the circumstances of their presence or absence, interesting observations can be made. A general feature is that where variation occurs, it is due to differences in the surrounding text (rewording or additional material) rather than the straightforward choice of an alternative conjunction.

IV.1 οὖν

There are relatively few occurrences of οὖν in the firm text of Acts generally, most being in speech with only rare instances in narrative passages. Whether in speech or narrative, the function of οὖν in Acts has been described by Levinsohn as being a marked form of δέ.[16] In reported speech, it serves 'to introduce a new assertion or

---

[16] Levinsohn, *Discourse Features*, 85.

exhortation which is to be inferred from the last premise'. In narrative, 'the second event is the direct result of the first, and closely conforms with its demands and implications'. It is always retrospective and in order to understand the clause it introduces reference must be made to what has just gone before. Although English translations often render οὖν by 'therefore', it does not always convey the idea of 'consequence' as such; it can simply mean 'in accordance with' rather than 'in consequence'. This is noticed especially in the course of a reasoned argument where οὖν expresses a logical relationship; it can either lead on to the next point inferred from the argument so far or, as an exhortation builds on an argument, it can present a consequence. These definitions need to be borne in mind as the variant readings are examined.

IV.1.i Variant readings of οὖν

οὖν is read eleven times by D05 but not the other two MSS:

2.32, 37; 4.17; 5.39; 6.3; 7.12; 13.23, 39; 16.10; 20.4, 26

It is not read by D05 four times when ℵ01/B03 read it:

10.23, 33; 16.11 (B03 only); 22.29

The number of occurrences in D05 is striking in view of the infrequency of οὖν in Acts generally. Most are found in reported speech and the two that occur in narrative (16.10; 20.4) belong to the 'we' sections of the book. Similarly, of the occurrences read by ℵ01 or B03, 10.33 and 16.11 arise within direct speech. The references at 10.23 and 22.29 are situated at the juncture of speech and narrative as the story is taken up after speech is reported; οὖν is replaced by D05 at both those places by τότε, in the midst of other variants and these two verses have been examined in the section on τότε where discussion of οὖν in the Alexandrian text can be found (§III.2.iv).

The Latin page of Codex Bezae reads *ergo* for οὖν at each additional occurrence in the Greek except at 7.12; 13.23, 39; 20.4, 26. Comment is made on the exceptions as the variant readings are discussed below.

2.32 It is possible that οὖν here should be read as an error for the accusative article τόν before the name of Jesus. On the other hand, the view may be taken that οὖν has its place in the development of Peter's demonstration of how the prophecies made by David were fulfilled through the resurrection of Jesus by God. It is already found as a similar aid to the unfolding of the argument at 2.30. It is also used in the same way in the course of Paul's preaching in Acts 13 at 2.23D05,38,39D05.

2.37 The consequential nature of οὖν is apparent in the way D05 uses it to introduce the reaction of some of Peter's audience to his preaching: in view of what Peter has explained (οὖν), what shall they do? Furthermore, the verb in this sentence in D05 is a future indicative (τί ποιήσομεν), instead of the aorist subjunctive in the ℵ01/B03 text (τί ποιήσωμεν), just as in the same question at 4.16D05. Together with οὖν, the indicative confers on the question a deliberateness and an urgency that are reflected in the additional words in the next line of the D05 text at 2.37: ὑποδείξατε ἡμῖν. The reaction is not just 'What might we do?' but 'So what shall we do? Show us.'

4.17 οὖν is found in the D05 version of the deliberations of the Sanhedrin over the action to be taken concerning Peter and John's healing of the lame man. The passage generally (4.13–22) displays some major divergences from the Alexandrian text with variant readings affecting the connectives at 4.13,15,17,18. It is unusual for so much structural reworking to be apparent between the two texts, an indication perhaps that the passage has posed some important problems during the early history of its transmission. In the discussion among the Sanhedrin 4.16–17, stronger feeling and a more decisive tone is conveyed by the Bezan text.

Ref.	D05	ℵ01/B03
4.16	τί ποιήσομεν τοῖς ἀνθρώποις τούτοις; ὅτι μὲν γὰρ γνωστὸν σημεῖον γεγονέναι δι᾽ αὐτῶν πᾶσιν τοῖς κατοικοῦσιν Ἰερουσαλὴμ φανερότερόν ἐστιν καὶ οὐ δυνάμεθα ἀρνεῖσθαι	τί ποιήσωμεν τοῖς ἀνθρώποις τούτοις; ὅτι μὲν γὰρ γνωστὸν σημεῖον γέγονεν δι᾽ αὐτῶν πᾶσιν τοῖς κατοικοῦσιν Ἰερουσαλὴμ φανερὸν ↑ καὶ οὐ δυνάμεθα ἀρνεῖσθαι·
4.17	↑ ἵνα μὴ ἐπὶ πλέον τι διανεμηθῇ εἰς τὸν λαὸν ἀπειλησόμεθα οὖν τούτοις μηκέτι λαλεῖν ἐπὶ τῷ ὀνόματι τούτῳ μηδενὶ ἀνθρώπων.	ἀλλ᾽ ἵνα μὴ ἐπὶ πλέον ↑ διανεμηθῇ εἰς τὸν λαὸν ἀπειλησώμεθα ↑ αὐτοῖς μηκέτι λαλεῖν ἐπὶ τῷ ὀνόματι τούτῳ μηδενὶ ἀνθρώπων.

The forceful impression in D05 is due firstly to the comparative φανερότερόν ἐστιν, 'it is more than manifest', and is further created by the variations in 4.17 where οὖν is read. Where the ℵ01/B03 text begins a new sentence with ἀλλά before the negative condition clause, D05 has several variants: it does not read ἀλλά and includes τι before the verb; a new sentence begins with ἀπειλησώμεθα, the future indicative being used instead of the subjunctive (cf. comments on 2.37 above) and οὖν serving as the connective. In this text, the ἵνα μή clause belongs to the last sentence of 4.16 so that this part of the speech reads thus: 'and we cannot deny, lest it spread more and more among the people. We shall therefore warn them to speak no more ...'. The firmness of the Sanhedrin's decision is restated in an additional comment in D05 following the speech:

4.18D05 συγκατατιθεμένων δὲ αὐτῶν τῇ γνώμῃ ...
'When they had agreed to the decision ...'.

5.39 In Gamaliel's warning to the Sanhedrin, there are several elements in D05 that are not read by the Alexandrian MSS and that reflect the Pharisaic outlook. Already in 5.38, there is the insistence that the Jewish leaders should keep well clear of the apostles (as they are so named in 5.34D05) for fear of being defiled, μὴ μιάναντες τὰς χεῖρας. The sentiment is echoed in the exhortation in 5.39D05, ἀπέχεσθε οὖν ἀπὸ τῶν ἀνθρώπων τούτων, 'keep away therefore from these men', where the verb is one used in legal requirements for abstaining from certain things (cf. 15.20). οὖν looks back on the reasoning of Gamaliel's speech and presents it as the basis for the exhortation. Leaving to the one side the question of what exactly these supplementary elements in D05 contribute in terms of meaning, it can be seen that from the point of view of the language they have the effect of producing a carefully constructed and rounded argument.

This study of variant readings that occur in the account of the two occasions on which the Sanhedrin is reported as discussing the apostles and their actions (4.13–21; 5.33–40) has shown that the D05 text presents a more developed and cohesive account of the speeches. These are characteristic features of further speeches in the Bezan text of Acts, where the choice of other connectives examined later in this chapter also make their contribution. The explanation that a later scribe has thought it desirable to neaten, or fill out, the original report does not account for the several peculiarly Jewish concerns that the variant readings reflect.

6.3 As the apostles propose arrangements to ensure fair treatment of the Hellenist widows, a reported speech is once more given in a slightly fuller and less summarized form in D05 than in ℵ01/B03. οὖν is found in additional material in D05 as part of a question that spells out the reasoning of the apostles. They do not want to abandon preaching for table service: τί οὖν ἐστίν, ἀδελφοί; 'So what is to be done, brethren?' οὖν here serves the purpose of indicating what follows from the argument so far. There is further additional material and word order variation in the answer given to the question, which is discussed in the chapter on word order (Chapter 4, §II.4.iii.a).

7.12 οὖν occurs in the Greek text only of Codex Bezae, in the course of Stephen's speech that relates the history of Israel from a very particular point of view. The period concerning Joseph in Egypt is given detailed attention from 7.6-16 and within it the Bezan text appears to have a special interest in Egypt, with a number of variant readings relating specifically to the country itself (7.11,12,15). It is within that episode that οὖν is used, to introduce Jacob's response to hearing that there was corn in Egypt at the time of a general famine. The conjunction οὖν specifies the close relationship between the lack of food in Canaan and the sending of Jacob's sons to Egypt: one leads to another. The relationship of consequence may be obvious enough in the alternative reading of δέ in all the other MSS; what οὖν does is to keep the interest on how Jacob comes to be in Egypt, rather than switching attention to Jacob as a character in his own right.

It is interesting to notice how this sentence fits into the wider narrative. There has been a long series of sentences linked with καί, beginning at 7.6 when God is reported as speaking to Abraham about his descendants being slaves in a foreign country (Egypt); 7.11, using δέ (no variants), introduces what is in effect an aside presenting information about the famine by which the patriarchs in Canaan were affected; 7.12 then moves back to Egypt. According to the choice of conjunction, Jacob's dealings with Egypt can either be seen as a new development in the story (δέ) or as an integral part (οὖν) of the longer section 7.6-16, unified by its focus on Egypt.

10.33 οὖν in ℵ01/B03 produces two consecutive occurrences of the particle (cf. 10.33a, no variant), the first expressing consequence and this second 'accordingly'. In its place, D05 reads ἰδού, conferring on the declaration by Cornelius of his readiness to listen to Peter a note reminiscent of stories from the Jewish Scriptures (e.g. the call of Samuel in I Kg 3.4). That is not, however, its sole function for, as in the Alexandrian text, the reading operates in association with other variants in the rest of the sentence: in ℵ01/B03, Cornelius presents himself and his household as waiting before God to hear what has been commanded by the Lord; in D05, the spotlight is clearly on Peter who is invited to take notice of the group gathered (ἰδού) and who, as a representative of the apostolic community, is seen to enter for the first time into direct communication with Gentiles.

13.23 Both this reference and the following one at 13.39 belong to Paul's preaching in the synagogue at Antioch in Pisidia. At both places, οὖν in D05 helps the development of the argument by clarifying the relationship between points and in this way has a function similar to that observed for οὖν in Peter's speech at 2.32.

At 13.23, οὖν shows how the words reported as spoken to David in 13.22 were accomplished by God in Jesus. As often, οὖν works in combination with other Bezan variants (only partially shared by the Latin page) the effect of which, in comparison with the word order and choice of words in ℵ01/B03, makes prominent the actions of God:

Ref.	D05	ℵ01/B03
13.23	[ὁ θεὸς <u>οὖν</u> ἀπὸ τοῦ σπέρματος <u>αὐτοῦ</u>] κατ' ἐπαγγελίαν <u>ἤγειρεν</u> τῷ Ἰσραὴλ σωτῆρα <u>τὸν</u> Ἰησοῦν	[<u>τούτου</u> ὁ θεὸς ↑ ἀπὸ τοῦ σπέρματος] κατ' ἐπαγγελίαν <u>ἤγαγεν</u> τῷ Ἰσραὴλ σωτῆρα ↑ Ἰησοῦν

In D05, this sentence constitutes the peroration of the first part of Paul's speech (13.16–25), all the earlier constituents being linked with καί. The structure of the speech is less clear in the Alexandrian text without the resumptive connective to indicate the peroration, and also without καί in 13.19B03. The other principal difference is that the Bezan text has God and his actions in focus: ὁ θεός is in first place as fore-fronted subject, and Jesus is mentioned with the article showing that it is not he who is salient so much as the actions of God. In the Alexandrian text, it is the person of David and his counterpart, Jesus who are in focus: the sentence connective is the relative pronoun τούτου, referring to David, and the name of Jesus is underlined without the article as the so far un-named fulfilment of the promise. The theological preoccupation of the Bezan text, of demonstrating how God has acted in fulfilment of prophecies made to Israel in the past, is consistent with its overall purpose of insisting to a Jewish audience that Jesus is part of God's plan for Israel.

13.39 Here, Paul continues to present arguments to show how Jesus fits into the plan of God for Israel. On the grounds that he was the one foreshadowed by David (οὖν, 13.38), it should be known that forgiveness of sins is announced through him (this, B03). The ℵ01/B03 text continues with a new sentence (no connective in ℵ01):

Ref.	D05	ℵ01/B03
13.38	καὶ <u>μετάνοια</u> ἀπὸ πάντων ὧν οὐκ ἠδυνήθητε ἐν νόμῳ Μωϋσέως δικαιωθῆναι,	καὶ (not ℵ01) ↑ ἀπὸ πάντων ὧν οὐκ ἠδυνήθητε ἐν νόμῳ Μωϋσέως δικαιωθῆναι,
13.39	ἐν τούτῳ <u>οὖν</u> πᾶς ὁ πιστεύων δικαιοῦται <u>παρὰ θεῷ</u>	ἐν τούτῳ ↑ πᾶς ὁ πιστεύων δικαιοῦται ↑

The Alexandrian text can be translated '(and) from all things from which you were not able to be freed by the law of Moses, by this man everyone who believes is freed'. The verb δικαιοῦμαι is used with ἀπό and a noun in the genitive to mean 'to be freed from something'. The verb can also be used in an absolute sense with the meaning of 'to be justified' or 'vindicated'. The double meaning is apparent in the Bezan text which has a different sentence structure in 13.38-39. First, μετάνοια is read after καί so continuing the previous sentence to the end of 13.38: '(forgiveness of sins is announced) and repentance from all things from which you were not able to be freed by the law of Moses.' It is the forgiveness of sins and the repentance announced through Jesus that bring about freedom from all the things from which the law of Moses was unable to offer release. That in turn leads to justification before God, expressed by the Bezan text in a new sentence beginning at 13.39 with the conjunction οὖν, and the words παρὰ θεῷ at the end of the verse: 'In this man, therefore, everyone who believes is justified before God'. There are exegetical issues to do with the force of ἐν used with Jesus (τούτῳ) that cannot be tackled here, but the function of οὖν is nevertheless clear: it presents the next step in the argument that follows on from what has previously been claimed.

As at 13:23, so here in the Bezan rendering of Paul's speech there is a more apparent concern to demonstrate that the God of Israel, known to Jews through their Scriptures and teachers and through his intervention in their history, is the same God who is the subject of the new teaching concerning the Messiah, Jesus. Paul is portrayed by D05 as anxious to communicate this continuity convincingly, in order for the new teaching to be acceptable to Jews.

16.10-11 οὖν occurs in 16.10 in D05 in the account of what happened after Paul had seen the vision of the man from Macedonia pleading for help. The ℵ01/B03 text leads without further ado into the decision of the group as a whole to go to Macedonia since they concluded that God was calling them to announce the gospel to them:

Ref.	D05	ℵ01/B03
16.10	↑ διεγερθεὶς οὖν [διηγήσατο τὸ ὅραμα] ἡμῖν· καὶ ἐνοήσαμεν ↑ [ὅτι προσκέκληται ἡμᾶς ὁ κύριος εὐαγγελίσασθαι τοὺς ἐν τῇ Μακεδονίᾳ].	ὡς ↑ δὲ [τὸ ὅραμα εἶδεν] ↑, εὐθέως ἐζητήσαμεν ἐξελθεῖν [εἰς ↑ Μακεδονίαν συμβιβάζοντες ὅτι προσκέκληται ἡμᾶς ὁ θεὸς εὐαγγελίσασθαι αὐτούς].

In contrast, D05 spells out the detail of Paul rising and recounting the vision to the 'we'-group who have the prophetic function of interpreting the vision. The role of the 'we'-group in this instance is typical of the way they are generally presented in D05. B03 introduces the subsequent departure from Troas in 16.11 with οὖν, unlike ℵ01 and D05, which both have δέ (Ἀναχθέντες δὲ ἀπὸ Τρῳάδος).

20.4 The texts of ℵ01/B03 and D05 at the beginning of Acts 20 contain a high number of divergences, producing in effect two different accounts of the incident that prompted Paul's departure from Greece and the start of his long journey to Jerusalem. The story according to most MSS is that an uprising of the Jews occurred just as Paul was about to set sail for Syria (20.3) and that the trouble prompted him to go back through Macedonia instead (20.4); he was accompanied by a group of men who went ahead to wait in Troas (20.5). It is not clear why the indirect route to Syria through Macedonia should have been preferable to the sea journey. The logic of the D05 text is different: it was the Jewish plot that made Paul want to set sail for Syria (cf. 17.4) and it was the Spirit who told him to go back through Macedonia instead (with no mention of a further destination beyond). It seems that Paul took advantage of this instruction, while acting in line with it (οὖν), to decide to pursue his journey to Asia where a group of men went on ahead to wait for him (and not 'us' as in the Alexandrian text) in Troas:

Ref.	D05	ℵ01/B03
20.4	μέλλοντος οὖν ἐξιέναι αὐτοῦ μέχρι τῆς Ἀσίας ↑ Σώπατρος κτλ …	↑ συνείπετο δὲ αὐτῷ Σώπατρος κτλ …
20.5	οὗτοι προελθόντες ἔμενον αὐτὸν ἐν Τρῳάδι	οὗτοι δὲ προελθόντες ἔμενον ἡμᾶς ἐν Τρῳάδι

20.26 D05 reads οὖν instead of διότι. In pronouncing his farewell speech to the Ephesian elders, Paul insists that he has fully accomplished his mission to preach the gospel among all the Ephesians (20.18–22), reiterating in 20.25 that he has proclaimed the kingdom among them. In 20.26ℵ01/B03, the sentence continues with Paul, on account of this ministry, testifying on this day that he is innocent of the blood of all; in contrast, D05 begins a new sentence with οὖν in 20.26 and has Paul stating that the consequence of his ministry is that up to this day he is innocent of the blood of all.

Ref.	D05	ℵ01/B03
20.26	↑ ἄχρι οὖν τῆς σήμερον ἡμέρας ↑ καθαρός εἰμι ἀπὸ τοῦ αἵματος πάντων·	διότι μαρτύρομαι ὑμῖν ἐν τῇ σήμερον ἡμέρᾳ ὅτι καθαρός εἰμι ἀπὸ τοῦ αἵματος πάντων·

οὖν, which links the new sentence back to what he has claimed about his preaching about the kingdom (of Jesus, 20.25D05), shows the consequential relationship not of his present testimony (ℵ01/B03) but of his being clean. The Bezan text portrays Paul as concerned with his record to date as he prepares to make what he has been warned is his dangerous journey to Jerusalem (20.22–24).

IV.1.ii Conclusions on the use of οὖν

The additional readings of οὖν in the MSS exist to indicate inferences and connections with what has been said previously. οὖν is never read as a variant reading on its own but occurs as part of a wider variation unit that may span several lines. Variation arises chiefly in speeches when the editor of one text appears to view the links between points in an argument or exposition differently from that of the other text. The careful and

IV.2 μέν

If οὖν looks back to the previous clause, μέν on the contrary has a prospective function when it is used as a connecting word. It anticipates a second contrastive clause, often beginning with δέ; the anticipated contrast may, however, be implied rather than be actually stated. When it looks ahead to a second sentence, the μέν clause is downgraded compared with the one linked with δέ. These rules, which have been deduced from an analysis of the NT documents generally, are borne out by a study of those places where the MSS differ.

IV.2.i Variant readings of μέν

μέν is read by only one of the two texts at the following five places:

> 3.13א01/B03, 3.17D05; 13.29D05, 13.36א01/B03; 19.15א01corr/B03

At 13.29D05, μέν is used adverbially rather than as a connective; the reference will be considered here, however, because it illustrates how contrast can be indicated without the use of a corresponding δέ.

3.13 μέν occurs, not only in א01/B03 but in most MSS, as Peter goes over the events leading up to the killing of Jesus; it introduces the statement that his audience handed over Jesus. Since μέν is prospective, it indicates that a contrast is anticipated; the contrast cannot be with the action of God in glorifying Jesus (3.13a) since this precedes the μέν clause. There is no contrastive δέ clause corresponding to the μέν clause for when δέ arises in 3.14 Peter continues to speak of the hostility of his audience (ὑμεῖς, again) against Jesus. There is a contrast, however, within the μέν clause itself that is found in the action of Pilate: '[Jesus] whom you handed over and denied before Pilate, that man having decided (κρίναντος ἐκείνου) to release him'. The implication of the aorist participle in the circumstantial genitive absolute construction is that the denying continued simultaneously with Pilate's decision to let Jesus go, so a conflict is presented. While the sentence in the א01/B03 text is very condensed, in D05 it is opened out somewhat and its meaning is different:

Ref.	D05	א01/B03
3.13	… ὃν ὑμεῖς ↑ παρεδώκατε εἰς κρίσιν καὶ ἀπηρνήσασθε αὐτὸν κατὰ πρόσωπον Πιλάτου τοῦ κρίναντος, ἐκείνου ἀπολύειν αὐτὸν θέλοντος	… ὃν ὑμεῖς μὲν παρεδώκατε ↑ καὶ ἠρνήσασθε ↑ κατὰ πρόσωπον Πιλάτου ↑ κρίναντος ἐκείνου ἀπολύειν ↑

The subtle construction of the speeches in D05 in particular suggests an editor who is not only sensitive to the Jewish viewpoint but who is also sufficiently familiar with it to be able to render the speeches of Paul in such a way that they set out an exposition of the Christian teaching that is favourable to a Jewish audience.

The sentence in D05 can be translated as '[Jesus] whom you handed over to judgement; and you denied him before Pilate who, when that man had judged, was wanting to release him'. Here, the meaning of κρίνω is 'to judge' rather than 'to decide', and the opposition is not between the people handing over Jesus and Pilate deciding to let him go, but rather between the people denying Jesus and Pilate wanting to release him. The successive timing of the actions of a) handing Jesus over for judgement and b) denying him once Pilate had judged does not bring the conflict into focus in the way that the other text does; it is in the next sentence (3.14) that the contrast between Pilate and the people is brought out, introduced with ὑμεῖς δέ.

3.17 Here, in the Bezan text Peter expresses a clear contrast between the ignorance of the Jews in having the Christ put to death and the foreknowledge inherent in the plan of God (3.18, δέ):

Ref.	D05	ℵ01/B03
3.17	Καὶ νῦν, ἄνδρες ἀδελφοί, ἐπιστάμεθα ὅτι ὑμεῖς μὲν κατὰ ἄγνοιαν ἐπράξατε πονηρὸν ὥσπερ καὶ οἱ ἄρχοντες ὑμῶν	Καὶ νῦν, ↑ ἀδελφοί, οἶδα ὅτι ↑ κατὰ ἄγνοιαν ἐπράξατε ↑ ὥσπερ καὶ οἱ ἄρχοντες ὑμῶν

The contrast is presented in D05 by the use of the emphatic pronoun ὑμεῖς followed by μέν, and is further intensified by the description of the Jews' action as πονηρόν, 'wicked'.

13.29 μέν in D05 is used adverbially and not to link sentences for it is found (in the main clause) following a subordinate clause of time that was linked by δέ to the preceding sentence. It nevertheless anticipates a second action and is considered here for the parallels it displays with the use of μέν as a conjunction.

μέν is found in additional material in the D05 text of Paul's speech as he presents the details of the crucifixion, material that exists in different forms in other MSS but not at all in ℵ01/B03. D05 (not d5) is alone in reading μέν; it is also alone in having Paul describe a two-fold request of the Jews ('the ones living in Jerusalem and their rulers', 3.26) to Pilate, namely to crucify Jesus and to give them the body back:

Ref.	D05	ℵ01/B03
13.29	ὡς δὲ ἐτέλεσαν πάντα τὰ περὶ αὐτοῦ γεγραμμένα εἰσίν, ᾐτοῦντο τὸν Πιλᾶτον τοῦτον μὲν σταυρῶσαι καὶ ἐπιτυχόντες πάλιν καὶ καθελόντες ἀπὸ τοῦ ξύλου καὶ ἔθηκαν εἰς μνημεῖον	ὡς δὲ ἐτέλεσαν πάντα τὰ περὶ αὐτοῦ γεγραμμένα ↑ ↑ ↑ καθελόντες ἀπὸ τοῦ ξύλου ↑ ἔθηκαν εἰς μνημεῖον.

μέν anticipates the second request which builds up to the final action of burying Jesus, underlined by Paul in the D05 text as being of special significance (participle + καί + finite verb, see §II.2.i above): 'They first of all asked Pilate to crucify him and, having obtained a second permission, they took him down from the tree and they even buried him'. A contrast is implied between the two requests, first for Jesus to be crucified and then for his body to be taken down from the cross. καί is not the usual connective to introduce a contrasting clause following μέν but it does happen elsewhere in Luke.[17] On this understanding, the opposition is between the cruelty of having Jesus killed and the more humane act of obtaining his body in order to lay it to rest.

13.36 Still in the context of Paul's speech, most MSS including ℵ01/B03 use μέν to set David, who saw corruption, in contrast to Jesus (δέ) who did not. There is no question that the contrast might not exist in D05 since it is the essence of the point that Paul is making, but in this text the contrast is conveyed throughout the speech by a range of means that make the contrast an altogether more forceful one than in the other MSS, for which the use of μέν is superfluous. On the one hand, contrast is created by the consistently heightened presence of the person of Jesus throughout Paul's speech. Concurrently, the importance of the role of David is downplayed in the D05 version of Paul's speech (unlike in Peter's speech in Acts 2 where the role of David is carefully explained). This has already been seen at 13.23 in examining the function of οὖν (§IV.1.i above) where it was observed that αὐτοῦ is read for τούτου and does not stand in first position; and that οὖν leads on from the prophecies given about David to focus on their outcome in Jesus. In the Bezan text, the focus remains on Jesus for the rest of the speech.

19.15 In the response of the evil spirit to the sons of Sceva who had commanded him to go out of a man, making reference to 'Jesus whom Paul preaches', the spirit replied that he knew both Jesus and Paul but not the exorcists. Most MSS introduce the contrast with μέν in the first part of the sentence, which is followed by ὑμεῖς δέ to refer to the exorcists. In not using μέν, D05 (along with other important witnesses, including ℵ01*) thus avoids any weakening of the double assertion of the first clause.

IV.2.ii Conclusions on the use of μέν

The variation in the use of μέν in the MSS studied here can be accounted for by the context. The variation reveals differences of emphasis and preoccupation and as such is unlikely to simply be due to scribal preference or custom.

IV.3 μὲν οὖν

μὲν οὖν incorporates in a way some of the separate functions of both μέν and οὖν in looking back to the previous event or element and forward to the next. Just as οὖν indicates a close relationship between the clause it introduces and the previous one, so μὲν οὖν also signals something that is in accordance with what has gone before or, in a weaker sense, is not in contradiction with it. μὲν οὖν in fact signals that there are two things that follow from what has gone before, the second being found in a subsequent δέ clause which presents the more significant effect and leads events on to a determined goal or to the next development.

---

[17] Cf. Lk. 8.5–6 where μέν…καί is used with a first and second type of seed.

IV.3.i Variant readings of μὲν οὖν

On three occasions, D05 uses μὲν οὖν where it is not read by ℵ01/B03:

11.2; 17.14; 19.9

11.2 The Bezan text at the beginning of Acts 11 is considerably fuller than the Alexandrian text which states simply that the Judaean church heard news of the conversion of some Gentiles (11.1) and that when (ὅτε δέ) Peter went to Jerusalem, the circumcision party took issue with him (11.2). In D05, the arrival of the news in Judaea (expressed impersonally in 11.1, ἀκουστὸν δὲ ἐγένετο) has a two-fold outcome introduced in 11.2 with μὲν οὖν...δέ:

Ref.	D05	ℵ01/B03
11.2	ὁ μὲν οὖν Πέτρος διὰ ἱκανοῦ ἠθέλησε πορευθῆναι εἰς Ἱεροσόλυμα καὶ προσφωνήσας τοὺς ἀδελφοὺς καὶ ἐπιστηρίξας αὐτούς, πολὺν λόγον ποιούμενος διὰ τῶν χωρῶν διδάσκων αὐτούς ὃς καὶ κατήντησεν αὐτοῦ καὶ ἀπήγγειλεν αὐτοῖς τὴν χάριν τοῦ θεοῦ. [οἱ δὲ ἐκ περιτομῆς ἀδελφοὶ διεκρίνοντο πρὸς αὐτὸν] λέγοντες...	↑ Ὅτε δὲ ἀνέβη Πέτρος ↑ εἰς Ἱερουσαλὴμ ↑ ↑ ↑ ↑ [διεκρίνοντο πρὸς αὐτὸν οἱ ἐκ περιτομῆς ↑] λέγοντες...

First, Peter wants to make the journey to Jerusalem which he does indeed accomplish and several details are described. Secondly, this in turn leads to the more significant event, the dispute among the brethren introduced with δέ at the end of 11.2. The importance of the circumcision party as opponents to Peter is conveyed by the reference to them standing in first place in the new sentence (and not in last place as in ℵ01/B03), and also by the presence of the word ἀδελφοί, not included in the other text. The use of μὲν οὖν is entirely in place in D05, indicating as it does that Peter's wish to go to Jerusalem derived from the knowledge that the Judaean church had heard about the Gentile conversions and would lead to further consequences, namely the dispute.

17.14 This verse has been considered with reference to τότε, read by the Alexandrian text as an adverb in this verse (see §III.3 above). The Bezan text reads μὲν οὖν in a passage full of variant readings from 17.12 to 17.15. The setting is Beroea where Paul and Silas have been preaching the gospel. μὲν οὖν at 17.12 in both texts introduces the two-fold effect of the eagerness of the Beroeans to study the gospel message. The first consequence was that many people believed, the Bezan text adding the comment that some did not (17.12D05 τινὲς δὲ ἠπίστησαν – this δέ clause would appear to be meant as a parenthetical aside and not as the δέ clause corresponding to μὲν οὖν). The second event that then happened (δέ, 17.13) was that Jews from Thessalonica came to stir up trouble. The strength of the disturbances is intensified in the Bezan text (οὐ διελίμπανον, 'they did not stop'), which also highlights the cause of their anger as the preaching of the word of God (fore-fronted D05) and the resulting belief (additional comment, 17.13).

Having reinforced the description of the Thessalonians' anger, the Bezan text then presents in two stages (μὲν οὖν ... δέ) the event that is the outcome of their troublemaking. Firstly, in 17.14 the brethren send Paul away to sea, Silas and Timothy remaining in Beroea, with δέ again introducing this background comment. Then, with δέ in 17.15, Paul is taken on to Athens, which represents the goal of his journey, the reason for which D05 explains in another parenthesis: <u>παρῆλθεν δὲ τὴν Θεσσαλίαν ἐκωλύθη γὰρ εἰς αὐτοὺς κηρύξαι τὸν λόγον</u>, 'he passed by Thessaly, for he was prevented from proclaiming the word to them'.

19.9 ℵ01/B03 use ὡς δέ to present the reason for Paul's move out of the synagogue, where he had been preaching to the Ephesians, to the school of Tyrannus – it was when some people did not accept his teaching and were criticizing it to the crowds. D05 uses μὲν οὖν at this point to present a two-stage outcome of Paul's preaching in the synagogue. A series of words and phrases peculiar to the Bezan text in 19.8 and 19.9 serve to portray a more detailed picture of Paul both in the synagogue and in the school of Tyrannus and thereby give support to μὲν οὖν as a stronger connective than simply ὡς δέ.

Paul is mentioned by name and is described as preaching 'with great power', ἐν δυνάμει μεγάλῃ, 19.8D05. The use of his name may indicate that the Bezan text considers this to be the beginning of a new unit that extends from 19.8 to 19.20, thus separating the initial work of Paul among the disciples in Ephesus (19.1–7) from the preaching, miracles and signs among a wider audience (19.8–20).

In 19.9D05, μὲν οὖν shows that the first outcome of his teaching in the synagogue was the hostility of some of the audience who disparaged it to the multitude, specified in D05 as being composed of Gentiles, τῶν ἐθνῶν. That in turn (τότε) led to Paul leaving the synagogue and teaching in another place. In this instance, τότε rather than δέ is used to introduce the second event following μὲν οὖν. T. This is the only example in the MSS under consideration of its being used to introduce the second element following μὲν οὖν. This variant is discussed with reference to τότε at §III.2.v above.

IV.3.ii Conclusions on the use of μὲν οὖν

In the three variant readings of μὲν οὖν in D05, the conjunction operates in the same way as it is observed to function generally in Acts; that is, it introduces a two-stage response to, or outcome of, the previous event. In the Alexandrian form of the text, the two-fold nature of the development of the story is either not present or is not made obvious. The Bezan text uses μὲν οὖν in combination with other narrative features to make clear how events and actions are linked together and as such it contributes to the cohesion of the narrative.

V. γάρ

γάρ is used in Acts to introduce an explanatory sentence looking back on what has just been said. It may provide a reason or cause for a prior assertion or action, or it may provide an amplified explanation. Sometimes, γάρ occurs as part of a logical argument;

at others, it presents a parenthetical comment. In its first use, its function overlaps with that of ὅτι; in its second, it parallels one of the uses of δέ with the difference that whereas δέ makes a parenthetical comment in anticipation of what will follow (cf. II.1.i above), γάρ comments on what has gone before. An examination of the variant readings involving γάρ can help to identify more closely its purpose.

V.1 Variant readings of γάρ

This study of the variant readings involving γάρ in the MSS under consideration (ℵ01/B03/D05) largely describes the situation rather than attempts to account for it. The reason for this is that the justification of some of the occurrences of γάρ where there are variant readings is of a theological nature and only becomes apparent when the passage as a whole is analysed exegetically in depth.[18]

Variant readings of γάρ arise as follows:

γάρ D05	ℵ01/B03 vl
1.15	τε
2.34; 12.9, 20	δέ
7.34; 10.36, 37	asyndeton
13.33	ὡς καί
5.15; 15.2; 17.15; 21.22, 25	sentence absent

γάρ ℵ01/B03	D05 vl
2.15	genitive absolute
8.21; 22.26	asyndeton
18.3	sentence absent

There are in all 17 variant readings of γάρ, of which 13 are found in D05 (the places where support from d5 is lacking are pointed out in the discussion). Some occur in place of an alternative conjunction or asyndeton, making clear the connection between two sentences; others (the last category in the lists above) arise in a comment not present in the other text. Variant readings are found in both speech and narrative; in the former, γάρ exists to make a step in a logical argument whereas in the latter it serves to present a parenthetical aside.

V.1.i Supplementary γάρ in speech

γάρ occurs as a variant reading in a speech passage as follows:

ℵ01/B03: 2.15; 8.21; 22.26
D05: 2.34; 7.34; 10.36,37; 13.33; 21.22,25

---

[18] See detailed discussion in Rius-Camps & Read-Heimerdinger, *The Message of Acts*.

V.1.i.a Preaching

γάρ occurs notably in the D05 text of the major speeches that present the gospel to a Jewish audience.

2.34 In his demonstration of the fulfilment of the prophetic words spoken by David, Peter seeks to show how they applied to Jesus and not to himself: οὐ γὰρ Δαυὶδ ἀνέβη εἰς τοὺς οὐρανούς, 'for David did not ascend to heaven'. ℵ01/B03 continues with a contrastive δέ clause to introduce the quotation from the Psalms that proves the point: λέγει δὲ αὐτός. D05 uses γάρ a second time to confirm the initial statement, with the perfect tense tending to treat the quotation more as a Scriptural record than as personal words of David's: εἴρηκεν γὰρ αὐτός. When γάρ is repeated in two successive clauses, it is common for the second clause to make a second assertion in confirmation of the first.

7.34 This part of Stephen's speech, from 7.30b to 7.34, is a condensation of the account in Exod. 3.1–10 of God's appearance to Moses, with sometimes the Alexandrian and sometimes the Bezan text following more closely the Greek of the LXX.

Ref. D05	ℵ01/B03
7.34 καὶ ἰδὼν γὰρ εἶδον τὴν κάκωσιν τοῦ λαοῦ τοῦ ἐν Αἰγύπτῳ καὶ τοῦ στεναγμοῦ αὐτοῦ ἀκήκοα, καὶ κατέβην ἐξελέσθαι αὐτούς·	↑ ἰδὼν ↑ εἶδον τὴν κάκωσιν τοῦ λαοῦ μου τοῦ ἐν Αἰγύπτῳ καὶ τοῦ στεναγμοῦ αὐτῶν ἤκουσα, καὶ κατέβην ἐξελέσθαι αὐτούς·

What the D05 text seems to do at the beginning of 7.34 is to bring together two sentences from Exod. 3.7LXX, the one repeating the other in expressing the idea that God has seen, or knows, the suffering of his people: Exod. 3.7b ἰδὼν εἶδον, and 3.7c οἶδα γάρ. The first expression of 3.7b is equivalent to the idiomatic infinitive absolute of the Hebrew which is an intensifying construction, conveying the idea that God has 'marked well', whereas γάρ in 3.7c translates the Hebrew כי. This is a particle that can be causal or explanatory in Hebrew but also emphatic, repeating or confirming what has just been said; this is its force here, shared by γάρ in the LXX clause. Although Stephen's summary in Acts omits the second sentence, the D05 text brings together in one sentence the intensity of feeling with a unique phrase: καὶ ἰδὼν γὰρ εἶδον, using both καί and γάρ as intensifying particles. Since in the Acts text there is no previous assertion for γάρ to confirm, it is perhaps possible to interpret γάρ in this case as answering the unspoken question as to why God has come to speak to Moses.

10.36,37 As Peter explains the gospel for the first time to a Gentile audience, he seems to get tangled up in a long and complex sentence which has been interpreted in various ways by editors, translators and commentators of the text. Without going into the possible renderings, it is sufficient to note that D05 has yet again two successive γάρ clauses. The first γάρ in 10.36D05 supports Peter's claim that from whatever nation 'the one who fears God and practises righteousness is acceptable to God'. The justification is that his audience knows the message sent by God to Israel, τὸν γὰρ λόγον … ὑμεῖς οἴδατε. Two parallel participial clauses standing either side of the main verb describe how this message was made known, with γάρ in the second one expanding on the information of the first: εὐαγγελιζόμενος εἰρήνην … ἀρξάμενος γὰρ ἀπὸ τῆς Γαλιλαίας, 'announcing peace … beginning, in fact, from Galilee'.

13.33 Paul is explaining here events concerning Jesus, arguing from the Scriptures. His concern in 13.32 is the fulfilment of God's promise to Israel. According to ℵ01/B03, the fulfilment is the resurrection of Jesus which has happened, 'just as it is written in the second Psalm: "You are my son, today I have begotten you"'. In D05, Paul is presented as seeing the contents of the promise in a wider sense, as the bringing of the Gentiles into Israel. Thus, the quotation from Psalm 2 LXX (known in early times as a prolongation of Psalm 1, hence the mention in D05 of ἐν τῷ πρώτῳ ψαλμῷ) is given as an amplification of his reasoning so far (γάρ), and includes Ps. 2.8 which is precisely the promise of the inheritance of the Gentiles (a theme Paul returns to in Acts 13.49, and cf. Rom. 11.17–24).

V.1.i.b Conversation

γάρ is also found in the course of short exchanges.

2.15 γάρ is read by ℵ01/B03 to explain why the men speaking in tongues cannot be drunk: ἔστιν γὰρ ὥρα [τρίτη τῆς ἡμέρας], 'for it is the third hour of the day'. D05 expresses the same information in a genitive absolute clause, a construction much more common in this text than in the other MSS: οὔσης [ὥρας τῆς ἡμέρας γ.].

8.21 The omission of γάρ from D05 may be due to haplography before καρδία: ἡ γὰρ καρδία σου. It is supplied by Corrector C who paid particular attention to correcting small omissions such as missing syllables. However, it is quite possible that the absence of connective is a way of highlighting this sentence, 'Your heart is not right before God', as a reference to the Psalms (Ps. 77.37 LXX) (cf. §VI below).

21.22, 25 The two-fold use of γάρ in D05 in the course of the conversation between the Jerusalem elders and Paul is important because it arises on each occasion from the inclusion of information that puts a different slant on the situation facing Paul compared with the Alexandrian text. In the first case, it is not just that people will hear that Paul has arrived in Jerusalem (21.22ℵ01/B03), but that a crowd is bound to assemble because of it: πάντως δεῖ πλῆθος συνελθεῖν· ἀκούσονται γὰρ ὅτι ἐλήλυθας (21.22D05). An interest in the Bezan text in the opposition of the crowd to Paul can be noticed in other places of variant reading (see e.g. 16.22, §III.2.ii above). In the second case, the elders' reminder that they have already given instructions concerning converted Gentiles is stated more strongly in D05 and is used as a reason why the Judaizers will not be able to criticize Paul:

Ref.	D05	ℵ01/B03
21.25	περὶ δὲ τῶν πεπιστευκότων ἐθνῶν οὐδὲν ἔχουσιν λέγειν πρός σε· ἡμεῖς γὰρ ἀπεστείλαμεν, κρίνοντες μηδὲν τοιοῦτον τηρεῖν αὐτοὺς εἰ μὴ φυλάσσεσθαι αὐτούς, κτλ.	περὶ δὲ τῶν πεπιστευκότων ἐθνῶν ↑ ἡμεῖς ↑ ἐπεστείλαμεν κρίναντες ↑ φυλάσσεσθαι αὐτούς, κτλ.

The Judaizing controversy is accentuated in D05 compared with its treatment in the ℵ01/B03 text, at the same time as the role of Paul is also given special attention.

22.26 It is the ℵ01/B03 text that reads γάρ in the report of the centurion to the tribune concerning Paul. There are a number of other differences in this episode that have been discussed in some detail in the section on τότε (§III.2.i).

V.1.ii Supplementary γάρ in narrative

γάρ is read as a variant reading in the following narrative passages:

D05: 1.15; 5.15; 12.9,20; 15.2; 17.15
ℵ01/B03: 18.3

1.15 γάρ makes explicit a connection between Peter's getting up to speak and the number of people present. The reason for his speaking is a theological one since the number is that required to be representative of Israel. τε as read by ℵ01/B03 is an unusual connective to introduce a parenthetical remark and it may be that δέ, read as a later correction to D05, was the original particle read by the ancestors of the ℵ01/B03 text.

5.15 A sentence is read by D05 that is not found in other Greek MSS but that has widespread support among the versions, notably in Latin. D05 is alone, however, in reading γάρ, rather than καί or *et* as in d5. With γάρ, the sentence gives a justification for the people attempting to have Peter's shadow fall on them, namely that they were set free from all the various sicknesses that they had: ἀπηλλάσαντο γὰρ ἀπὸ πάσης ἀσθενείας ὡς εἶχεν ἕκαστος αὐτῶν.

12.9, 20 In these two places, what is elsewhere a descriptive aside introduced by δέ, in D05 is linked to the preceding narrative by γάρ. In 12.9ℵ01/B03, δέ looks ahead to the point when Peter will become quite sure that he was not seeing things when the angel led him out of the prison (12.11), whereas γάρ in D05 dwells on the reason that he thought that the event was unreal: he thought it was a vision (such as he had previously, see Acts 10). This insistence on Peter's misunderstanding accounts for the word order of 12.11D05: νῦν οἶδα [ὅτι ἀληθῶς] ἐξαπέστειλεν κύριος τὸν ἄγγελος αὐτοῦ.

In 12.20D05, Herod's stay in Caesarea following the escape of Peter from prison is linked to his anger with the Tyrians and Sidonians: ἦν γὰρ θυμομαχῶν, suggesting that he diverted his anger over Peter to dealing with another difficult problem. The ℵ01/B03 text uses δέ as the connective, thus making a simple aside preparing for the meeting between Herod and the people from Tyre and Sidon.

15.2 The context of an additional explanatory γάρ sentence in D05, the disagreement between Paul and the circumcision party, has been examined above with reference to 21.22,25 (§V.1.i.b). D05 spells out the reason Paul and Barnabas disputed the teaching of those who had come to Antioch from Judaea: ἔλεγεν γὰρ ὁ Παῦλος μένειν οὕτως καθὼς ἐπίστευσαν διϊσχυριζόμενος, 'for Paul said that they should remain just as they were when they believed, insisting forcefully'. This is clearly an important issue for D05, highlighted in so many ways throughout the MS.

17.15D05 provides explanatory information about Paul's itinerary, introduced with γάρ, which the other MSS do not include: παρῆλθεν δὲ τὴν Θεσσαλίαν ἐκωλύθη γὰρ εἰς αὐτοὺς κηρύξαι τὸν λόγον, 'He passed by Thessaly, for he was forbidden to preach the word to them'. A greater interest in Paul's movements and the influences behind them is apparent in D05 generally.

18.3 The information (introduced with γάρ) that the reason for Paul working with Aquila and Priscilla was that they shared a common trade is not given by D05 (supported by Old Latin g). The absence of detail can be compared with the absence of information about Tarsus at 21.39 in the D05 text.

V.2 Conclusions

The additional occurrences of γάρ in D05 frequently serve the purpose of defining steps in a logical argument that occurs as the gospel is announced to a Jewish audience; elsewhere, they aid careful explanation about the conflict between Paul and the circumcision party. Other usage is more general, providing narrator's comments on participants' actions or motives. Overall, they reflect, and indeed contribute to, the heightened interest displayed in this MS in Jewish concerns. The impression is of a text that is familiar with Jewish ways of thinking, not least in the argumentation of the major speeches.

From a linguistic point of view, many of the passages in which γάρ is read as a variant reading acquire thereby a greater cohesiveness by the way links are built between ideas and events.

VI. Asyndeton

Complete asyndeton in the narrative text of Acts is rare. Several times, a demonstrative pronoun is used with no conjunction at the start of a new sentence (1.14; 8.26b; 13.7b; 14.9; 16.3,17) but, except for one place where the sentence so introduced is an aside (8.26b), the reason for the demonstrative seems to be either to avoid a second relative clause or because the description of the referent is extensive (notably 1.14). In only a few other examples common to ℵ01, B03 and D05 is the new sentence linked to its preceding context without a connective as such: 10.44 (ἔτι); 17.33 (οὕτως); 19.20 (οὕτως).

In speech, asyndeton is a natural and rather more common way of moving on to a fresh thought, or making a new point in a reasoned argument, or starting a new section of a speech, all instances when there is no direct continuity with what has gone before. Conversely, asyndeton is used for making restatements of a previous assertion, such as repeating a thought in different words. In many cases, it forms part of a rhetorical device to attract or hold the hearers' attention. The examples that are to be found in Peter's speeches in Acts 1 and Acts 2 (common text) illustrate the usage of asyndeton in speech: 2.22 (vocative, following quotation), 2.28 (x 2, parallel statements), 2.29 (vocative, following quotation); 2.37 (command following speakers' question); 3.13 (answer following speaker's question); 3.25 (new section following quotation), 3.26 (parallel statement).

VI.1 Variant readings

VI.1.i Narrative

The scarcity of asyndeton in the narrative sections of the common text of Acts makes the abundance of references in D05 all the more striking. Asyndeton is found in narrative passages as follows (variant reading in brackets):

ℵ01/B03: 1.7B03 (δέ ℵ01; καί D05); 8.1ℵ01 (δέ); 18.1 (δέ)
D05: 2.5 (δέ), 2.43 (δέ); 6.2 (δέ); 8.2 (δέ); 14.19 (δέ); 17.2 (καί); 19.19a,b (δέ, καί); 20.7 (τε); 22.26 (δέ)

In the following examination of these references, analysis will be made of the circumstances in which asyndeton is found, and of the effect on the impact of the narrative where it is possible to do so without entering into extended discussion.

1.7 The absence of connective in B03 is unusual to introduce a speaker in the course of a conversation. καί, however, in D05 is also unexpected since Luke's usual conjunction in a speech exchange is δέ. Both asyndeton and καί would seem to express the fact that when Jesus speaks, he does not answer the apostles' question but changes the subject of the conversation. In D05, in fact he interrupts their question when he speaks (see §II.2.i above).

2.5 The sentence presents background information about the presence of Jews from every nation in Jerusalem at the time that the Holy Spirit came on the disciples at Pentecost. Whereas the usual connective for such an aside is δέ as in ℵ01/B03, D05 employs no connecting word or phrase. There are other indications in the D05 order of words (ἐν Ἰερουσαλήμ, fore-fronted, εὐλαβεῖς ἄνδρες, adjective fronted) and the periphrastic tense, that the Bezan narrator views this as information of the greatest importance, an importance that asyndeton further underlines.

2.43 In this instance, the connective has dropped out of D05 through haplography (ΠΟΛΛΑΤΕΤΕΡΑΤΑ). That the connective was intended can be seen from an examination of the literary structure of the passage.

6.2 The absence of connective in D05 stands out because at first sight there seems to be no reason for it. The use of δέ in ℵ01/B03, is expected: following the description of the discontent of the Hellenists, the action taken by the Twelve of calling together the disciples and speaking with them about the problem of table service is viewed as building on the preceding sentence. It is the next logical event in the narrative sequence. Asyndeton, in contrast, suggests some kind of hiatus. The reason for this is to be found in the sudden reappearance of 'the Twelve' who, in the Bezan text, have not been mentioned since 1.26 (cf. 2.14ℵ01/B03, 'Peter... with the eleven', where D05 has the number 'ten'). It is a term full of irony, for the narrator of the Bezan text has made it clear that the apostles no longer hold the leadership function originally expressed by the symbolic number twelve. Not having understood this, they continue to regard themselves as 'the Twelve' but the incident related here will demonstrate their loss of power as the Hellenists become according to the D05 narrator, the real heroes.

8.1B03 uses asyndeton to introduce a parallel statement about the effects of the persecution on the Jerusalem church.

8.2 This is another aside that D05 introduces without a connective. The comment is linked to the context of the persecution in Jerusalem following Stephen's death, but it stands out from the surrounding description of the effects of the persecution itself. Asyndeton serves to detach the comment from its context in order to highlight it. Special attention is drawn within the sentence to the lamentation of the men who recovered Stephen's body, it being referred to emphatically by the use of an adverbial καί following a participle (see §II.2.i above).

14.19 The text of D05 includes information about the stay of Paul and Barnabas in Lystra that is absent from ℵ01/B03. At 14.7D05, it was said that they 'tarried' (διέτριβον) in the city following which an incident occurred involving the healing of a lame man. Following the conclusion of that incident at 14.18, the Bezan text picks up the reference to their tarrying in Lystra to give the context for some Jews who came from Iconium and Antioch to Lystra to stir up trouble: διατριβόντων αὐτῶν καὶ διδασκόντων..., 'While they were tarrying and teaching...'. The absence of connective suggests that it was not after the conclusion of the previous incident but during it that the Jews arrived in Lystra, and the outcome produced by the healing of the lame man was their stoning of Paul and Barnabas.

17.2 A parallel statement about Paul's activities in the synagogue in Thessalonica is underlined in D05 by the use of asyndeton. The Bezan text generally expresses a negative attitude towards Paul's preaching in the synagogues and in various ways draws critical attention to it.

18.1 The ℵ01/B03 text apparently views Paul's departure (χωρίσθεις) from Athens as the start of a completely new episode, introducing it simply with μετὰ ταῦτα. The hiatus thus created is absent from D05 where the choice of verb (ἀναχωρήσας) connects his departure to the previous context as a fleeing from Athens, and the appropriate connective used is δέ.

18.7 The reading of D05 is not certain but the evidence of the MS suggests a sentence that has no connecting particle: μεταβὰς ἀπὸ τοῦ Ἀκύλα καὶ ἦλθεν.... The reference is to Paul who, following the hostility of his fellow-Jews, leaves Aquila's house to go to that of the Gentile Justus, a God-fearer. Asyndeton underlines the rupture represented by his action, further emphasied by the particle καί between a participle and a main verb (cf. §II.2.i above).

19.19a,b Asyndeton occurs in D05 twice in two separate parallel statements that serve to reveal the nature and extent of the former occult activities of the Ephesian converts. The double use of asyndeton as this revelation is made suggests a slowing down of speed in the oral telling of the story, with dramatic pauses at the crucial points.

20.7D05 introduces a parallel statement about Paul's speaking to the church in Troas without a connective, adding that he continued until midnight. ℵ01/B03 uses δέ, as do both texts in the following verse to present further parenthetical information.

22.26a The D05 text provides an example of a sentence introduced with a demonstrative pronoun but no other connective. The sentence describes the response of the centurion on learning that Paul is a Roman: τοῦτο ἀκούσας ὁ ἑκατοντάρχης ὅτι Ῥωμαῖον ἑαυτὸν λέγει.... By the use of τοῦτο and in spelling out what 'this' consisted of, the new sentence restates the essential information revealed in the previous question spoken by Paul and leads directly into the subsequent events. Asyndeton highlights the dramatic tension as Paul's claims about his Roman citizenship become known. The ℵ01/B03 text does not repeat the information gleaned from Paul's question, drawing less attention to it.

VI.1.ii Direct speech

Asyndeton occurs as a variant reading in speech in the following passages (*vll* in brackets):

ℵ01/B03: 7.34 (καί + γάρ); 10.36, 37 (γάρ x 2); 13.8bℵ01/B03 (καί B03)
D05: 2.14 (καί); 5.28 (καί); 6.3 (δέ); 7.15 (καί ℵ01/δέ B03); 7.21 (καί); 11.9 (δέ); 11.12 (δέ); 15.18 (omit ℵ01/B03); 20. 29 (ὅτι B03); 22.26 (γάρ)

2.14 At the opening of Peter's speech in Jerusalem, he gives two parallel exhortations to his audience to listen, with no connective between them in D05 but καί in ℵ01/B03.

5.28 The representative of the Sanhedrin begins his interrogation of the apostles by reminding them of the charge they had been given not to preach in the name of Jesus. As his speech continues with his reproving them for disobeying the order, ℵ01/B03 uses καὶ ἰδού to present the evidence where D05 uses simply ἰδού. The absence of connective is justified by the rhetorical question of the preceding sentence in D05 (<u>οὐ</u> παραγγελίᾳ παρηγγείλαμεν. . .;), which reads as a statement of fact in ℵ01/B03.

6.3 There is another example here of asyndeton to introduce the response to the speakers' own rhetorical question, a question that is not included in the ℵ01/B03 text.

7.15 It is possible that καί was omitted in D05 through haplography (ΚΑΙΚΑΤΕΒΗ). There is, however, a range of support for asyndeton among the early versions; furthermore, καί is not a certain reading in the Greek MSS, for B03 reads δέ. The sentence parallels the previous verse in saying that Jacob went down to Egypt in response to Joseph's call (7.14) which may well account for the asyndeton. What happens in this case as elsewhere (cf. 7.21D05; 11.12D05) is that an initial assertion is reinforced in a parallel statement that then moves the story being related on to a new idea. Here, 7.16 leads on to several sentences describing the burial of Jacob in Sechem.

7.21 Another set of parallel statements, this time about the rearing of Moses by Pharoah's daughter, is connected with καί in ℵ01/B03 but is not formally connected in D05. The new sentence moves the story on to Moses' time in Egypt.

7.34 D05 reads γάρ where ℵ01/B03 has no connective. This sentence has been discussed in §V.1.i.a above where it was observed that γάρ seems to be in answer to an unexpressed question. Asyndeton is nevertheless also appropriate as the speech of Yahweh to Moses moves from an initial command ('Loosen your sandal') to the purpose of his appearing to him ('I have seen the ill-treatment of my people').

10.36,37 These two verses present a long and complex sentence that has been construed in a number of ways. It has been discussed at §V.1.i.a above because of the two variant readings of γάρ in D05 where there is no connective in ℵ01/B03. According to the way the verses are understood, there may be one or two instances of asyndeton in the Alexandrian text, both of them difficult to justify as the usual circumstances are absent.

11.9 As Peter relates his vision on the roof-top in Joppa, he describes how a voice from heaven answered his refusal to touch the food that was presented to him. This is the key point of the vision, introduced in D05 without a connective even though the voice is clearly a reponse to Peter's words: ἐγένετο φωνὴ ἐκ τοῦ οὐρανοῦ, 'A voice came from heaven'. The asyndeton, together with the choice of verb ἐγένετο in place of ἀπεκρίθη (א01/B03), heightens the dramatic suspense at the moment when the radical new teaching is about to be declared.

11.12 Peter's obedience to the Spirit's command to go back with the three men to Caesarea is linked without a connective in D05, the response echoing the command (εἶπεν δὲ τὸ πνεῦμά μοι συνελθεῖν αὐτοῖς. ἦλθον σὺν ἐμοὶ καὶ οἱ ἓξ ἀδελφοὶ οὗτοι, 'The Spirit said to me to go with them. These six men also came with me'). The sentence leads on to an account of the events that followed. א01/B03 link the two sentences with δέ, Luke's usual practice when a response follows a command.

13.38b This verse has been examined in the section on οὖν (§IV.1.i) along with 13.39. It was seen that D05 has a rather different sentence structure with 13.38 representing one sentence, but in both א01 and B03 a new sentence starts in the second half of 13.38. B03 has the connective καί whereas א01 starts the new sentence with no connecting word. The sentence, declaring freedom in Jesus for all believers, echoes that of the previous one announcing forgiveness of sins. Asyndeton in א01 is in keeping with the element of repetition.

15.17–18 As James argues from the prophets concerning the acceptance of Gentiles, he concludes his reasoning by citing the Lord as author of the prophecy. The wording is different according to the texts of א01/B03 or D05:

Ref.	D05	א01/B03
15.17	… λέγει κύριος. ποιήσει ταῦτα	… λέγει κύριος ποιῶν ταῦτα
15.18	γνωστὸν ἀπ' αἰῶνός ἐστιν τῷ κυρίῳ τὸ ἔργον αὐτοῦ	γνωστὰ ἀπ' αἰῶνος ↑

Since the א01/B03 text qualifies κύριος with a participial phrase, no connective is required to start a new sentence. The D05 text, though, reads one, or possibly two, sentences following κύριος. The first, ποιήσει ταῦτα, may have arisen through the omission by homeoteleuton of the relative pronoun ὅς after κύριος. If it is intentional, it is very brief and all the more emphatic for that, the future tense echoing the series of future verbs in 15.16. The absence of connective to the second sentence is clear, producing a firm and again emphatic conclusion to James' recollection of prophecy.

20.29 The absence of connective occurs in the text of Paul's speech to the Ephesian elders at Miletus according to א01 and D05. Having exhorted the elders to be careful of the flock for which they are responsible, he goes on to say that he knows that wolves will come to attack them once he has gone away. The sentence begins with the emphatic personal pronoun: ἐγὼ οἶδα ὅτι, made even more prominent by asyndeton. B03, on the other hand, makes explicit the causal link between Paul's exhortation and his knowledge of what will happen, by using ὅτι (cf. other MSS which read γάρ).

22.26b The dramatic tension noted in the narrative in this verse (see 22.26a at §V.1.i above) is continued in the Bezan text when the centurion reports what he has heard to the tribune.

Ref.	D05	ℵ01/B03
22.26	ὅρα τί μέλλεις ποιεῖν· ὁ (D*, *erasum*) ↑ ἄνθρωπος οὗτος Ῥωμαῖός ἐστιν	↑ τί μέλλεις ποιεῖν; ὁ γὰρ ἄνθρωπος οὗτος Ῥωμαῖός ἐστιν

The centurion's words in the Bezan text convey a greater sense of surprise and urgency created in part by the asyndeton before the declaration, 'This man is Roman'.

VI.2 Conclusions on the use of asyndeton

There are occasional variant readings of asyndeton that arise where there is a complete break of sense between two sentences. Used in this way, asyndeton indicates a new section within a speech or the narrative or some other kind of rupture. The unusual abruptness of the break highlights the start of a new section or a quite unexpected development.

Much more commonly, asyndeton expresses a close relationship between sentences. The relationship can be one of time but is usually one of meaning. In these cases, asyndeton functions essentially as a rhetorical device to draw attention to the information of the second sentence by creating tension or introducing surprise, for example. The second sentence may be an aside, or an element of critical information, or a response to a rhetorical question or, finally, a parallel statement. A parallel statement that reiterates or expands on a previous assertion occurs at several places as a way to move the story on to new sequence of events.

VII. Conclusions on variant readings concerning connectives

There is a range of connectives that Luke uses to join sentences together, and the force he attributes to them in Acts can be identified from the patterns of use in the text common to the three MSS under consideration. It is evident that the choice of connective is dependent on the way that Luke wishes to construct his narrative or relate the speeches of his characters. Successive editors, in transmitting the text to different audiences than the one intended by Luke, sometimes chose to express the connections between sentences differently. Thus, sentence connectives in Acts are affected by a large number of variant readings scattered throughout Acts but clustering in the speech sections. Of the two forms of text considered, it is the D05 form that uses with striking frequency the more complex connectives and also asyndeton, in line with the patterns of use in the common text. The choice of connective, or indeed its absence, can often be seen in D05 to serve as a means to make clear the narrator's or speaker's attitude to events or characters. The overall effect is a text that 'hangs together' well, with a cohesiveness that appears to be carefully crafted.

From this point of view, it is contrary to reason to regard the readings of D05 as haphazardly arising as modifications to an Alexandrian-type text over the course of time. On the contrary, it is the Alexandrian text that has the characteristics of a secondary text, with its weaker links between events and episodes and its more simplistic telling of the story.

4

Word order[1]

I. Theoretical considerations

I.1 The importance of studying word order

Some languages have a word order that is said to be 'fixed', in other words determined by grammatical or syntactical rules that are very rarely altered (English is an example). Typically, languages with a fixed word order do not have case-markings and word order is used to show grammatical relations. Greek is often said to have a word order that is 'free' as opposed to 'fixed', and to differ in that respect from English. It is true that in a language that has case-markings, such as Greek has, word order plays a lesser role in indicating grammatical relations than in languages without case-markings.[2] Aside from a few aspects (e.g. the second position of δέ and γάρ) that are determined by grammatical or syntactical considerations, it has usually been assumed in traditional grammar books of NT Greek that word order is largely a matter of a speaker's choice. Variation is ascribed to personal custom or style, whether an unconscious habit on the part of the speaker or deliberately crafted for rhetorical effect.[3] Thus, differences can be

---

[1] This chapter was revised and updated in consultation with John Callow of the Summer Institute of Linguistics (GB), prior to its publication in Jenny Read-Heimerdinger, *The Bezan Text of Acts: A Contribution of Discourse Analysis to Textual Criticism* (JSNTSup. 236; Sheffield: Sheffield Academic Press, 2002), Chapter 3, 62–115, where his help was gratefully acknowledged. The work has been updated for the present study.

[2] B. Comrie, 'Linguistic Typology', in *Linguistics: The Cambridge Survey*. I, *Linguistic Theory: Foundations*, ed. F. J. Newmeyer, 455-7 (Cambridge: CUP, 1988); cf. T. Givón, *Syntax* (Amsterdam/Philadelphia: John Benjamins, 1984), 188.

[3] Grammars of New Testament Greek traditionally tend to assign little importance to variation in word order except where a change in meaning is involved, e.g. the position of πᾶς in relation to the noun (with or without an article) it qualifies. In the field of general linguistics, there is evidence of a greater interest in exploring the importance of word order, much of it prompted by the work on language typology of J.H. Greenberg, 'Some Universals of Grammar with Particular Reference to the Order of Meaningful Elements', in *Universals of Language*, ed. J. H. Greenberg, 2nd edn, 73–113 (1963; Cambridge, MA: MIT Press, 1966), which was followed by that of Comrie, 'Linguistic Typology' cited above, and T. Givón, 'The Pragmatics of Word Order: Predictability, Importance and Attention', in *Studies in Syntactic Typology*, ed. M. Hammonds, E.A. Moravcsik and J.R. Wirth, 243–84 (Amsterdam/Philadelphia: John Benjamins, 1988). A comprehensive collection of articles on word order studied from a discourse perspective is that edited by P. Downing and M. Noonan (eds), *Word Order in Discourse* (Typological Studies in Language, 30; Amsterdam/Philadelphia: John Benjamins, 1995). The need to update and revise the notion of style in the light of contemporary linguistic research is presented, with examples and reference to Greek grammars, by J. E. Botha, 'Style in the New Testament: The Need for Serious Reconsideration', *JSNT* 43 (1991): 71–87.

observed in the word order used by different authors in the NT, or in different books, and also in different MSS.

However, as the reasons for one order of words being chosen in preference to another are being studied by linguists, two things are becoming apparent with reference to languages generally. First, it is clear that the notions of 'fixed' and 'free' are only relative. Even in a language dependent on word order to indicate grammatical structure, some things may still be flexible, such as the position of adverbs, the order of pronouns, or the order of clauses. Flexibility in a 'fixed' word order language is a matter of degree, with the amount of freedom varying from one language to another. In English, for example, the order of the direct and indirect object pronouns is not rigid whereas in French, in contrast, it is governed by strict rules. Conversely, in a language with a so-called 'free' word order, there are, in fact, constraints that all authors are bound by; they cannot move words around just as they please. In his work on NT Greek, Porter usefully differentiates the varying degrees of flexibility in Greek word order, referring to those patterns that are never altered as 'fully codified', those that are generally followed as 'partially codified' and those that are only sometimes applied as 'marginally codified'.[4] He suggests that an individual writer may adopt his or her own level of codification.

Secondly, in line with the interest of discourse analysis in looking at language in its real life context, it is now recognized that the constraints operating on Greek word order are of a semantic and pragmatic nature rather than a grammatical one.[5] In other words, the constraints are connected with the function of the words and sentences within the discourse, not the grammatical relations that exist between the words or sentences. They operate on a deep level rather than a surface level. They have to do with such purposes as introducing a new idea, indicating a contrast or conflict, or signaling which part of the sentence is the most important. Word order choice is thus not a matter of style, dependent on a writer's or scribe's preference or habit, but is a device that forms an integral part of the communication of the message.[6]

Accordingly, the typical or most common word order for different types of discourse is liable to vary from one type to another because of the different purposes and intentions. This is indeed seen to be the case in the NT, especially when the Gospels (mainly narrative) are compared with the Epistles (discursive). In the narrative portions of the NT, events and people are essentially what the writing is about; in the discursive sections, it is ideas, reasoned argument and exhortation that are prominent. So, in

---

[4] Stanley E. Porter, 'Word Order and Clause Structure in New Testament Greek: An Unexplored Area of Greek Linguistics, Using Philippians as a Test Case', *FilNeo* 6/12 (1993): 179–81; for detailed examples, see Porter, *Idioms of New Testament Greek* (Biblical Languages: Greek, 2; Sheffield: JSOT Press, 1992), 290–2.

[5] Factors affecting word order are covered in Parts 3 and 4 of Steven E. Runge, *Discourse Grammar of the Greek New Testament* (Lexham Bible Reference Series; Peabody, Mass.: Hendrickson Publishers), 2010. For discussion with multiple examples, see also Stephen H. Levinsohn, *Discourse Features of New Testament Greek: A Coursebook on the Information Structure of New Testament Greek*, 2nd edn (1992; Dallas: SIL International, 2000), Part I, 1–67. See also A. Kirk, *Word Order and Information Structure in New Testament Greek* (LOT 311) 2012; available at https://scholarlypublications.universiteitleiden.nl/handle/1887/20157.

[6] Comrie, 'Linguistic Typology', 457.

establishing what the rules are that govern word order in the books of the NT, it is important, in the initial stages at least, to take one book at a time and to work out the principles specific to that book before moving on to make comparisons with other books.

The aim of this chapter will be to examine the text of Acts in order to show how an awareness of discourse factors gives an insight into how Luke makes use of word order flexibility to communicate his message to Theophilus. Only passing mention will be made of the Gospel of Luke, for which focused and detailed research into the use he makes there of word order patterns is needed.[7] As a by-product, some reasons will be suggested for variation that is found in word order patterns among the chief Greek MSS of Acts. Following a discussion of some general issues associated with the study of word order, one specific aspect will be considered, namely, the order of constituents within the noun phrase. Attention will, as usual, focus on the texts of Codex Sinaiticus (ℵ01) and Codex Vaticanus (B03), as representatives of the more familiar Alexandrian tradition and that of Codex Bexae (D05) as the principal Greek MS that differs from the familiar text. At each stage, analysis will begin with the text that is common to all three MSS before examining how the patterns thus established correspond to the diverse readings at places of variation.

I.2 Statistical analyses

The availability of computer-generated data has made the process of collecting and analysing information on a large scale so much quicker than it would be otherwise. Statistical analyses of word order in NT books that can be thereby generated, consisting in a numerical count of the word order patterns, are useful for determining the relative frequency of particular orders that occur. However, they do not show why a usual order is disrupted nor even if the most frequently occurring order is the 'unmarked' one. Indeed, relating frequency to markedness is not quite as simple as it looks, for it may well be that a particular book or author has occasion to modify the default word order more often than not.

The use of statistics to analyse word order is especially misleading in textual criticism when they are appealed to in order to determine an author's 'original' word order. Numerical counts have been used for some time by textual critics (certainly before the invention of computers) to define a writer's 'usual' practice, which is then used as a guide to decide the authenticity of variant readings.[8] Statistical analyses are

---

[7] A work devoted to the study of word order in Luke's Gospel is Ivan Shing Chung Kwong, *The Word Order of the Gospel of Luke: Its Foregrounded Messages* (LNTS 298. London: T&T Clark, 2005). The approach he adopts pays careful attention to sentence word order, allowing the usual patterns to be distinguished from 'rare' ones. He then goes on, however, to assume that the whole of the sentence with the unusual order is of special prominence which he identifies as 'foregrounding'. These last two steps are derived from the blunt tool of statistical counts (of the N-A text) and would benefit from being considered on a more refined linguistic and textual basis. See the review by Steven E. Runge in *Review of Biblical Literature*, no. 4 (2008), available at http://rblnewsletter.blogspot.com/2008/ (last accessed 29/09/2021).

[8] The appeal to the criterion of 'usual style' established on the basis of frequency of use lies behind some of the textual decisions taken by eclectic textual critics. As an illustration of this thinking, see J.K. Elliott, *Essays and Studies in New Testament Textual Criticism* (Estudios de Filología Neotestamentaria 3; Cordoba: Ediciones El Almendro, 1992), e.g. Chapter 12, 153.

not, however, a reliable tool when it comes to textual criticism (see Chapter 1, §III.2). In using them to establish which is likely to be the original reading among one or more variants, there is a danger of imposing a false rigidity on a language. It is true that they allow a description to be made of the occurrence of typical patterns and of departure from them, but they do not explain the patterns nor the reasons for their disruption. So, whilst the relative frequency of a certain pattern (say, the order of noun and attached adjective in Acts) shows that noun–adjective was the usual order for Luke, it does not mean that the reversal of the usual order was erroneous and should be rejected on those grounds if found as a variant reading.[9] Each instance of departure from the usual order – in the common text and within the particular MSS being examined – needs to be analysed and the reasons for its occurrence looked for. The reasons will often be found to lie within the surrounding co-text, or else outside the written text within the discourse context. The inadequacy of explanations for variation in word order that are drawn from the level of sentence-based grammar, as happens in most grammars of NT Greek, means that it is imperative to base the analysis of word order on a study of how the language functions on the level beyond the sentence. It will be seen in the analyses of this chapter that there are many factors operating on that level that affect the order of words. Research into varying word orders in Greek, as in other languages, demonstrates that variation arises on the whole neither for its own sake nor because of a writer's/scribe's fancy or carelessness but as a device that is an integral part of the communication of the message.

I.3. Foreign influence

Foreign influence is frequently appealed to as a cause of word order variation.[10] In the first-century setting of the NT writers, there was indeed a great mixture of languages, namely Greek, Hebrew, Aramaic as well as local dialects, whose importance varied according to geographical location, social class, racial group and even purpose of communication.[11] And certainly, languages are known to bring about changes in one another in some respects and foreign influence can be detected in the Greek of the NT

---

[9] To impose a particular order on a book because it is the most common is, as Winer has said in another context, 'empirical pedantry' (see G. B. Winer, *A Treatise on the Grammar of New Testament Greek*, trans. W. F. Moulton (1882. Repr., Eugene, OR: Wipf and Stock 2001), 686, where he speaks of the various possible ways of referring to the Spirit of God and the dangers of imposing one particular way on an author.

[10] Note, e.g. how the examination of the various possible strands of Semitic influence makes up much of the discussion on the style of Luke–Acts in N. Turner, *A Grammar of New Testament Greek*. iii, *Syntax* (Edinburgh: T&T Clark, 1963), 45–63. Cf. J.D. Yoder, 'Semitisms in Codex Bezae', *JBL* 78 (1959): 317–21. Although Yoder argues that Codex Bezae is not characterized by Semitisms, his conclusions are based on a numerical count of what he regards as Semitisms. The difficulty with this debate generally is the lack of a framework for identifying a genuinely foreign Semitic construction.

[11] See James Barr, 'Hebrew, Aramaic and Greek in the Hellenistic Age', in *The Cambridge History of Judaism*, ed. W. D. Davies and L. Finkelstein, 79–114 (Cambridge: CUP, 1989), for a comprehensive study of the situation. Cf. Martin Hengel, *The Hellenization of Judaea in the First Century*, trans. J. Bowden (London: SCM Press, 1989), 7–18; B. Lifschitz, 'L'héllenisation des juifs de la Palestine', *Revue Biblique* 72 (1965): 520–38.

in the borrowing of fixed idioms, of lexical items or of spelling from Semitic languages (less frequently from Syriac).[12]

That said, when it comes to seeing foreign influence on word order, problems arise, for not only do patterns of word order vary from one language to another but so do the constraints that determine the order of words. For a language to use, therefore, the word order of another language, even intermittently, it is these constraints that would have to be violated in addition to the pattern of word order having to be altered in the receptor language. In view of the complexity of these modifications, it is not too surprising that studies of bilingual cultures and of inter-language contamination indicate that the influences that can be detected with certainty are very largely in the semantic field and do not affect the structure of the receptor language.[13]

Among the foreign influences supposed to be acting on the Greek text of Codex Bezae, the Latin side of the MS is appealed to. The suggestion has been made that the peculiarities of the Greek text derive in part from the Latin, assuming that the Latin side preceded and acted as a model for the Greek. As far as word order is concerned, it is true that there are similarities between the two pages at many places where the Greek of Codex Bezae differs from that of the Alexandrian textual tradition. The use of the Latin side as a model for the Greek is, however, a matter open to a great deal of question. In a recent investigation of the bilingual tradition by David Parker the conclusions reached indicate that the influence of the Latin text on the word order of the Greek pages is unlikely: 'The chief influence was of the Greek on the Latin. Examples of the reverse are very rare'.[14]

Consequently, much caution must be exercised when considering the validity of explanations of word order variation between MSS that depend on seeing the influence of Hebrew, Aramaic or any other language. This does not mean that any possibility of foreign influence must categorically and definitively be ruled out, but that in the present circumstances it should be viewed as an unlikely cause of word order variation, and one almost impossible to determine in any case given the present linguistic knowledge and research in the area.[15]

I.4. Factors affecting word order

Some of the factors affecting word order have already been mentioned in passing in the previous section. A principle that operates in many languages is that the usual order in

---

[12] See Matthew Black, *An Aramaic Approach to the Gospels and Acts* (Oxford: Clarendon Press, 1967); D. F. Payne, 'Semitisms in the Book of Acts', in W. W. Gasque and R. P. Martin (eds), *Apostolic History and the Gospel*, 134–50 (Exeter: Paternoster, 1970); Max Wilcox, *The Semitisms of Acts* (Oxford: Clarendon Press, 1965).

[13] Porter, *Idioms*, 13; M. Silva, 'Bilingualism and the Character of Palestinian Greek', *Bib.* 61 (1980): 198–219, see esp. 216–19.

[14] The relationship between the Greek and the Latin texts of Codex Bezae is discussed in detail by D. C. Parker, *Codex Bezae: An Early Christian Manuscript and its Text* (Cambridge: CUP, 1992), 183–93 (esp. 193).

[15] It would be interesting and worthwhile to re-examine the examples of the verb-final sentences of the Gospel of Mark which C. H. Turner adduces as evidence of a Latin influence on Mark's style – see his 'Notes on Marcan Usage' X, *Journal of Theological Studies* 29 (1928): 346–61 (352–6) (repr. in *The Language and Style of the Gospel of Mark: An Edition of C. H. Turner's 'Notes on Marcan Usage' Together with Comparable Studies*, ed. J. K. Elliott, 120–36 (Leiden: Brill, 1993) (126–30).

which elements of a sentence or phrase appear is for the known elements ('given') to be presented first and the 'new' information to occur last.[16] In other words, what has already been mentioned before in the discourse (sometimes referred to as the 'topic', where 'topic' is used as a technical term) is repeated in some form before additional information about the topic (referred to by some as the 'comment', again as a technical term) is provided. An example in English can serve as a general illustration:

Sentence 1: 'Two books are addressed to Theophilus.'
Sentence 2: 'The second is known as the Acts of the Apostles.'
         given   *new*

If the expected pattern of constituents in a discourse may be referred to as 'unmarked', then disruption of the anticipated pattern produces in contrast a 'marked' word order. Essentially, 'marked' word order patterns are utilized by the speaker in order to draw the attention of the addressee to something in the text, in a process of 'highlighting' (see Chapter 1, §III.2).[17] In Koine Greek, the way to do this is to employ a device common to many languages by shifting the element to be highlighted forward ('front-shifting'), to occur sooner (more to the left) in the phrase or clause in which is belongs. Normally, of course, such arranging of words is spontaneous, although where a written MS is changed by a subsequent editor or copyist, the re-positioning of words is likely to be more conscious and deliberate.

When this front-shifting occurs within a sentence, it can be said in broad terms that it indicates that the front-shifted element is of some special significance to the message being communicated. It is a means for the speaker to draw attention to an element because it indicates something unusual or unexpected or of particular interest; in the case of Acts, as will be seen, it also includes instances where the author deliberately chooses a word or phrase for its theological significance and draws attention to it by displacing it from its usual position.

Additionally, when front-shifting occurs at the start of a sentence (sometimes called 'fore-fronting'), it typically signals some change from the previous sentence in the topic (what is being talked about), the time or the location.[18] Both within and between sentences, front-shifting could be described in a rather general way as 'emphasis'. Emphasis, however, is a somewhat vague term that covers a broad range of reasons for drawing attention to an element in a sentence;[19] it is more useful to break down the general category and identify the different purposes being served by emphasis.

---

[16] These concepts are helpfully set out in Levinsohn, *Discourse Features*, chapters 1, 5, 6. For a detailed study, see also Kirk, *Word Order and Information Structure*.

[17] See Iver Larsen, 'Word Order and Relative Prominence in New Testament Greek', *Notes on Translation* 15, no. 2 (2001): 13–27.

[18] See Stephen H. Levinsohn, *Textual Connections in Acts* (Atlanta: Scholars Press, 1987), 61–82, where he uses the term 'change of basis'; see also Levinsohn, *Discourse Features*, 13–30.

[19] This vagueness is a problem in J. K. Elliott's article on Marcan word order, 'The Position of the Verb in Mark with Special Reference to Chapter 13', *NovT* 38 (1996): 136–44. 'Emphasis' is the term used by Levinsohn (*Discourse Features*, 83, 85–6) in a more specific way to describe the type of fronting that 'usually involves strong feelings or as matter expected to surprise the hearer' (83).

I.5. As a category of variant readings

Word order variation was noted in Chapter 1 §IV as one of the four types of variation present between ℵ01/B03 and the extant text of D05, where the same words occur in both texts but arranged in different orders. When word order varies, it is usually a matter of the order varying within the same sentence; only twice are words found in different sentences (5.29 and 7.31/33). The form of the displaced words is generally the same, except where a change in the syntactical structure of the sentence resulting from the word order variation demands a grammatical modification.

There are a great many variant readings among the Greek MSS that involve the order of words but they are by no means regularly indicated in the critical apparatus of editions of the Greek NT. They reflect the kind of variation that is also apparent between different writings of the NT, and indeed within the work of any individual writer. No single cause for this fluctuation can be readily identified; rather, the reasons for variation in word order tend to be diverse and often depend on the context of the discourse. The variants thus provide valuable data for the study of word order patterns in NT Greek and of the reasons underlying the variation. It can be hoped that making use of variant readings will enable a clearer picture of Luke's own patterns to be constructed and thereby serve to further understanding of the importance of the role played by word order in the task of communication.

In citations below of the variant readings, words that are present in only one of the texts are underlined with a solid line; lexical or grammatical alternative material is underlined with a dotted line; brackets [. . .] are used to indicate variation in word order, with brackets (. . .) within them where there is further internal variation in word order.

I.6. The speaker's purpose

The differences in word order between the two main textual traditions of Acts are in many cases indicative of a deeper difference in the perceived purpose of the book. A thorough comparison of the texts reveals that whereas the Alexandrian text reads largely as a historical account albeit with an underlying theological message, the Bezan text reads primarily as a theological exposition with a different historical perspective than the one which is apparent in the more familiar text (cf. Chapter 1 §II.3). In view of the distinctive characteristics of the two texts, it is sometimes likely that, for example, the use of word order as a device to highlight certain words, a clear tendency of the D05 text, may be for the purpose of underlining their theological importance. Conversely, employing a usual rather than a marked word order, a tendency seen in the Alexandrian text, may be a means of downplaying a contrast in order to give a more neutral, or literal, account of events. Clearly, the interpretation of word order variation along these lines requires detailed exegetical discussion. In order to avoid lengthy digressions from the linguistic analysis, questions of interpretation will not be treated extensively here; where exegetical interpretation, especially of Codex Bezae, is referred to, detailed discussion can be found at the relevant places in the commentary on Acts co-authored by myself and Josep Rius-Camps.[20]

---

[20] Josep Rius-Camps and Jenny Read-Heimerdinger, *The Message of Acts in Codex Bezae: A Comparison with the Alexandrian Tradition*. 4 vols. JSNTSup 257/LNTS 302, 365, 415. London: T&T Clark, 2004–09.

I.7. Classification of word order variation

When words are found in a different order in MSS of Acts, this is occasionally brought about by other syntactical changes in the co-text but, more usually, is independent of other variation.

I.7.i Word order variation is secondary

Some instances of variation in word order among the Greek MSS are brought about indirectly by modification to some other aspect of the sentence or paragraph, a modification that necessitates a change in the order of words for grammatical reasons (e.g. 16.3: ℵ01/B03, ᾔδεισαν γὰρ ἅπαντες [ὅτι Ἕλλην ὁ πατὴρ αὐτοῦ] ὑπῆρχεν; cf. D05, ᾔδεισαν γὰρ πάντες [τὸν πατέρα αὐτοῦ ὅτι Ἕλλην] ὑπῆρχεν). Such instances of word order change are secondary and do not provide any fresh information about the rules for the order of words in the sentence. There are 13 examples of this kind in Acts:

    10.33; 12.5,20a; 15.2,35a; 16.3,35,36,40; 17.12; 18.4; 19.20; 21.18.

I.7.ii Word order variation is primary

There are some 160 remaining instances of word order variation that do not arise solely because of the presence of other types of variation occurring in the same co-text. These can be grouped into two categories according to the level at which they occur within a sentence:

- within noun phrases where a verb is not directly involved
- within clauses where the verb is involved

A complete examination of word order variation requires both groups to be considered separately as well as together. Such exhaustive analysis is needed in order to arrive at the most comprehensive results, for discourse studies generally demonstrate that what happens on the level of the clause, for example, may well influence what happens on both the lower level of the noun phrase or the higher level of the sentence or paragraph. The demands of this kind of investigation are best met by an interdisciplinary approach with input from linguists, textual critics and exegetes working as a team. In this way, the form of a text can be considered in conjunction with its meaning, and the contribution of each to word order patterns can be held in balance.[21] What is proposed in this chapter is a detailed study of word order within noun phrases. In Chapter 8, word order in relation to the verb at the front of sentence will be discussed for the ways Luke uses it to mark the narrative structure of the book of Acts.

---

[21] Disagreement among the authors of studies in the field arises not so much because some of the research is faulty but because investigators adopt different approaches and do not always treat the subject in equally fine detail. The work of Porter on Greek word order (e.g. Stanley E. Porter, 'Word Order and Clause Structure in New Testament Greek: An Unexplored Area of Greek Linguistics, Using Philippians as a Test Case', *Filologia Neotestamentaria* 6 (1993): 177–206, which refers to the principal studies that have been carried out in the field), provides a fair reflection of the conflicting views.

II. Word order variation within the noun phrase

Word order variation within the noun phrase represents a little more than a quarter of the total of 160 instances of word order variation in Acts, in which the word order changes generally affect words adjacent to each other. They will all be examined in this section except for the expression used to refer to the Holy Spirit (τὸ πνεῦμα; πνεῦμα ἅγιον; τὸ πνεῦμα τὸ ἅγιον; τὸ ἅγιον πνεῦμα), which is dealt with separately in Chapter 5 where attention can also be given to other aspects of variation associated with the phrase.

In order to make meaningful comparisons, for the present study, word order variation in the noun phrase has been broken down according to the syntactical or semantic function of the elements involved:

- pairs of nouns
- words in apposition
- ὀνόματι
- possessive or partitive genitive
- descriptive adjectives and noun/noun phrase
- cardinal numbers
- ordinal numbers
- πᾶς
- τίς
- demonstratives

The first four categories are examined in turn in this section. The last six categories all concern adjectives of one kind or another. They are analysed in §III below, where they are treated as separate topics because it appears that the position of adjectives depends to some extent on the nature of the adjective. It is therefore essential to examine each type of adjective independently in order to establish the significance of the word order patterns.[22]

From an examination of these categories in each of ℵ01, B03 and D05, it is possible to establish the patterns of usage that occur in the text shared by both MS traditions, that is, in what will be referred to as the 'common text'. It can generally be seen from the examples of noun phrases in the common text that there is an order of words that is usual for Luke, and that when he disrupts the usual order, reasons for the disruption can be deduced.[23] Whether 'usual' also means 'neutral' can likewise be tested, checking

---

[22] Porter comments ('Word Order and Clause Structure', 182, n. 19; 183, n. 21) that he finds unhelpful a comparable method adopted by M. E. Davison in 'New Testament Greek Word Order', *Literary and Linguistic Computing* 4 (1989): 19–28, of separating adjectival modifiers into semantic categories. The findings of the present study suggest, in contrast, that to group all adjectives in the same syntactic analysis, as Porter advocates, produces confusing results.

[23] The existence of noun phrase patterns in the common text of Acts that are sometimes disrupted can be expressed using the terms adopted by Porter ('Word Order and Clause Structure', 179–80) as 'partial codification', meaning that there is 'a general tendency but not an invariable rule'. My analysis of Acts confirms Porter's statement that 'at the level of the group or phrase Greek (or at least certain writers of Greek) has a tendency for a far more fixed word order than may have been recognized, especially in terms of partially codified rules' (181).

whether the most frequent order is, in fact, the unmarked one since this is not necessarily the case.

In order for the appropriateness or significance of variant readings among MSS to be evaluated, they must be compared not only with the usual patterns but also with the deviations from the usual patterns that are apparent in the common text. The methodology adopted in this analysis will take account of these factors. For each category, the most frequent order of words in the common text will be worked out from a count of the occurrences of the particular elements in question. Instances within the common text of departure from the usual pattern will then be examined and an explanation for both word orders sought. As a second step, the variant readings of the MSS will be evaluated in the light of the findings relating to the common text. Finally, any additional readings occurring in only one of the two texts under consideration will be discussed.

II.1 Pairs of nouns

This category of readings groups together nouns that are conjoined with καί.

II.1.i In the common text

There is no regular occurrence in the common text of general nouns that are presented in this way. On the other hand, there is a number of pairs of proper nouns that can be used as a basis for partial comparison with some of the variant readings.

The conjunction καί establishes the two proper nouns as of equal status (see Chapter 3, §II.1.ii). Nevertheless, the first-named of the pair appears to enjoy some kind of prominence. This can be seen in the common text of Acts in the references to Paul and Barnabas. Initially, Barnabas is mentioned as the head of the pair, when they are both first chosen by the Holy Spirit (13.2). As Paul emerges as the dominant character, he is mentioned on his own (13.9,13,16) and then as the first-named before Barnabas (13.43). Indeed, in a number of lists in Luke's work, special importance is accorded to the noun at the head of the list. Thus, Peter's role as leader of the apostles is indicated by the mention of his name in first place in the list of apostles in 1.13. Peter is also consistently mentioned before John in the references to their joint activity (3.1, 3, 4, 11).

II.1.ii Variant readings

Four variant readings occur:

Ref.	D05	ℵ01/B03
14.19	ἀπὸ [Ἰκονίου καὶ Ἀντιοχείας]	ἀπὸ [Ἀντιοχείας καὶ Ἰκονίου]
17.8	[τοὺς πολιτάρχας καὶ τὸν ὄχλον]	[τὸν ὄχλον καὶ τοὺς πολιτάρχας]
18.26	[Ἀκύλας καὶ Πρίσκιλλα]	[Πρίσκιλλα καὶ Ἀκύλας]
20.20	[κατ' οἴκους καὶ δημοσίᾳ]	[δημοσίᾳ καὶ κατ' οἴκους]

The pairs of words are found in the reverse order in each text. The two words are of equal syntactical value and there is no grammatical reason for one order to be used in preference to the other. However, the particular order adopted by the different MSS can be seen to reflect a certain preoccupation of the editor or to match the intention of other neighbouring variant readings. Each of the variant readings will be considered in the light of its context, taking into account other occurrences of the particular nouns in question.

14.19 The two towns, Antioch (of Pisidia) and Iconium, are cited as being the places from where some Jews came to attack Paul when he was in Lystra (14.7). To appreciate the importance of the difference in word order, the whole clause must be viewed as it stands in each of the two texts:

Ref.	D05	ℵ01/B03
14.19	διατριβόντων αὐτῶν καὶ διδασκόντων ἐπῆλθόν ↑ τινες [Ἰουδαῖοι ἀπὸ (Ἰκονίου καὶ Ἀντιοχείας)]	↑ ἐπῆλθαν δὲ ↑ [ἀπὸ (Ἀντιοχείας καὶ Ἰκονίου) Ἰουδαῖοι]

Paul had taken refuge in the cities of Lycaonia after suffering persecution in both Antioch and Iconium which he had previously visited in that order, travelling from north-west to south-east. The order in which the names are given in the Alexandrian text reproduces the north-south order, the first-named, Antioch, also being the larger of the two places. A series of factors illustrate a concern in the Bezan text with the geographical detail. Twice Paul is said to have been specifically in the Lycaonian town of Lystra when the attack by certain (omit τινες ℵ01/B03) Jews took place (14.8,20; ℵ01/B03 omit the name of the town, 14.20); and twice he is said to have spent some time there with Barnabas (14.8,19, both mentions omitted by ℵ01/B03). The order of the place names, Iconium and Antioch, represents the south-north order in which they are found looking back from Lystra, rather than the order in which Paul had visited them. All these factors taken together indicate that closer attention is paid to the local geographical setting in the Bezan text than in the Alexandrian one. It is not clear, even so, what is the importance of the particular order of names nor why one text should have felt it necessary to alter it.

17.8 The situation is again one of Jewish persecution of Paul, this time as he is accompanied by Silas in the town of Thessalonica (17.1, 4). The Jewish agitators had intended to bring Paul and Silas out to the crowd (17.5 εἰς τὸν δῆμον) from Jason's house where they supposed them to be hiding. Not finding them, they brought out instead Jason and some of the brethren to the city leaders (17.6 ἐπὶ τοὺς πολιτάρχας). They shouted out their accusation and, as the narrator says 17.8, disturbed both the crowd (τὸν ὄχλον) and the leaders. The order of these two elements varies according to the MSS.

The ℵ01/B03 text specifies that the Jews initially gathered a crowd together (17.5, καὶ ὀχλοποιήσαντες), a reference to the crowd that is absent from D05. The order τὸν ὄχλον καὶ τοὺς πολιτάρχας in 17.8ℵ01/B03is a way of maintaining the focus on the crowd by mentioning them as the first of the pair. The order of D05, on the other hand, creates a chiastic structure that is typical of Luke's writing:

(17.5) τὸν δῆμον   (17.6) τοὺς πολιτάρχας
(17.8) τοὺς πολιτάρχας   (17.8) τὸν ὄχλον

The use of synonyms (δῆμος – ὄχλος) to designate the crowd does not negate the structure, for Luke often deliberately uses two parallel terms to designate the same entity. The chiasmus is all the stronger in D05 that it operates across the conjunction καί (17.8) rather than δέ as in ℵ01/B03 for, whereas δέ signals a new development in the narrative, καί adds another element to the same unit of development in the story (see Chapter 3, §II.1.ii). The word order of 17.8D05 combines with the absence of the mention of gathering a crowd in 17.5D05 to draw less attention to the crowd than the other text. Conversely, attention is focused on the leaders for whom, indeed, the accusation of the Jews (17.6b-7) is intended.

18.26 This is the third joint mention by name of the husband and wife whom Paul met in Corinth. They are first introduced as 'a certain Jew named Aquila, a native of Pontus who had recently come from Italy, and Priscilla his wife...' (18.2), with Aquila as the dominant figure since the reference to Priscilla is made in relation to him. The Alexandrian text then says that Paul went to them (plural, 18.2) and stayed with them (plural, 18.3); in the Bezan text, Paul went to him (singular, 18.2) and stayed with them (plural, 18.3), so continuing to give a certain prominence to Aquila. Aquila is yet again singled out in 18.7D05, this time by name as Paul decides to leave his house (μεταβὰς ἀπὸ τοῦ Ἀκύλα); ℵ01/B03, like all other Greek MSS, say simply that he left 'there' (ἐκεῖθεν).

The pair next reappear as Paul travels away from Corinth accompanied by 'Priscilla and Aquila', in that order without any variant reading (18.18). The context does not give any obvious clues as to the reason for the change. It is worth pointing out, however, that the pair are mentioned in relation to Paul (σὺν αὐτῷ), and not independently, and this fact, along with other variants in this verse, may have some bearing on the order of names. Paul separates from the couple (ἐκείνους) when he goes on his own to the synagogue in Ephesus (18.19), eventually continuing with his journey towards Jerusalem (18.21).

At the final appearance of the couple (18.26), they are still in Ephesus where they come to the assistance of a newly introduced participant, Apollos, who has been teaching in the synagogue. It is now that there is a variant reading in the order of names:

Ref.	D05	ℵ01/B03
18.26	καὶ ἀκούσαντες αὐτοῦ [Ἀκύλας καὶ Πρίσκιλλα] προσελάβοντο αὐτόν	ἀκούσαντες δὲ αὐτοῦ [Πρίσκιλλα καὶ Ἀκύλας] προσελάβοντο αὐτόν

The ℵ01/B03 text, with only some support, repeats the order of names previously found at 18.18 although the text offers no evidence for Priscilla having become the leading figure of the pair. D05, along with most Greek minuscules, places Aquila once more in the first place, reflecting the dominant position that he occupied in the opening sequences of the chapter. When the reading of this verse is taken together with the series of variants in 18.1–7D05, Aquila's role is considerably strengthened in comparison to his wife's. The overall effect is to cause the order of names at 18.18, where Priscilla is the first named member of the couple, to stand out in the Bezan text even more than in the Alexandrian text.

20.20 Here, Paul is speaking to the elders of Ephesus whom he has called down to meet him during a break in his journey at Miletus (20.17). He reminds them of his work in Ephesus, carried out despite plots against him by the Jews. He says that he was unrestrained in his announcing of anything that was useful and, furthermore, in his teaching both publicly and from house to house (20.20). It is in the order of the places that ℵ01/B03 and D05 differ:

Ref.	D05	ℵ01/B03
20.20	οὐδὲν ὑπεστειλάμην τῶν συμφερόντων τοῦ ↑ ἀναγγεῖλαι ὑμῖν καὶ διδάξαι ↑ [κατ' οἴκους καὶ δημοσίᾳ]	οὐδὲν ὑπεστειλάμην τῶν συμφερόντων τοῦ μὴ ἀναγγεῖλαι ὑμῖν καὶ διδάξαι ὑμᾶς [δημοσίᾳ καὶ κατ' οἴκους]

The notion of activities of the Christian communities taking place both publicly and in private, in that order, has already been put forward twice by Luke, at 2.46 and 5.42 (in the Temple and in houses). The previous order is repeated at 20.20 by ℵ01/B03, whereas D05 reverses it. D05 also omits the second person pronoun after the second verb (διδάξαι), with the dual result that the activity of 'declaring' refers only to the Ephesian elders (cf. 20.27), and the phrase 'in the houses and publicly' is limited to the activity of 'teaching': 'I did not shrink from declaring to you anything that was useful, nor from teaching in the houses and publicly'. The prominence thus given to the teaching in private may seem strange given the narrative account of Paul's teaching activity in Ephesus (19.8–10): he is seen firstly in the synagogue for an initial period of three months (19.8), and ἐν τῇ σχολῇ Τυράννου for two further years (19.9–10). In ℵ01/B03, this 'school' appears to be a public building belonging to Tyrannus; accordingly, the order in that text of the public declaration and teaching (δημοσίᾳ καὶ κατ' οἴκους) fits to some extent with this picture, though there is missing any portrayal of private discussion. In D05, the mention of the school is heavily ironic, for it is said to be that of 'a certain little tyrant' (and not a person called Tyrannus) who had little pity on his disciples for he lectured them during the hottest part of the day, 'between the fifth and the tenth hour': ἐν τῇ σχολῇ τυραννίου τινὸς ἀπὸ ὥρας πέμπτης ἕως δεκάτης. The school, in this case, does not refer to a building but to Paul's own didactic programme, and it would have been in the houses that the teaching took place once the public meeting place of the synagogue became problematic.

There are no additional occurrences in either text of pairs of nouns whose order requires investigation.

II.2 Words in apposition

II.2.i In the common text

In the text common to the two textual traditions, where a noun or phrase is placed in apposition to a name, it is generally the name that is placed first. For example:

4.25   Δαυὶδ παιδός σου
5.1   σὺν Σαπφίρῃ τῇ γυναικὶ αὐτοῦ
10.6   παρά τινι Σίμωνι βυρσεῖ

In such cases, it would seem that it is the name that is the most significant piece of information to be communicated. Sometimes, however, it is not the name but the phrase in apposition that is placed first, as in the following example:

4.27   ἐπὶ τὸν ἅγιον παῖδά σου Ἰησοῦν

The phrase is repeated at 4.30. This verse is part of a prayer addressed to God by the Jerusalem Jesus-believers in which they speak of those of the city who had attacked 'your holy servant, Jesus'. The principal reason that this was shocking was the fact that Jesus was God's servant and the one whom he anointed (ὃν ἔχρισας); this is duly indicated by the occurrence of the epithet before the name of Jesus. The association of Jesus with the term 'God's holy servant' is strikingly new, as signalled by the omission of the article before his name (see Chapter 2, §II.3.iii). The second position, then, of the name of Jesus does not mean that the name is in any way insignificant but that, in the situation in question, it is the attribute or function that is in focus.

II.2.ii Variant readings

The order of words in apposition varies at four places:

4.36; 11.5; 12.1; 18.8

At these places, the order name/appositional noun phrase varies, except at 4.36 where it is the order of two nouns in apposition to a name that varies.

4.36 Barnabas is presented as a member of the community of believers in Jesus; according to both texts, he is described as a Cypriot and a Levite:

Ref.	D05	ℵ01/B03
4.36	Ἰωσὴφ δὲ ὁ ἐπικληθεὶς Βαρναβᾶς ὑπὸ τῶν ἀποστόλων, ὅ ἐστιν μεθερμηνευόμενον υἱὸς παρακλήσεως, [Κύπριος, Λευίτης] τῷ γένει	Ἰωσὴφ δὲ ὁ ἐπικληθεὶς Βαρναβᾶς ἀπὸ τῶν ἀποστόλων, ὅ ἐστιν μεθερμηνευόμενον υἱὸς παρακλήσεως, [Λευίτης, Κύπριος] τῷ γένει

In this pair of readings, the variation does not so much alter the relative importance of 'Levite' or 'Cypriot', but rather causes a difference of meaning. In D05, he is a Levite by race (τῷ γένει) whereas in ℵ01/B03 he is a Cypriot by race. Throughout the narrative of Acts, there are some highly significant variant readings concerning the role of Barnabas, and this particular variant is part of the larger picture first introduced into the Bezan text at 1.23.[24] From a Jewish perspective, a Levite could be viewed as being a Levite τῷ γένει whatever his place of birth or upbringing, in so far as γένος expresses a blood relationship; the fact that Barnabas was from Cyprus is a secondary factor as far as his identity as a Levite is concerned. Thus, it is the Bezan reading of 4.36 rather than the Alexandrian one that reflects a Jewish understanding of Barnabas' identity within the Jerusalem community. For another variant involving γένος, see on 18.24 (§II.3.ii below).

11.5 *Joppa* is introduced differently in the two texts:

ℵ01/B03   ἐν [πόλει Ἰόππῃ]
D05   ἐν [Ἰόππῃ πόλει]

In order to determine the significance of the different word order, the context of the reference needs to be carefully considered. It is Peter who speaks here of Joppa in explaining to the Jerusalem disciples the sequence of events leading up to his visit to a Gentile household in Caesarea. In the first-century CE, Joppa was a predominantly Jewish town of some strategic importance in Palestine[25] and, in his defence, Peter makes it clear that it was to there that he had initially travelled; he had not gone to Caesarea, a Roman town in contrast to Joppa, on his own initiative. In ℵ01/B03, the name of the town is not underlined. In D05, on the other hand, the name of Joppa is given prominence, possibly for Peter's purpose of stressing that he had intended to remain within Jewish circles in his missionary activity.[26]

12.1 Herod is introduced in a phrase with three different word orders:

ℵ01   ἐπέβαλεν [ὁ βασιλεὺς Ἡρῴδης τὰς χεῖρας]
B03   ἐπέβαλεν [Ἡρῴδης ὁ βασιλεὺς τὰς χεῖρας]
D05   ἐπέβαλεν [τὰς χεῖρας Ἡρῴδης ὁ βασιλεύς]

The text of ℵ01 focuses on the function of Herod as king by placing ὁ βασιλεὺς before his name. The other two texts place less emphasis on his function by retaining the more usual order of name before title. However, D05 draws special attention to his person by displacing the subject after the direct object in clause-final position.[27] The tendency of D05 throughout Acts 12 is, in fact, to insist on the persecution of the Jesus-believers by

---

[24] See my article, 'La tradition targumique et Le Codex de Bèze: Ac 1:15-26', in *La Bíblia i el Mediterrani*, ed. Agustí Borrell, Alfonso De la Fuente and Armand Puig, 2 vols, 171–80 (Associació Bíblica de Catalunya: L'Abadia de Montserrat, 1997), II; 'Barnabas in Acts: A Study of his Role in the Text of Codex Bezae', *Journal for the Study of the New Testament* 72 (1998): 23–66.

[25] S. Applebaum *Judaea in Hellenistic and Roman Times* (Leiden: Brill, 1989), 20; E. Schürer, *The History of the Jewish People in the Age of Jesus-Christ 175 BC – AD 135*, trans., rev. and ed. G. Vermes, F. Millar, M. Black (Edinburgh: T&T Clark, 1987), 110–14. The term πόλις indicates that under Roman rule of Judaea, the town had probably achieved city status (but cf. Schürer, *History of the Jewish People*, 196-7) for which there must have been at least some element of Greek population (Applebaum, *Judaea*, 83; see also 165, on the use of Greek by the Jewish inhabitants).

[26] It is in keeping with the overall purpose of the D05 narrator to pay attention to the fine detail of the conflict caused among the Jerusalem disciples by the evangelization of the Gentiles.

[27] This observation is based on the usual order in Acts of verb followed by subject, see Chapter 8, §II.

Herod (cf. 12.3D05), a character whose role in the re-enactment of the history of Israel through the unfolding of events in the early Church is brought out with special force in that text.[28]

18.8 Crispus is mentioned as the leader of the synagogue:

ℵ01/B03   [Κρίσπος δὲ ὁ ἀρχισυνάγωγος]
D05   [ὁ δὲ ἀρχισυνάγωγος Κρίσπος]

It is D05 that, in this instance, focuses on the function rather than on the name of the person mentioned. In 18.7, reference has just been made to the synagogue to which its ruler is closely linked by appearing as a contiguous term, before his name. The order of the elements is thus 'given – new', following the usual pattern of presenting information (see §I.4 above). The ℵ01/B03 text, in comparison, gives prominence to the name of the ruler by placing it in the initial position in the new sentence. The focus of D05 is in keeping with the main interest of the episode, which is the impact of Paul's preaching in Corinth on the Jews as a collective group.

There are no additional readings of nouns in apposition in the MSS examined. It is a striking fact that all four variants involving the order of nouns in apposition indicate a Jewish concern of some kind. This is a feature of the variant readings concerning word order that will be observed as other kinds of word order variation are analysed.

II.3 ὀνόματι

A common formula found in Acts to introduce a person by name consists of ὀνόματι together with the name of the person. The formula is typical of Luke's Gospel, too, but it is not found in the other Gospels. Indeed, the interest with the names of characters is typically Lukan. The phrase in Acts is often:

noun + ὀνόματι + name

where the noun is either general (ἀνήρ, γυνή) or specific (e.g. παιδίσκη, μαθητής).

II.3.i In the common text

In the common text, the order is always ὀνόματι + name. It is unfortunate that D05 is missing for the two occurrences of ὀνόματι in Acts 9, where there are two instances in ℵ01/B03 of the name appearing before ὀνόματι (Saul, 9.11, Ananias, 9.12 D05 *lac.*). In each case, the name of the person in question is necessary information, provided by the speaker for the purpose of identification. Most of the other occurrences of the

---

[28] For the role of Herod in the D05 text of Acts as a re-enactment of the Prince of Tyre, see J. (Read-)Heimerdinger, 'The Seven Steps of Codex Bezae: A Prophetic Interpretation of Acts 12', in *Codex Bezae. Studies from the Lunel Colloquium June 1994*, ed. D. C. Parker and C.-B. Amphoux, 303–10 (Leiden: Brill, 1996).

formula with ὀνόματι introduce a participant with the indefinite τις (noun + τις + ὀνόματι + name), or occasionally with an anarthrous noun (e.g. a servant, 12.13; a centurion, 27.1 D05 *lac.*). As such, the characters can be understood to be representatives of a type, the name being a descriptive detail rather than information needed for identification.

From the data available in the common text, it may be concluded that Luke's practice is to place the name of the person after ὀνόματι unless the name is provided specifically for identification.

II.3.ii Variant readings

Two variant readings occur:

5.1; 18.24

At these two places, where a new participant is introduced, ℵ01/B03 read the name before ὀνόματι, contrary to the usual word order.

5.1 Ananias is referred to as he is introduced at the beginning of the epsiode with the phrase ἀνὴρ δέ τις Ἀνανίας ὀνόματι. It is followed by the introduction of his wife, σὺν Σαπφίρῃ τῇ γυναικὶ αὐτοῦ (cf. §II.2.i above). Attention is drawn to the name of Ananias in ℵ01/B03 by mentioning it before ὀνόματι, since the usual order is thereby disrupted. Thereafter in the Alexandrian text of the incident, attention is noticeably focused on events rather than on the participants of the drama. It looks as if the name 'Ananias' could be a signal that reminds the addressees of an incident instead of referring to an important person in his own right but this device is not used elsewhere in either text unless the following variant reading (18.24ℵ01/B03, see below) can be construed as another example of the same procedure. It may be that because of the nature of the incident, Ananias acquired a notoriety that allowed his name to act as a signal in this way.

In contrast, D05 introduces Ananias with the formula in its usual order. A chiastic pattern is thus obtained with the following phrase, the effect of which is to juxtapose the names of Ananias and Sapphira. The D05 text, written as it is in sense lines, looks like this:

5.1D05 ἀνὴρ δέ τις [ὀνόματι Ἀνανίας]
σὺν Σαπφίρῃ τῇ γυναικὶ αὐτοῦ

In the account of the incident overall, D05 maintains attention on the participants of the story.

18.24 Apollos ℵ01/B03/Apollonius D05 is introduced as a new character into the narrative following the departure of Paul from Ephesus; he is presented both by name and by race. Three variant readings combine here to form one unit (the word order of the two appositional phrases and the spelling of the man's name):

Ref.	D05	ℵ01/B03
18.24	Ἰουδαῖος δέ τις [ὀνόματι Ἀπολλώνιος], [↑ γένει Ἀλεξανδρεὺς] ἀνὴρ λόγιος	Ἰουδαῖος δέ τις [Ἀπολλῶς ὀνόματι], [Ἀλεξανδρεὺς τῷ γένει] ἀνὴρ λόγιος

The next four verses (18.25–28) relate the arrival of Apollos/Apollonius in Ephesus and Corinth with considerable variation between the two texts, D05 providing more detailed information about his background and about the circumstances of his stay in Corinth. Alexandria, as his place of origin is of greater significance for the Bezan version of the story than for the other text.

This is the second time that a variant reading has been seen to occur in connection with the γένος of a Jewish person.[29] The other occasion was in Acts 4 with respect to Barnabas (4.36, see §II.2.ii above), but there the variant concerns the reference of γένος (Levite or Cypriot) rather than the position of γένος, which is read after the tribe/country in all MSS. Country – race is also the order found at the other occurrence in Acts of γένος at 18.2 where Aquila is presented as τινα Ἰουδαῖον ὀνόματι Ἀκύλαν, Ποντικὸν τῷ γένει. The effect of placing the country first, at both 4.36D05 and 18.2, is to draw attention to the place of origin of a Jewish person as being outside Palestine. In this way, the word order reflects the situation of the dispersion of the Jews in the first century and of their attachment to countries other than Israel.

In both texts of 18.24, the aspect of the man's identity that is of primary importance is the fact that he is a Jew, for Ἰουδαῖος is the initial identification label provided. The ℵ01/B03 text then highlights both the specific name and the origin of the participant by placing them as first constituent in their respective phrases. The reason for drawing attention to the name of Apollos is not apparent from the account of his part in the story (as it was not with Ananias, cf. 5.1 above); however, the underlining of his place of origin outside Israel is in line with the other references to Jews of the Diaspora as noted above. D05, on the other hand, leaves the name and the origin of the participant in the usual position. That the origin is of interest is signalled, nonetheless, by the absence of the article before γένει.[30]

Comparison of 18.24D05 with the presentation of Barnabas at 4.36D05 (see §II.2.ii above) as a 'Cypriot, a Levite by race' is instructive. It suggests that whereas Barnabas' racial identity as a (Jewish) Levite is important because it is in contrast to his Cypriot (Hellenistic) nationality, in the case of Apollonius it is the fact that his place of origin was the town of Alexandria that is important to the story. This focus is confirmed by the additional reference to his homeland in 18.25D05: κατηχημένος ἐν τῇ πατρίδι τὸν λόγον τοῦ κυρίου. It is in the context of Alexandria, too, that the Bezan form of the name, 'Apollonius' may have special significance.[31]

---

[29] Outside Acts, the γένος of a person is only specified once at Mk 7.26, when the Syrophoenecian woman is presented: ἡ δὲ γυνὴ ἦν Ἑλληνίς Συροφοινίκισσα τῷ γένει. Here, there is a clear reason within the story itself for highlighting the place of origin of the woman who comes to Jesus for help. The meaning of γένος needs to be carefully defined. According to J. P. Louw and E. A. Nida, *Greek-English Lexicon of the New Testament Based on Semantic Domains*, 2 vols, (New York: UBS, 1988), I, 112, n.1), 'the feature of biological descent is focal while group functioning is secondary'. According to this definition, the implication for those Jews in Acts whose γένος is defined in relation to a country outside Palestine, whether Cyprus (4.36ℵ01/B03), Pontus (18.2) or Alexandria (18.24), is that they were descendants of proselytes who were natives of those Diaspora countries, rather than of Jewish families who had been exiled there.

[30] Levinsohn, *Discourse Features*, 107.

[31] Cf. P.-F. Beatrice, 'Apollos of Alexandria and the Origins of Jewish-Christian Baptist Encratism', *Aufstieg und Niedergang der römischen Welt* II, 26/2, 1232–75 (Berlin: W. de Gruyter, 1995).

II.3.iii Additional reading

One reading is found at 13.6D05 that is absent from ℵ01/B03. Here, D05 reads ὀνόματι καλούμενον in place of ᾧ ὄνομα in the Alexandrian text to present the name of Bar-Jesus, the magician at Paphos. The phrase follows the usual pattern with ὀνόματι before the name. The sentence is discussed in Chapter 7, §II.4.i with other instances of the parallel terms ὀνόματι/ ᾧ ὄνομα.

II.4 Possessive or partitive genitive

This final category of word order within the noun phrase considers the order of two nouns when one of them is in the genitive because it is belongs to, or is part of, the other.

II.4.i In the common text

An examination of the examples of noun with dependent genitive in the common text of Acts shows that the genitive, be it possessive or partitive, usually follows the noun it qualifies. The same pattern is found elsewhere in the NT writings: 'It is generally agreed that the form τὸ βιβλίον τοῦ πατρός is the predominant form in the NT'.[32] This would seem to be because it is the noun that is the chief element, the noun or pronoun in the genitive being dependent on it. When the genitive is placed before the noun, on the other hand, it is a means of drawing attention to that element, either because there is a reason to emphasize it or because, as Winer puts it, it 'contains the principal notion'.[33]

II.4.ii Variant readings

These affect both pronouns and nouns.

a) Personal pronouns in the genitive

There are five instances of variation:

    2.26; 3.7, 19; 4.27; 12.20b

The genitive is read before the noun by ℵ01/B03 at 2.26; 3.19; 12.20b, and by D05 at 3.7; 4.27.

---

[32] Porter, 'Word Order and Clause Structure', 184.
[33] Winer, *Grammar*, 240. Several grammars cite occurrences in the New Testament (few of them in Acts) of a genitive preceding a noun where it is claimed that there is no particular cause to underline the first word. It is possible that light may be shed on these references by a careful analysis of the discourse context – for examples, see Porter, 'Grammatical Study', 8–11; Turner, *Syntax*, 189–90; Winer, *Grammar*, 192. Porter's two examples in Acts (4.13; 19.27) are not, in fact, straightforward instances of genitive/noun. Even so, in both cases there is reason to highlight the preceding genitive. At 4.13, Peter is distinguished from John as speaker (as Porter suggests, p. 8), and at 19.27 it is not the temple of Artemis that is being 'emphasized' as the new subject of the clause, but rather the focus is on the great divinity herself, albeit by means of a stock phrase (see §II.4.2.b below).

2.26; 3.19; 4.27 These three references belong to either an explicit or implicit scriptural quotation.³⁴ ℵ01/B03 read the pronoun before the noun at 2.26 (μου ἡ καρδία) and 3.19 (ὑμῶν τὰς ἁμαρτίας), whereas D05 has it before the noun at 4.27 (τὸν ἅγιόν σου παῖδά Ἰησοῦν). As the immediate context in none of the instances provides a reason for emphasizing the pronoun, it is possible that the variation arises because different textual or interpretative traditions are familiar to the different editors of the MSS, and that an emphasis belongs to those earlier traditions rather than to the time of Acts.

3.7 When the lame man is healed by Peter, D05 reads the possessive pronoun before a pair of nouns, αὐτοῦ αἱ βάσεις καὶ τὰ σφυδρά,³⁵ 'his feet and his ankles', whereas ℵ01/B03 read the possessive between the two nouns, after αἱ βάσεις. When a pronoun in the genitive is governed by two nouns as here, it happens on a number of occasions in the NT that the genitive is placed at the head of the phrase. The explanation for this may be to avoid repeating the pronoun before each of the two entities as Turner suggests,³⁶ but in every case in Luke–Acts it is plausible to interpret the position of the pronoun as an indication of contrast or focus on the person to whom the pronoun refers. In Acts 3.7, the Bezan text has a series of variant readings preceding the inversion of word order:

Ref.	D05	ℵ01/B03
3.7	καὶ πιάσας αὐτὸν τῆς δεξιᾶς χειρὸς ἤγειρεν ↑ καὶ παραχρῆμα ἐστάθη καὶ ἐστερεώθησαν [αὐτοῦ αἱ βάσεις] καὶ τὰ σφυρά	καὶ πιάσας αὐτὸν τῆς δεξιᾶς χειρὸς ἤγειρεν αὐτόν· παραχρῆμα δὲ ↑ ἐστερεώθησαν [αἱ βάσεις αὐτοῦ] καὶ τὰ σφυδρά

The presence of the main verb in D05, ἐστάθη, 'he stood up', brings the lame man more into focus than in the other text and the placing of the possessive pronoun before the feet and ankles maintains the focus on the man.

12.20b In ℵ01/B03, the country of the Tyrians and the Sidonians is viewed as one country, set in antithesis to the country of the king (Judea). The antithesis is achieved by the highlighting of the genitive possessive pronoun αὐτῶν before τὴν χώραν:

Ref.	D05	ℵ01/B03
12.20	Ἦν γὰρ θυμομαχῶν Τυρίοις καὶ Σιδωνίοις· οἱ δὲ ὁμοθυμαδὸν ἐξ ἀμφοτέρων τῶν πόλεων παρῆσαν πρὸς τὸν βασιλέα καὶ πείσαντες Βλάστον, τὸν ἐπὶ τοῦ κοιτῶνος αὐτοῦ, ᾐτοῦντο εἰρήνην διὰ τὸ τρέφεσθαι [τὰς χώρας αὐτῶν] ἐκ τῆς βασιλικῆς.	Ἦν δὲ θυμομαχῶν Τυρίοις καὶ Σιδωνίοις· ↑ ὁμοθυμαδὸν δὲ ↑ παρῆσαν πρὸς αὐτὸν καὶ πείσαντες Βλάστον, τὸν ἐπὶ τοῦ κοιτῶνος τοῦ βασιλέως, ᾐτοῦντο εἰρήνην διὰ τὸ τρέφεσθαι [αὐτῶν τὴν χώραν] ἀπὸ τῆς βασιλικῆς.

---

[34] 2.25–8 is a quotation from Ps. 15.8–11 of which D05 follows the LXX word order. Peter's speech in Acts 3 is based on a variety of scriptural traditions including the Palestinian Targum of Isaiah (see (Read-)Heimerdinger, 'Unintentional Sins in Peter's Speech: Acts 3:12–26', *Revista Catalana* 20 (1995): 269–76). The reference at 4.27 belongs to a prayer addressed by the apostles to God that is couched throughout in scriptural/liturgical language.

[35] The reading σφυρά instead of σφυδρά is shared by ℵ01² and B03² along with other MSS.

[36] Turner, *Syntax*, 190; cf. Winer, *Grammar*, 239. Their references for Luke–Acts are Lk. 12.35; 22.53; Acts 21.11, with the latter, in fact, using the emphatic form of the pronoun ἑαυτοῦ.

The antithesis is less apparent in the Bezan text with the possessive pronoun in post-noun position. But in this text the two peoples are viewed as coming from two separate countries (τὰς χώρας), in keeping with the rest of the Bezan version of this episode (cf. οἱ ... ἐξ ἀμφοτέρων τῶν πόλεων, D05).[37]

b) Nouns in the genitive

There are eight variant readings:

4.33; 5.13,36; 8.23; 17.5,28; 19.27b; 21.14

The majority of these variants occur within a wider variation unit and sometimes at places where the text is uncertain.

4.33 The three MSS, ℵ01, B03 and D05 differ at the end of the first clause in this verse:

Ref. D05	ℵ01/B03
4.33 καὶ δυνάμει μεγάλῃ ἀπεδίδουν τὸ μαρτύριον οἱ ἀπόστολοι τῆς ἀναστάσεως [τοῦ κυρίου Ἰησοῦ χριστοῦ]	καὶ δυνάμει μεγάλῃ ἀπεδίδουν τὸ μαρτύριον οἱ ἀπόστολοι τῆς ἀναστάσεως [Ἰησοῦ χριστοῦ τοῦ κυρίου, ℵ01] / [τοῦ κυρίου Ἰησοῦ τῆς ἀναστάσεως, B03]

In speaking of the resurrection of the Lord Jesus Christ, ℵ01 and D05 use a set phrase with only the order of the words of the personal title varying. B03, on the other hand, has τοῦ κυρίου Ἰησοῦ without χριστοῦ and places it before τῆς ἀναστάσεως. The B03 order is unusual in speaking of the resurrection in Acts, a probable indication that, in fact, τοῦ κυρίου Ἰησοῦ qualifies the apostles and not the resurrection at all. If the phrase is read with τῆς ἀναστάσεως, it has the effect of focusing attention on the Lord Jesus rather than on the resurrection. This form, which is less of a set formula, could be considered to represent an earlier reading but since liturgical phrases are by no means unknown in either the Jewish literature of the time or the writings of Paul, this argument is far from being as conclusive as is commonly suggested.[38]

5.13 The text for the beginning of this verse has several variants:

Ref. D05	ℵ01/B03
5.13 [καὶ οὐδεὶς τῶν λοιπῶν] ἐτόλμα κολλᾶσθαι αὐτοῖς	[τῶν δὲ λοιπῶν οὐδεὶς] ἐτόλμα κολλᾶσθαι αὐτοῖς

---

[37] See (Read-)Heimerdinger, 'The Seven Steps of Codex Bezae', for further discussion.
[38] In his *Commentary*, Metzger frequently appeals to the argument from Christian liturgy in evaluating variant readings and it is often found in commentaries on the Gospels or Acts. Cf. M.-E. Boismard and A. Lamouille, *Le texte occidental des Actes des Apôtres*, 2 vols (Paris: Editions Recherches sur les Civilisations, 1984), II, 32, who believe that the existence of the variant readings for this verse indicates that the mention of the resurrection was absent from the original text altogether.

The meaning of τῶν λοιπῶν has been much debated. It stands in contrast to one of the groups of the previous verse (apostles/people/all), but which one is a matter of interpretation. With regard to the word order, suffice it to say that the use of the connecting particle δέ in ℵ01/B03 is appropriate to signal contrast in the change of subject,[39] and is therefore compatible with the forefronting of τῶν λοιπῶν, which also heightens the contrast. In D05, where the contrast is lessened with the use of the unmarked word order, the particle καί corresponds to the downplaying of contrast.

5.36 D05 conveys the size of the threat posed by Theudas in a series of variant readings:

Ref.	D05	ℵ01/B03
5.36	ἀνέστη Θευδᾶς λέγων εἶναί τινα <u>μέγαν</u> ἑαυτόν, ᾧ <u>καὶ</u> προσεκλίθη [ἀριθμὸς ἀνδρῶν] ὡς τετρακοσίων	ἀνέστη Θευδᾶς λέγων εἶναί τινα ↑ ἑαυτόν, ᾧ ↑ προσεκλίθη [ἀνδρῶν ἀριθμὸς] ὡς τετρακοσίων

In D05, μέγαν adds to the notion of the power held by Theudas and secondly, an emphatic καὶ stresses the presence of a large number of followers. ἀριθμός is probably placed after the genitive in the ℵ01/B03 text to be nearer the number quoted rather than to give prominence to 'the men', which would be unnecessary here.

8.23 The varying order of the noun and its dependent genitive in this verse occurs amidst a number of other variants:

Ref.	D05	ℵ01/B03
8.23	ἐν γὰρ [<u>πικρίας</u> χολῇ] καὶ σύνδεσμον ἀδικίας ὁρῶ σε ὄντα	εἰς γὰρ [χολὴν <u>πικρίας</u>] καὶ σύνδεσμον ἀδικίας ὁρῶ σε ὄντα

D05's initial ἦν must clearly be read as an error for ἐν for the verse to make sense. The difference in preposition brings about the change in case of the governing nouns. In ℵ01/B03, εἰς tends to be used in place of ἐν without losing its static force.[40] The phrase χολή πικρίας reflects a Hebrew construction in which the noun in the genitive has the force of an adjective, so 'the gall of bitterness' means 'bitter gall'.[41] Though not common in non-biblical Greek, the idiom is found elsewhere in the NT,[42] always with the order noun–dependent genitive, which is the Hebrew word order. Here, D05 goes against that pattern and in so doing creates a chiastic structure with the second noun–dependent genitive, the force of which is to strengthen Peter's description of Simon's inner state. If the phrase χολή πικρίας represents something of a fixed expression, the D05 narrator displays a freedom in his use of Greek which allows him to modify a standard formula and thereby underline its force.

---

[39] Levinsohn, *Textual Connections*, 87–9.
[40] It may be, however, that in ℵ01/B03 Peter is saying that he sees Simon as heading towards 'the gall of bitterness and the bond of iniquity' whereas in the D05 text he sees him as already in that state.
[41] M. Zerwick, *Biblical Greek*, trans., rev. and ed. J. Smith (Rome: Scripta Pontificii Instituti Biblici, 1963), §40.
[42] In Luke's writings, see e.g. Lk. 4.22; 16.9; Acts 9.15.

17.5, 38 The readings of these two verses are discussed in the section on τις (§III.5.ii below) since that is the noun on which the genitive is dependent in each case.

19.27 The text of this verse in all three MSS is confused. The word order variation concerns the placing of the name of the goddess Artemis in the genitive before or after 'the temple':

Ref.	D05	ℵ01/B03
19.27	οὐ μόνον δὲ τοῦτο [ἡμῖν κινδυνεύει] τὸ μέρος εἰς ἀπελεγμὸν ἐλθεῖν ἀλλὰ καὶ τὸ τῆς μεγάλης θεᾶς [ἱερὸν Ἀρτέμιδος] εἰς οὐδὲν λογισθήσεται, [ἀλλὰ καθαιρεῖσθαι μέλλει] ↑ ἣν ὅλη ἡ Ἀσία καὶ ἡ οἰκουμένη σέβεται	οὐ μόνον δὲ τοῦτο [κινδυνεύει ἡμῖν] τὸ μέρος εἰς ἀπελεγμὸν ἐλθεῖν ἀλλὰ καὶ τὸ τῆς μεγάλης θεᾶς [Ἀρτέμιδος ἱερόν] εἰς οὐθὲν λογισθῆναι, [μέλλειν τε καὶ καθαιρεῖσθαι] τῆς μεγαλειότητος αὐτῆς ἣν ὅλη ἡ Ἀσία καὶ ἡ οἰκουμένη σέβεται

The variant arises in a sentence described as 'monstrous' in ℵ01/B03,[43] with words that are absent in D05. The question of a possible shift of emphasis is complicated by the presence of a name in apposition to the dependent genitive, τῆς μεγάλης θεᾶς. If emphasis does lie behind this variant, there would seem to be a conflict of interests between drawing attention to the goddess and to the temple.[44]

21.14 The word order variation occurs in the phrase 'the will of God/the Lord be done' as spoken by Paul's companions ('we') at Caesarea when they saw that Paul was determined to go to Jerusalem despite the prophetic warnings of the danger waiting for him there.

Ref.	D05	ℵ01/B03
21.14	μὴ πειθομένου δὲ αὐτοῦ ἡσυχάσαμεν οἱ εἰπόντες πρὸς ἀλλήλους· [τὸ θέλημα τοῦ θεοῦ] γινέσθω	μὴ πειθομένου δὲ αὐτοῦ ἡσυχάσαμεν ↑ εἰπόντες ↑· [τοῦ κυρίου τὸ θέλημα] γινέσθω

In ℵ01/B03, with the order τοῦ κυρίου τὸ θέλημα, Paul's friends appear to be contrasting the will of the Lord with the conflict between their own wishes and those of Paul. This contrast is not apparent in D05, where the narrator furthermore makes it clear that the friends are not talking in Paul's hearing but among themselves: πρὸς ἀλλήλους. In D05 generally, the role of the 'we'-group is heightened, with those who belong to it presented as having an accurate understanding of the will of God even when Paul does not.[45] Here, in so far as the companions address each other, the reference to the will of God is an indication of their dependence on God to bring his plan to fruition despite Paul.

---

[43] J. H. Ropes, *The Text of Acts*, III, in *The Beginnings of Christianity*, Part I *The Acts of the Apostles*, ed. F. J. Foakes-Jackson and K. Lake (London: Macmillan, 1926), 186, n. 27.

[44] Porter, 'The Adjectival Attributive Genitive in the New Testament: A Grammatical Study', *Trinity Journal* 4 (1987): 3–17 (8–9), argues that ἱερόν is emphatic.

[45] The function of the first-person plural passages in Acts, including the references absent from the Alexandrian text, is examined in J. Read-Heimerdinger, 'Paul, a Fallible Apostle: Luke's Evaluation of Paul's Mission in the Manuscript Tradition of Acts' (unpublished post-doctoral Licentiate in Divinity thesis, University of Wales, Lampeter, 2010).

II.4.iii Additional readings

A high number of partitive or possessive genitives are found in D05, whether as pronouns or nouns.

a) Personal pronouns in the genitive

D05 frequently adds the personal possessive pronoun to a noun (one or two instances in most chapters), chiefly in the third person, where none is specified in the text of the other MSS. With one exception (6.3), it is always placed following the noun, in accordance with the usual pattern of the common text.

6.3 The exception occurs within the context of a wider variation unit spanning 6.1-5 which will be considered in part in the section dealing with demonstratives (§III.6 below).

Ref.	D05	ℵ01/B03
6.3	τί οὖν ἐστίν [ἀδελφοί; ἐπισκέψασθε] [ἐξ ὑμῶν αὐτῶν ἄνδρας] μαρτυρουμένους .ζ.	↑ [ἐπισκέψασθε δέ, ἀδελφοί], [ἄνδρας ἐξ ὑμῶν ↑] μαρτυρουμένους ἑπτά.
6.4	ἡμεῖς δὲ ἐσόμεθα τῇ προσευχῇ... προσκαρτεροῦντες	ἡμεῖς δὲ ↑ τῇ προσευχῇ... προσκαρτερήσομεν

In D05, ἐξ ὑμῶν before ἄνδρας and is rendered emphatic by the presence of the adjacent αὐτῶν. ὑμῶν refers to οἱ Ἑλληνισταί (6.1), the Hellenistic members of the church in Jerusalem in contrast to the 'twelve', the apostles. They are already designated in 6.2D05 where they are specified as the intended addressees of the apostles' speech, πρὸς αὐτούς. On its own, the additional pronoun in 6.3 could be construed as a rather unnecessary attempt to clarify the shorter text. It is, in fact, in keeping with a concern pervading the D05 text of Acts, that of underlining the apostles' preoccupation during the early stages of the Church with their distinctive spiritual function within the Jerusalem community. The contrast they seek to maintain in this collective speech is indicated by the emphatic pronoun ἡμεῖς at the head of the clause in 6.4, again reinforced in D05 by the 1st p.pl verb ἐσόμεθα. A greater tension between the two groups, of the apostles on the one hand and the disciples on the other, is created by the D05 text.

b) Nouns in the genitive

Where D05 has additional instances of a possessive or partitive genitive, all but one of the 25 occurrences have the unmarked order noun + genitive. The exception is at 4.24 where, in an entire additional phrase, clear prominence is given to the noun θεός by the word order:

4.24D05 οἱ δὲ ἀκούσαντες καὶ ἐπιγνόντες τὴν τοῦ θεοῦ ἐνέργιαν ὁμοθυμαδὸν ἦραν

The word θεός is already present in both texts in the following part of the sentence, and is further highlighted in D05 by a second additional mention in the address of the prayer later in the same verse. When D05 specifies elsewhere God (or Jesus, or Lord) as the possessor, the usual order of noun + genitive is followed: 16.6D05; 18.25D05; 20.25D05.

III. Adjectives in the noun phrase

In this section, Luke's pattern of ordering adjectives and nouns is considered, examining the different types of adjectives in turn.

III.1. Descriptive adjectives and noun/noun phrase

III.1.i In the common text
Different patterns can be observed according to whether the noun is arthrous or not.

a) With the article
There are only 16 occurrences in the text of Acts extant in ℵ01, B03 and D05 of an arthrous noun qualified by a descriptive adjective (3.7,10; 11.17; 12.10; 13.46; 17.18; 19.12,13,15, 16; 20.28; 21.26,27, 40; 22.2,25) and there are no variants involving change of word order. The data is therefore somewhat limited and conclusions about word order are necessarily the more tentative for that. The more frequent order is article–adjective–noun. In such cases, the order may express a familiar association of the adjective and the noun it qualifies (e.g. 3.7 'the right hand', τῆς δεξιᾶς χειρός; 3.10 'the Beautiful Gate', τῇ ὡραίᾳ πύλῃ; 13.46 'the eternal life', τῆς αἰωνίου ζωῆς); or it may accord equal attention to the adjective and the noun (22.25 'the standing-by centurion', τὸν ἑστῶτα ἑκατόνταρχον); or it may confer special importance on the adjective (11.17 'the equal gift', τὴν ἴσην δωρεάν; 21.40 + 22.2 'the Hebrew language', τῇ Ἑβραΐδι διαλέκτῳ).

When the adjective follows the arthrous noun (and the article is thereby repeated), the context is sometimes explanatory – explanatory rather than emphatic.[46] The repetition of the article and the separation of the adjective from the noun that it qualifies seem to be factors that achieve this purpose. One example can be seen at 12.10: τὴν πύλην τὴν σιδηρᾶν, 'the-gate-the-iron', where the situation is one of defining which gate rather then simply naming it, as is the case with 'the Beautiful Gate' at 3.10 (see above). Again, at 20.28, 'by his own blood', διὰ τοῦ αἵματος τοῦ ἰδίου, occurs as an integral part of an explanation about the sacrifice of Jesus, made all the clearer in the Bezan text by the additional ἑαυτῷ and κυρίου in place of θεοῦ earlier in the verse.[47]

The place of the article after a definite noun occurs in each of the references to the evil spirits at 19.12,13,15,16 (τὰ πνεύματα τὰ πονηρά), where the phrase stands in

---

[46] This is noticeably true of τὸ πνεῦμα τὸ ἅγιον, see Chapter 5, §V.1.iii.
[47] James D. G. Dunn, *The Partings of the Ways Between Christianity and Judaism and their Significance for the Character of Christianity* (London: SCM Press, 1991) overstates the textual difficulty of 20.28 when he speaks of it as one of 'the most difficult textual questions in Luke-Acts', 59.

contrast to the form of expression for the Holy Spirit used when the context for the mention is not a familiar one.

The small number of examples of adjectives following an arthrous noun can be accounted for by the relatively few occasions in the Book of Acts when an adjective is associated with a noun in the context of an explanation. Further instances will be noted in connection with the Holy Spirit (τὸ πνεῦμα τὸ ἅγιον, see Chapter 5, §III.2.iii).

b) Without the article

Here, the picture is much easier to see, there being a greater number of examples and some variation. When the adjective is adding more detail to the noun, the noun being the more important of the two elements, then the adjective follows the noun. This is especially the case in any kind of standard epithet accompanying a noun such as 5.12 'many signs and wonders', σημεῖα καὶ τέρατα πολλά; 8.1 'great persecution', διωγμὸς μέγας; 13.48 'eternal life', ζωὴν αἰώνιον; 18.14 'evil villainy', ῥᾳδιούργημα πονηρόν. The adjective in these cases is often the expected one. It is not of special importance or it may even be redundant. No contrast or emphasis is implied.

When the adjective is placed before the anarthrous noun, the epithet is usually more carefully chosen than when it is in post position. This may be because it is significant of itself, or because special emphasis is being given to it and attention is being focused on it. Examples occur at 2.4 'other tongues', ἑτέραις γλώσσαις; 4.16 'a notable sign', γνωστὸν σημεῖον; 12.21 'an appointed day', τακτῇ ἡμέρᾳ; 14.10 'a loud voice', μεγάλῃ φωνῇ; 17.23 'an unknown god', Ἀγνώστῳ θεῷ; 19.26 'a considerable crowd', ἱκανὸν ὄχλον.

In summary, the pattern is:

- adjective–noun
  - without the article: the adjective is being highlighted
  - with the article: the adjective is not necessarily being highlighted but may be.
- noun–adjective
  - without the article: the adjective is not of special importance
  - with the article: the adjective is being underlined as part of an explanation.[48]

III.1.ii Variant readings

There are only five variant readings affecting the position of the descriptive adjective with respect to the noun and none of these occur in a phrase with the article.

---

[48] H. H. Hess analysed the order of words within the noun phrase in Mark's Gospel ('Dynamics of the Greek Noun Phrase in Mark', *Optat* 4 (1990): 353–69), and comes to the opposite conclusion regarding the marked and unmarked position of the adjective, claiming that emphasis is conveyed by the post-noun position. Since he does not, however, define in what way such adjectives are emphatic in their context, nor in what way the pre-noun adjectives are not emphatic, it is difficult to discuss his conclusions.

Ref.	D05	ℵ01/B03
2.2	βιαίας πνοῆς	πνοῆς βιαίας
2.5b	εὐλαβεῖς ἄνδρες	ἄνδρες εὐλαβεῖς
13.32	γενομένην ἐπαγγελίαν	ἐπαγγελίαν γενομένην
16.28	φωνῇ μεγάλῃ (+ ℵ01)	μεγάλῃ φωνῇ (B03 only)
22.3a	Ἰουδαῖος ἀνήρ	ἀνὴρ Ἰουδαῖος

On four occasions, the order adjective is placed before the noun in D05 indicating that the adjective is of special importance for the Bezan text. In one instance (16.28), the adjective is placed before the noun in B03, where it is a matter of how a happening is perceived rather than the special significance of the adjective.

2.2 God's speaking by means of a violent wind was a fact familiar to Jews from the Scriptures (cf. 1 Kgs 19.11) and drawing attention to it may be understood as a way of underlining that it was indeed the same God who intervened through the Pentecost drama.

2.5 The men who witnessed the Pentecost event are described as 'devout men from every nation' where the word εὐλαβεῖς is a religious qualification of high value. The text of the first part of this verse, as far as ἀπό, has been transmitted in almost as many forms as there are words but the variation that concerns us here is the highlighting by D05 of the devoutness of the men, people who were not Jewish (cf. §III.4.ii below). In addition, the Bezan text carefully sets the scene as Jerusalem by placing the name of the location in first position in the sentence.

13.32 γενομένην is a participial adjective, describing the promise as having been made. Its position before the noun links the action closer to the recipients of the promise, the ancestors, whom the Bezan text has Paul further qualify as ἡμῶν in a speech in which he preaches to Jews.

16.28 The phrase 'in a loud voice' occurs at two other places in the common text of Acts, at 7.57: φωνῇ μεγάλῃ and at 14.10: μεγάλῃ φωνῇ. With other nouns, μέγας is read after the noun, except at 19.27 where the greatness of Artemis is being focused upon (τὸ τῆς μεγάλης θεᾶς Ἀρτέμιδος ἱερόν) especially in the Alexandrian text which speaks of her majesty, τῆς μεγαλειότητος αὐτῆς, which D05 omits). Looking at the picture overall, it is noticeable that μέγας is placed after the noun unless there is a reason for drawing special attention to the quality of greatness. Thus, Paul's 'loud voice' as he addresses the lame man in Lystra (14.10) is significant because had he spoken quietly to the man, he would not have been heard by the crowds standing around; it is therefore highlighted. The 'loud voice' of the enraged crowd, on the other hand, as they attack Stephen (7.57) is not surprising and the order is unmarked. As Paul calls to the jailor in prison at 16.28, it seems that ℵ01 and D05 (in common with most MSS) view it as not unnatural that he should call 'in a loud voice', whereas in B03 Paul's reaction to the jailer is set in stronger terms by the initial position of the adjective. The order in B03 may possibly be conditioned by the fact that in that MS the adverbial noun phrase is separated from the verb by the subject:

Ref.	ℵ01/D05	B03
16.28	ἐφώνησεν δὲ [φωνῇ μεγάλῃ] ὁ (D05) Παῦλος	ἐφώνησεν δὲ ↑ Παῦλος [μεγάλῃ φωνῇ]

22.3a It is Paul again who is speaking here as he introduces himself as a Jewish man. In the common text of Acts, at all eight occurrences of ἀνήρ except two (15.22,25), the adjective is found after ἀνήρ even though it is the adjective that is important. Presumably, the adjective does not usually need to be fronted in order to insist on its importance because ἀνήρ is in any case an almost redundant noun in Luke. In the Bezan text of 22.3, Ἰουδαῖος is not only emphatic but it also closely associated with Tarsus in Cilicia as Paul's birthplace, which the Bezan text places before the verb in the next phrase. Both emphases are relevant to Paul's purpose of establishing his identity:

Ref.	D05	ℵ01/B03
22.3	ἐγώ εἰμι [Ἰουδαῖος ἀνὴρ] [ἐν Ταρσῷ τῆς Κιλικίας γεγεννημένος]	ἐγώ εἰμι [ἀνὴρ Ἰουδαῖος] [γεγεννημένος ἐν Ταρσῷ τῆς Κιλικίας]

It is interesting to note that all four variant readings of adjective–noun in D05 arise in a context involving peculiarly Jewish questions. While it is the D05 text that underlines the Jewish significance of the subject matter, that text specifically does not reproduce the typical Hebraic word order of noun–adjective. In other words, it is a text that is conscious of the Jewish setting of contemporary events but that draws attention to their Jewishness in ways in keeping with the Greek language and not by imitating the Hebraic idiom.

III.1.iii Additional readings

Adjectives occur in material present in only one of the two textual traditions.

a) ℵ01/B03

There is only one instance of an adjective present in ℵ01/B03 and absent from D05.

15.32 The reference is to Judas and Silas who were part of the group responsible for handing the apostolic letter to the church in Antioch (15.30). The letter was well received (15.31) and 'furthermore', so the Alexandrian text goes on, 'since Judas and Silas were prophets, they exhorted the brethren with much speech'.

Ref.	D05	ℵ01/B03
15.32	Ἰούδας δὲ καὶ Σιλᾶς καὶ αὐτοὶ προφῆται ὄντες πλήρεις πνεύματος ἁγίου διὰ λόγου ↑ παρεκάλεσαν τοὺς ἀδελφούς	Ἰούδας τε καὶ Σιλᾶς καὶ αὐτοὶ προφῆται ↑ διὰ λόγου πολλοῦ παρεκάλεσαν τοὺς ἀδελφούς

The adjective πολλοῦ is non-emphatic; it may have dropped out of D05 through haplography, the next word also beginning with π, but there is a more likely explanation that depends on the presence of two other adjacent variant readings: firstly, D05 starts a new development at 15.32, with δέ rather than τε, so that the prophetic activity of Judas and Silas is separated off from the reading of the letter instead of being closely associated with it. Then, the participle ὄντες relates to a phrase absent from ℵ01/B03, 'because they were full of the Holy Spirit', which (within the terms of the ideology of the D05 narrator) draws a contrast between the legal nature of the apostolic document and the spiritual nature of the prophets. In consequence, the expression διὰ λόγου describes simply the manner in which Judas and Silas exercised their prophetic minstry, that is, verbally. Without the mention of the Holy Spirit in ℵ01/B03 and in view of the conjunction τε, διὰ λόγου on its own has little purpose but is more meaningful if it is qualified with πολλοῦ.

b) D05

There are many more instances of adjectives that only occur in the D05 text. On three occasions, these adjectives qualify a noun common to both texts:

12.5D05   <u>πολλὴ</u> προσευχή
16.22D05 <u>πολὺς</u> ὄχλος
17.5D05   οἱ <u>ἀπειθοῦντες</u> Ἰουδαῖοι

In all three cases, the adjective is found before the noun. One of two explanations for the variation can be proposed: either the adjective was not present when the Bezan editor read the text but it was felt to be needed; the adjective was thus likely to be prominent and naturally occurs before the noun. Alternatively, the prominence of the adjective is to be viewed as an indication of its underlying significance for the message of the text in its immediate context, which ℵ01/B03 sought to attenuate. The justification for the latter interpretation depends on the specific intention of the narrator of the D05 text at each point.

That the fronted position of the adjective in the above examples is not accidental is demonstrated by the observation that when an adjective occurs in a supplementary phrase in D05 (that is, qualifying a noun not read by ℵ01/B03), its position varies:

D05 adjective pre-noun: 8.24; 11.2a,2b, 27; 12.20; 18.6,27
D05 adjective post-noun: 15.30; 16.39a,39b; 19.8

Most of these adjectives are to do with size (e.g. πολύς) or extent (ἱκανός). The pattern observed in the common text can be used to determine the importance of the adjective at each of these points. For example, at 11.27D05 when the prophets went down from Jerusalem to visit the newly established community in Antioch, the joy experienced was noteworthy: ἦν δὲ πολλὴ ἀγγαλίασις, with the clause standing on its own as a single sentence. In contrast, at 16.39D05 when the magistrates heard that Paul and Silas were Romans, they went to see them accompanied by 'many friends', μετὰ φίλων πολλῶν, where the strength of the reinforcements is not an especially significant feature.

III.2. Cardinal numbers

III.2.i *In the common text*

Cardinal numbers occur with nouns that are both arthrous and anarthrous.

a) Arthrous nouns

In the text of Acts common to ℵ01/B03 and D05, the practice is for cardinal numbers to be placed before a noun with the article, which is to be expected in so far as, if the numbers are stated at all, it is because they are significant.

b) Anarthrous nouns

The order varies in the common text. For lengths of time, the adjective usually comes second (5.7; 7.30,36,42; 13.20,22; 19.8,10; 20.3,6) with only one departure from this order (7.23, see below). In all such cases, the number is not apparently of particular significance. The same can be said of occurrences of a number other than to express time where the number follows the noun (1.10; 7.29; 12.10; 21.33).

Where the numeral adjective comes first, the explanations that were found to account for this order with the general nouns (§III.1.i.b) may be appealed to. Either the fronting of the adjective expresses an instrinsic quality: 11.5 'lowered by four corners', τέσσαρσιν ἀρχαῖς καθιεμένην; 12.6 'bound between two soldiers', μεταξὺ δύο στρατιωτῶν δεδεμένος; or it is an indication of surprise: 11.11 'three men appeared', τρεῖς ἄνδρες ἐπέστησαν, at the house where Peter was staying (introduced by καὶ ἰδοὺ and ἐξαυτῆς); 12.4 Peter was handed over to be guarded by 'four quaternions of soldiers', παραδοὺς τέσσαρσιν τετραδίοις στρατιωτῶν, a number of guards that may be presumed to be unusually large.

At the one place, 7.23, where the number is placed before the noun in an expression of time, the reference is to the age of Moses in Stephen's speech: ἐπληροῦτο αὐτῷ τεσσερακονταετὴς [τεσσερακονταετὴς αὐτῷ, D05] χρόνος. Two further periods of forty years in the life of Moses are mentioned in the speech (7.30,36) in a way that divides the life of Moses into three equal periods but, after the first reference in 7.23, the order of the phrase is noun–number. At 7.23D05, the detail about the age of Moses is further underlined by its unusual position next to the verb before the pronoun (cf. 7.30D05, where an additional pronoun comes first: πληρωθέντων αὐτῷ ἐτῶν τεσσεράκοντα). As the first element of a threefold pattern, the reference at 7.23 signals the importance of the specification of time by the dual highlighting of the time expression and the number within it.[49]

III.2.ii Variant readings

There are no variant readings involving the place of a cardinal number before an arthrous noun.

---

[49] The age of Moses when he died is given as 120 by Deut. 34.7. Apart from a reference to Moses entering the desert of Sinai at the age of 80 (Exod. 7.7), the division of the life of Moses into three equal periods does not appear to be known in any tradition before Acts. However, it is mentioned in association with Rabbi Aquibah (d. 132–5 CE) (see Bernard Barc, *Les Arpenteurs du Temps. Essais sur l'histoire religieuse de la Judée á la période hellénistique* (Histoire du texte biblique 5; Lausanne: Éditions du Zèbre, 2000), 49–53). In view of the Jewish use of the tradition, it is unlikely to be an invention of Luke as some commentaries suggest (see e.g. L.T. Johnson, *The Acts of the Apostles* (Sacra Pagina 5; Collegeville, Minnesota: The Liturgical Press, 1995), 126). The threefold division of Moses' life is a theme found in some Patristic writings, see A. Le Boulluec and P. Sandevoir, 'L'Exode', *La Bible d'Alexandrie*, II, ed. M. Harl (Paris: Le Cerf, 1989), 83.

Before an anarthrous noun, the usual order of anarthrous noun–number is reversed in one variant reading of D05 in Acts 1 where Luke introduces the second volume of his work and describes Jesus as appearing over a period of 40 days:

Ref. D05	ℵ01/B03
1.3 ↑ [τεσσεράκοντα ἡμερῶν] ὀπτανόμενος αὐτοῖς	δι' [ἡμερῶν τεσσεράκοντα] ὀπτανόμενος αὐτοῖς

The mention of 40 days in this summary of Jesus' resurrection appearances is introduced in the narrative of Acts for the first time here. In the Jewish Scriptures, the number 40 was a figure of special significance and it was a point of some importance to the first Christians that Jesus was seen as re-enacting an ancient pattern. This is a point underlined by D05 through the fronted position of the number, but not by ℵ01/B03.

III.2.iii Additional readings

There are three additional readings of a cardinal number in D05:

2.14; 10.41; 12.10

At 2.14D05 and 12.10D05, the number occurs with an arthrous noun and is placed before the noun, following the pattern of the common text.

At 10.41D05, the noun is anarthrous and here the number is placed last. It is an additional reference to the resurrection appearances of Jesus happening over 40 days: ἡμέρας .μ (=40). D05 mentions '40 days' in Peter's speech to Cornelius where, in referring to the appearances of Jesus after his death, the Bezan text specifies that this happened over a 40-day period. The adjective is placed last. This is the usual order for time phrases, as was mentioned above (§III.2.1.ii), but it is in contrast to the D05 order of the phrase in the same context at 1.3 (§III.2.ii). Although in speaking to Cornelius, Peter introduces the detail of the number of days in D05, he does not draw particular attention to it, suggesting that it had become a part of the telling of the traditional story. Only when the purpose of the mention of 40 days is to establish the role of Jesus in the history of Israel, as at 1.3, is there a need to draw attention to its significance.

III.3. Ordinal numbers

III.3.i In the common text

Ordinal numbers function grammatically as ordinary adjectives, whether the noun is arthrous or anarthrous, and they follow the same pattern as set out above (see §III.1).

III.3.ii Variant readings

Two variant readings involving ordinal numbers arise in Acts, requiring careful attention:

3.1; 12.10

3.1 At the beginning of Acts 3, Luke mentions the time at which Peter and John went to the Temple:

Ref.	D05	ℵ01/B03
3.1	ἐπὶ τὴν ὥραν [↑ ἐνάτην τῆς προσευχῆς]	ἐπὶ τὴν ὥραν [τῆς προσευχῆς τὴν ἐνάτην]

The ℵ01/B03 text, with its double repetition of the article, uses an explanatory form (see §III.I.i above) whereas the D05 text mentions the hour of prayer without particular emphasis. At the two other places where the time is specified in Acts (10.3,9ℵ01/B03, D05 *lac.*), it is the order noun-number that is found, but there the noun (ὥραν) is without the article. In the absence of the D05 text of Acts 10 for comparison, it is not possible to comment in detail on the reasons for the variation at 3.1 except to say that the D05 narrator appears to view the reference to the hour of prayer as a familiar and self-explanatory one.

12.10 In the account of Peter's miraculous escape from prison, the angel is described as leading him through two prisons:

Ref.	D05	ℵ01/B03
12.10	διελθόντες δὲ πρώτην [καὶ δευτέραν φυλακὴν]	διελθόντες δὲ πρώτην [φυλακὴν καὶ δευτέραν]

The D05 order has both 'first' and 'second' highlighted in their position before the noun. The text of ℵ01/B03 can be said to underline further the existence of a second prison: by separating δευτέραν off and removing it further from the noun it qualifies, attention is thereby drawn to the second prison. The D05 narrator appears to be treating the existence of the two prisons more as an acknowledged fact while at the same time giving them prominence by the position of the numbers before the noun. This is in accordance with the overall metaphorical meaning of the prison that can be detected in the D05 version of the account of Peter's escape from prison.

III.4. πᾶς

III.4.i In the common text

πᾶς is always read before the noun in the common text. Its position is to be expected in view of the inherently emphatic implication of 'all'. This is an example of how analysis based simply on statistical comparisons could have distorted our conclusions, for we have seen that the basic order for adjectives that qualify anarthrous nouns is for the adjective to follow the noun, and for the order to be reversed for the general purpose of stressing the adjective. If the occurrences of πᾶς had been included in an overall count of nouns with qualifying adjectives, the basic pattern would not have emerged clearly.

III.4.ii Variant readings

The meaning of πᾶς when placed before an arthrous noun may change according to whether it is read before the article (meaning 'all' or 'every') or after (meaning 'the whole').[50] However, none of the variants involve the position of πᾶς in relation to the article, so no change of meaning from 'all' to 'whole' is implied.

At four places, א01/B03 read the adjective πᾶς after the noun:

2.14; 4.29; 7.50; 15.36

2.14 By placing πάντες at the front of the phrase [πάντες οἱ κατοικοῦντες Ἰερουσαλήμ], D05 treats the phrase 'all those living in Jerusalem' as referring to people not included in the initial ἄνδρες Ἰουδαῖοι. This corresponds to the interpretation given above to ἄνδρες εὐλαβεῖς in 2.5, that they were non-Jews (cf. §III.1.ii above on this variant). In א01/B03, the two phrases can be co-referential, the one being parallel to the other. The D05 narrator has Peter display an awareness of the application of his message extending beyond the Jewish people, even as early as Pentecost.[51]

4.29 The order of D05, μετὰ [παρρησίας πάσης], places greater stress on the quality of boldness that the apostles pray for.

7.50 In the LXX and MT forms of Isa. 66.2 that Stephen refers to here, there is a clear focus on 'all these things': πάντα ταῦτα ἐποίησεν ἡ χείρ μου. The focus is maintained by the D05 order in Acts 7.50: οὐχὶ ἡ χείρ μου ἐποίησεν [πάντα ταῦτα]; ('Did not my hand make all these things?'), where the א01/B03 text has the reverse order.[52]

15.36b Paul proposes to Barnabas to visit 'the brethren in every city', τοὺς ἀδελφοὺς τ κατὰ [πόλιν πᾶσαν], א01/B03) / τοὺς ἀδελφοὺς τοὺς κατὰ [πᾶσαν πόλιν], D05. As at 4.29, there is a shift in emphasis between the two readings, according to the position of the adjective pre- or post-noun. The D05 text is once again the more emphatic one, with the additional article τούς confirming the care taken to specify that it is the people who are in all the cities that they will visit.

III.4.iii Additional readings

There are 12 occurrences of adjectival πᾶς in D05 that are absent from א01/B03:

2.2,37,46; 4.31; 5.15,32; 6.10; 15.26; 16.4,15; 20.2,23

πᾶς is always read before the noun at these places, just as it is in the common text.

---

[50] On πᾶς and the article, see C. F. D. Moule, *An Idiom Book of New Testament Greek*, 3rd edn (Cambridge: CUP, 1977) 93–4; Zerwick, *Biblical Greek*, §§188–90.

[51] W. Strange, *The Problem of the Text of Acts* (Cambridge: CUP 1992), 153, believes that the displacement of πάντες from the end of one line to the end of the previous one in D05 is a typical Bezan error. Boismard and Lamouille (*Le texte occidental*, II, 12) indicate that the position of πάντες following the noun is 'anormale' by which they mean that it is statistically infrequent. Whilst a scribal error behind the D05 reading cannot be definitely ruled out, it is legitimate to suppose that the change was intentional since the alteration to the meaning is significant and in keeping with the overall insistence of the D05 narrator on the place of the Gentiles in the plan of salvation.

[52] Winer, *Grammar*, 686, observes that there is furthermore a difference between πάντα ταῦτα meaning 'all these things', and ταῦτα πάντα meaning 'these things all taken together'. The same order of πᾶς–demonstrative is found in 5.32D05 with the addition of πάντων and 21.20D05 with the addition of τοῦτοι (*sic*). As often, D05 displays a high degree of regularity in this respect.

III.5. τις

III.5.i In the common text

Adjectival τις is more often than not placed after the noun. This usual order is to be expected for, by its very indefiniteness, τις is not emphatic. When the adjective is placed before the noun, it can be seen that there is a reason for focusing attention on the person it refers to:

>   3.2; 16.14; 17.34; 21.10

3.2 τις ἀνήρ introduces the lame man as a new participant at the beginning of the episode with Peter and John in the Temple. The narrator of D05 draws particular attention to this introduction with an additional ἰδού. In this instance of τις with a person, the name of the person is not mentioned. A similar absence of a name occurs in an introduction at 16.16. Here, τις follows the noun (παιδίσκη τινά). The explanation for this may be that there is a deliberate focus on 'we' in this epsiode (the pronoun occurs four times between the end of 16.15 and the beginning of 16.17, and is distinguished from 'Paul' at the last mention), an indication that it is not the servant girl who is the main object of attention. It may be, therefore, that τις at 3.2 is operating as a device of salience underlining the importance of the lame man.

16.14 τις precedes γυνή in the introduction of Lydia when she is singled out from the group of women mentioned in the previous line. This would seem to confirm the suggestion above that τις before the noun is a way of focusing attention on the person.

17.34 There is a switch of focus in this parenthetical sentence from Paul to τινὲς ἄνδρες who became believers. The order of words here may be compared to that of the Bezan text at 17.5 and 18.26 (see §III.5.ii below). τινές here may convey not so much indefiniteness as a limitation of Paul's influence: only some of the men became believers.

21.10 τις here refers to a specific member of the group of Judaean prophets, Agabus, who has been mentioned before in the narrative of Acts (11.28). Like Lydia (16.14), he is singled out from among the prophets and τις stands before the noun.

III.5.ii Variant readings

There are two variant readings involving the position of τις:

>   17.5, 28

17.5 D05 places τις before the noun. The reading is part of a variation unit spanning several lines that has already been partially commented upon in §II.1.ii above:

Ref. D05	ℵ01/B03
17.5 [οἱ δὲ ἀπειθοῦντες Ἰουδαῖοι] ↑ συστρέψαντες [(τινὰς ἄνδρας) τῶν ἀγοραίων] πονηροὺς ↑ ἐθορύβουσαν τὴν πόλιν	[ζηλώσαντες δὲ οἱ Ἰουδαῖοι] καὶ προσλαβόμενοι [τῶν ἀγοραίων (ἄνδρας τινὰς)] πονηροὺς καὶ ὀχλοποιήσαντες ἐθορύβουν τὴν πόλιν

In the D05 text, ἄνδρας is in focus since it is the only group mentioned as being gathered by the Jews to stir up the city. τινὰς ἄνδρας is placed in front of the adjectival genitive τῶν ἀγοραίων, reinforcing their importance (cf. §II.4 above). In view of what has already been seen of the function of fronted τις, it looks probable that it is the more prominent position of ἄνδρας that accounts for the placing of τινάς before the noun.

17.28 Adjectival τις in ℵ01/B03 is a pronoun in D05 and is found in a different position in the phrase:

Ref.	D05	ℵ01/B03
17.28	ὥσπερ καὶ [τῶν καθ' ὑμᾶς τινες] ↑ εἰρήκασιν	ὡς καί [τινες τῶν καθ' ὑμᾶς] ποιητῶν εἰρήκασιν

The omission of ποιητῶν in D05 may well be the cause of τῶν καθ' ὑμᾶς being placed in first position before τινες. In the ℵ01/B03 order of words, the genitival phrase τῶν καθ' ὑμᾶς is highlighted by being placed between the adjective and the noun; D05 maintains the focus on the absence of the noun by keeping the gentival phrase before the pronoun (cf. §II.4).

III.5.iii Additional readings

There are ten additional occurrences of adjectival τις in D05, both before the noun and following it.

a) Pre-noun

D05 has five occurrences of τις + noun where τις is not present in ℵ01/B03:

10.22; 14.19; 17.34; 18.27; 21.15

At 10.22; 17.34, τις occurs in an appositional phrase in which the person introduced (Cornelius, Dionysius) is salient and τις is placed before the complement. These two references may be compared with another appositional phrase at 8.27 (see below) where mention is made of Candace, Queen of Ethiopia, who is not salient; there, D05 adds τις after the complement.

14.19 In ℵ01/B03, the subject of the sentence is read after the adverbial phrase of place (cf. discussion on this verse in §II.1.ii above):

Ref.	D05	ℵ01/B03
14.19	καὶ ἐπῆλθάν τινες [Ἰουδαῖοι ἀπὸ (Ἰκονίου καὶ Ἀντιοχείας)]	ἐπῆλθαν δὲ ↑ [(ἀπὸ Ἀντιοχείας καὶ Ἰκονίου) Ἰουδαῖοι]

D05 gives greater prominence to the subject, both by placing Ἰουδαῖοι before the adverbial phrase and by qualifying it with τινες.

18.27 In an extended D05 reading that is absent from ℵ01/B03, the subject of the verb, τινες Κορίνθιοι, is again given prominence by being introduced in a participial clause before the main verb: ἐν δὲ τῇ Ἐφέσῳ ἐπιδημοῦντές τινες Κορίνθιοι καὶ ἀκούσαντες αὐτοῦ παρεκάλουν διελθεῖν σὺν αὐτοῖς..., D05

21.15 While ℵ01/B03 have μετὰ δὲ τὰς [ἡμέρας ταύτας], D05 reads μετὰ δὲ [τινας ἡμέρας]. The word order of the former is the one usually employed in Acts to indicate the general sequence of events (see §III.6.i below on demonstratives). The narrator of D05 underlines that Paul and his company spent some more time at Caesarea before leaving for Jerusalem. There are other details, too, that are given by the D05 narrator concerning the departure of Paul from Caesarea[53] and that combine to make more of Caesarea as the point of departure for the highly significant visit to Jerusalem. μετὰ δὲ τινας ἡμέρας, then, is a coherent part of a larger picture. The verse can be compared with the use of τις at 17.19D05 where the additional reference to time is simply an indication of a lapse of time and τις follows the noun: μετὰ δὲ ἡμέρας τινας.

b) Post-noun

D05 has five more occurrences of τις not present in ℵ01/B03, where the adjective follows the noun:

7.58; 8.27; 17.19; 19.9; 20.16

Where τις follows the noun, the noun is not salient. 8.27 and 17.19 have already been mentioned in the preceding discussion.

7.58; 19.9 The use of τις by D05 draws attention to both the characters in question but in an understated way. At 7.58, παρὰ τοὺς πόδας νεανίου τινός, 'at the feet of a certain young man' the understatement provides an instance of narrative irony since this is the first mention of someone whom the hearers know will subsequently become the central character of the narrative. At 19.9, ἐν τῇ σχολῇ τυραννίου τινὸς, 'in the school of a certain little tyrant', the significance of 'the little tyrant' is likewise ironic, coupled as it is in the D05 text of this verse with the time phrase ἀπὸ ὥρας πέμπτης ἕως δεκάτης (see discussion §II.1.ii above).[54]

20.16 Paul is the indirect object of an impersonal verb in the Bezan text: μήποτε γενηθῇ αὐτῷ κατάσχεσις τις ἐν τῇ Ἀσίᾳ, 'lest there be some delay for him'. It is not the subject (the delay) that is in focus, although some attention is drawn to it in D05 by the use of τις following κατάσχεσις. The ℵ01/B03 text uses an active verb χρονοτριβῆσαι in place of the D05 clause, which has a similar effect of maintaining Paul in focus but the importance to Paul of a possible delay is not so apparent.

---

[53] In 21.15, the participle in D05 is from the verb 'to say farewell' (ἀποταξάμενοι) rather than 'to make preparations' (ἐπισκεθασάμενοι) as in ℵ01/B03. Only the first letters of the following verse are visible in the Greek text of D05 but it can be deduced with the help of the Latin side that the party is described as going 'from (ἐκ)' Caesarea, with a multitude of variant readings apparent in the Latin text that relates the remainder of the journey.

[54] The D05 detail concerning the time at which Paul lectured has been taken as an authentic piece of local knowledge (Metzger, *Commentary*, 417), in much the same way as have the 'seven steps' of Acts 12.10 (*Commentary*, 347). As suggested at §II.1.ii, the time reference may be an oblique way of criticizing Paul by specifying that he taught at the hottest time of the day; alternatively, it may be a veiled allusion to something that Theophilus would have understood but that is not accessible to a modern reader.

III.6. Demonstratives

While the position of the demonstrative adjective in relation to the noun is variable, there emerge clear reasons for the different positions of the adjective.

III.6.i In the common text

The large number of demonstrative adjectives in Acts allows patterns to be identified with relative ease.

a) Following the noun

By far the most usual order of demonstrative adjective and noun in the common text is for the adjective to be placed after the noun it qualifies (39 times, to eight times when the demonstrative adjective precedes the noun). This order has been found to be the more usual one in biblical Greek generally.[55] In these instances, 'this' and 'that', οὗτος and ἐκεῖνος, are a way of indicating which is the noun in question, and that it is known because it has just been referred to (e.g. 15.2, περὶ τοῦ ζητήματος τούτου, 'about this matter'); or is about to be presented (e.g. 2.22, ἀκούσατε τοὺς λόγους τούτους, 'hear these words'); or can be pointed to as the speaker talks (e.g. 19.37, ἠγάγετε γὰρ τοὺς ἄνδρας τούτους, 'you have brought these men').

Demonstrative adjectives following the noun in a time expression are discussed in §III.6.i.c below because they constitute a special case.

b) Preceding the noun

When the demonstrative adjective precedes the noun, it has an emphatic value in that it implies 'this rather than another' or 'this very person'. An example can be seen at 19.25 where, in the phrase ἐκ ταύτης τῆς ἐργασίας ἡ εὐπορία ἡμῖν ἐστιν, 'from this trade we make our living', the importance of the trade under threat is underlined (doubly, in fact, because it is also placed at the front of the clause). Similarly, at 16.20, the subject of the sentence, οὗτοι οἱ ἄνθρωποι ἐκταράσσουσιν ἡμῶν τὴν πόλιν, 'these men', is also given prominence by being placed at the beginning of the clause before the verb and by the demonstrative being in first position; the emphasis is echoed by the naturally salient position of the final participle at the end of the clause, Ἰουδαῖοι ὑπάρχοντες, 'being Jews'. The same emphasis is seen when Jesus is proclaimed as the focus of attention at 1.11 and 2.36: οὗτος ὁ Ἰησοῦς.

Demonstrative adjectives that precede the noun in a time expression are discussed in the next section because again, they are a special case.

c) Expressions of time

Phrases denoting the time of an event and that include a demonstrative adjective require careful examination. Most time phrases with a demonstrative adjective occur in a summary of events, or at the beginning of a new development, and serve the

---

[55] Davison, 'New Testament Greek Word Order', 24; Turner, *Syntax*, 193, 349; Winer, *Grammar*, 686.

purpose of helping the story to move on. They are often found in first position in the sentence and as such provide a new basis for the following events.

When the demonstrative is placed after the time noun, it is the straightforward sequence of events that is being described (1.15, ἐν ταῖς ἡμέραις ταύταις, 'in these days'; 7.41, ἐν ταῖς ἡμέραις ἐκείναις, 'in those days'; 12.6, τῇ νυκτὶ ἐκείνῃ, 'on that night'; 19.23, κατὰ τὸν καιρὸν ἐκεῖνον, 'about that time'). There is no need to emphasize the particular time since it is not of special significance nor is there any possibility of confusion. The only exception to this pattern is found at 1.6, which is discussed at the end of this section.

The demonstrative is found before the time noun in special circumstances. It happens when a new event is of special importance or apparently represents something very different from the event just related, and yet (and this is the crucial thing) the narrator wishes to connect it closely with the previous incident. The chronology is thus underlined for the purpose of the narrative; there is an insistence on the particular time at which a thing happened. This is the case at 8.1, Ἐγένετο δὲ ἐν ἐκείνῃ τῇ ἡμέρᾳ διωγμὸς μέγας, '... on that very day'; 11.27, Ἐν ταύταις δὲ ταῖς ἡμέραις, 'it was in these days'; 12.1, κατ' ἐκεῖνον δὲ τὸν καιρόν, 'it was around that time'. The persecution at 8.1 represents a major shift of direction in the activities of the Church and Luke associates its occurrence directly with the preceding death of Stephen by the emphatic time expression. The timing of the arrival of the prophets who had come from the Jerusalem church (11.27) is similarly carefully linked to the earliest days of the church in Antioch. At 12.1, the persecution of the Jerusalem church by Herod appears to be a completely new developement but it is closely connected, by the underlining of the timing of his hostility, to the visit of Barnabas and Saul who have come from Antioch with financial help for the brethren. The sequence of events from the founding of the Antioch church through Herod's persecution to his eventual death is being shown by Luke to be more than coincidental. In all of these cases, the exact timing is not necessarily historically accurate; in emphasizing the timing of events, Luke's concern is not to situate them in 'real time' but to show how incidents and developments in the early days of the Church were intertwined from a theological perspective.[56]

On three occasions, the demonstrative adjective is read before the time noun where no connection is being made with a previous event but the reference to 'these days' is to the present time: 1.5, οὐ μετὰ πολλὰς ταύτας ἡμέρας, 'not many days from now'; 5.36; 21.38, πρὸ τούτων τῶν ἡμερῶν, 'before these present times'. The pre-noun position of the adjective serves to makes it clear that 'these days' means 'the present time'. This use of the pre-noun position is distinguished from the other use discussed above (a new development, time being underlined) by the context. When 'the present time' is intended in the above cases, there is no previous time to which the demonstrative could refer.

---

[56] From the point of view of Luke, literal or actual time is not as important as the narrative time which he assigns to events. This is not the mark of a bad or a dishonest historian, but it does reflect a typically Jewish concept of history and of reality, whereby the spiritual or symbolic association between events and people is more significant, more 'real', than a literal association might be. For a presentation of the Jewish view of history and time, see e.g. Jonathan Sacks, *Crisis and Covenant* (Manchester: Manchester University Press, 1992), 208–46.

This function of the pre-noun position to express the present can help to clarify the reason for the place of the demonstrative adjective after the noun at 1.6, ἐν τῷ χρόνῳ τούτῳ, 'at that time'. The disciples enquire of Jesus whether the time when the Holy Spirit will come (1.5) is also the time when the kingdom will be restored to Israel (or, something will be restored to the kingdom of Israel, D05; for discussion of this variant reading, see Chapter 3, §II.2.i). τούτῳ could have been expected before the noun χρόνῳ since it expresses the purpose of the question and means 'this time rather than any other' (cf. §III.6.i.b above). However, if the demonstrative had been placed before the noun (giving ἐν χρόνῳ τῷ τούτῳ), it could have been understood to mean 'now, at the present time' (as at 1.5; 5.36; 21.38). Clearly, this is not the meaning intended by the disciples who are referring rather to the time when they will be baptized in the Holy Spirit. The potential ambiguity may be the reason for the demonstrative being placed after the noun in this case.

III.6.ii Variant readings

There are only three instances where the position of the demonstrative adjective varies:

2.41; 6.1; 7.60

D05 has the adjective before the noun in all three cases; B03 shares the reading of D05 at 7.60. A similar picture, of D05 tending to have the adjective in the emphatic position where there are differences between the MSS, was also seen with respect to variant readings concerning general adjectives (see §III.1.ii above). The first two references are expressions of time.

2.41 In the summary describing the response to Peter's speech, the Bezan text stresses that the addition of 3,000 people happened on the very same day as the day of Pentecost, by placing the demonstrative before the noun, ἐν ἐκείνῃ τῇ ἡμέρᾳ.

6.1 The position of the demonstrative before the time noun in D05, Ἐν δὲ ταύταις ταῖς ἡμέραις, is in keeping with the new development of events in the Jerusalem church. The reading of ℵ01/B03, which does not place the adjective in front of the noun, suggests that in that text the new episode concerning the problems of table-service is viewed as only loosely connected on the basis of time to the problems faced by the apostles with the Sanhedrin authorities. The Bezan editor, in contrast, is using the pre-noun position to tie the new episode more closely to previous events. The Bezan readings that occur in the rest of this episode confirm that the author did indeed make a connection (see §II.4.iii.a above). In other words, this variant reading confirms that the post-noun position of the demonstrative in a time expression introducing a new development is appropriate unless the new development is to be signalled as being closely related to the previous action.

7.60 The context in this verse is Stephen's cry to God before his death:

B03/D05 κύριε, μὴ στήσῃς αὐτοῖς ταύτην τὴν ἁμαρτίαν (τὴν ἁμαρτίαν ταύτην, ℵ01)

The implication of the pre-noun position of the demonstrative adjective is that Stephen's reference is to 'this sin rather than any other', that is, the particular sin of killing him. To represent Stephen as asking for only this one wrongdoing not be held against his persecutors may have been seen as potentially contentious: what, it may have been asked, are the other sins of the Jews that Stephen is excluding from his request? What are the implications of his singling out this one crime? The answers to such theological difficulties are best found within a Jewish framework; the difficulties are avoided by placing the demonstrative in simple deictic position after the noun, as in ℵ01.

III.6.iii Additional readings

There are no further occurrences of a demonstrative adjective qualifying a noun in the text of ℵ01/B03; there are seven in the text of D05:

    2.1; 3.1; 4.1; 5.39; 6.5; 17.30; 19.38

In all of these instances, the demonstrative follows the noun. Three of them (6.5; 17.30; 19.38) qualify a noun that exists in both texts; the other four (2.1; 3.1; 4.1; 5.39) are part of a whole phrase absent from the other text. The first two of the latter group are expressions of time in the early chapters of Acts where the time-scale is large and events are painted on a broad canvas. With the demonstrative in the non-emphatic position, the time phrases add an element of structure to the account without making close connections between the events. All the other additional occurrences are examples of simple deixis and as such follow the pattern observed in the common text.

Considering the picture that can be built up of the use of the demonstrative adjective overall, it is apparent that the Bezan narrator displays a greater interest in the relationships between episodes of the narrative than does the ℵ01/B03 text. It makes use of the demonstrative adjective in time phrases to express a narrative purpose by signalling links and ties between incidents and in so doing follows consistently the pattern of use observable in the common text. In its readings of the demonstrative in other types of phrases, it likewise follows the regular pattern of noun–demonstrative unless the demonstrative is used emphatically in some way.

III.7 Conclusions on the word order of adjectives in the noun phrase

When general descriptive adjectives follow the noun they qualify, they are not of special importance unless in an arthrous construction, in which case they have an explanatory function. In contrast, the position of the adjective in front of the noun often draws attention to it, especially if the noun is anarthrous, for a reason that may depend on the co-text or on the situation of the discourse. The usual position of other types of adjectival modifiers does not necessarily reflect that of general adjectives, but the underlying highlighting function of the fronted position can be seen to be operative in most cases. In other words, it looks as if the reason for the flexibility in the pre- or post-noun position among the various adjectival modifiers is not that they follow different rules, but that the basic principle itself governing the order of nouns and qualifying adjectives causes them to occupy a different position. In addition, it emerges that the position of πᾶς, τις, numbers and demonstratives in relation to the noun is governed by a variety of conditions that do not apply to general descriptive adjectives.[57] Although these adjectival modifiers all fall into the same syntactic category, there are semantic factors that affect their place in relation to the noun they qualify and that cause the usual position they occupy in the noun phrase to vary.

IV. General conclusions

The differences in word order occurring within the noun phrase in the MSS studied can generally be accounted for. Sometimes, explanations are to be found in the immediate co-text of the variant where there are other differences that reflect the way in which the story is being told. At other times, the explanation lies in the wider context of the book of Acts where there is a difference in the overall perspective of the separate textual traditions. In particular, there is a striking number of variants in D05 that reflect a preoccupation with matters of typically Jewish concern. There remain some instances of word order variation that are difficult to account for, or whose significance appears to depend on questions of interpretation that cannot be discussed fully in this present study.

What the investigation carried out here ascertains is that the word order patterns of the respective texts tend to conform to the patterns that can be established from an examination of the common text, with variation arising because of varying intentions rather than varying stylistic habits. To say that a scribe 'preferred' one order of words rather than another is an inadequate explanation, nor is it necessary. That is because reasons can be seen for variation in word order even within the common text and where there is variation between the readings of the MSS, similar reasons can be appealed to in order to account for the differences in word order.

At places of variation, it is frequently D05 that displays a more emphatic word order, whether it be for purposes of focusing attention on a character, or drawing a contrast, or linking episodes together. The ℵ01/B03 text, in comparison, tells a more straightforward story inasmuch as it has a less structured narrative. It could be argued that in the successive tellings of any story, the tendency is to move from a more emphatic, more polemical form to a less elaborate and more neutral form. If this position can be substantiated, then there is evidence in this analysis of word order

---

[57] Porter ('Word Order and Clause Structure', 183, n. 22) finds that the variety of unmarked word order followed by different NT authors for the different kinds of adjectival modifiers in Greek does not support the description of universal word order features given by Greenberg ('Some Universals of Grammar', 86-7). In Acts, in fact, where the descriptive adjective usually follows the noun, the observation of Greenberg's 'universal 19' is applicable: 'When the general rule is that the descriptive adjective follows [the noun], there may be a minority of adjectives which usually precede...'. It seems to be the semantic content of certain non-descriptive adjectives that causes them to appear to behave differently to more generally descriptive adjectives.

variation that the text of D05 pre-dates that of the Alexandrian MSS and that subsequent editors have toned the Bezan account down.[58]

Where additional readings are present, they are almost all to be found in the D05 text. Here, the unmarked word order is more prominent; where the marked order is used, the reason for it can usually be found either within the local or the wider context. This finding is clear proof that the marked order that tends to be typical of the D05 text at places of variation is not simply 'scribal preference'. Rather, it can be seen as representing the mark of an narrator who had in mind a clear purpose for his narrative, which he was well able to express through the subtleties of Greek word order.

---

[58] A comparison of the word order in parts of Mark's Gospel common to that of Luke shows that it is Mark that generally has a more emphatic word order (Elliott, 'The Position of the Verb', 142–4). On the assumption that Luke's Gospel dates from after the writing of the Gospel of Mark, this confirms the conclusions about the more emphatic word order belonging to the primary rather than the secondary text.

5

Expressions for the Holy Spirit[1]

Divine names and titles in the Luke's writing have been subject to a fair bit of alteration in the course of the NT textual history and there are many variant readings in the MSS under consideration in this study: Codex Sinaiticus (א01), Codex Vaticanus (B03) and Codex Bezae (D05). The terms used to designate God, Jesus and the Holy Spirit are all extensively affected. It is commonly supposed that variation crept in as ecclesiastical practices developed and so influenced the NT text through its use as a liturgical document. While this is most certainly true, the situation is much more complex than that and any explanation of it needs to take account of linguistic factors. This chapter will look at forms of expression used to refer to the Holy Spirit, seeking to establish Luke's patterns of usage. Capitals are used for references in English to the Holy Spirit in order to distinguish the divine from the human spirit. The study will draw on the findings set out in earlier chapters concerning both the use of the article (Chapter 2) and word order (Chapter 4). Word order is an issue because of the variation in the position of the adjective ἅγιον, the presence of which also varies; there is further variation in the presence or absence of the article. Detailed exegetical discussion of passages of Acts mentioned here can be found in the commentary co-authored by myself and Josep Rius-Camps.[2]

While exegetical issues are inevitably bound up with some of the linguistic questions, discussions concerning the theology of the Holy Spirit rarely treat the subject of the different forms of expression used to refer to the Spirit, except for occasional mention of the possible significance of the article.[3] The variant readings are a phenomenon more often alluded to in textual discussions, in which certain generalized ideas tend to be repeated, principally that the 'Western' text (in which is included D05) has a tendency to add mentions of the Spirit, especially with the adjective ἅγιον, and that this tendency reflects a late ecclesiastical tradition rather than the original text.[4] The situation is, in

---

[1] A study of the different forms of expression that Luke uses to speak of the Holy Spirit in Acts was first published in my *The Bezan Text of Acts: A Contribution of Discourse Analysis to Textual Criticism* (JSNTSup. 236; Sheffield: SAP, 2002), Chapter 5, 145–72. The work has been updated and developed here to give some further attention to the way Luke refers to the divine Spirit in his Gospel.
[2] Josep Rius-Camps & Jenny Read-Heimerdinger, *The Message of Acts in Codex Bezae: A Comparison with the Alexandrian Tradition*. 4 vols (JSNTSup 257/LNTS 302, 365, 415; London: T&T Clark, 2004–09).
[3] M. M. B. Turner, *Power from on High: The Spirit in Israel's Restoration and Witness in Luke-Acts* (Sheffield: SAP, 1996), reviewed all the major theological positions in an exhaustive analysis of the references to the Spirit in Luke-Acts. See also M.M.B. Turner, 'The Work of the Holy Spirit in Luke-Acts', *Word & World* 23 (2003): 146–53.

fact, far from being as settled as is often implied. As a clearer picture is being sought, it will be helpful to bear in mind two points. The first is that the 'Western' text represents much too diverse a tradition for the label to be interchangeable with any one MS, and D05 in particular does not, as the analysis will show, demonstrate a preference for the use of ἅγιον with πνεῦμα. Secondly, it is simplistic to state that modifications were made to Luke's text in order to bring it into line with the practice of the established Church, for the practices that influenced the inclusion of ἅγιον with the mention of πνεῦμα may just as well be Jewish as later Christian.

I. Identification of expressions used

Before any analysis of the problem can be successfully undertaken, the references to the Spirit in the writings of Luke need to be identified, as they stand in the common text as well as the variant readings.[5] The lists for the Gospel and Acts are set out in Table 5.1, which notes who makes mention of the Spirit and to whom, and also the context of the mention, for these are all factors that often have an influence on linguistic choices. At places of variant reading, the familiar ℵ01/B03 text is given first with the D05 reading underneath.

I.1 In the common text

The lists of Table 5.1 show that three references to the divine Spirit are made with a singular expression that occurs only once in each book: Lk.4.18 (τὸ D05) πνεῦμα (τοῦ D05) κυρίου; Acts 5.9 τὸ πνεῦμα (τοῦ D05) κυρίου; 16.7 τὸ πνεῦμα Ἰησοῦ. Since specific exegetical issues are involved in these mentions of the Spirit, they will not be included in the analysis that follows. Three mentions of τὸ πνεῦμα at Acts 18.25; 19.21; 20.22, which may be interpreted as meaning the human rather than the divine spirit, are likewise not included in the count.

In two further instances in Acts at 2.17,18, the personal pronoun μοῦ qualifies the Spirit. Lest it be thought that it is the possessive pronoun that causes the absence of the adective, comparison should be made with 1 Thess. 4.8 ('his Holy Spirit') and Tg. Isa.

---

[4] See B. M. Metzger, *A Textual Commentary on the Greek New Testament*, 2nd edn (1975; Stuttgartt: Deutsche Bibelgesellschaft, 1994), 225–6. Matthew Black notably devoted one study entirely to an examination of Western readings concerning the Holy Spirit in Acts, 'The Holy Spirit in the Western Text of Acts', in *New Testament Textual Criticism: Its Significance for Exegesis. Essays in Honour of B. M. Metzger*, ed. E. J. Epp and G. D. Fee (Oxford: Clarendon Press, 1981), 159–76. E. J. Epp, *The Theological Tendency of Codex Bezae Cantabrigiensis in Acts* (Cambridge: CUP, 1966), 116, states that 'D shows a preference for the formal expression "the Holy Spirit"'. Black speaks of the 'D text ... employing its usual fuller expression "Holy Spirit"' ('The Holy Spirit', 161). Boismard and Lamouille have a rather different perspective on the matter, for their interpretation of the MS evidence is that the purest (earliest) form of their reconstruction of the Western text never reads ἅγιον before πνεῦμα (M.-E. Boismard and A. Lamouille, *Le texte occidental des Actes des Apôtres: Reconstitution et réhabilitation*, 2 vols (Paris: Editions Recherche sur les Civilisations, 1984), I, 107).

[5] J. H. E. Hull, *The Holy Spirit in the Acts of the Apostles* (London: Lutterworth Press, 1967), provides an analysis of the references to the Holy Spirit based on the N-A[25] text. Although his presentation shows the presence or absence of the article it does not indicate the position of the adjective.

Table 5.1 Expressions referring to the Holy Spirit

Ref.	Expression	Speaker–hearer	Context
LUKE			
1.15	πνεῦμα ἅγιον	angel–Zacariah	will be filled with the HS
1.35	πνεῦμα ἅγιον	angel–Mary	the HS will come on Mary
1.41	πνεῦμα ἅγιον	narrator	was filled with the HS
1.67	πνεῦμα ἅγιον	narrator	was filled with the HS
2.25ℵ01/B03	πνεῦμα ἦν ἅγιον	narrator	the HS was on Simeon
D05	πνεῦμα ἅγιον		
2.26	τὸ πνεῦμα τὸ ἅγιον	narrator	revealed by the HS
2.27	τὸ πνεῦμα	narrator	had gone in the Spirit
3.16	πνεῦμα ἅγιον	John the Baptist–people	will baptize with the HS
3.22	τὸ πνεῦμα τὸ ἅγιον	narrator	the HS came down on Jesus
4.1a	πνεῦμα ἅγιον	narrator	full of the HS
4.1b	τὸ πνεῦμα	narrator	taken by the Spirit
4.14	τὸ πνεῦμα	narrator	in the power of the Spirit
4.18ℵ01/B03	πνεῦμα κυρίου	Jesus–synagogue	The Spirit of the Lord is upon me
D05	τὸ πνεῦμα τοῦ κυρίου		(Isaiah)
10.21	τὸ πνεῦμα τὸ ἅγιον	narrator	rejoiced in the HS
11.13ℵ01/B03	πνεῦμα ἅγιον	Jesus–disciples	the father will give the HS
12.10ℵ01/B03	τὸ ἅγιον πνεῦμα	Jesus–disciples	speaking against the HS
D05	τὸ πνεῦμα τὸ ἅγιον		
12.12	τὸ ἅγιον πνεῦμα	Jesus–disciples	the HS will teach them what to say
ACTS			
1.2	πνεῦμα ἅγιον	narrator	Jesus instructed the apostles through the HS
1.5	πνεῦμα ἅγιον	Jesus–apostles	baptized with the HS
1.8	τὸ ἅγιον πνεῦμα	Jesus–apostles	the HS will come on them
1.16	τὸ πνεῦμα τὸ ἅγιον	Peter–120 disciples	the HS foretold through the Scriptures
2.4	πνεῦμα ἅγιον	narrator	all were filled with the HS
2.17	τὸ πνεῦμά μου	Peter–Jews	the Lord pours out his Spirit (Joel)
2.18	τὸ πνεῦμά μου	Peter–Jews	the Lord pours out his Spirit (Joel)
2.33ℵ01/B03	τὸ πνεῦμα τὸ ἅγιον	Peter–Jews	Jesus has received the promise of the HS
D05	τὸ ἅγιον πνεῦμα		
2.38	τὸ ἅγιον πνεῦμα	Peter–Jews	the gift of the HS
4.8	πνεῦμα ἅγιον	narrator	Peter filled with the HS
4.25	πνεῦμα ἅγιον	apostles–God	God spoke through the HS
4.31	τὸ ἅγιον πνεῦμα	narrator	all were filled with the HS
5.3ℵ01/B03	τὸ πνεῦμα τὸ ἅγιον	Peter–Ananias	Ananias deceived the HS
D05	τὸ ἅγιον πνεῦμα		
5.9ℵ01/B03	τὸ πνεῦμα κυρίου	Peter–Sapphira	Ananias and Sapphira tested the Spirit of the Lord
D05	τὸ πνεῦμα τοῦ κυρίου		
5.32	τὸ πνεῦμα τὸ ἅγιον	Peter–Sanhedrin	God gave the HS who is a witness
6.3	πνεῦμα	apostles–other disciples	7 men full of the Spirit
6.5	πνεῦμα ἅγιον	narrator	Stephen full of the HS
6.10ℵ01/B03	τὸ πνεῦμα	narrator	the (H)Spirit with which Stephen spoke
D05	τὸ πνεῦμα τὸ ἅγιον		
7.51	τὸ πνεῦμα τὸ ἅγιον	Stephen–Jews	they resist the HS
7.55	πνεῦμα ἅγιον	narrator	Stephen full of the HS
8.15	πνεῦμα ἅγιον	narrator	the Samaritans will receive the HS
8.17	πνεῦμα ἅγιον	narrator	the Samaritans received the HS

(*Continued*)

Table 5.1 Continued

Ref.	Expression	Speaker-hearer	Context
8.18א01/B03	τὸ πνεῦμα	narrator	Simon saw that the (H)Spirit was given
D05	τὸ πνεῦμα τὸ ἅγιον		
8.19	πνεῦμα ἅγιον	Simon Magus–Peter	people will receive the HS
8.29	τὸ πνεῦμα	narrator	the Spirit spoke to Philip
10.19	τὸ πνεῦμα	narrator	the Spirit spoke to Peter
10.38א01/B03	πνεῦμα ἅγιον	Peter–Cornelius	God anointed Jesus with the HS
D05	ἅγιον πνεῦμα		
10.44	τὸ πνεῦμα τὸ ἅγιον	narrator	the HS fell on Cornelius' house
10.45א01	τὸ ἅγιον πνεῦμα	narrator	the gift of the HS was poured out on Gentiles
B03	τὸ πνεῦμα τὸ ἅγιον		
D05	τὸ πνεῦμα ἅγιον		
10.47	τὸ πνεῦμα τὸ ἅγιον	Peter–brethren from Joppa	Gentiles have received the HS
11.12	τὸ πνεῦμα	Peter–Jerusalem church	the Spirit had spoken to Peter
11.15	τὸ πνεῦμα τὸ ἅγιον	Peter–Jerusalem church	the HS fell on Gentiles
11.16	πνεῦμα ἅγιον	Peter–Jerusalem church	baptism in the HS
11.17D05	πνεῦμα ἅγιον	Peter–Jerusalem church	God gave the HS to those believing in Jesus
11.24	πνεῦμα ἅγιον	narrator	Barnabas full of the HS
11.28	τὸ πνεῦμα	narrator	Agabus spoke through the Spirit
13.2	τὸ πνεῦμα τὸ ἅγιον	narrator	the HS spoke
13.4א01/B03	τὸ ἅγιον πνεῦμα	narrator	men sent out by the HS
D05	τὸ πνεῦμα ἅγιον		
13.9	πνεῦμα ἅγιον	narrator	Paul filled with the HS
13.52	πνεῦμα ἅγιον	narrator	the disciples were filled with the HS
15.7D05	πνεῦμα	narrator	Peter stood up in the Spirit
15.8	τὸ πνεῦμα τὸ ἅγιον	Peter–Jerusalem church	God gave the HS to Gentiles
15.28א01/B03	τὸ πνεῦμα τὸ ἅγιον	apostles–Antioch church	it was decided by the HS
D05	τὸ ἅγιον πνεῦμα		
15.29D05	τὸ ἅγιον πνεῦμα	apostles–Antioch church	sustained by the HS
15.32D05	πνεῦμα ἅγιον	narrator	Judas and Silas full of the HS
16.6	τὸ ἅγιον πνεῦμα	narrator	prevented by the HS
16.7	τὸ πνεῦμα Ἰησοῦ	narrator	the Spirit of Jesus did not allow
18.25	τὸ πνεῦμα	narrator	Apollo(nius) fervent in the Spirit/spirit
19.1D05	τὸ πνεῦμα	narrator	the Spirit spoke to Paul
19.2a	πνεῦμα ἅγιον	Paul–Ephesian disciples	did they receive the HS?
19.2b	πνεῦμα ἅγιον	Ephesian disciples–Paul	the HS exists א01/B03/is received D05
19.6	τὸ πνεῦμα τὸ ἅγιον	narrator	the HS fell upon the Ephesians
19.21	τὸ πνεῦμα	narrator	Paul resolved in the Spirit/spirit
20.3D05	τὸ πνεῦμα	narrator	the Spirit spoke to Paul
20.22	τὸ πνεῦμα	Paul–Ephesian elders	Paul is bound by the Spirit/spirit
20.23א01/B03	τὸ πνεῦμα τὸ ἅγιον	Paul–Ephesian elders	the HS testifies to Paul
D05	τὸ ἅγιον πνεῦμα		
20.28א01/B03	τὸ πνεῦμα τὸ ἅγιον	Paul–Ephesian elders	the HS placed them as overseers
D05	τὸ ἅγιον πνεῦμα		
21.11	τὸ πνεῦμα τὸ ἅγιον	Agabus–Paul	thus says the HS

42.1b; 44.3b; 59.21 ('my Holy Spirit') where the adjective 'holy' is included along with the pronoun; these two personal references are therefore included in the analysis.

In summary, Luke makes use of four recurring expressions, whose frequency in the text common to ℵ01, B03 and D05 is displayed in Table 5.2.

Table **5.2** Four recurring expressions for the Holy Spirit

Form	Gospel	Acts
A: τὸ πνεῦμα	3	6
B: πνεῦμα ἅγιον	7	17
C: τὸ πνεῦμα τὸ ἅγιον	3	10
D: τὸ ἅγιον πνεῦμα	1	4
Total	14	37

In Luke's writings overall, there are thus 51 references to the Holy Spirit for which the form of expression is the same in ℵ01, B03 and D05.

I.2 Variant readings

For all that the wording of the references to the Holy Spirit varies in a number of places, the similarity between the three MSS under consideration is striking. Compared with the 51 references in common, there are only 12 others that have a variant reading. The pattern of variant readings is set out in Table 5.3, where the letters refer to categories of forms listed in Table 5.2.

The following comments on the variants may be made:

- At Lk. 2.25, ℵ01/B03 express the holiness of the Spirit on Zachariah as a predicate rather than with the adjective. πνεῦμα is used without the article, a unique occurrence (see §IV below).
- D05 reads an additional ἅγιον at only two places. At least as significant as these additions are the ten mentions of πνεῦμα common to both texts that D05 does not see a need to qualify (cf. Table 5.1).
- Most variants concern the place of the adjective.
- No variants arise over the presence of the article before πνεῦμα as such except at Lk. 2.25; variants involving the article generally concern the repetition of the article before the adjective in post-position at Acts 10.45; 13.4.

Table **5.3** Variant readings

D05	ℵ01/B03	Ref.
B	A	Lk. 2.25 (ℵ01/B03: πνεῦμα ἦν ἅγιον)
C	A	Acts 6.10; 8.18
C	D	Lk. 12.10
		Acts 10.45 (D05: τὸ πνεῦμα ἅγιον; ℵ01: τὸ ἅγιον πνεῦμα; B03: τὸ πνεῦμα τὸ ἅγιον) 13.4 (D05: τὸ πνεῦμα ἅγιον)
D	B	Acts 10.38
D	C	Acts 2.33; 5.3; 15.28; 20.23,28

Finally, there is one reference in Luke's Gospel read only by ℵ01/B03 and six in Acts read by D05 alone:

Table 5.4 Additional readings

Form	ℵ01/B03	D05
A: (τὸ) πνεῦμα		Acts 15.7; 19.1; 20.3
B: πνεῦμα ἅγιον	Lk. 11.13	Acts 11.17; 15.32
C: τὸ πνεῦμα τὸ ἅγιον		Acts 15.29

At Acts 15.7D05, πνεῦμα is used without the article (cf. Lk. 2.25ℵ01/B03), on which see §V.1.i.b below. It is clear from the additional mentions that D05 does not display a preference for the inclusion of ἅγιον for it has as many additional references without the adjective (form A) as with (B and C).

Preliminary comparison with the forms used in the Jewish Scriptures will make clearer the significance of the forms of expression used by Luke.

II. Expressions used in the Jewish Scriptures

II.1 In the Hebrew and Greek Bible

In the Hebrew Bible (MT), the noun רוּחַ ('spirit') is used on its own to designate the Spirit of God except for three occasions when the Spirit it qualified as 'holy', using the noun קֹדֶשׁ ('holiness'), with possessive suffix, equivalent to 'of his holiness'): Ps. 50.13 (MT); Isa. 63.10,11. In the LXX, the situation is identical, with the Greek expression for the Holy Spirit taking the form τὸ πνεῦμα τὸ ἅγιον (Luke's form C) at each of these three same places. Elsewhere, the divine Spirit is referred to without further qualification.

Questions may be legitimately asked as to when and where 'holy' became associated with 'Spirit' with more frequency than in the Hebrew Bible or the LXX translation for, as was seen in the previous section, by the time of Luke the adjective is usually used, with even a variety of phrase structures. It may be thought that the inclusion of 'holy' must reflect a later Christian understanding deriving from the gift of the Holy Spirit at Pentecost and attributed anachronistically by Luke to the time of the Gospel. Some such supposition may have been the obvious explanation were there not earlier evidence for more extensive use of the adjective 'holy' qualifying the mention of the Spirit of God, evidence that is found notably in the Targum of Isaiah (Tg. Isa.).[6]

---

[6] For an exploration of extra-scriptural influences on the notion of the Spirit in first-century Judaism, see John Levison, *The Spirit in First Century Judaism* (Arbeiten Zur Geschichte Des Antiken Judentums Und Des Urchristentums, 29; Leiden: Brill, 1997).

II.2 In the Isaiah Targum

The relevance of the targums to NT writings has long been recognized. Of particular relevance to the study of the terms used for the Holy Spirit is the Targum to Isaiah where the prophet's theme of divine revelation is reinforced and developed.[7] As God communicates his will, his word, even his presence to the people of Israel, he does so through his Spirit who, in this context, is referred to according to the targumic tradition as the 'Holy Spirit'. The Holy Spirit represents God taking action in relation to man, action that is conveyed by means of the Holy Spirit and through the prophets.[8] The presence of the Holy Spirit with the prophets is an expression of their relationship to God, not their own personal relationship but one that places them between God and the people to whom they are to convey God's message. The prophet is further empowered throught the Holy Spirit to carry out his prophetic task, whether speaking or acting. When the Spirit is mentioned alone without the adjective in Tg. Isa., reference is being made to an aspect of God rather than to the relationship between God and his prophets.[9]

Tg. Isa. is, of course, not alone in presenting the Spirit of God as the Spirit of prophecy for in the Jewish Scriptures generally this is a characteristic of the Spirit,[10] but, unlike the Hebrew text or the LXX, Tg. Isa. includes the word 'holy' as an epithet when the context is one of prophecy. A comparison of the text of Tg. Isa. with that of the MT brings to light four places where 'holy' is read by the targum but not by the Hebrew text: Isa. 40.13a; 42.1b; 44.3b; 59.21. At these four places, the prophetic thrust is thus amplified in Tg. Isa.

Nevertheless, there are other references to the Spirit of God in Isaiah where the context is similarly prophetic and where 'holy' is not added in Tg. Isa., but instead the phrase 'of my Memra' is found, a complex concept embodying the principal notion of the word of God (Isa. 30.1; 34.16; 48.16; 63.24).[11] Again, the declaration of Isa. 61.1, attributed to Jesus by Luke ('The Spirit of the Lord is upon me' Lk. 4.18), where the context is so obviously prophetic, is modified to become: 'A spirit of prophecy before the Lord God is upon me'.

In addition, at the two places noted above where 'holy' is used with the Spirit in both the Hebrew and the LXX text of Isaiah (Isa. 63.10,11), Tg. Isa. curiously does not use the adjective but accentuates the nature of the prophetic action in other ways:

---

[7] The date of the written Tg. Isa. is uncertain, not least because it is derived from oral sources. Tradition has attributed the written from to Jonathan ben Uzziel in the first century CE. For an excellent edition in English, see Bruce Chilton (ed.), *The Isaiah Targum: Introduction, Translation, Apparatus, Notes* (The Aramaic Bible, II; Edinburgh: T&T Clark, 1987).

[8] See Chilton, *Isaiah Targum*, 49.

[9] See https://www.jewishencyclopedia.com/articles/7833-holy-spirit (last accessed 4/01/2022).

[10] For a summary of the discussions on this point, see R. P. Menzies, *The Development of Early Christian Pneumatology with Special Reference to Luke-Acts*, (JSNT Supplement, 54; Sheffield: JSOT Press, 1991), Part I and, for his own contribution, Part II, chs. 2–5, esp. 99–104 on the targums.

[11] The description 'of my Memra' is commented on in detail by Bruce Chilton in *The Glory of Israel: The Theology and Provenience of the Isaiah Targum* (JSOT Supplement, 23; Sheffield: JSOT Press, 1982), 56–69.

Isa. 63.10 MT 'they rebelled and grieved his Holy Spirit.'
Tg. Isa. 'they provoked the words of his holy prophets.'
63.11MT 'Where is he who put in the midst of them his Holy Spirit?'
Tg. Isa. 'Where is he who made the Memra of his holy prophets dwell among them?'

The lack of consistency in the way in which the references to the Spirit of God are qualified in Tg. Isa. is possibly to be accounted for by the fluidity and mixture of the targumic tradition. In particular, there are strands in Tg. Isa. that can be dated as reflecting the political and religious situation after 70 CE, interwoven with earlier strands from the intertestamental period.[12] In the case of the addition of 'holy' to the references to the Spirit, it is the presence of the expression 'Holy Spirit' in the NT writings that witnesses to its probable appearance at an earlier date in Tg. Isa. In other words, it may be legitimately surmised that when Luke used the adjective ἅγιον in referring to the πνεῦμα, he was not inventing something new but were using an association of terms that was familiar within Aramaic-speaking Jewish circles, not only at the time at which he was writing but already at the time about which he was writing.

One of the forces that seems to have prompted change in the terms used to refer to the Spirit is the progressive awareness of the importance of the role of the Spirit as the means by which God communciated with his people, an awareness that matched the progressive revelation of the Spirit. As this revelation developed, with the coming of the Messiah and the sending of the Spirit in a new way at Pentecost, it may be expected that terms and forms of expression would undergo further modification, with the variant readings possibly testifying to varying degree of conservatism in adapting to the changing language.

III. Essential linguistic considerations

In seeking for some kind of rationale behind the choice of expression at each place in Luke's writings, there are two linguistic matters that need to be considered: the use of the article, and the presence and place of the adjective. These factors are also the variable factors in the variant readings.

III.1 The role of the article

The article is found in the three forms A, C and D: τὸ πνεῦμα, τὸ πνεῦμα τὸ ἅγιον and τὸ ἅγιον πνεῦμα. The presence versus the absence of the article in referring to the Holy Spirit in the NT has been the subject of some discussion, which tends to attribute a theological function to the role of the article. It has been suggested that when the article

---

[12] Chilton, *Isaiah Targum*, pp. xx–xxv; *A Galilean Rabbi and His Bible* (London: SPCK, 1984), 40–6; see also Roger Le Déaut, *The Message of the New Testament and the Aramaic Bible (Targum)*, trans. S. F. Miletic (Rome: Biblical Institute Press, 1982), 25.

is used, the Holy Spirit is active as a person and without the article it is rather the effects of the activity of the Holy Spirit, that is the power, that are being referred to.[13]

This distinction between person and power is tempting in view of the more general nature of the references to the Holy Spirit that are anarthrous (see §V.1.ii.a below). It is questionable, however, that 'God gave the Holy Spirit' (Acts 5.32; 15.8), for example, refers to the Spirit as a person in a way that 'receiving the Holy Spirit' (8.15,17,19; 19.2a,2bD05) does not. It is also doubtful whether a writer such as Luke could consider the Holy Spirit to be an indeterminate divine spirit.[14] There is, moreover, every reason to expect the article to operate as a linguistic rather than a theological marker in view of the conclusions about of the discourse function of the article in other situations (see Chapter 2). The personal nature of the references to the Holy Spirit in Acts makes the analysis of the use of the article with names of persons particularly relevant. In Chapter 2, §II.2, it was argued that the unmarked pattern was for the article to be present; the absence of the article, in cases where the person was known and particular, indicated, in contrast, that the mention was being highlighted, that the person was in some way salient. Applied to the reference to the Holy Spirit, the Spirit is salient when the focus of the sentence is on the mention, or when the Spirit is introduced as new information. On this understanding, an anarthrous reference to the Spirit or the Holy Spirit by no means signals a vague, unidentified spirit. Not only is the Spirit as definite as in a reference with the article but, furthermore, it is being highlighted.

Two qualifying comments need to be made. First, although the absence of the article signifies salience, the opposite is not necessarily true; in other words, it should not be maintained that when the article is present before πνεῦμα the noun is never salient. The absence of the article, when the referent is clearly a particular individual, is the marked form; omission indicates marked salience, but the expression can still enjoy natural salience, with the article present. It will be seen in the analysis that follows that that sometimes is indeed the case.

The second point is that even though salience may be the chief reason for omitting the article before πνεῦμα, it need not be the only one (just as it is not the only factor in the omission of the article before names of people). With πνεῦμα ἅγιον in particular, the possibility of a stereotyped expression will also be seen to be relevant.

---

[13] G. B. Winer (*A Treatise on the Grammar of New Testament Greek*, trans. W. F. Moulton (1882; repr., Eugene, Ore.: Wipf and Stock, 2001) 151) quotes Westcott: 'When the term occurs in this form [i.e. without the article] it marks an operation, or manifestation, or gift of the Spirit, and not the personal Spirit'. In a similar vein, Nigel Turner, *A Grammar of New Testament Greek*. III, *Syntax*, ed. J. H. Moulton (Edinburgh: T&T Clark, 1963), 176, concludes his consideration of the use of the article by saying 'it is not the personal Holy Spirit, but the influence of a divine spirit which is intended, if Luke omits the article'. Turner would furthermore see a preposition or dependent genitive as liable to cause the omission of the article and thus to override his rule (175). The obvious difficulty with this view is that there are many instances of the article being retained in the presence of both prepositions and dependent genitives.

[14] 'An unknown power' is how Turner describes it (*Syntax*, 175). Cf. C. F. D. Moule, *An Idiom-Book of New Testament Greek*, 2nd edn (1953; repr. Cambridge: CUP, 1975) 112–13, who disagrees with Turner.

III.2 Word order

It was seen in Chapter 4 that the flexibility of word order in Greek allows a speaker to move a word from its expected, 'default' position as a way to draw attention to that word. It was observed that when an adjective qualifies a noun without the article it is normally, 'by default', placed after the noun; in contrast, when the noun has the article, the adjective is usually placed before it. Changing the expected order has the effect of underlining the adjective (Chapter 4, §III.1). When applied to the expressions referring to the Holy Spirit, these principles result in the following distinctions:

- *adjective first*
  - with the article (τὸ ἅγιον πνεῦμα): the adjective is not highlighted, but expresses an intrinsic quality of holiness
  - without the article (ἅγιον πνεῦμα): the adjective is highlighted; it draws attention to the holiness of the Spirit.
- *adjective second*
  - with the article (τὸ πνεῦμα τὸ ἅγιον): the adjective is highlighted; the expression is frequently found in the context of an explanation
  - without the article (πνεῦμα ἅγιον): the adjective is not highlighted; the focus is on the Holy Spirit and not on the quality of holiness; the expression is found in stereotypical formulas.

IV. Expressions used in the Gospel of Luke

Luke has 16 references to the Holy Spirit in his Gospel, of which three are variant in the MSS under consideration, and one additional reference in ℵ01/B03. The context on most of these occasions is singularly Jewish, notably in the early chapters, Luke 1–4, where Luke relates the births and early ministries of John the Baptist and Jesus. Then, in Luke 10 Jesus' rejoicing in the Holy Spirit is occasioned by the way the message about the kingdom has been received among the ordinary Jewish people as opposed to the leaders; and in his teaching in Luke 12 he speaks of the Holy Spirit in preparing his followers for persecution from the Jewish authorities.

The simple noun πνεῦμα (A) is used three times of Jesus as he is led into the desert and returns and then when he speaks in the synagogue, although on this last occasion the full expression is 'Spirit of the Lord' (Lk. 4.18). At 2.25, ℵ01/B03 have ἅγιον as a predicate of πνεῦμα to speak of the Spirit upon Simeon being 'holy' before he entered the Temple; this is the only place that such a variant occurs, and its significance would require separate detailed exegetical analysis. D05 uses πνεῦμα ἅγιον (B) here, just as both texts do on the other occasion at 1.35 when the Spirit is said to be upon someone in a general sense. This second form is also the one associated with being full or filled or baptized with the Holy Spirit. At 11.13 ℵ01/B03 where D05 omits any reference to the Holy Spirit, the use of πνεῦμα ἅγιον stands out as unusual for the context of the heavenly father giving good gifts is quite unlike the context of the other occurrences of this form. It is form C, τὸ πνεῦμα τὸ ἅγιον, that is found referring to a specific incident of the Holy Spirit descending upon Jesus (3.22) and the specific nature of the phrase is also seen in the Holy Spirit making a revelation (2.26). This is also the form used to contrast the Holy Spirit with evil spirits (10.21; 12.10), although ℵ01/B03 has τὸ ἅγιον πνεῦμα for the latter. This is again unusual, for elsewhere the form τὸ ἅγιον πνεῦμα (D) is found when it is a matter of the Holy Spirit teaching the disciples in a personal relationship (12.12).

A pattern is apparent in the choice of the forms as they stand in the D05 text of Luke's Gospel: whereas πνεῦμα ἅγιον refers to the effect of the Holy Spirit on a person in a general sense, τὸ πνεῦμα τὸ ἅγιον identifies the Holy Spirit more specifically and τὸ ἅγιον πνεῦμα focuses on the relational aspect. πνεῦμα on its own is more difficult to account for, though the element of anaphoricity may possibly be responsible for the absence of qualifying adjective at 2.27; 4.1b,14. The pattern emerging from the references to the Spirit in the Bezan text of Luke's Gospel will be found to be confirmed when the references in Acts are studied in §V below. A pattern is less apparent for the ℵ01/B03 readings in Luke's Gospel.

V. Expressions used in Acts

In turning to the forms of expression used in Acts to refer to the divine Spirit, the four recurring forms of expression will be considered in turn, examining first the readings shared by ℵ01, B03 and D05, together with any readings read by D05 alone (there being no additional mentions of the Holy Spirit in Acts ℵ01 or B03). A second section will then evaluate the variant readings in the light of that analysis.

V.1 Common text and additional readings

As each expression is examined, the limits of the field of its meaning will be traced by means of the context of its occurrence. These limits will become more clearly defined for each expression as the alternatives are considered and as successive expressions are compared with the former ones. As with all componential analysis, some overlap between the various fields is to be expected and it may well be impossible to define clearly the nuances of meaning within the area of overlap in the absence of a native speaker.

V.1.i τὸ πνεῦμα

a) Common readings

References shared by all three MSS are found at:

2.17,18; 6.3 (anarthrous); 8.29; 10.19; 11.12,28; 20.22

These references to the Spirit occur in narrative as well as in direct speech. The article is present on all occasions except at 6.3.

In the first two of the references at 2.17,18, the Spirit is mentioned in a quotation from Joel 2.28–29 (3.1–2 MT/LXX). As was seen in §II above, the qualification 'holy' is not generally included in the Jewish Scriptures even when the context is as clearly prophetic as it is here.[15]

Aside from these verses, when πνεῦμα is a reference to the Spirit of God, the presence or activity of the Spirit is mentioned in connection with Jesus-believers. Either the Spirit directs them or they act in association with him. The context of these references is not generally prophetic, that is, the person in communication with the Spirit is not required nor empowered to transmit in God's name what they receive. Two examples do, nevertheless, involve some kind of prophetic activity:

6.3 This is the only anarthrous reference, which can be accounted for on the grounds of salience in that 'full of the Spirit' is spelt out as being of decisive importance in selecting the seven men to serve at tables. There is, however, a difficulty in the absence of the adjective with πνεῦμα here, for in every other case, the expression 'full of' is followed by πνεύματος ἁγίου (cf. 6.5). It may be that the coupling of 'full of Spirit' with wisdom has affected the choice of expression here: πλήρεις πνεύματος καὶ σοφίας. A further possibility to be considered, however, is that the apostles avoided qualifying the Spirit as 'holy' here, given their sense of the spiritual inferiority of the Hellenists.[16] The choice to include the adjective ἅγιον at 6.10D05 in the narrator's account of Stephen's way of speaking with the Holy Spirit is thus all more telling, for it implicitly contrasts with the apostles' terms and reinforces the criticism made elsewhere in D05 of the apostles' inflated sense of their importance.

11.28 The context is that of the prophecy of Agabus concerning the impending famine. In such circumstances, the adjective ἅγιον would be expected in the light of the conclusions below (§V.1.ii) on its prophetic force. It is possible that the nature of the prophecy in this case, a straightforward telling of a natural event rather than a revelation of the will of God, has something to do with the absence of the adjective.

b) Additional readings of τὸ πνεῦμα

Three references are found only in D05 at:

15.7D05 (anarthrous); 19.1D05; 20.3D05

The references at 19.1 and 20.3 are similar to those found in the common text where the Spirit gives instructions to Jesus-believers (cf. 8.29; 10.19). The other example is a unique case:

15.7D05 As Peter stands to address the Jerusalem Jesus-believers, the Bezan text reads ἐν πνεύματι after the verb (ἀνέστησεν D05; ἀναστάς ℵ01/B03). There is no other reference like this one in either Luke or Acts: no article, no ἅγιον, and prefaced by ἐν.[17]

---

[15] Tg. Joel reads 'Holy Spirit' at Joel 3.1,2. It should be noted that the D05 text in particular does not adhere to the LXX of Joel 3 generally in this quotation.

[16] This possibility was not considered in Read-Heimerdinger & Rius-Camps, *The Message of Acts* II, 23–4; cf. IV, 26 on 18.25.

[17] The form does arise, however, in Mt. 22.43, 45D05 (cf. Mk 12.36).

The absence of the article can be taken as an indication that the information that Peter acted in the Spirit is highlighted. However, the reason attention is being drawn to this aspect of his speech is precisely because his message is so crucial to the revelation of the divine plan and the examination of the use of the adjective ἅγιον in the next section §V.1.ii shows that the prophetic content would generally call for the adjective to be used. This may be another reference to be grouped with 11.28, where the surprising omission of the adjective in a prophetic context was commented on in the previous section (§V.1.i.a).

V.1.ii πνεῦμα ἅγιον

a) Common readings

All three MSS have this form at:

1.2,5; 2.4; 4.8,25; 6.5; 7.55; 8.15,17,19; 11.16,24; 13.9,52; 19.2a,b

In this form of the expression, the one found most frequently, there is no article and the adjective follows the noun.

Seven of the 16 references are to being filled with, or full of, the Holy Spirit; of the rest, there are two to baptism in the Holy Spirit; five to receiving the Holy Spirit; and two to Jesus/God speaking through the Holy Spirit. Whenever the divine Spirit is mentioned in Acts in any of these ways, the expression always takes the form πνεῦμα ἅγιον (but cf. on 6.3, discussed above (§V.1.i.a). In all cases, the Holy Spirit is referred to in a general way; he is not specifically active or present for a definite action but is rather God's means of self-revelation, very much in the sense of the promises of the Isaiah Targum (see §II.2 above). Furthermore, πνεῦμα ἅγιον occurs in what seem to be stereotyped expressions ('filled with', baptised in', etc.). This particular feature matches the conclusion reached in Chapter 4 on word order (see §III.2 above), namely, that when the adjective follows an anarthrous noun it is often being used as a standard epithet.

The absence of the article can often be accounted for by the salience of the clause in which it is found. The mention of the Holy Spirit is sometimes the main point of the sentence: 2.4; 8.15,17 (cf. 8.18 where it is the laying on of the apostles' hands that is the important factor for Simon); 13.52; 19.2a. At 1.2, διὰ πνεύματος ἁγίου is given exceptional prominence by its position before the relative clause to which it belongs.[18] At several other places, the phrase that includes the mention of the Holy Spirit is placed before the main verb and so is highlighted: 1.5; 4.8,25; 7.55; 13.9. It is also sometimes part of a contrast: 1.5; 11.16. As was pointed out above, however, many of the expressions used are, by their very frequency, stereotyped phrases and it is possible that at some point this has had an influence on the article (see e.g. 8.19, where it could be argued that the salient part of the sentence is the laying on of hands by Simon (+ κἀγώ D05).

---

[18] Other commentators take διὰ πνεύματος ἁγίου with ἐντειλάμενος, but even so the position of the expression between τοῖς ἀποστόλοις and the relative clause that qualifies them, is unusual. Cf. Mk 13.20: διὰ τοὺς ἐκλεκτοὺς οὓς ἐξελέξατο.

The position of the adjective after the noun has also been described as the non-emphatic position for anarthrous nouns (see §III.2 above). This is an indication that the focus is on the presence of the Spirit as Spirit, rather than on the quality of holiness, and reinforces the idea of a fixed expression.

The semantic force of ἅγιον is best seen in comparing the references in Acts that simply have τὸ πνεῦμα with those that use πνεῦμα ἅγιον. In the former case, the interaction that takes place between the Spirit and the people is of a short-term, punctual nature, for a specific purpose that is generally limited to the person with whom the Spirit communicates. In the latter case where the adjective is used, the interaction between the Spirit and the people is of a different nature and on a different scale: it is a declaration or fulfilment of promises made to Israel in the Jewish Scriptures and, more recently, by Jesus during his lifetime. It signals the arrival of a new era. Its effect is to bring about change in people and is frequently accompanied by a demonstration of God's power. People themselves are empowered to act or speak on God's behalf. This includes witnessing to the Messiah, an aspect of revelation that is communicated only after Pentecost as an extension of the contents of the Jewish prophetic preaching.

The same action of the Holy Spirit, signalling the fulfillment of God's promises to send his Spirit, is already evident in the references in Luke's Gospel that use the form πνεῦμα ἅγιον (Table 5.1); except for the ℵ01/B03 variant reading at 11.13, they are all connected with the birth of either John the Baptist or Jesus, or with the outset of Jesus' ministry. They all speak of being filled with the Holy Spirit or of the Holy Spirit coming/being on a person.

On two occasions in Acts, the references are to words spoken through the Holy Spirit (Jesus 1.2; God/David 4.25). In Tg. Isa., the Holy Spirit is the vehicle through which God himself communicates prophecy or teaching, particularly concerning the development of history and the expression πνεῦμα ἅγιον is quite in place here.[19]

Of all the four forms (A, B, C and D), this is the one that appears to be the most securely established for there is only one place of disagreement over its use (10.38, discussed in §V.2.ii below). This fact can be taken as a further indication that πνεῦμα ἅγιον became part of set phrases whereas, in comparison, the other forms of the expression were used more spontaneously, leaving them thereby more open to variation.

b) Additional readings of πνεῦμα ἅγιον

Two references occur in D05 at:

11.17D05; 15.32D05

11.17D05 Peter is asking about the giving of the Holy Spirit to the Gentiles and it is the main point of his question; the use of πνεῦμα ἅγιον is in line with its use in the instances in the common text.

---

[19] The text of 4.25 has attracted a number of variant readings, apparently because of the difficult Greek. Metzger, *Commentary*, 279–80, also finds theological difficulty with text, asking rhetorically, 'Where else does God speak through the Holy Spirit?', to which question one may suggest the answer, 'In the Isaiah Targum'.

15.32D05 The Bezan text makes a point of adding that the prophets Judas and Silas were 'full of the Holy Spirit'. The very fact that it was felt necessary to mention it is a sign of its importance in the sentence. The expression is the expected one given similar examples in the common text.

V.1.iii τὸ πνεῦμα τὸ ἅγιον

a) Common readings

References shared by all three MSS are found at:

1.16; 5.32; 7.51; 10.44,47; 11.15; 13.2; 15.8; 19.6; 21.11

Most of these references fall into three categories: the Holy Spirit falls on people, speaks about future events of spiritual significance or is given by God as a witness. The exceptions are 7.51 (Stephen accuses his Jewish audience of resisting the Holy Spirit) and 10.47 (Peter speaks of the Gentiles who have received the Holy Spirit), but these, too, nevertheless share some of the features that are noted in the following discussion.

What is immediately striking is that, except for 7.51 and 10.47, the Holy Spirit (or God, 15.8) is directly active and is the subject of the verb. The context is frequently one of explanation, expounding a teaching that is new to the hearers (e.g. 5.32; 15.8) and that requires careful introduction. More often than not, τὸ πνεῦμα τὸ ἅγιον occurs in direct speech during the course of an evangelistic proclamation or speech of defence. The context is always prophetic in the sense that the Holy Spirit acts through people to communicate the words or power of God. This is true even at 7.51 where the Holy Spirit is not the subject: ὑμεῖς ἀεὶ τῷ πνεύματι τῷ ἁγίῳ ἀντιπίπτετε, 'you always resist the Holy Spirit', is a reference to the rejection by the Jews of the activity of the Holy Spirit communicated through the prophets. τὸ πνεῦμα τὸ ἅγιον is likewise found in the LXX text of Isa. 63.10 (see §II above) in a context of rejecting the prophets, and also in Lk. 12.10D05 where it is a matter of speaking against the Holy Spirit.

A comparison of 13.2 with what appear at first sight to be similar mentions of the Holy Spirit is illuminating. When the Spirit gives instructions to Jesus-believers at 13.2, ἅγιον is included in post-position whereas elsewhere (e.g. 8.29; 10.19) it is simply the Spirit who gives instructions. There is a difference, however, in the nature of the instructions in each case. Where ἅγιον is used, the Spirit gives directions concerning the sending out of Jesus-believing leaders to preach, about who should go and to whom they should speak, as part of the broad plan of the Church's mission to spead the good news. Where ἅγιον is omitted, in contrast, the instructions are to do with a more immediate situation; they are concerned with a practical detail on a smaller scale than the general direction of the Church's mission.

There are two references in Luke's Gospel that have the expression τὸ πνεῦμα τὸ ἅγιον in similar circumstances in so far as Lk. 2.26 describes a revelation made by the Holy Spirit to Simeon, and Lk. 3.22 the coming down of the Holy Spirit on Jesus.

It is the direct, specific action of the Spirit in these references that may account for the retention of the article. There is often here a quality of particularity about the presence and activity of the Spirit which, by comparison, is absent in the mentions of the Spirit without the article.

The explanatory nature of the references explains the position of the adjective after the noun. In examining the position of the adjective in the chapter on word order (Chapter 4, §III.i), it was noted that an important function of the adjective following an arthrous noun was an explanatory one. To the few examples in Acts of the pattern arthrous noun–adjective noted there can now be added the references to the Holy Spirit that take the form τὸ πνεῦμα τὸ ἅγιον, references that confirm the earlier conclusions.

The occurrence of τὸ πνεῦμα τὸ ἅγιον at 10.47 illustrates the quality of specificity and explanation inherent in the expression. It was noted above (§V.1.ii) in discussing the force of πνεῦμα ἅγιον without the article, that 'receiving the Holy Spirit' does not normally call for the article (cf. 8.15,17,19; 19.2a,2bD05). When Peter, however, asks the Jesus-believers, 'Can anyone forbid water for baptizing these people who have received the Holy Spirit just as we have?', he is first of all referring to a specific manifestation of the Holy Spirit which has just occurred in front of their eyes; secondly, he is spelling out what has happened in order to cause questions to be asked and answers provided. In other words, he is using the phrase 'receive the Holy Spirit' as more than a customary, fixed expression; he is drawing attention to its implications in the present situation.

There are no additonal Bezan readings of τὸ πνεῦμα τὸ ἅγιον, although there are many variant readings which is not surprising since the expression is not being used as a set phrase but spontaneously, and with deliberate care attached to the weight of its connotations. The variant readings are examined below (§V.2).

V.1.iv   τὸ ἅγιον πνεῦμα

a) Common readings

Four references shared by all three MSS:

1.8; 2.38; 4.31; 16.6

This is the most difficult form of expression to explain from the occurences of τὸ ἅγιον πνεῦμα in the common text; fortunately, the relatively large number of variant readings makes a useful contribution to establishing the boundaries of its use as will be seen when they are examined below. Meanwhile, some preliminary observations may be made. It can be noted that all four references have distinct prophetic connotations in so far as the Holy Spirit is mentioned either in fulfilment of God's promises (1.8; 2.38) or as directly associated with the preaching of the gospel (4.31; 16.6). Thus, the presence of ἅγιον is in line with what has already been observed about the force of its meaning when allied with πνεῦμα.

The article can be accounted for at 1.8. and 16.6 by the fact that the mention of the Holy Spirit is not salient information, being contained in a participial clause. The action of the Holy Spirit is also specific in each case. Levinsohn explains the presence of the article in the clause referring to the apostles being 'filled with the Holy Spirit' at 4.31 by describing it as an event that is 'supportive' of the more salient 'they spoke the word of God with boldness'.[20] The verse can be compared to 2.4 where the article is omitted in a very similar phrase referring to the filling of the apostles at Pentecost; on that occasion, the filling of the Holy Spirit was the salient event.

At 2.38, Peter mentions τὸ ἅγιον πνεῦμα as the goal of his explanation to the Jews about the gospel message; in this case, it seems that the reason for retaining the article (explanation) is stronger than that (salience) for omitting it.

It remains to find the reason for the placing of the adjective before the noun. πνεῦμα ἅγιον was found to be to a large extent a fixed, stereotyped expression with the focus on the presence of the Spirit and no particular emphasis on the quality of 'holy' (§V.1.ii). τὸ πνεῦμα τὸ ἅγιον was seen, in contrast, not to be a fixed expression but to be used spontaneously, often within the context of an explanation or declaration about the coming of the Holy Spirit who was portrayed as acting as an agent without an intermediary (§V.1.iii).

The direct intervention of the Holy Spirit also characterizes the references that use the expression τὸ ἅγιον πνεῦμα at 1.8 and 16.6. An important difference, however, which becomes apparent when comparing these two verses with the τὸ πνεῦμα τὸ ἅγιον references, is that the context is not one of explanation. In Jesus' teaching at 1.8, at the point at which he mentions the Holy Spirit he is explaining that the disciples will receive power when the Holy Spirit comes, having already spoken about the baptism in the Holy Spirit with the set phrase ἐν πνεύματι . . . ἁγίῳ at 1.5. His explanation is not about the Holy Spirit himself at 1.8. Similarly, the reference at 16.6 is not specifically an explanation about the Holy Spirit nor an account of his coming. The same can be said of 4.31.

The reference at 2.38 is instructive. Here, Peter says to the Jews that, following repentance and baptism for the forgiveness of sins, λήμψεσθε τὴν δωρεὰν τοῦ ἁγίου πνεύματος, 'you will receive the gift of the Holy Spirit'. It was seen in the previous section that explanatory discourse, especially about the fulfilment of God's purposes in history, usually called for the article and the adjective to be placed in post-position, τὸ πνεῦμα τὸ ἅγιον. The placing of the adjective before the noun in Peter's speech in this instance suggests that his teaching about the gift of the Holy Spirit following repentance and baptism was not something new that his audience needed instruction about; rather, he is telling them what they already know from their traditional teaching.

To summarize: where the Holy Spirit is mentioned in a non-explanatory context, the usual way for Luke to refer to him would seem to be with the adjective ἅγιον before the noun πνεῦμα. This conclusion will be seen to be confirmed by the variant readings. The pattern fits with what has been identified as a typical feature of the fronted position of the adjective before an arthrous noun, namely that the adjective can refer to an intrinsic quality, one that belongs to the noun it qualifies (Chapter 4, §III.1.i.a). This is indeed the case with the Holy Spirit whose very essence, as the Spirit of God, is to be holy. It is only when attention is being drawn to the activity of the Holy Spirit in the

---

[20] Stephen H. Levinsohn, *Discourse Features of New Testament Greek* (Dallas: Summer Institute of Linguistics, 1992), 142.

course of an unfamilar teaching, within a declaration or explanation, that the adjective is separate from the arthrous noun and placed in post-position.

From the limited number of references examined so far, it may be suggested that τὸ ἅγιον πνεῦμα refers to the Holy Spirit as a known and familar personal manifestation of God, in an active role. The forms of the expression Luke uses to refer to the Holy Spirit in his Gospel bear out this analysis. There is one firm reading of τὸ ἅγιον πνεῦμα at Lk. 12.12 where Jesus speaks of the Holy Spirit who will teach the disciples what to say to their accusers. It is significant that in the Gospel this form is used only by Jesus and in referring to a personal relationship that the Spirit will have with the disciples after Pentecost.

b) Additional reading of τὸ ἅγιον πνεῦμα

Only one additional reading occurs at:

15.29D05

This additional reference to the Holy Spirit is made at the end of the apostolic letter to the Antioch church and speaks of the recipients being 'sustained in the Holy Spirit', φερόμενοι ἐν τῷ ἁγίῳ πενύματι. The Spirit is thus spoken of in the context of a personal relationship with disciples, not as part of an explanation or declaration; furthermore, the mention is not the salient part of the sentence. All the conditions so far defined for choosing to use the phrase τὸ ἅγιον πνεῦμα are thus met.

V.2 Variant readings

The variant readings are set out in Table 5.3 above, where the alternative readings in each case are shown. When citations from the MSS are given in this section, variant words are indicated as follows: material that is not read by all three MSS is underlined with a solid line, and the corresponding absence in the other MS(S) is indicated with ↑; material that is read in a alternative form in another of the MSS is underlined with a dotted line; words that vary in their order are enclosed within square brackets.

V.2.i τὸ πνεῦμα in ℵ01/B03 is τὸ πνεῦμα τὸ ἅγιον in D05

6.10; 8.18

The variant here involves the presence versus the absence of the adjective, which is placed in post-position. The mention of the Spirit is in relation to a specific event where ἅγιον is an expression either of the prophetic context or of the insistence on the identity of the Spirit.

6.10 The reference is to Stephen's manner of speech as he explained to the Jews the divine purpose behind the history of Israel; it is typical of D05 to stress the prophetic tradition within which the Jesus-believing leaders spoke and acted. This example resembles that of 7.51 in the common text.

8.18 The reference is to the gift of the Spirit through the laying on of hands by Peter and John in Samaria, as seen through the deliberations of Simon the Magician. The expression (adjective following arthrous noun) is different from that used for the people receiving the Holy Spirit in 8.15,17,19 (πνεῦμα ἅγιον) because the reference is made from the point of view of Simon and not of the narrator. The absence of ἅγιον in ℵ01/B03 is perhaps an indication that Simon was thought to be unable to properly recognize the holy quality of the spirit he witnessed being given.

It is important to recognize that these are the only two instances where the Bezan text includes the adjective ἅγιον where ℵ01/B03 read πνεῦμα alone, even though there would have been at least one other place (6.3, see §V.1.i above) where the noun on its own could have been considered to be incomplete.

V.2.ii πνεῦμα ἅγιον in ℵ01/B03 is ἅγιον πνεῦμα in D05

10.38

The reference to the Holy Spirit occurs in the course of Peter's explanation to his Gentile audience about Jesus. He tells them that Jesus was anointed by God with the Holy Spirit and power. The structure of the sentence is different in the two texts:

Ref.	D05	ℵ01/B03
10.38	Ἰησοῦν τὸν ἀπὸ Ναζαρέθ, ὄν ἔχρισεν ↑ ὁ θεὸς [ἁγίῳ πνεύματι] καὶ δυνάμει, οὗτος διῆλθεν εὐεργετῶν...	Ἰησοῦν τὸν ἀπὸ Ναζαρέθ, ὡς ἔχρισεν αὐτὸν ὁ θεὸς [πνεύματι ἁγίῳ] καὶ δυνάμει, ὃς διῆλθεν εὐεργετῶν...

The expression used in ℵ01/B03 (πενύματι ἁγίῳ) is in accordance with its use elsewhere (see §V.1.ii above). The Holy Spirit is salient which accounts for the absence of the article; he is not referred to as directly active but in the same way as in the other occurences of the phrase where it is a question of being baptized in, or filled with, the Holy Spirit, for example. In D05, the clause in which the Holy Spirit is mentioned is introduced by the relative pronoun ὅν referring to Jesus and, secondly, the next clause is introduced by the emphatic pronoun οὗτος, again referring to Jesus. Focus is thus maintained on the person of Jesus although the salience of the Holy Spirit as the new element is not affected. The effect of the fronting of the adjective (ἁγίῳ πνεύματι), a form not found elsewhere in Acts or Luke's Gospel, is to draw attention to it, possibly because of the context of the anointing (ἔχρισεν) of Jesus.

V.2.iii τὸ πνεῦμα τὸ ἅγιον in ℵ01/B03 is τὸ ἅγιον πνεῦμα in D05

2.33; 5.3; 15.28; 20.23,28

The divergence over the position of the adjective in these readings throws some light on the significance of the form τὸ ἅγιον πνεῦμα. This is the expression that was previously seen (§V.1.iv) to be reserved chiefly to express the relationship between the Holy Spirit and Jesus-believers.

In all the places where variant readings arise, the Holy Spirit is mentioned in close relation to either Jesus-believers or Jesus himself and in respect of this feature the D05 form is thus appropriate. The mentions do not occur in the context of an explanation or a declaration, except at 2.33 where Peter is explaining to his Jerusalem audience about Jesus receiving the promise of the Holy Spirit from God. The word order of the D05 expression there can be accounted for by the fact that the dominant theme at this point is the special relationship Jesus enjoyed with the Father.

At 5.3, Ananias deceives the Holy Spirit; the incident takes place within the newly formed Jesus-believing community, which enjoys an intimacy in its relationship with the Holy Spirit (unlike those who resisted the Holy Spirit at 7.51, for example, where τὸ πνεῦμα τὸ ἅγιον is used, see §V.1.iii above). Likewise, the occurrence at 15.28 is part of a letter from the church in Jerusalem to Gentile believers, the writers indicating the guidance of the Holy Spirit in their decisions about the regulations they are to pass on to the recipients. Finally, in his discourse with the Ephesian elders, Paul mentions twice, at 20.23,28, activities of the Holy Spirit that are closely related to himself or to the church and in this context the familiar, intimate expression is quite appropriate.

In the alternative reading of τὸ πνεῦμα τὸ ἅγιον in ℵ01/B03, the portrayal of the Holy Spirit is, by comparison, one of a less intimate presence. The overall resultant effect is all the stronger because of the relatively low number of readings of τὸ ἅγιον πνεῦμα in the ℵ01/B03 text anyway; to the D05 readings listed here must be added the supplementary Bezan reading of 15.29 (see §V.1.iv.b above) although there are two supplementary ℵ01/B03 readings of τὸ ἅγιον πνεῦμα (see §V.2.iv below) that counterbalance the effect to some extent.

From its restricted use to express the relationship between the Holy Spirit and Jesus-believers, it may be deduced that the term τὸ ἅγιον πνεῦμα is the most recent of the four that Luke uses to refer to the Holy Spirit in Acts (and indeed, in his Gospel too). It is also possible that the prophetic force of the adjective ἅγιον in this form is diminished. In the instances where Luke uses πνεῦμα ἅγιον and τὸ πνεῦμα τὸ ἅγιον, the prophetic aspect is generally much more marked than in the references with τὸ ἅγιον πνεῦμα.

V.2.iv τὸ ἅγιον πνεῦμα in ℵ01/B03 is τὸ πνεῦμα ἅγιον in D05

10.45; 13.4

At 10.45, ℵ01 and B03 are divided in their readings. Whereas ℵ01 reads τὸ ἅγιον πνεῦμα, B03 reads τὸ πνεῦμα τὸ ἅγιον. At both places, the Bezan text reads ἅγιον after πνεῦμα and omits the second article. A corrector has added the omitted article at 10.45 to read τὸ πνεῦμα τὸ ἅγιον,[21] thus bringing it into line with the B03 reading. The omission of the second article at 13.4, on the other hand, is supported by the Byzantine text.

The pattern of the D05 original reading in these two verses, of an arthrous noun followed by an anarthrous qualifying adjective, is not found anywhere else in Acts (see

---

[21] David C. Parker, *Codex Bezae: An Early Christian Manuscript and its Text* (Cambridge, UK: CUP, 1992), 137, 138, 139.

Chapter 4, §III). The absence of possible comparison makes it difficult to determine what is the force of the anarthrous adjective ἅγιον in post-noun position. It has already been observed that with the adjective in the pre-noun position, τὸ ἅγιον πνεῦμα, is used to refer to the Holy Spirit by Jesus-believers from the point of view of their relationship with him and that is how it can be understood in the MSS that have this reading at both 10.45 and 13.4 (see below). With the adjective in post-noun position and the repetition of the article (τὸ πνεῦμα τὸ ἅγιον), the expression was found to be the one used for explanations or declarations (§V.1.iii above). That could possibly account for the use of this form at 10.45B03, although it is not entirely satsfactory to see the comment as either an explanation or declaration. In looking at the two references more closely, some further suggestions will be made for the D05 reading.

10.45 The reference to the Holy Spirit is made by the narrator who reports the amazement of Peter's companions that 'even on the Gentiles the gift of the Holy Spirit has been poured out', καὶ ἐπὶ τὰ ἔθνη ἡ δωρεὰ τοῦ ἁγίου πνεύματος [τοῦ πνεύματος ἁγίου D05] ἐκκέχυται. In so far as the comment is made from the point of view of the onlookers (Jewish Jesus-believers), they themselves may think of the Holy Spirit in two different ways: subjectively, as the Holy Spirit with whom they have a relationship (τὸ ἅγιον πνεῦμα, א01), or objectively, as the Holy Spirit who is given to the Gentiles (τὸ πνεῦμα τὸ ἅγιον, B03). It may be that the objective perspective is sufficient to warrant placing the adjective in post-position and that the article is not repeated in D05 because the context is not one of explanation or proclamation.

13.4 Barnabas and Saul are sent out by the Holy Spirit. The setting of the gathering of the Jesus-believers in Antioch could, on the basis of what has been said about the intimacy of situations using τὸ ἅγιον πνεῦμα, explain the choice of this term in א01/B03. With τὸ πνεῦμα ἅγιον, the Bezan text in comparison seems to bring the incident out into the wider context of the church's mission, leaving behind the closeness of the immediate church setting.

It should also be noted concerning these two Bezan readings of τὸ πνεῦμα ἅγιον that, in each case, the Holy Spirit has been mentioned in the immediately preceding co-text (10.44; 13.2). The article before πνεῦμα could then have arisen because the references are anaphoric, and the form τὸ πνεῦμα ἅγιον should be viewed as an arthrous form of the fixed expression πνεῦμα ἅγιον.

VI. Conclusions on Luke's choice of expressions for the Holy Spirit

This survey of the different expressions used by Luke to refer to the divine Spirit has shown that there is more than one reason for the variety of forms.

To some extent, the fluidity reflects the changing nature of the revelation of the Spirit as it progresses from the historical intervention and prophecies recorded in the Jewish Scriptures, to the manifestation of the Spirit and the teaching concerning him in the life of Jesus, to the outpouring of the Spirit at Pentecost and his subsequent presence with and through the Church. Within the setting of the narrative of Acts, when mention of the Spirit arises in a quotation from the Jewish Scriptures the choice of expression follows the LXX text. But there is a variety of other circumstances in which the Spirit is referred to and here the choice of expression depends on the particular situation in which the reference made.

When ἅγιον is used with πνεῦμα, the adjective has a prophetic force and is included more often than not, on two occasions by D05 where the ℵ01/B03 text does not use it. In references to the Holy Spirit, both the noun/adjective word order and the use of the article follow patterns observed in earlier chapters when examining these factors more generally. Variant readings affecting the form of the expression apparently occur because at some places the circumstances of the mention are viewed differently by each text. Concerning D05, the overall picture is that use of the various forms is controlled and the choice justifiable from the context.

Typical factors that influence the choice of expression in both the D05 and the ℵ01/B03 texts are whether the Spirit is presented as acting directly or rather as the subject of teaching, and whether he is mentioned in relation to believers or, on the contrary, unbelievers. The most common form of expression, πνεῦμα ἅγιον, comes to be used as a stereotyped phrase in fixed expressions speaking of characteristic manifestations of the Holy Spirit, whereas the arthrous form τὸ πνεῦμα τὸ ἅγιον is found in contexts of explanation or instruction. It is the form τὸ ἅγιον πνεῦμα that is preferred to refer to the relationship between the Holy Spirit and Jesus-believers. This is a term not used before the time of Jesus in the Scriptures and, judging from his Gospel and Acts, is one inaugurated by him. It occurs as the most frequent of the variant readings and is preferred overall by D05.

While ℵ01/B03 have one reference in Luke's Gospel to the Holy Spirit that is not present in D05, there are six references in Acts that are present in D05 but absent in ℵ01/B03. In addition, twice D05 includes the adjective ἅγιον where ℵ01/B03 do not. It has been argued that the interest of D05 in the Holy Spirit reflects a Montanist interest,[22] adding to Luke's text references to the Holy Spirit, and qualifying the Spirit as holy by inserting the adjective at places where it was absent. Three points need to be made in response to this interpretation. First of all, it has been noted in the present study that the addition of the adjective is by no means systematic, and that there are additional references to the Spirit without the adjective. Secondly, the notion that D05 is a revision to bring the text of Acts into line with Montanist concerns depends on seeing the text as a secondary one. If this presupposition is put to one side, then it can be equally argued that references to the Holy Spirit were removed or toned down at a time when the Church was taking care to protect itself against movements such as Montanism, which emphasised the intervention of the Holy Spirit in the life of Christians; there is evidence that this was happening at least by the time of Irenaeus in the latter part of the second century.[23] Finally, several of the references to the Spirit in Acts indicate criticism of Paul's final journey to Jerusalem, which there would be good reason to eliminate once he had acquired the status of a infallible apostle, again some time in the second century.

---

[22] J. Rendel Harris, *Codex Bezae: A Study of the So-called Western Text of the New Testament* (Cambridge: CUP, 1891): 'The conclusion which we draw ... is that the Western text of Luke and Acts is a Montanist text', 152.
[23] Eusebius, *Historia Ecclesiae*, 5.3.4, available at https://www.newadvent.org/fathers/250105.htm (last accessed 29/09/2021).

The fluidity of expression in referring to the Spirit of God may reflect the language of the Greek-speaking Jesus-believing communities. Comparison of Luke's patterns of use with Paul's in his letters would be worthwhile but care would need to be exercised as references to the Holy Spirit are subject to variant readings there just as in Luke–Acts. What is apparent is that as a writer Luke makes deliberate use of the parallel expressions as a means to distinguish among the various operations and manifestations of the Spirit. The use of parallel terms to convey different nuances is a literary device that Luke was familiar with and that he employs in other instances, as illustrated in Chapter 7.

6

The tracking of participants[1]

I. Introduction

The purpose of this study is to examine the use of the third person pronoun (αὐτός) as a device to track participants in the narrative of Acts. More specifically, leaving aside the rare occurrences of αὐτός as a subject pronoun, analysis will be made of the use of αὐτός to designate participants as the direct object (in the accusative) or indirect object (in the dative, or preceded by a preposition) of a verb. It is possible, and even good style in Greek, to leave out the pronoun if the meaning is clear, as frequently it is after a verb with the same object as the preceding one, for example. The omission of the pronoun does not always happen, however, and in the narrative of Acts there is a number of variant readings on this point. Rather than summarily conclude that it is simply a matter of style and that scribes imposed their own habits on their copies of the text, it is more prudent, and fruitful, to examine the question in detail. The starting point is to look at the pattern of use in the text without variant in the main textual traditions, in order to establish if particular circumstances call for omission of the pronoun or, on the contrary, its repetition; and the second step is to compare the variant readings with the non-variant text. In order to work from a controlled quantity of data, representative MSS will be taken from each of the two principal textual traditions of Acts: Codex Sinaiticus (ℵ01) and Codex Vaticanus (B03) for the Alexandrian text will be compared with Codex Bezae (D05) as the most extensive extant Greek manuscript of the so-called 'Western' text of Acts, bearing in mind that there are lacunae in D05 at 8.29–10.14; 21.2–10; 22.11–20; 22.29–end.

To restate the problem under investigation: when a participant is the object, direct or indirect, of two or more verbs in succession, it is possible in Greek for the participant to be specified more than once, but repeated mention is not obligatory. The first reference can be either by name or by third person pronoun in the appropriate case; if

---

[1] This chapter was originally published as 'The Tracking of Participants with the Third Person Pronoun: A Study of the Text of Acts', *Revista Catalana de Teologia* 31 (2006): 439–55. The organization of the material has been slightly modified here. Where reference is made to the interpretation of Luke's message, especially in Codex Bezae, detailed discussion can be found in Josep Rius-Camps and Jenny Read-Heimerdinger, *The Message of Acts in Codex Bezae: A Comparison with the Alexandrian Tradition*. 4 vols (JSNTSup 257/LNTS 302, 365, 415; London: T&T Clark, 2004–09).

the reference is repeated, the third person pronoun is typically used in the appropriate case. The study looks at why the reference is repeated on some occasions and not on others. While the data examined is restricted to the book of Acts, the findings may be used subsequently to deduce patterns of use in other writings.

All the occurrences in Acts of two or more verbs with the same object will be examined and classified according to various categories. For ease of reference, the full list of occurrences is given at the end of the study.

II. Verb 2 is a verb of saying

The situation under consideration occurs when a participant undergoes action as the object (direct or indirect) of a verb and then, with the following verb, is addressed in direct speech. While the participant could be specified after the second verb using the third person pronoun, the pronoun is often not stated.

II.1 In the common text

The references shared by all three MSS are:

1.6,10–11; 3.4; 5.19, 40; 13.2,10; 14.9; 15.13; 17.19

A general pattern emerges from looking at the firm text:

RULE 1: when the second verb is one of speaking, the pronoun is generally omitted.

For example:

1.10–11 καὶ ὡς ἀτενίζοντες ἦσαν εἰς τὸν οὐρανὸν πορευομένου αὐτοῦ, καὶ ἰδοὺ ἄνδρες δύο παρειστήκεισαν αὐτοῖς ἐν ἐσθήσεσιν λευκαῖς (ἐσθῆτι λευκῇ, D05), οἳ καὶ εἶπαν· ...

The object of the first verb, παρειστήκεισαν, is specified, αὐτοῖς, and is not repeated after the second verb, εἶπαν.

Observations

Two references in the above list require further comment.

5.40 The verb of speaking is the third in a series of verbs which have the same object: the apostles are the direct object of the first, second and fourth verbs, and the implied addressee of the third verb of speaking. They are explicit after the first verb (and also the fourth in D05):

5.40 καὶ προσκαλεσάμενοι τοὺς ἀποστόλους δείραντες παρήγγειλαν μὴ λαλεῖν ἐπὶ τῷ ὀνόματι τοῦ Ἰησοῦ καὶ ἀπέλυσαν (+ αὐτούς, D05).

In this instance, even though the verb παρήγγειλαν has an implied indirect object the addressee is not made explicit, following the general rule after verbs of speaking. The pronoun after the fourth verb in D05 may be prompted by the change from indirect to direct object (see §IV.2 below). It may be observed that in D05, the apostles are again spelt out with the nominative noun, οἱ ἀπόστολοι, in the following clause (5.41) instead of the simple article on its own.

17.19 The text varies considerably in the first half of the verse. The absence of the pronoun after the participle λέγοντες in ℵ01/B03 follows the rule. even though it is the third verb of the sentence:

Ref.	D05	ℵ01/B03
17.19	μετὰ δὲ ἡμέρας τινὰς ἐπιλαβόμενοι αὐτοῦ [ἤγαγον αὐτὸν ἐπὶ ↑ Ἄρειον Πάγον] πυνθανόμενοι καὶ λέγοντες...	↑ ἐπιλαβόμενοί τε αὐτοῦ [ἐπὶ τὸν Ἄρειον Πάγον ἤγαγον] ↑ λέγοντες...

The text of D05 is even more striking, for there the verb of speaking is the fourth in a series (see §V below), yet the pronoun is not specified.

An exception to the above rule arises once at 19.2, where the pronoun is used to refer to the addressee even when they have already been specified as the object of the previous verb.

19.1-2 The people addressed are encountered for the first time as new participants on the scene as the direct object of the first verb that precedes the one of speaking. This factor may account for the use of the pronoun after the verb of speaking:

Ref.	D05	ℵ01/B03
19.1-2	↑ ↑ διελθὼν δὲ τὰ ἀνωτερικὰ μέρη ἔρχεται εἰς Ἔφεσον καὶ εὑρὼν τινας μαθητὰς, εἶπεν ↑ πρὸς αὐτούς...	Ἐγένετο δὲ ἐν τῷ τὸν Ἀπολλῶ εἶναι ἐν Κορίνθῳ Παῦλον διελθόντα τὰ ἀνωτερικὰ μέρη κατελθεῖν (ἐλθεῖν B03) εἰς Ἔφεσον καὶ εὑρεῖν τινας μαθητάς, εἶπέν τε πρὸς αὐτούς...

II.2 Variant readings

The pronoun is included after the verb of speaking in D05 but not in ℵ01 and/or B03 at:

3.3; 10.19; 12:17; 16.30; 22.26

Explanation for the presence of the pronoun is found within the context of the reference.

3.2-3 Two successive verbs have Peter and John as direct objects, where the second verb is one of asking:

Ref.	D05	ℵ01/B03
3.2-3	εἰσπορευομένων αὐτῶν εἰς τὸν ἱερὸν οὗτος ἀτενίσας τοῖς ὀφθαλμοῖς αὐτοῦ καὶ ἰδὼν Πέτρον καὶ Ἰωάννην μέλλοντας εἰσιέναι εἰς τὸ ἱερόν, ἠρώτα αὐτοὺς ἐλεημοσύνην ↑	↑ ὅς ↑ ἰδὼν Πέτρον καὶ Ἰωάννην μέλλοντας εἰσιέναι εἰς τὸ ἱερόν, ἠρώτα ↑ ἐλεημοσύνην λαβεῖν

ℵ01/B03 do not include the pronoun to make explicit the addressee of ἠρώτα, whereas D05 does. D05's inclusion of the pronoun tallies with the heightened prominence given to the apostles in the narrative of this text – it was Peter and John that the lame man was specifically waiting for at the gate of the Temple. ℵ01/B03 complete the verb ἠρώτα with the infinitive λαβεῖν.

12.17 The dative pronoun is included after the verb διηγήσατο in D05 and B03 but not ℵ01:

Ref.	D05	ℵ01/B03
12.17	κατασείσας δὲ αὐτοῖς τῇ χειρὶ <u>ἵνα σιγῶσιν εἰσῆλθεν καὶ</u> διηγήσατο αὐτοῖς	κατασείσας δὲ αὐτοῖς τῇ χειρὶ ↑ <u>σιγᾶν</u> ↑ διηγήσατο αὐτοῖς (*om.* ℵ01)

In B03, the second dative pronoun is anomalous since the addressees have just been specified with the dative pronoun following the previous verb; in fact, the pronoun is omitted by a number of MSS including ℵ01, and is placed in square brackets in N-A²⁸ as an indication of the uncertainty over the reading. Its presence in D05 is normal, for there is an additional finite verb separating the two verbs κατασείσας and διηγήσατο.

16.30 The third person pronoun may be repeated in D05 because of a participial clause intervening between the first verb and the verb of speaking:

Ref.	D05	ℵ01/B03
16.30	καὶ <u>προήγαγεν</u> αὐτοὺς ἔξω <u>τοὺς λοιποὺς ἀσπαλισάμενος καὶ εἶπεν</u> αὐτοῖς…	καὶ <u>προαγαγὼν</u> αὐτοὺς ἔξω ↑ ↑ <u>ἔφη</u> ↑ …

22.26 The use of the pronoun after the verb of speaking in D05 can be explained by the fact that the words spoken have already been reported in indirect speech earlier in the sentence. Thus, the pronoun gives emphasis to the fact that what the centurion heard, he repeats to the tribune:

Ref.	D05	ℵ01/B03
22.26	<u>τοῦτο</u> ἀκούσας δὲ ὁ ἑκατοντάρχης <u>ὅτι Ῥωμαῖον ἑαυτὸν λέγει</u> προσελθὼν τῷ χιλιάρχῳ ἀπήγγειλεν ↑ <u>αὐτῷ</u>…	↑ ἀκούσας δὲ ὁ ἑκατοντάρχης ↑ ↑ προσελθὼν τῷ χιλιάρχῳ ἀπήγγειλεν <u>λέγων</u> ↑ …

III. Verb 2 is παρακαλέω

A particular case arises when the second verb is παρακαλέω, often followed by a further verb which is one of speaking. On each occasion, variant readings are involved.

III.1 General principle

A typical pattern emerges from the occurrences of παρακαλέω:

RULE 2: the object is not made explicit after παρακαλέω when it is the second of two verbs with the same object.

This is particularly the case when παρακαλέω is found alongside a verb of speaking. Where the pronoun is present, it is because particular circumstances require it.

III.2 Variant readings

Variant readings occur as follows:

8.18–19; 16.9,39a,b,40; 20.1

An examination of these occurrences of παρακαλέω shows that whenever it is found as the second verb alongside another verb of speaking, the texts disagree over the presence of the pronoun.

8.18–19 Only D05 has the verb παρακαλέω, after which the pronoun is omitted: προσήνεγκεν αὐτοῖς χρήματα παρακαλῶν καὶ λέγων.... The pronoun is repeated after the verb of speaking λέγων in neither text, following the general rule observed in §II.1 above.

16.9 D05 omits the pronoun after παρακαλέω where ℵ01/B03 have it:

Ref.	D05	ℵ01/B03
16.9	καὶ ἐν ὁράματι διὰ νυκτὸς [ὤφθη τῷ Παύλῳ] ὡσεὶ ἀνὴρ Μακεδών τις ↑ ἑστὼς κατὰ πρόσωπον αὐτοῦ παρακαλῶν ↑ καὶ λέγων...	καὶ ὅραμα διὰ τῆς (om. B03) νυκτὸς [τῷ Παύλῳ ὤφθη] ↑ ἀνὴρ Μακεδών τις ἦν ἑστὼς ↑ καὶ παρακαλῶν αὐτὸν καὶ λέγων...

In D05, the Macedonian is the subject of the main verb ὤφθη of which Paul is the indirect object, as well as of the two participles παρακαλῶν καὶ λέγων of which Paul is the implied object. The different construction in B03, however, means that the Macedonian is not the subject of ὤφθη, and that Paul thus needs to be specified as the object of the participle παρακαλῶν.

16.39 D05 twice includes the pronoun after παρακαλέω:

Ref.	D05	ℵ01/B03
16.39	καὶ παραγενόμενοι μετὰ φίλων πολλῶν εἰς τὴν φυλακὴν παρεκάλεσαν αὐτοὺς ἐξελθεῖν εἰπόντες... καὶ ἐξαγαγόντες παρεκάλεσαν αὐτοὺς ↑ λεγόντες...	καὶ ἐλθόντες ↑ παρεκάλεσαν αὐτοὺς ↑ ↑ καὶ ἐξαγαγόντες ἠρώτων ↑ ἀπελθεῖν ἀπὸ τῆς πόλεως ↑

At the first occurrence of παρακαλέω in D05, the subject is the magistrates and since the participants referred to as αὐτούς (Paul and Barnabas) have not been mentioned with a preceding verb, the pronoun is expected. At the second occurrence, the pronoun is associated with two verbs (ἐξαγαγόντες, παρεκάλεσαν, λεγόντες) and the choice to place the pronoun with παρεκάλεσαν, especially in view of the repetition of the clause in the previous sentence, confers on it particular emphasis (cf. 16.40 below). In accordance with the Rule 1, the pronoun is not repeated after the verb of speaking at either occurrence (εἰπόντες, λεγόντες). The question of the omission of the pronoun with a series of three verbs is looked at below (§V). ℵ01/B03 reads here only the first occurrence of παρακαλέω as a verb on its own, with the meaning not so much of 'begged' as in D05 but of 'called them', and the pronoun is expected since the verb is the only one.

16.40, Here and at 20.1 παρακαλέω is found on its own, not accompanying a verb of speaking, and the object pronoun is read by D05, but not by ℵ01/B03:

Ref.	D05	ℵ01/B03
16.40	καὶ ἰδόντες <u>τοὺς ἀδελφοὺς διηγήσαντο ὅσα ἐποίησεν κύριος αὐτοῖς</u>. παρεκαλέσαντες <u>αὐτοὺς</u> καὶ ἐξῆλθαν	καὶ ἰδόντες ↑ ↑ παρεκάλεσαν <u>τοὺς ἀδελφοὺς</u> καὶ ἐξῆλθαν

In ℵ01/B03, the direct object τοὺς ἀδελφούς serves both the participle ἰδόντες and the verb παρεκάλεσαν. In D05, the pronoun αὐτούς following παρακαλέσαντες is accounted for by the fact that a sentence in indirect speech separates the pronoun from its referent τοὺς ἀδελφούς.

20.1 the pronoun is not read by ℵ01/B03 after the verb παρακαλέω, where D05 has an alternative verb:

Ref.	D05	ℵ01/B03
20.1	μετὰ δὲ τὸ παύσασθαι τὸν θόρυβον <u>προσκαλεσάμενος</u> ↑ Παῦλος τοὺς μαθητὰς καὶ <u>πολλὰ</u> <u>παρεκαλεύσας</u> ἀσπασάμενος ἐξῆλθεν ↑ εἰς Μακεδονίαν	μετὰ δὲ τὸ παύσασθαι τὸν θόρυβον <u>μεταπεμψάμενος</u> <u>ὁ</u> Παῦλος τοὺς μαθητὰς καὶ ↑ <u>παρακαλέσας</u>, ἀσπασάμενος ἐξῆλθεν <u>πορεύεσθαι</u> εἰς Μακεδονίαν

In ℵ01/B03, the direct object of παρακαλέσας has already been specified (τοὺς μαθητάς) as the direct object of the preceding participle μεταπεμψάμενος and is not repeated. D05, on the other hand, reads the verb παρακαλεύω, 'give instructions', of which the direct object is πολλά.

IV. Two successive verbs (not verbs of saying)

IV.1 Pronoun omitted after verb 2

At the listed places in Table 6.1, the object pronoun is omitted after the second verb (its form, had it been present, is given in brackets). There are no variant readings.

On the majority of occasions, the omitted pronoun corresponds to the direct object of the second verb, where this is also the function of the referent with respect to the first verb.

RULE 3a: the pronoun is omitted after the second verb when it is the direct object of two successive verbs.

Whether the verb is a finite verb, infinitive or a participle seems to have no bearing on the presence of the second pronoun.

Table 6.1 Omission of pronoun verb 2

Ref.	Vb1 form	noun/pro.	Vb2 form	(noun/pro.)
4.3	vb (part. D05)	dat. pro.	vb	(acc. pro.)
5.2	part.	acc. noun	vb	(acc. pro.)
5.15	inf.	acc. noun	inf.	(acc. pro.)
5.27	part.	acc. pro.	vb	(acc. pro.)
6.12	vb	acc. pro.	vb	(acc. pro.)
8.3	part.	acc. noun	part.	(acc. pro.)
12.19	part.	acc. pro.	part.	(acc. pro.)
13.3	part.	dat. pro.	vb	(acc. pro.)
14.19	part.	acc. noun	vb	(acc. pro.)
15.32	vb	acc. noun	vb	(acc. pro.)
16.32	part.	acc. pro.	vb	(acc. pro.)
17.15a	part.	acc. noun	vb	(acc. pro.)
18.17	part.	acc. noun	vb	(acc. pro.)
21.33	vb	gen. pro.	inf.	(acc. pro.)

Observations

In addition to the list above, 16.3 presents a comparable example of the direct object of two successive transitive verbs being specified only once. But here, it is given after the second verb, not the first (part. – *acc.* – part. + acc. pro.):

16.3: τοῦτον ἠθέλησεν ὁ Παῦλος σὺν αὐτῷ ἐξελθεῖν, καὶ λαβὼν περιέτεμεν αὐτὸν διὰ τοὺς Ἰουδαίους

For four of the references in Table 6.1, the pronoun is omitted after the second verb even though there would have been a change in case, because the first verb is intransitive and the second is transitive:

4.3; 13.3; 20.10; 21.33

The first two examples express similar ideas with the same structure:

4.3 καὶ ἐπέβαλον (ἐπιβαλόντες D05) αὐτοῖς τὰς χεῖρας καὶ ἔθεντο εἰς τήρησιν εἰς τὴν αὔριον
13.3 καὶ ἐπιθέντες τὰς χεῖρας αὐτοῖς ἀπέλυσαν (*om.* D05)

The first verb is followed by the indirect object; the second verb follows without the direct object being specified. In 4.3D05, which reads the participle for the first verb, καί before ἔθεντο is adverbial (see Chapter 3, §II.2.i). The second verb of 13.3, ἀπέλυσαν, was probably omitted by D05 accidentally since the sentence is incomplete without it.[2] These two examples may be contrasted with 5.18 below (§IV.2.i) where the verb ἐπέβαλον is followed by ἐπὶ τοὺς ἀποστόλους and the next verb repeats the accusative pronoun αὐτούς.

20.10 The object (Eutyches) is specified after the first verb alone, even though the second verb requires a change of case:

Ref.	D05	ℵ01/B03
20.10	καταβὰς δὲ ὁ Παῦλος ἐπέπεσεν ἐπ'αὐτῷ καὶ συμπεριλαβὼν καὶ εἶπεν...	καταβὰς δὲ ὁ Παῦλος ἐπέπεσεν ↑ αὐτῷ καὶ συμπεριλαβὼν ↑ εἶπεν...

The pronoun is in the dative, with or without the preposition ἐπί, following the finite verb ἐπέπεσεν. It is omitted after the participle συμπεριλαβών, where the accusative would be required. Because the pronoun would normally be expected in view of the change of case, its omission has the effect of taking attention away from Paul's holding of the young man and focusing it instead on his next action of speaking to the onlookers. The focus is underlined in D05 by the adverbial καί before εἶπεν (see Chapter 3, §II.2.i). The absence of pronoun after the verb of speaking εἶπεν is present because the addressee is the onlookers in general, and not the same object as the object of the previous verbs (cf. §II above).

21.33 The situation is comparable though not identical to that of 4.3 and 13.3: τότε ἐγγίσας ὁ χιλίαρχος ἐπελάβετο αὐτοῦ καὶ ἐκέλευσεν δεθῆναι ἁλύσεσιν δυσίν. The first verb is one of arrest followed by the indirect object in the genitive, and the second verb δεθῆναι follows without the direct object being specified. The pattern of these three similar examples that involve verbs of persecution is found again at 16.23 where there are three successive verbs (see §V.2.i below).

IV.2 Pronoun included after verb 2

This pattern is also found in the text of Acts, but with some variant readings.

IV.2.i In the common text

There are 10 occurrences of the object being specified after the second of two verbs. They are listed in Table 6.2, showing the form of the two verbs and also the form of the two objects.

In all of these instances except 22.24, the role of the noun/pronoun is not identical with respect to both verbs: the case may be different or there may be a preposition following one of the verbs.

> RULE 3b: The pronoun is included after the second verb if there is a difference in case or if a preposition is necessary after one of the verbs.

---

[2] The manuscript is illegible here, but it is possible that the object pronoun was also read by D05, and that ἀπέλυσαν αὐτούς stood on a separate line that a copyist has jumped over.

Table 6.2 Presence of pronoun after verb 2

Ref.	1st vb form	noun/pro.	2nd vb form	noun/pro.
5.18	vb	prep. + acc. pro.	vb	acc. pro.
8.2	part.	acc. noun	vb	prep. + dat. pro.
13.43	vb	dat. pro.	part.	acc. pro.
13.50	vb	prep. + acc. noun	vb	acc. pro.
14.23	part.	dat. pro.	vb	acc. pro.
16.29	vb	dat. noun	vb	acc. pro.
17.2	vb	prep. + acc. pro.	vb	dat. pro.
17.9	part.	prep. + gen. noun	vb	acc. pro.
20.37	part.	gen. pro.	vb	acc. pro.
22.24	inf.	acc. pro.	inf.	acc. pro.

Observations

At 22.24, the direct object pronoun is repeated after two successive infinitives, where the repetition can be accounted for by the fact that the infinitives are separated by a participle in a new clause:

22.24: ἐκέλευσεν ὁ χιλίαρχος εἰσάγεσθαι αὐτὸν εἰς τὴν παρεμβολήν, εἴπας μάστιξιν ἀνετάζεσθαι (ἀνετάζειν D05) αὐτόν

IV.2.ii *Variant readings*

Variation in the presence or absence of the pronoun after the second verb occurs at:

3.7; 17.19; 18.12; 21.30

3.7 Two verbs are used successively both with the lame man as the direct object. D05 omits the pronoun after the second verb: καὶ πιάσας αὐτὸν τῆς δεξιᾶς χειρὸς ἤγειρεν αὐτόν (*om.* D05). The omission of the pronoun tends to direct attention to Peter's first action, the shocking gesture of touching an unclean man; the inclusion, contrary to Rule 3a above, underlines the raising of the man.

17.19 The verse has been discussed at §II.1 above. Material present only in D05 involves a repetition of the pronoun referring to Paul with two successive verbs, ἐπιλαβόμενοι and ἤγαγον. The pronoun is repeated because a change of case is required. The absence of a pronoun after the two verbs of speaking is in accordance with Rule 1.

18.12 In ℵ01/B03, the occurrence of the pronoun after the second verb is expected because of a change in case from that required after the first verb (vb + dat. noun – vb + acc. pro.). In D05, the situation is more complex, for there are three verbs instead of two and the pronoun is omitted after the second but not the third verb (cf. §V.2 below):

Ref.	D05	ℵ01/B03
18.12	κατεπέστησαν ὁμοθυμαδὸν οἱ Ἰουδαῖοι συν λαλήσαντες μεθ᾽ ἑαυτῶν ἐπὶ τὸν Παῦλον καὶ ἐπιθέντες τὰς χεῖρας ἤγαγον αὐτὸν ἐπὶ τὸ βῆμα	κατεπέστησαν ὁμοθυμαδὸν οἱ Ἰουδαῖοι ↑ τῷ Παύλῳ καὶ ↑ ἤγαγον αὐτὸν ἐπὶ τὸ βῆμα

As in the examples of §IV.1 above, the omitted pronoun following the second verb ἐπιθέντες would have been in the same case with the same preposition ἐπί as that which belongs to the first verb; this may account for its omission. The inclusion of the pronoun after the third verb ἤγαγον is expected, since here it is the simple direct object (acc. pro.) and no preposition is needed.

21.30 The pronoun is included after the second verb in ℵ01/B03 where a different case is called for: καὶ ἐγένετο συνδρομὴ τοῦ λαοῦ, καὶ ἐπιλαβόμενοι τοῦ Παύλου εἷλκον αὐτὸν (*om.* D05) ἔξω τοῦ ἱεροῦ. In omitting the pronoun after the finite verb εἷλκον, D05 appears to contravene Rule 3b. It is interesting to note, however, that the context of physical attack is similar to that of 4.3; 13.3; 21.33 where, as noted above §IV.1), the pronoun is omitted after the second verb despite a different case being required.

V. Three or more successive verbs

In general, the same rules as have been formulated for two successive verbs (Rule 3a, 3b) are equally valid for a series of three verbs or even more, giving rise to the formulation of Rule 4 in two parts:

> RULE 4a: the pronoun is omitted with the second and successive verbs if the same case is required with no preposition
> RULE 4b: the pronoun is included if there is a change of case or a preposition is required with one or more of the verbs

V.1 Pronoun omitted after verb 2 or 3 (or 4)

V.1.i *In the common text*

There is only one reference in this category, at 5.10.

5.10 Sapphira is established as the topic of the narrative (5.7–10), and is referred to by the accusative pronoun after the first verb:

Ref.	D05	ℵ01/B03
5.10	εἰσελθόντες δὲ οἱ νεανίσκοι εὗρον αὐτὴν νεκρὰν καὶ συνστείλαντες ἐξήνεγκαν καὶ ἔθαψαν πρὸς τὸν ἄνδρα αὐτῆς	εἰσελθόντες δὲ οἱ νεανίσκοι εὗρον αὐτὴν νεκρὰν καὶ ↑ ἐξένεγκαντες ↑ ἔθαψαν πρὸς τὸν ἄνδρα αὐτῆς

Sapphira is the direct object of each of the verbs, including the participle συνστείλαντες in D05. The pronoun αὐτήν is used only after the first verb, and the pronoun is not repeated thereafter, except as the possessive genitive at the end of the sentence.

V.1.ii Variant readings

Variant readings occur at:

11.25-26; 12.4

11.25-26 Where ℵ01/B03 has three verbs of which Saul is the direct object, the sentence in D05 is more complex:

Ref.	D05	ℵ01/B03
11.25-26	ἀκούσας δὲ ὅτι Σαῦλός ἐστιν εἰς Θαρσὸν ἐξῆλθεν ἀναζητῶν αὐτὸν καὶ ὡς συντυχὼν παρεκάλεσεν ἐλθεῖν εἰς Ἀντιόχειαν	↑ ἐξῆλθεν δὲ εἰς Ταρσὸν ἀναζητῆσαι Σαῦλον, καὶ ↑ εὑρὼν ↑ ἤγαγεν εἰς Ἀντιόχειαν

In ℵ01/B03, Saul is mentioned after the infinitive ἀναζητῆσαι with the noun in the accusative, and is not explicitly referred to after the second and third verbs εὑρών, ἤγαγεν. This is in accordance with Rule 4a, which states that the pronoun is omitted with the second and successive verbs if the same case is required with no preposition. In D05, Saul has already been mentioned as a nominative noun in a clause of indirect speech. Thus, the pronoun is used to refer to him as the direct object of the participle ἀναζητῶν. The absence of the dative pronoun with the following participle συντυχών, is accounted for by the fact that, introduced by ὡς, the participle is an oblique aside: 'as if running into him by chance'. Its omission after the finite verb παρεκάλεσαν is expected in accordance with Rule 2.

12.4 There are four verbs, all referring to Peter as the direct object:

Ref.	D05	ℵ01/B03
12.4	τοῦτον ↑ πιάσας ἔθετο εἰς φυλακὴν παραδοὺς τέσσαρσιν τετραδίοις στρατιωτῶν φυλάσσειν ↑ βουλόμενος μετὰ τὸ πάσχα ἀναγαγεῖν αὐτὸν τῷ λαῷ.	ὃν καὶ πιάσας ἔθετο εἰς φυλακὴν παραδοὺς τέσσαρσιν τετραδίοις στρατιωτῶν φυλάσσειν αὐτόν, βουλόμενος μετὰ τὸ πάσχα ἀναγαγεῖν αὐτὸν τῷ λαῷ.

Peter is specified as the direct object after the first verb πιάσας, with the relative pronoun in ℵ01/B03 and the demonstrative in D05. The pronoun is omitted after the second (ἔθετο) and the third (παραδοὺς) verbs; after the fourth verb (φυλάσσειν), ℵ01/B03 include the pronoun but not D05. The inclusion of the pronoun can be explained by change of subject of the fourth verb (from Herod to the soldiers; cf. §VI below). The omission of the pronoun in D05 may be due to the fact that it is Herod's will that continues to be behind the action of the fourth verb; the initial demonstrative pronoun, more emphatic than the relative pronoun in ℵ01/B03, may also play a part.

V.2 Pronoun omitted after verb 2 but included after verb 3

V.2.i In the common text

Table 6.3 sets out the successive verb forms with the dependent noun or pronoun; where it is omitted, the form it would have had is given in brackets.

Table 6.3 Omission of pronoun after verb 2 but not verb 3

Ref.	1st vb form	noun/pro.	2nd vb form	noun/pro.	3rd vb form	noun/pro.
16.19–20	part.	acc. noun	vb	(acc. pro.)	vb ℵ01/B03 part. D05	acc. pro.
16.23	part.	dat. pro.	vb	(acc. pro.)	inf.	acc. pro.
17.5–6	vb	acc. pro.	inf.	(acc. pro.)	part.	acc. pro.

16.19–20 Paul and Silas are the direct object of three successive verbs as they are arrested in Philippi: ἐπιλαβόμενοι τὸν Παῦλον καὶ τὸν (*om.* D05) Σιλᾶν εἵλκυσαν εἰς τὴν ἀγορὰν ἐπὶ τοὺς ἄρχοντας καὶ προσαγαγόντες αὐτοὺς τοῖς στρατηγοῖς εἶπαν... The accusative pronoun is omitted after the second verb εἵλκυσαν in accordance with Rule 3, for Paul and Silas are the direct object of two successive verbs. They are also the direct object of the third verb προσαγαγόντες, where they are referred to with the accusative pronoun. This can be explained by the change from the general intention expressed by the second verb (to drag Paul and Silas before the rulers in the agora) to the specific outcome expressed by the third (they present them to the magistrates).

16.23 Paul and Silas are again the object of three successive verbs: πολλάς τε (δὲ B03) ἐπιθέντες αὐτοῖς πληγὰς ἔβαλον εἰς φυλακὴν παραγγείλαντες τῷ δεσμοφύλακι ἀσφαλῶς τηρεῖν (τηρεῖσθαι D05) αὐτούς. The dative pronoun is used after the first verb (ἐπιθέντες); the second requires the accusative pronoun but it is omitted; the third has a change of subject – in ℵ01/B03, from the soldier to the jailors, so it is normal for the object to be specified; in D05, the infinitive is passive, with Paul and Silas as the subject expressed by the accusative pronoun αὐτούς. The omission of the direct object pronoun after ἔβαλον, despite a change of case compared with the previous verb, may be compared to the examples of 4.3 and 21.33 cited at §IV.1 above, where the pronoun was omitted despite a change in case and where, as here at 16.23, the verbs express actions of persecution.

17.5–6 The participant is the direct object of each of the three verbs, and is specified with the first and the third, but not the second: ἐζήτουν αὐτοὺς προαγαγεῖν (ἐξ- D05) εἰς τὸν δῆμον· μὴ εὑρόντες δὲ αὐτοὺς ἔσυρον Ἰάσονα καί τινας ἀδελφούς... The pronoun referring to Paul and Silas is made explicit with the third verb, because at that point they are being contrasted with other participants, Jason and some brethren.

V.2.ii Variant readings

Variant readings occur at:

2.45; 7.57–58

2.45 The pattern of omitting the pronoun after the second verb but including it with the third is found in D05: vb–acc. noun + vb–vb–acc. pro:

Ref. D05	ℵ01/B03
2.45 καὶ ὅσοι κτήματα εἶχον ἢ ↑ ὑπάρξεις ἐπίπρασκον καὶ διεμέριζον αὐτά	καὶ τὰ κτήματα ↑ καὶ τὰς ὑπάρξεις ἐπίπρασκον καὶ διεμέριζον αὐτά

In both texts, the neuter accusative pronoun αὐτά refers to κτήματα. In ℵ01/B03, there are only two verbs with the same object, and the pronoun is used after the second. In D05, κτήματα is the direct object of the first verb εἶχον; it is followed by an aside (ἢ ὑπάρξεις) and is then referred as the object of the second and third verbs equally. It may be that the pronoun is included with the third verb (jointly with the second) because of the intervening aside as well as the marked word order (object before verb, see Chapter 8, §II). In ℵ01/B03, the sentence is structured differently, without the first verb of D05, and here the repetition of the pronoun is contrary to the pattern of Rule 3 above, namely, that when the noun/pronoun is the direct object of two successive verbs, the pronoun is omitted after the second verb. Again, it may well be the marked word order that prompts the use of the pronoun.

7.57–58 D05 omits the pronoun with the second verb but includes it with the third (vb–prep. + acc. noun–part.–vb. acc. pro.), whereas ℵ01/B03 omit it with both the second and the third verbs: καὶ ὥρμησαν ὁμοθυμαδὸν ἐπ' αὐτὸν καὶ ἐκβαλόντες ἔξω τῆς πόλεως ἐλιθοβόλουν αὐτόν (*om.* ℵ01/B03). The absence of the pronoun with the second verb ἐκβαλόντες is similar to its absence with other occurrences of verbs such as ἐκβάλλω (cf. 4.3, §IV.1; or 12.7, §VII). However, the omission in ℵ01/B03 of the pronoun with the third verb is anomalous.

V.3 The pronoun is included with verbs 2 and 3

There are two instances of three verbs where the pronoun is repeated after each one, as set out in Table 6.4.

Table 6.4 Presence of pronoun after verb 2 and verb 3

Ref.	Verb 1	noun/pro.	Verb 2	noun/pro.	Verb 3	noun/pro.
18.26	part.	gen. pro.	vb	acc. pro.	vb	dat. pro.
19.16	part	prep. + acc. pro.	part.	gen. pro.	vb	prep. + gen. pro.

In both cases, there is a change of case and/or preposition from one verb to another. This change justifies the repetition of the pronoun, despite the variant readings in other parts of the verse:

Ref.	D05	ℵ01/B03
18.26	ἀκούσαντες δὲ αὐτοῦ [Ἀκύλας καὶ Πρίσκιλλα] προσελάβοντο αὐτὸν καὶ ἀκριβέστερον αὐτῷ ἐξέθεντο τὴν ὁδόν ↑	ἀκούσαντες δὲ αὐτοῦ [Πρίσκιλλα καὶ Ἀκύλας] προσελάβοντο αὐτὸν καὶ ἀκριβέστερον αὐτῷ ἐξέθεντο τὴν ὁδὸν <u>τοῦ θεοῦ</u>
19.16	καὶ <u>ἐναλλόμενος</u> [εἰς αὐτοὺς ὁ ἄνθρωπος] ἐν ᾧ ἦν τὸ πνεῦμα τὸ πονηρόν, <u>κυριεύσας</u> ἀμφοτέρων ἴσχυσεν κατ' αὐτῶν	καὶ <u>ἐφαλόμενος</u> [ὁ ἄνθρωπος ἐπ' αὐτούς] ἐν ᾧ ἦν τὸ πνεῦμα τὸ πονηρόν, <u>κατακυριεύσας</u> ἀμφοτέρων ἴσχυσεν κατ' αὐτῶν

VI. Change of subject

VI.1. General principle

When the object of two or more successive verbs is the same but there is a change of subject, then the pronoun is regularly repeated, giving rise to Rule 5:

<u>Rule 5</u>: The object of two or more successive verbs is repeated when the subject of the verbs is different.

An example is found at 5.27–28:

5.27–28: Ἀγαγόντες δὲ αὐτοὺς ἔστησαν ἐν τῷ συνεδρίῳ. καὶ ἐπηρώτησεν αὐτοὺς ὁ <u>ἀρχιερεὺς</u> (<u>ἱερεὺς</u> D05) λέγων …

VI.2 Genitive absolute

VI.2.i In the common text

Rule 5 accounts for those instances where a subject of an introductory genitive absolute becomes the object of the following verb at:

10.19; 18.6,27

By definition, the genitive absolute implies a change of subject in the main verb and so it is normal for the object pronoun to be made explicit even though it refers to the just mentioned subject of the genitive absolute. Most examples, however, are affected by variant readings, as set out in §VI.2.ii below. Particular comment is needed on 18.6.

18.6 The pronoun is used to specify the participant addressed by Paul although they have been mentioned in the previous clause: ἀντιτασσομένων δὲ αὐτῶν καὶ βλασφημούντων ἐκτιναξάμενος (<u>ὁ Παῦλος</u> D05) τὰ ἱμάτια (<u>αὐτοῦ</u> D05) εἶπεν πρὸς αὐτούς…On this occasion the participant has not been the object of previous action, but rather was mentioned as the subject of a genitive absolute clause.

VI.2.ii Variant readings

At several places, variant readings arise in the context of a genitive absolute where the repetition of the pronoun is a relevant issue:

1.9; 4.1; 10.19; 18.6,20; 19.1,30

1.9 D05 has a genitive absolute with Jesus as the subject and then as the direct object of the main verb. ℵ01/B03 word the sentence differently and do not have two references to Jesus with a pronoun:

Ref.	D05	ℵ01/B03
1.9	καὐτὰ εἰπόντος αὐτοῦ ↑ νεφέλη ὑπέλαβεν αὐτόν	καὶ ταῦτα εἰπὼν βλεπόντων αὐτῶν ἐπήρθη καὶ νεφέλη ὑπέλαβεν αὐτόν

The pronoun is repeated in D05 since there is a change of subject (Rule 5).

4.1 The sentence begins with a genitive absolute where Peter and the other apostles are talking to the people:

Ref.	D05	ℵ01/B03
4.1	λαλούντων δὲ αὐτῶν πρὸς τὸν λαὸν τὰ ῥήματα ταῦτα ἐπέστησαν ↑ οἱ ἱερεῖς	λαλούντων δὲ αὐτῶν πρὸς τὸν λαὸν ↑ ἐπέστησαν αὐτοῖς οἱ ἱερεῖς (ἀρχιερεῖς B03)

Following the main verb, ἐπέστησαν, ℵ01/B03 refer to the apostles with the indirect object, αὐτοῖς, taking the verb with the meaning 'approach someone'. D05 has no pronoun following ἐπέστησαν, but the reason for that is not that it chooses to omit it (which would be an anomaly given Rule 5 concerning change of subject) but rather that the verb is taken as standing on its own, meaning 'appear', with no object.[3] Comparison may be made with a similar absolute use of the verb at 6.12, where no indirect object is mentioned because the verb has the sense of 'appear'.

10.19 The first mention of the participant, Peter, is by his name in a genitive absolute clause; D05 then includes the pronoun as the addressee of the verb of speaking, though ℵ01/B03 omit it: Τοῦ δὲ Πέτρου διενθυμουμένου περὶ τοῦ ὁράματος εἶπεν αὐτῷ (om. ℵ01/B03) τὸ πνεῦμα.

18.20 Following the genitive absolute, D05 repeats the third person subject pronoun, in a prepositional phrase dependent on the following verb, where ℵ01/B03 omits it: ἐρωτώντων δὲ αὐτῶν ἐπὶ πλείονα χρόνον μεῖναι παρ' αὐτοῖς (om. ℵ01/B03) οὐκ ἐπένευσεν. The omission by B03 is justified by the fact that the verb can be used in an absolute sense, without any need for an indirect object.

19.1 A similar instance of a genitive absolute clause, where the subject in the genitive becomes the addressee of the main verb, occurs in supplementary material at D05. Here, the pronoun is used for the addressee, Paul, who was previously mentioned as the

---

[3] B-A-G, s.v. ἐφίστημι, 1a.

subject of a genitive absolute clause: θέλοντος δὲ τοῦ Παύλου κατὰ τὴν ἰδίαν βουλὴν πορεύεσθαι εἰς Ἱεροσόλυμα εἶπεν αὐτῷ τὸ πνεῦμα…

19.30 The construction of the genitive absolute is straightforward in ℵ01/B03, with the repetition of the genitive subject pronoun as the direct object of the main verb εἴων:

Ref.	D05	ℵ01/B03
19.30	[βουλομένου δὲ τοῦ Παύλου] εἰσελθεῖν εἰς τὸν δῆμον [οἱ μαθηταὶ ἐκώλυον ↑]	[↑ Παύλου δὲ βουλομένου] εἰσελθεῖν εἰς τὸν δῆμον [οὐκ εἴων αὐτὸν οἱ μαθηταί]

D05 omits the accusative pronoun αὐτόν, using a different verb, κωλύω, in its absolute sense of 'stand in the way' (cf. Lk. 9.50).

VII. Special cases

Three instances merit special attention because of the complexity of the sentence in which the verbs and objects are found, and the nature of the MS variation:

1.4; 11.2; 12.7

1.4 The opening verses of Acts (1.1b–5) form a long series of verbal forms, between which the connection is not always clear. The subject of them all is Jesus, and the object is the apostles, referred to initially in the dative (τοῖς ἀποστόλοις) in the second clause of 1.2. Thereafter, they are referred to with the relative pronouns (οὕς οἷς), and then twice by the dative pronoun (αὐτοῖς). After the participle λέγων in 1.3, they are not specified in accordance with the general rule for verbs of speaking (Rule 1). The same is true of a supplementary sentence in 1.2D05: καὶ ἐκέλευσεν κηρύσσειν τὸ εὐαγγέλιον. At 1.4, the MSS disagree over the presence of the pronoun:

Ref.	D05	ℵ01/B03
1.4	καὶ συναλισκόμενος μετ' αὐτῶν παρήγγειλεν αὐτοῖς ἀπὸ Ἱεροσολύμων μὴ χωρίζεσθαι	καὶ συναλιζόμενος ↑ παρήγγειλεν αὐτοῖς ἀπὸ Ἱεροσολύμων μὴ χωρίζεσθαι

In ℵ01/B03, the meaning of the participle συναλιζόμενος is uncertain. It may be 'come together' or 'eat a meal with'; in either case, the singular is strange, standing as it does on its own without specifying with whom Jesus met; a pronoun with a preposition (whether σύν or μετά) is required. In view of this, it would be abnormal for the following αὐτοῖς to serve the participle as well as παρήγγειλεν since the dative pronoun is not appropriate for the participle (Rule 3b). In D05, it is conjectured that συναλισκόμενος arose through phonetic confusion with συναλιζόμενος, since the meaning of συναλίσκομαι ('be taken captive with') is inappropriate here. On the other hand, the inclusion of μετ' αὐτῶν is expected.

11.2D05 is a verse that is considerably longer than in ℵ01/B03 where a complex series of sentences is absent:

Ref. D05	ℵ01/B03
11.2 ὁ μὲν οὖν Πέτρος <u>διὰ ἱκανοῦ χρόνου</u> ἠθέλησε πορευθῆναι εἰς Ἱεροσόλυμα καὶ <u>προσφωνήσας</u> τοὺς ἀδελφοὺς καὶ ἐπιστηρίξας αὐτούς, πολὺν λόγον ποιούμενος διὰ τῶν χωρῶν <u>διδάσκων</u> αὐτούς ὅς καὶ κατήντησεν αὐτοῦ καὶ ἀπήγγειλεν αὐτοῖς τὴν χάριν τοῦ θεοῦ. [οἱ δὲ ἐκ περιτομῆς <u>ἀδελφοὶ</u> διεκρίνοντο πρὸς αὐτὸν] λέγοντες...	↑ Ὅτε δὲ ἀνέβη Πέτρος ↑ εἰς Ἱερουσαλήμ ↑ ↑ ↑ ↑ [διεκρίνοντο πρὸς αὐτὸν οἱ ἐκ περιτομῆς ↑] λέγοντες...

The conjecture of κατήντησεν αὐτοῦ ('he arrived there', where αὐτοῦ is locative) as the original reading of D05 in place of the manuscript reading αὐτοῖς, is made on the grounds that 1) καταντάω is always followed by εἰς/ἐπί + accusative and never the dative; 2) Luke is the only NT author to use the verb καταντάω, and only in Acts (x 9 + x 3 D05), where he always uses εἰς + accusative except at 20.15 (ἄντικρυς + genitive); 3) the repetition of αὐτοῖς as the indirect object of two successive verbs, with no intervening material, is anomalous according to the findings of this study (Rule 3b).

By understanding κατήντησεν αὐτοῖς as κ. αὐτοῦ in this way, the relationship between the various propositions of the sentence, as well as the referents of the pronouns, are clear. Peter is the subject of the finite verb and its dependent infinitive, ἠθέλησε πορευθῆναι, and is taken up in a second main clause with a relative pronoun and a second finite verb, κατήντησεν. In the first main clause, there is a series of two aorist participles (προσφωνήσας, ἐπιστηρίξας), followed by two present participles (ποιούμενος, διδάσκων). The direct object of the two aorist participles and also the present participle is τοὺς ἀδελφούς, first expressed with the accusative noun, then twice with the accusative pronoun. The repetition is explained by the immense importance of the action that D05 attributes to Peter at this point: he is fulfilling the command Jesus gave to him at the Last Supper (Lk. 22.32), that when he 'turned again' he must 'strengthen your brethren' (στήρισον τοὺς ἀδελφούς σου). It is only here, in the D05 text of Acts 11.2, that Peter is recorded as 'strengthening (ἐπιστηρίξας) the brethren', having finally understood that God accepted the Gentiles as equals to the Jews (10.34–35, cf. 10.47) (see also Chapter 3, §IV.3.i).

The final dative pronoun αὐτοῖς refers not to the brethren, as do the accusative pronouns in the first main clause, but to the people of Jerusalem to whom he announced the grace of God once he arrived there (κατήντησεν αὐτοῦ). The pronoun is expected since the referents have not been mentioned beforehand.

12.7 Peter undergoes a series of actions:

Ref. D05	ℵ01/B03
12.7 νύξας δὲ τὴν πλευρὰν τοῦ Πέτρου ἤγειρεν αὐτὸν λέγων· ἀνάστα ἐν τάχει. καὶ ἐξέπεσαν [αἱ ἁλύσεις ἐκ τῶν χειρῶν αὐτοῦ]	πατάξας δὲ τὴν πλευρὰν τοῦ Πέτρου ἤγειρεν αὐτὸν λέγων· ἀνάστα ἐν τάχει. καὶ ἐξέπεσαν [αὐτοῦ αἱ ἁλύσεις ἐκ τῶν χειρῶν]

He is first specified by name in the genitive following πατάξας (א01/B03; νύξας D05) τὴν πλευρὰν τοῦ Πέτρου; thereafter the pronoun is used in the appropriate case, which changes from accusative for the direct object of ἤγειρεν to genitive. After the verb of speaking, λέγων, which intervenes between the second and third verbs, there is no pronoun, following Rule 1.

VIII. Conclusions

The following general rules emerge from the study, concerning the presence of the third person pronoun after a verb after the referent has already been specified in relation to the preceding verb. They may be described as the 'default' patterns that Luke adopts, or his 'unmarked' pattern of usage:

Rules:
1. The pronoun is omitted when the second verb is one of speaking.
2. The pronoun is omitted after παρακαλέω.
3a. The pronoun is omitted after the second verb when it is the direct object of both the first and second verbs.
3b. The pronoun is included after the second verb if the case is different from that required by the first verb, or if a preposition is necessary after one of the verbs.
4a. The pronoun is omitted with the second and successive verbs if the same case is required with no preposition.
4b. The pronoun is included if there is a change of case, or a preposition is required with one or more of the verbs.
5. When the object of two or more successive verbs is the same but there is a change of subject, then the pronoun is repeated.

The presence of the pronoun is not affected by the form of the verbs, whether they be finite, infinitives or participles. The variant readings can usually be accounted for by differences in the immediate context. It is the context that causes the pronoun to be omitted or included rather than an editor's or scribe's habit or style.

7

Parallel terms

A striking feature of Luke's writing in both the Gospel and Acts is the use he makes of alternative phrases or words as a system, for distinguishing between different aspects of a topic. Synonyms, grammatical alternatives and variations in the spelling of names are distinguished in such a way that each member of the set communicates a specific and characteristic meaning. This dual system is a vehicle for communication used with such great precision that its value for expressing Luke's message cannot be ignored; as has already been seen with the different ways he refers to the Holy Spirit, it has the function of an internal code that needs to be recognized and understood. Exegetical discussion of passages mentioned, especially of Luke's text in Codex Bezae (D05) can be found in the commentary on Acts co-authored by myself and Josep Rius-Camps.[1] Three examples will serve to illustrate the point: πρός + noun/pronoun or the dative case to specify the addressee of direct speech; different means to introduce a new character by name; ὡς or ὡςεί to make comparisons.[2]

I. Introducing the addressee of direct speech[3]

It is a common observation that the use of prepositions with nouns is closely related to the function of nominal case, not only because prepositions are associated with certain cases but also because the role of the preposition to some extent overlaps with the use of case – for example, where the genitive case alone of a noun/pronoun can express location corresponding to the use of ἐν with the dative case of the noun/pronoun; or

---

[1] Josep Rius-Camps and Jenny Read-Heimerdinger, *The Message of Acts in Codex Bezae: A Comparison with the Alexandrian Tradition* 4 vols (JSNTSup 257/LNTS 302, 365, 415; London: T&T Clark, 2004–09).
[2] Analysis of further semantic examples (God/the Lord; the spelling of Jerusalem) have been discussed in Jenny Read-Heimerdinger, *The Bezan Text: A Contribution of Discourse Analysis to Textual Criticism* (JSNTSup.236; Sheffield: SAP, 2002), 275–344. See also Rius-Camps & Read-Heimerdinger, *The Message of Acts*, III 47–51; IV, 6–8.
[3] The three sections of this chapter have previously appeared separately. Section 1 was part of Chapter 6, which examined Luke's use of prepositions in my *The Bezan Text of Acts*, 176–82. A shortened form was published in French in Jenny Read-Heimerdinger, 'L'analyse du discours au service de la critique textuelle: illustrations à partir du livre des Actes des Apôtres', in *Actes du Colloque Philologie du Nouveau Testament 2014*, ed. Christian-Bernard Amphoux and Jacqueline Assaël, 261–82 (Aix-en-Provence: Presses Universitaires de Provence, 2018).

similarly, where the dative case can express the notion of indirect object, equivalent to the use πρός with the accusative case. It has been suggested[4] that the use of the preposition increased over time in order to make more clear the function of the case of a noun, and this reasoning has no doubt contributed to variant readings involving a preposition versus case being interpreted as a reflection of scribal preference.

The example of πρός may be taken to illustrate how the approach of discourse analysis is able to identify the difference between the two constructions and the reasons for a speaker to prefer one over the other. The alternation of πρός with the accusative or the dative case alone is particularly evident in Luke's writings to introduce the addressee following a verb of speaking (e.g. λαλέω, λέγω, ἀποκρίνομαι). When the addressee is specified, the preposition πρός is sometimes used to introduce the addressee (more usually in the form of a pronoun rather than a noun) in the accusative; alternatively, the noun/pronoun referring to the addressee is in the dative case with no preceding preposition. Not only does Luke appear to switch between the two constructions at random, but the occurrences of both are also affected by a fair number of variant readings. This could be dismissed as the simple desire to avoid repetition on the part of Luke, or personal preference on the part of the scribe. However, close scrutiny of the text reveals some interesting clues as to the reason for variation by both Luke and the copyists.

An examination of all the occurrences in the firm text of verbs of speaking that are followed by a specified addressee allows some general observations to be made about the grounds for choosing to use either a preposition or the dative case. Readings that are common to ℵ01/B03 will be examined first in order to establish the basis on which Luke chooses one form or the other. Variant readings among the three MSS will then be considered.

I.1 The common text

I.1.i πρός + accusative

The prepositional construction is the more common means that Luke uses to introduce direct speech in the course of the narrative account (31 occurrences in the common text). The addressee is usually a third person, expressed either as a pronoun or a name/noun clause. Examples are:

> Lk. 24.17 εἶπεν δὲ πρὸς αὐτούς – Jesus to the disciples on the road out of Jerusalem
> Acts 8.26 Ἄγγελος δὲ κυρίου ἐλάλησεν πρὸς Φίλιππον λέγων ... The angel of the Lord to Philip
> Acts 18.14: εἶπεν ὁ Γαλλίων πρὸς τοὺς Ἰουδαίους ... Gallio to the Jews

I.1.ii Dative case

This form is less frequent (19 occurrences in the common text). It is used only occasionally by the narrator himself, and otherwise by participants in certain circumstances:

---

[4] See e.g. Daniel B. Wallace, *Greek Grammar beyond the Basics* (Grand Rapids: Zondervan, 1996), 360.

- within a speech when a participant is relating indirectly what someone said to him or to another person, e.g. Acts 11.12 when Peter relates that the Spirit told him to go with the men from Caesarea: εἶπεν δὲ τὸ πνεῦμά μοι συνελθεῖν αὐτοῖς ...)
- the speaker is a divine participant commanding someone to speak to another person, e.g. Acts 5.20 when the angel of the Lord tells the apostles to speak to the people, λαλεῖτε ἐν τῷ ἱερῷ τῷ λαῷ πάντα τὰ ῥήματα τῆς ζωῆς ταύτης
- with first or second person pronouns, in such phrases as λέγω ὑμῖν, or εἶπέν μοι
- when the addressee has already been introduced by πρός at the opening of a dialogue

This last circumstance is particularly helpful for explaining the distinction between the use of πρός + accusative case of the addressee rather than simply the dative case of the addressee. When the dative case is used, it frequently happens that the relationship between speaker and addressee has already been established in a previous clause. This is apparent, for example, on the occasion that Jesus addresses the two disciples on their journey to 'Emmaus'.[5] The narrator says (Lk. 24.17), εἶπεν δὲ πρὸς αὐτούς, but as the story continues the dative case is used (24.19), καὶ εἶπεν αὐτοῖς. Equally, in the response of the disciples to Jesus, it is first said that Cleopas speaks for them both (24.18), ἀποκριθεὶς δὲ εἷς ὀνόματι Κλεοπᾶς εἶπεν πρὸς αὐτόν, and then as they continue the dialogue (24.19), οἱ δὲ εἶπαν αὐτῷ. Likewise, when the angel gives to Peter the command to put on his belt and sandals (Acts 12.8a), εἶπεν δὲ ὁ ἄγγελος πρὸς αὐτόν is used but καὶ λέγει αὐτῷ for the second command to put on his cloak in the following clause (12.8b).

In other words, it appears that πρός with the accusative case is used to establish a relationship between the speaker and the hearer within the narrative, and that the dative case with no preposition is used once it has been established. This accounts for the absence of the preposition with first or second person pronouns where the relationship does not usually need to be underlined since immediacy is already inherent in the presence of the speaker and/or the addressee.

When the default pattern as noted in the points above is disrupted, attention is directed to the addressee for one reason or another. A striking example is found at Acts 11.14 where Peter reports to the Jerusalem leaders that Cornelius was informed by an angel that Peter would tell him things that would lead to his salvation: λαλήσει ῥήματα πρὸς σέ. In such indirect speech (at two removes) and with a second person pronoun, the dative case would be expected. However, at this juncture in Luke's narrative, Peter is at pains to persuade his critics that it was an angel who ordered him to go into a Gentile's house to speak with him about matters of salvation, a practice that was considered unacceptable among many Jews; the preposition has the effect of underlining that the angel informed Cornelius that Peter's message would be addressed specifically to him.

---

[5] The identity of the village in Lk. 24.13 is uncertain. Where most MSS read ᾗ ὄνομα Ἐμμαοῦς, D05 reads ὀνόματι Οὐλαμμαοῦς (see J. Read-Heimerdinger, 'Where is Emmaus?', in *The Early Text of the Gospels and Acts*, ed. D. J. Taylor, 229–44 (Birmingham: Birmingham University Press, 1998); and Josep Rius-Camps and Jenny Read-Heimerdinger, 'Emmaous or Oulammaous? Luke's Use of the Jewish Scriptures in the Text of Luke 24 in Codex Bezae', *Revista Catalana de Teologia* 27 (2002): 23–42. See also §II.4.i below.

The distinct force of the prepositional construction is apparent in the account of the testing of Jesus by the devil in Luke 4. It is the devil who initiates the dialogue with Jesus, whom Luke introduces with the dative pronoun. However, when Jesus responds to the devil's challenge, the prepositional phrase is used to express the devil as Jesus' addressee:

Lk. 4.3 Εἶπεν δὲ αὐτῷ ὁ διάβολος …
4.4 καὶ ἀπεκρίθη πρὸς αὐτὸν ὁ Ἰησοῦς …

Thereafter, for the rest of the dialogue the dative case is used (Lk. 4.6, 8, 9, 12). What Luke would seem to be indicating is that when the devil addressed Jesus he was not seeking to set up a personal relationship with him, he remained at a distance from him. In contrast, in his response, Jesus does demonstrate an attempt to create a more personal engagement with his adversary. The dative case for the subsequent exchanges in the dialogue is in accordance with normal practice to introduce the addressee after the first mention.

I.2 Variant readings

Interesting variant readings arise with respect to the alternative possibilities for introducing the addressee of speech. In the analysis that follows, the readings of א01/B03 will be compared with those of D05. The variants will be identified according to the usual categories as follows: material read by only one of the MSS is underlined with a solid line; an arrow is placed at the corresponding place in the text of the other manuscript to indicate an absence; lexical or grammatical variation is shown by a dotted underline; words that vary in order are in square brackets.

A telling example is seen in Acts 12.15, as Peter arrives at Mary's house in Jerusalem following his escape from prison. Luke relates the dialogue between the servant Rhoda and the people in the house who had been praying for Peter's release. A variant reading, where א01/B03 use a preposition and D05 uses the dative case, occurs in the context of the announcement of Rhoda to the gathering in Mary's house in Jerusalem that Peter was at the door (12.14):

Ref.	D05	א01/B03
Acts 12.15	οἱ δὲ [ἔλεγον αὐτῇ], Μαίνῃ. ἡ δὲ διϊσχυρίζετο οὕτως ἔχειν. οἱ δὲ ἔλεγον πρὸς αὐτήν, Τυχὸν ὁ ἄγγελος [αὐτοῦ ἐστιν]	οἱ δὲ [πρὸς αὐτὴν εἶπαν], Μαίνῃ. ἡ δὲ διϊσχυρίζετο οὕτως ἔχειν. οἱ δὲ ἔλεγον ↑, ↑ Ὁ ἄγγελός [ἐστιν αὐτοῦ].

The response of the assembly is that Rhoda is mad, introduced in B03 by οἱ δὲ πρὸς αὐτὴν εἶπαν but in D05 by οἱ δὲ ἔλεγον αὐτῇ. In א01B03, the preposition with the accusative pronoun can be explained by the fact that this is the first time that mention is made of the relationship between those assembled and the servant Rhoda since it has not been made explicit in the account so far of Rhoda's announcement to them. The preposition underlines the relationship. Nevertheless, in the א01B03 text the relationship is not developed further, for when the assembly next speaks in response to her insistence, their comment is addressed to no-one in particular but is more of a supposition uttered among the gathering, Οἱ δὲ ἔλεγον, Ὁ ἄγγελός ἐστιν αὐτοῦ. The narrator in D05 appears to view the situation differently. The use of the dative pronoun at 12.15a can be taken as indicating that the conversation is seen as already underway since Rhoda spoke to them first (cf. ἀπήγγειλεν, 12.14). When, however, the assembly respond that it is Peter's angel at the door, their suggestion is directed quite specifically to Rhoda in the Bezan text, οἱ δὲ ἔλεγον <u>πρὸς αὐτήν</u>, <u>Τυχὸν</u> ὁ ἄγγελός αὐτοῦ ἐστιν, thus creating an interest in the relationship with the servant, which is an important element in the Bezan text.[6]

The D05 narrator specifies the addressee more frequently than does that of ℵ01/B03, always in accordance with the principles derived from the firm text. Thus, at Acts 7.1D05, when the High Priest questions Stephen about the truth of his accusers' charges, it is the dative case that is used to name his addressee, Εἶπεν δὲ ὁ ἀρχιερεὺς <u>τῷ Στεφάνῳ</u>, where other MSS omit the name. The dative is appropriate in a formal situation such as a trial before the Sanhedrin, where the role of the High Priest is to preside over the proceedings, and not to enter into a personal conversation with Stephen for which the preposition πρός with the accusative would have been appropriate. Conversely, at Acts 16.38D05, as the officers report back to the magistrates in Philippi what Paul has said about their orders for him and his companions to be secretly released, D05 specifies that Paul's words had been deliberately intended for the magistrates themselves:

Ref.	D05	ℵ01/B03
Acts 16.38	ἀπήγγειλαν δὲ <u>αὐτοῖς</u> τοῖς στρατηγοῖς οἱ ῥαβδοῦχοι τὰ ῥήματα ταῦτα <u>τὰ ῥηθέντα πρὸς τοὺς στρατηγούς</u>	ἀπήγγειλαν δὲ (τε ℵ01) ↑ τοῖς στρατηγοῖς οἱ ῥαβδοῦχοι τὰ ῥήματα ταῦτα ↑ ↑

The use of the preposition is appropriate to spell out for whom Paul had formulated his response, even though the words are reported indirectly.

1.3 Conclusion on Luke's means to introduce the addressee

In brief, an analysis of the choice of preposition versus the dative case in Luke's writings shows that πρός has a real function, serving to underline the relationship between the speaker and the addressee. Consequently, as far as the use of πρός to introduce the addressee is concerned at the time of Luke's writing, it is inaccurate to view the use of the preposition as simply arising as a way to clarify the purpose of the dative case. The cause of the variant readings can be found in the different attitudes that the narrator of the respective texts has towards the characters, each using the preposition or the dative appropriately.

---

[6] It is not without purpose that the relationship between the assembly in Jerusalem and the servant Rhoda is underlined. Rhoda is, in fact, much more than an incidental character in this scene, serving as she does to bring out the parallels between the insistent knocking of Peter at the door of the community and his threefold denial of Jesus during the trial scene.

II. Introducing a character by name[7]

Individual characters in Luke's two volumes abound and almost all of them who play an active part are named. Some are even assigned two different names; still others are known by a pseudonym. Luke uses a range of expressions to present the people by name, in a way that could appear to be for the sake of stylistic variety but, once more, a system can be discerned, one that serves to distinguish between the nature of the various kinds of names.

II.1 ὀνόματι

The expression that Luke uses most frequently to introduce a character into his narrative by his or her own name is ὀνόματι followed by the proper noun. It is found at the following places without variant in ℵ01/B03/D05, although sometimes, the order of the expression is reversed (^{s} indicates the reverse order, name + ὀνόματι) and in places the name itself varies:

Lk. 1.5 (Zachariah); 10.38 (Martha); 16.20 (Lazarus); 23.50 (Joseph of Arimathea)

Acts 5.1 (Ananias [ℵ01/B03^s]); 5.34 (Gamaliel); 8.9 (Simon); 11.28 (Agabus); 12.13 (Rhoda); 16.1 (Timothy), 16.14 (Lydia); 18.2 (Aquila); 18.7 (Titius ℵ01/B03/Ioustos D05); 18.24 (Apollos ℵ01/B03^s/Apollonios D05); 20.9 (Eutychus); 21.10 (Agabus)

At a further eight places in Acts, ὀνόματι + name occurs where D05 is lacunous:

Acts 9.10 (Ananias), 9.11 (Saul^s), 9.12 (Ananias^s), 9.33 (Aeneas), 9.36 (Tabitha); 10.1 (Cornelius); 27.1 (Julius); 28.7 (Publius).

II.2 The dative expression, ᾗ/ᾧ ὄνομα

An alternative expression to present a person by name consists of the dative expression ᾗ/ᾧ ὄνομα followed by the proper name. In the text common to ℵ01, B03 and D05, there are only three occurrences of this expression, all in the Gospel:

Lk.1.27 (Joseph); 2.25 (Simeon); 8.41 (Jairos; *cui nomen* d05)[8]

The force of this construction is not clear from these three occurrences. By examining the variant readings, where the dative construction is an alternative for another form

---

[7] Section II develops a summary examination of the topic which was published in Rius-Camps & Read-Heimerdinger, *The Message of Acts*, III, 52–3, n. 80, 81, 82.
[8] The copyist of the Greek page left out the mention of Jairus in error, but the equivalent Latin expression is read by the Latin page of Codex Beaze, d5, and also the Greek text corrected by later correctors H and L; see Jenny Read-Heimerdinger and Josep Rius-Camps (eds), *Luke's Demonstration to Theophilus: The Gospel and Acts of the Apostles according to Codex Bezae*, English expanded edn (London: Bloomsbury, 2013), 343–4.

of expression (see §II.4 below), it becomes apparent that Luke uses the expression ᾗ/ᾧ ὄνομα to indicate that the name has a special significance associated with the role played by the character in the narrative – for example, Joseph as re-enacting the aspects of Joseph the son of Jacob; Simeon as echoing the exalted hopes for Israel for which the High Priest Simeon the Just was esteemed.

II.3 The verb καλέω

καλέω is found in association with a name in various circumstances, as the simple conjugated verb in both the active and the passive or as a passive participle, as well as a compound verb.

II.3.i *καλέω followed directly by a given name or epithet*

There are numerous instances in Luke's Gospel but only two in Acts:

> Lk. 1.32 (Son of the Most High), 35 (Son of God), 60 (John), 76 (Prophet of the Most High); 2.4 (Bethlehem), 23 (holy to the Lord); 6.13 (apostles), 46 (Lord, Lord); 15.19 (your son), 21 (your son); 20.4 (Lord); 22.25 (benefactors)
> Acts 1.19 (Akeldama); 14.12 (Zeus)

II.3.ii *καλέω followed by τὸ ὄνομα and a given name*

This construction is found only in Luke 1:

> Lk. 1.13 (John), 31 (Jesus), 59 ([ἐπὶ τῷ ὀνόματι] Zechariah), 61 (John)

II.3.iii *Passive participle καλούμενος followed by a name*

The name is generally mentioned as a secondary or customary one, rather than the original name:

> Lk. 1.36 (Barren); 6.15 AT (Zealot); 7.11 (Nain; *om.* א01*); 8.2 (Magdalene); 10.39 (Maria); 19.29 (Olivet: ⁵D05); 21.37 (Olivet); 22.3 (Iscariot); 23.33 (The Skull)
> Acts 1.12 (Olivet), 23 (Barsabbas B03/Barnabas D05); 3.11 (Solomon's); 7.58 (Saul); 8.10 (Great); 15.22 (Barsabbas B03/Barabbas D05)

At a further eight places in Acts, the passve participle καλούμενος occurs where D05 is lacunous:

> Acts 9.11 (Straight); 10.1 (The Italian [Cohort]); 27.8 (Fair Havens), 14 (the North-Easter), 16 (Cauda); 28.1 (Malta)

The force of καλέω to indicate a customary or given name can be seen with the name of places: Bethsaida, Olivet, The Skull (Golgotha), Fair Havens, The North-Easter, Cauda and Malta.

II.3.iv The compound verb ἐπικαλέω

Other than in the sense of 'invoke', 'appeal to', the compound verb in the passive occurs both as a reading shared by א01/B03/D05 and as a variant in Acts, and in the Gospel only as a variant reading (see §II.4 below). The readings of the common text occur at:

> Acts 1.23 ὃς ἐπεκλήθη (Justus); 4.36 ὁ ἐπικληθείς (Barnabas); 10.18 ὁ ἐπικαλούμενος (Peter), 32 ὃς ἐπικαλεῖται (Peter); 11.13 τὸν ἐπικαλούμενον (Peter); 12.12 τοῦ ἐπικαλουμένου (Mark), 25 τὸν ἐπικκληθέντα (Mark; τὸν ἐπικαλούμενον א01)

A further occurrence is found in Acts where D05 is lacunous:

> Acts 10.5 ὃς ἐπικαλεῖται (Peter)

It is striking that the compound verb is used only for names that are secondary, where the given name is not just in addition to an original name but is one that was given to indicate the function or quality of the person in some way. This aspect is confirmed by the two variant readings (see §II.4 below).

II.4 Variant readings

The nature of the variants is diverse but falls into two distinct groups consisting of ὀνόματι and ᾗ/ᾧ ὄνομα on the one hand, and the verbs καλέω and ὀνομάζω on the other. At several places, the name is not mentioned at all by one MS. There are some further differences in the word order or in the name itself.

II.4.i ὀνόματι and ᾗ/ᾧ ὄνομα

Table 7.1 shows that twice in B03 and once in D05, ᾗ/ᾧ ὄνομα is read as a variant in place of ὀνόματι. Two variants arise because D05 omits any mention of the name, and on two further occasions B03 and D05 each simply gives the name without ὀνόματι. Each MS also adds καλούμενον once after ὀνόματι.

It is striking that the two expressions ὀνόματι and ᾗ/ᾧ ὄνομα are only found as variants of each other (Lk. 24.13,18), and never in place of καλέω and ὀνομάζω to introduce a name. The example at 13.6, where the Jewish magician and false prophet is attributed the name (ᾧ ὄνομα) of Bar-Jesus in א01/B03 and called by the given name (ὀνόματι καλούμενον) of Bar-Jesoua in D05, suggests the force of the dative construction. It was seen above (§II.3.iii) that the passive particple καλούμενος used here by D05 presents a customary or given name, rather than a person's original one. By means of an elaborate play on words over the following verses, the name Bar-Jesoua is seen in 13.8D05 to be full of powerfully symbolic significance for the scene at Paphos, derived from the meaning of the Hebrew as Ἑτοιμᾶς (from ἕτοιμος, 'ready').[9] Though less

---

[9] The complexity of the play on words in D05 is discussed in Read-Heimerdinger & Rius-Camps, *The Message of Acts*, III, 29–31, 37–42.

Table 7.1 Variant readings involving ὀνόματι and ᾗ/ᾧ ὄνομα

Ref.	D05	ℵ01/B03	Name
Lk.			
1.26	om. mention	ὀνόματι	Nazareth
5.27	ὀνόματι	om. ὀνόματι	Levi
19.2	ὀνόματι	+ καλούμενον	Zacchaeus
24.13	ὀνόματι	ᾗ ὄνομα	Emmaus (Oulammaous D05)
24.18	ᾧ ὄνομα	ὀνόματι	Cleopas
Acts			
13.6	ὀνόματι + καλούμενον	ᾧ ὄνομα Βαριησοῦς	Bar-Jesus (Bar-Jesoua D05)
17.34	om. mention	ὀνόματι	Damaris
19.24	om. ὀνόματι	ὀνόματι	Demetrios [*]

developed in the text of ℵ01/B03, the special significance of the name for this passage is pointed to in ℵ01/B03 by the corresponding dative expression ᾧ ὄνομα.

The other two instances when ὀνόματι and ᾗ/ᾧ ὄνομα arise as alternative readings occur in close proximity in the story of the two disciples in Luke 24. Here, too, there is an intricate play on the names of both the village and the disciple referred to as Cleopas, with each text viewing the status of the two names differently.[10]

II.4.ii καλέω and ὀνομάζω

The variants are set out in Table 7.2. The two verbs occur as variant readings of each other twice in Luke's Gospel. There is some alternation between the simple and

Table 7.2 Variant readings involving καλέω and ὀνομάζω

Ref.	D05	ℵ01/B03	Name
Lk.			
2.21	ὠνομάσθη τὸ ὄνομα αὐτοῦ	ἐκλήθη τὸ ὄνομα αὐτοῦ	Jesus
2.39	κληθήσεται	om. mention	Nazorene
6.13	ἐκάλησεν	ὠνόμασεν	apostles
6.14a	ἐπωνόμασεν	ὠνόμασεν	Peter
6.14b	ἐπωνόμασεν	om. mention	Boanerges
6.15	τὸν ἐπικαλούμενον	om. Mention	Didymos
9.10	τὴν λεγομένην	τὴν καλουμένην	Bethsaida
22.47	ὁ καλούμενος	ὁ λεγόμενος	Judas
Acts			
13.1	ὁ ἐπικαλούμενος	ὁ καλούμενος	Niger
15.37	τὸν ἐπικαλούμενον	τὸν καλούμενον	Mark

[10] See Read-Heimerdinger, 'Where is Emmaus?'; and Rius-Camps & Read-Heimerdinger, 'Emmaous or Oulammaous?'

compound forms of the verbs (× 3), as well the use of verb λέγω (× 2). Three variants arise because ℵ01/B03 omit any mention of the name.

The simple ὀνομάζω verb or its compound ἐπονομάζω is found only as a variant reading in Luke's work. In the absence of any firm readings, no conclusions can be drawn about Luke's own use of the verb.

II.5 Conclusions on the means to introduce a character by name

Some patterns emerge from this analysis, which suggest that Luke is consciously choosing one form or the other. A difficulty in understanding the reasons for the variability is that there is also an unusually large number of variant readings which, while increasing the amount of data, at the same time complicate the picture for they do not readily fall into clear alternative groups. It is likely that the relative closeness of the narrator to the characters affects the way he views them. Another factor is the way that Luke makes use of characters in his narrative as the representative of a group, or to illustrate a point, and it can be expected that his particular purpose at any point affects the wording he uses to name them.

In order to know whether the system Luke makes use of is of his own creation, or whether he is adopting one already in use among Greek speakers, the analysis presented here would need to be compared with a similar analysis of other Greek narrative writing that also uses a variety of means to introduce characters by name.

III. Making comparisons with ὡς and ὡσεί[11]

The final part of this study of dual expressions examines how Luke uses the particles ὡς and ὡσεί as discrete means to make comparisons, in such a way that the choice of particle allows him to convey his message through the distinctive meanings that he assigns to them. The two words are often assumed in exegetical work to be interchangeable terms, both signifying 'about' or 'like'.[12] Grammar books, likewise, tend to view the two particles as equivalent, expressing a degree of comparison or approximation. Certainly, Luke uses both throughout his two volumes (the Gospel and the book of Acts), and there are frequent occurrences of variant readings with some MSS reading ὡς where others read ὡσεί. For two reasons, however, it is reasonable to assume that there exists some real distinction between the terms. First, from a linguistic

---

[11] Section III of this chapter was first published as 'Luke's Use of ὡς and ὡσεί: Comparison and Correspondence as a Means to Convey his Message', in *Grammatica Intellectio Scripturae: Saggi filologici di Greco biblico in onore di padre Lino Cignelli, OFM*, ed. R. Pierri, 251–74 (Studium Biblicum Franciscanum, Analecta 68; Jerusalem: Franciscan Printing Press, 2006).

[12] The use of ὡς as a temporal conjunction introducing a subordinate clause of time (meaning 'when', e.g. Acts 1.10) or as a content conjunction introducing, for example, indirect speech (meaning 'that' or 'how', e.g. Lk. 22.61) is not relevant to this analysis and will not be included.

point of view, it is unlikely that two words overlap completely in their connotation, even though there may be some areas that are covered by both. Secondly, from the point of view of Luke's style, it would be atypical of a writer whose language is characterized by a high degree of regularity and careful attention to detail to use two terms without distinction.

Here, as so often in the studies of this volume, the question of the text of Luke's work is important. In order for a linguistic analysis to be valid, it must be based on a text that actually existed. That is not the case of the text presented in the current editions of the Greek New Testament, which present an eclectic text composed of readings from a variety of MSS. For the purposes of this investigation, therefore, the analysis will be based on the chief representatives of the two main textual traditions of Luke's work, the Alexandrian represented here by Codex Vaticanus (B03)[13] and the so-called 'Western' represented by Codex Bezae (D05).

It is common to ascribe textual variation to the custom or whim of scribes but, as has been seen in earlier chapters, variation is more likely to reflect different ways of viewing the story than the simple mechanical habits of scribes. In examining the occurrences of ὡς and ὡσεί, therefore, particular attention will be paid to their context. In order to make the analysis as rigorous and as complete as possible within the stated parameters, every reading will be examined, those that are attested by both MSS and also those affected by variant readings. The procedure that will be followed is to examine ὡς and ὡσεί in turn and for each, to list first the occurrences of the particle that are common to both MSS; secondly, to note the occurrences that have an alternative reading in one or other of the MSS; and finally, to list the occurrences that are found in one MS only. The tables of references set out in §§III.1, 2 are followed by detailed discussion in §III.3.

It will be seen in the tables that as a particle of comparison, both ὡς and ὡσεί introduce either a clause, or a noun/noun phrase/adjective, or a number. The first use is described here as 'adverbial' and the second as 'adjectival' or 'expressing a quality' according to its function. The third use, introducing a number, is a particular application of the adjectival use which will be considered in a separate section (§III.3.v). The English translation seeks to reflect the Greek as closely as possible. Some of the meanings given in the tables, particularly before numbers, are indicated as possibilities with a question mark; the analysis will seek to ascertain those meanings with greater clarity.

III.1 Occurrences of ὡς in Luke's writings

III.1.i Readings of ὡς common to B03 and D05

Table 7.3 sets out every occurrence of ὡς in the Luke's Gospel and Acts where B03 and D05 agree. An English translation is suggested for each reference, as well as the

---

[13] The readings of Codex Sinaiticus (א01), the other chief representative of the Alexandrian tradition will be noted where they differ from B03, though this is an infrequent occurrence.

Table 7.3 Occurrences of ὡς in the common text

Ref.	Reading	Function
Lk.		
3.4	as it is written	adverb
3.22	came down in bodily form like a dove upon him	adjective (adverb?)
3.23	Jesus was, as it seemed, the son of Joseph	adverb
6.22	treat your name as evil	expressing a quality
6.40	everyone will be like his master	adjective
10.3	I send you like lambs among wolves	adjective
10.18	Satan falling from the sky like lightning	adverb (adjective?)
10.27	love your neighbour as yourself	adverb
12.27	Solomon was not dressed like one of these	adverb
15.19	treat me like one of your servants	adverb (adjective?)
17.6	faith like a mustard seed	adjective
18.11	I am not like this publican	adjective
18.17	receive the kingdom like a little child	adverb
21.35	that day will come like a snare	adverb
22.26 × 2	become like the smallest (D05 = youngest), like the one who serves	expressing a quality
22.27	I am among you as one who serves	expressing a quality
22.31	Satan has demanded to sift you like wheat	adverb
22.52	you have come out as if against a robber	adverb
23.14	you have brought this man as one perverting	expressing a quality
Acts		
1.15 ℵ01 ὡσεί	the crowd numbered as? 120	number
2.15	it is not as you imagine	adverb
3.12	as if we did it by our own power	adverb
3.22	listen to him as to me (μου gen. D05)	adverb D05
	God will raise a prophet like me (ἐμέ acc. B03)	adjective? B03
4.4 ℵ01 om.	the number of men became as? 5,000	number
5.7	as? a 3 hour interval	number
5.36	a number of men as? 400	number
8.32 × 2	as a sheep is led to slaughter … as a lamb is dumb …	adverb
11.5	some object coming down like a great sheet	adjective
11.17	God gave to them as also to us	adverb
22.5	as indeed the HP witnesses (will witness, D05)	adverb

grammatical function of each. A question mark indicates places of ambiguity of meaning; this is notably a problem with numbers, which will be addressed in §III.3.v below.

III.1.ii Variant readings of ὡς

The 15 variant readings noted in Table 7.4 reveal a marked difference between the Gospel, where D05 has ὡς in preference to other words or expressions, and Acts where it is more often B03 that reads ὡς.

Parallel Terms

Table 7.4 Occurrences of ὡς as a Variant Reading

Ref.	Reading	Function	Variant Reading
Lk.			
3.23D05	Jesus began when he was <u>as</u>? 30 years	number	B03 ὡσεί
9.14aD05	there were <u>as</u>? 5,000 men	number	B03 ὡσεί
11.4D05	forgive us <u>as</u> we forgive others	adverb	B03 καὶ γάρ
18.11D05	I am not <u>like</u> other men	adjective	B03 ὥσπερ
24.44D05	just <u>like</u> they said	adverb	B03 καθώς
24.47D05	<u>certainly,</u> to all nations (+ ἐπί D05)	adverb	B03 εἰς
Acts			
7.37B03	God will raise up a prophet <u>like</u> me	adverb (adjective?)	D05 ὡσεί
7.48D05	<u>as</u> the prophet said	adverb	B03 καθώς
7.51B03	you oppose the Holy Spirit <u>like</u> your fathers	adverb	D05 καθώς
10.47B03	they received the Spirit just <u>as</u> we did	adverb	D05 ὥσπερ
13.20B03	<u>as</u>? 450 years	number	D05 καὶ ἕως
13.33B03	<u>as</u> indeed it is written	adverb	D05 οὕτως γάρ
17.15B03	<u>as</u> quickly as possible	superlative adverb	D05 ἐν τάχει
17.28B03	<u>as</u> indeed one of your own said	adverb	D05 ὥσπερ
19.34א01.D05	<u>well</u> over 2 hours (+ ἐπί)	adverb	B03 ὡσεί

III.1.iii Additional readings of ὡς

The 14 occurrences of ὡς found in only one of the two MSS are fairly evenly divided between them, as seen in Table 7.5.

Table 7.5 Readings of ὡς present in one MS

Ref.	Reading	Function	Variant Reading
Lk.			
1.56B03	<u>as</u>? 3 months	number	D05 *om.* ὡς
6.10D05	his hand was restored <u>like</u> the other	adjective	B03 *om.* ὡς
8.42B03	<u>as</u>? 12 years old	number	D05 *om.* ὡς
9.54D05	tell fire ... just <u>as</u> Elijah did	adverb	B03 *om.* clause
11.2aD05	do not babble <u>like</u> the rest	adverb	B03 *om.* clause
11.2bD05	your will be done <u>as</u> in heaven so on earth	adverb	B03 *om.* clause
11.36B03	it will be wholly bright ... <u>as</u> when a lantern illuminates	adverb	D05 *om.* v.
11.44B03	you are <u>like</u> graves	adjective	D05 *om.* ὡς
22.27D05 × 2	I came not <u>as</u> a diner ... but <u>as</u> one serving	expressing a quality	B03 *om.* clause
22.44D05	his sweat became <u>like</u> drops of blood	adjective	B03 *om.* v.; א01 ὡσεί
Acts			
9.18B03	[something] <u>like</u> fishscales fell from his eyes	adjective	D05 *lac.*; א01² ὡσεί
10.11B03	some object coming down <u>like</u> a great sheet being let down by the four corners	adjective	d5 *om*; D05 *lac.*
10.26D05	I am a man just <u>like</u> you	adjective	B03 *om.* ὡς

III.2 Occurrences of ὡσεί in Luke's writings

The tables in this section demonstrate that in the common text ὡσεί is less frequently used than ὡς; there are, correspondingly, few variant readings.

III.2.i Readings of ὡσεί common to B03 and D05

These are presented in Table 7.6.

Table 7.6 Occurrences of ὡσεί in the common text

Ref.	Reading	Function
Lk.		
9.14b	make them sit in groups of <u>about</u>? 50	number
9.28	<u>about</u>? 8 days after this conversation …	number
22.41	he moved away from them <u>about</u>? a stone's throw	distance
22.59	<u>about</u>? an hour later someone else insisted	number
23.44	it was <u>about</u>? the 6th hour	number
24.11	these words seemed to them <u>like</u> madness	adjective
Acts		
2.3	divided tongues <u>like</u> fire appeared	adjective
2.41	there were added on that day <u>about</u>? 3,000 persons	number
6.15	his face was <u>like</u> the face of an angel	adjective
19.7	there were altogether <u>about</u>? 12 men	number

III.2.ii Variant readings of ὡσεί

ὡσεί is consistently read as an alternative for ὡς at the five places of variant reading, as set out in Table 7.7, with D05 reading ὡς at four of the places and B03 at one of them. One occurrence is located in a passage not extant in D05. These variants have already appeared in Table 7.4.

Table 7.7 Occurrences of ὡσεί as a variant reading

Ref.	Reading	Function	Variant Reading
Lk.			
3.23B03	Jesus began when he was <u>about</u>? 30 years	number	D05 ὡς
9.14aB03	there were <u>about</u>? 5.000 men	number	D05 ὡς
Acts			
7.37D05	God will raise up a prophet <u>like</u> me	adjective	B03 ὡς
10.3B03	he saw clearly in a vision at <u>about</u> the 9th hour (+ περί)	number	ℵ01 ὡς; D05 *lac.*
19.34B03	<u>about</u>? over two hours (+ ἐπί)	adjective	ℵ01, D05 ὡς

III.2.iii Additional readings of ὡσεί

There is only one additional occurrrence of ὡσεί, located in Acts, presented in Table 7.8.

Table 7.8 Reading of ὡσεί present in one MS

Ref.	Reading	Function	Variant Reading
Acts			
16.9D05	there appeared a man <u>like</u> a Macedonian	adjective	B03 *om.* ὡσεί

III.3 Analysis of the use of ὡς and ὡσεί

III.3.i Adverbial use of ὡς

In a number of instances among the common readings of ὡς, the particle is used to introduce a clause (or a phrase where the verb is understood) and so serves as an adverbial conjunction: Lk. 3.4,23; 10.18,27; 12.27; 15.19; 18.17; 21.35; 22.31,52; Acts 2.15; 3.12,22; 8.32 × 2; 11.17; 22.5). In contrast, ὡσεί is never used to introduce a clause, whether the verb is explicit or elided.

The adverbial function of ὡς to introduce a clause of comparison can also be observed among the variant readings in both D05 and B03, where the alternative is καθώς (Lk. 24.44 D05; Acts 7.48 D05, 51B03) or ὥσπερ (Acts 10.47B03; 17.28B03) or a phrase with γάρ (καὶ γάρ, Lk.11.4 D05; οὕτως γάρ, Acts 13.33B03). There are four similar readings of a clause introduced by ὡς that is present in only one or the other text: Lk. 9.54D05; 11.2aD05, 2bD05, 36B03.

The element of comparison found in a clause introduced by ὡς may be of various kinds:

- ὡς introduces a clause that relates something back to what was written or said in Scripture, or to what someone has said (or imagined) more recently, at Lk. 3.4; 24.44D05; Acts 2.15; 7.48D05; 13.33B03; 17.28B03; 22.5. The parenthetical 'as it seemed' concerning Jesus' relationship to Joseph at Lk. 3.23 could also be included in this category.
- An action is compared with a hypothetical situation at Lk. 22.52; Acts 3.12, with ὡς meaning 'as if' in such examples.
- A noun may be compared with another noun because the same action is performed by both: Lk. 9.54D05; 11.2aD05; 12.27; 18.17; Acts 7.51B03; 10.47B03. The purpose of such a comparison is sometimes to create a simile where the action of one noun is compared with the action of another in order to make a point more graphically, as at Lk. 21.35, where the coming of the day of judgment is likened to the falling of a trap; and Lk. 22.31, where Jesus likens his disciples to wheat that Satan wants to sift. A complex example of this kind occurs at Acts 8.32, where Jesus' silent acceptance of his mistreatment is compared with the muteness of a sheep being taken to be shorn or a lamb to be slaughtered. The simile is based

on appearance as well as action at Lk. 11.36B03 where the metaphorical brightness of a body is likened to a lamp shining.
- In some cases, an action is performed by one subject with respect to two objects which are thus compared: Lk. 10.27; 15.19; Acts 3.22D05; 11.17.
- At Lk. 11.4 D05, it is the action itself that is compared with respect to two different subjects, God and people.
- The location is the focus of comparison at Lk. 11.2bD05

There are several examples of comparisons introduced by ὡς where there is ambiguity as to whether the comparison is adverbial (involving a whole clause with a verb) or whether it is a matter of simply comparing two nouns: Lk. 3.22; 10.18; Acts 3.22B03; 7.37B03. Such instances will be considered in the section below (§III.3.iv) which examines comparisons between nouns. Among these references, although ὡς is read by both texts at Acts 3.22, the wording of the verse varies in other respects with the result that while it is clear that ὡς introduces a clause in D05 and is adverbial, it is possible that in B03 the comparison is adjectival.

III.3.ii *ὡς or ὡσεί followed by a preposition*

At Lk. 24.47D05 and Acts 19.34, ὡς is followed by ἐπί. In the first instance, B03 simply reads εἰς with neither ὡς or ὡσεί, where the context is the command of Jesus to the apostles to preach the gospel to all nations. In the Bezan text, ὡς intensifies the force of the preposition that follows it[14] and underlines the inclusion of the Gentiles in the programme of proclamation Jesus sets out for his apostles.[15]

At Acts 19.34, the force of ὡς could again be to underline the length of time for which the Ephesians cried out in praise of their goddess Artemis ('for a full two hours'). The alternative reading ὡσεί is usually taken as expressing the weaker sense of 'approximately', so understating the time that the uproar in the town lasted (cf. §III.3.v below).

At Acts 10.3, where unfortunately D05 is lacunous, B03 reads ὡσεί before the preposition περί and a time phrase (ὥραν ἐνάτην τῆς ἡμέρας) to explain the time of day when Cornelius was praying in Caesarea and had a vision. The use of ὡσεί in this case is pleonastic, since both the particle and the preposition convey the idea of approximation ('about', 'around'), and it is probably for this reason that some MSS omit περί.[16] On the other hand, in line with the observations on the use of ὡς before other prepositions, ὡς before περί would have drawn attention to the time of Cornelius' prayer – a fact that was worth underlining since, corresponding as it did to the hour of

---

[14] Cf. 1 Macc. 5.29 (*vl.* ἕως); Acts 17.14 (*vl.* ἕως; D05*om*.). G. B. Winer, *A Treatise on the Grammar of New Testament Greek*, trans. W. F. Moulton (1882; repr. Eugene, Ore.: Wipf and Stock, 2001), 771: 'ὡς, when joined with a preposition denoting direction ... expresses either the definite intention of following a certain direction or feint of doing so'; cf. Nigel Turner, *A Grammar of New Testament Greek*. III, *Syntax*, ed. J. H. Moulton (Edinburgh: T&T Clark, 1963), 321, who states that 'in Hell. Gk. ὡς ἐπί = against, *versus*', but that can hardly be the meaning at Lk. 24.47.

[15] In Luke's Gospel according to D05, the Gentiles have not previously been mentioned as beneficiaries of the good news, since Simeon's speech omits the reference to 'the nations' (Lk. 2.32D05).

[16] The majority of minuscules omit the preposition, as does the Latin tradition.

the Jewish afternoon sacrifice, it was noteworthy that the Gentile Cornelius should be displaying piety in observing a Jewish practice. Cornelius will comment on the time of his vision when he reports its content to Peter (10.30) and in the Bezan text at this point particularly heavy emphasis is laid on the time of day and Cornelius' piety.[17] These factors lend weight to the surmise that ὡς (as in ℵ01) rather than ὡσεί was Luke's intended particle at 10.3: ὡσεί is not only redundant but avoids drawing attention to the importance of the 'ninth hour', just as the Alexandrian text will later play down the importance of the time at 10.30.

III.3.iii Expressing a quality

Another use of ὡς is seen in several examples where it denotes a quality, whether expressed as an adjective or a noun (Lk. 6.22; 22.26 [× 2], 27 [+ 2 D05]; 23.14). The example of the superlative adverbial phrase, ὡς τάχιστα, at Acts 17.15B03 (where D05 simply reads the phrase ἐν τάχει) could also be included as an expression of quality. ὡσεί is never used in this way by either text.

III.3.iv Adjectival comparison of noun/pronoun

In order to distinguish between the force of ὡς and ὡσεί when they introduce an adjectival comparison, it will be useful to classify such occurrences into smaller groups.

a) 'A prophet/man like . . .'

This type of expression occurs four times altogether, with both ὡς and ὡσεί. Two occurrences are found only in D05: at Acts 10.26D05, Peter declares to Cornelius, 'I am a man just like (ὡς) you'; and at 16.9D05, the narrator describes the man who appeared in a vision to Paul, 'a man like (ὡσεί) a Macedonian'. The choice of particle can be explained by the underlying meaning: Peter wants to convey to Cornelius that he must not bow down to him because he is a man just as Cornelius is. In this case, the verb ἐστίν is to be understood, and so ὡς is used as in other examples of an elliptical clause (cf. §III.3.i above). In Paul's vision, on the other hand, the man whom Paul saw 'looked like' a Macedonian in his physical appearance, and ὡσεί is used to express this resemblance. In the first example, it is a matter of intrinsic identity, whereas in the second the comparison is more superficial.

The two other occurrences in this category concern the similarity between Moses and Jesus, and involve the declaration, 'God will raise up a prophet like me' (προφήτην ὑμῖν ἀναστήσει κύριος ὁ θεὸς ὑμῶν ἐκ τῶν ἀδελφῶν ὑμῶν ὡς ἐμέ, Acts 3.22B03; προφήτην ὑμῖν ἀναστήσει ὁ θεὸς ἐκ τῶν ἀδελφῶν ὑμῶν ὡς [D05 ὡσεί] ἐμέ, 7.37). The pronouncement takes up Deut. 18.15, which in the Septuagint reads: προφήτην ἐκ τῶν ἀδελφῶν σου ὡς ἐμὲ ἀναστήσει σοι κύριος ὁ θεός σου, αὐτοῦ ἀκούσεσθε (cf. 18.18:

---

[17] Compare Acts 10.30B03: ἀπὸ τετάρτης ἡμέρας μέχρι ταύτης τῆς ↑ ὥρας ἤμην ↑ τὴν ἐνάτην ↑ προσευχόμενος, with D05: ἀπὸ τῆς τρίτης ἡμέρας μέχρι ταύτης τῆς ἄρτι ὥρας ἤμην νηστεύων τὴν ἐνάτην τε προσευχόμενος.

προφήτην ἀναστήσω αὐτοῖς ἐκ τῶν ἀδελφῶν αὐτῶν ὥσπερ σέ). B03 twice uses ὡς in Acts to make the comparison, echoing the wording of Deut. 18.15LXX. It is possible to see the particle as relating to the verb ἀναστήσει, 'he will raise up', in which case its function is to introduce an underlying clause: 'he will raise up a prophet from among your brethren as he raised up me'. By referring this prophecy to Jesus, Peter first, then Stephen, make a play on the word ἀναστήσει, which has the figurative sense of 'cause to appear' as well as the specific sense of 'resurrect'. But it could also be that the intention is to compare the new prophet with Moses as a person: 'a prophet like me'. Other comparable occurrences of ὡς (see §III.4.iii below) suggest that on this interpretation of the sentence, Jesus is being presented as a 'new Moses' who embodies the essential qualities and characteristics of the first Moses.

As has already been noted (see §III.1 above), the wording of D05 at Acts 3.22 differs from that of the B03 text, so that the comparison is no longer between Moses and the new prophet as it is in the LXX and the B03 text, but rather it is between the *hearing* of Moses and the *hearing* of the new prophet, Jesus. The freedom with which the Bezan narrator adapts the LXX text is characteristic of the way the D05 text of Luke's work generally presents a modification of sources to suit the narrative purpose.[18] The rewording also causes Peter to play down the similarity between Moses and Jesus, insisting instead on the importance of Jesus by demanding that the attention paid to his teaching be as great as that paid to Moses, which was, of course, immeasurable.

Likewise at Acts 7.37D05, Stephen avoids the suggestion that Jesus is to be viewed as reproducing the essence of Moses by reading ὡσεί in place of ὡς. The new prophet will be *like* Moses but will not be identical to him since Jesus will, in fact, be greater than Moses.

At three further places in Luke's Gospel, one person is compared with another on the level of behaviour or attitudes, where ὡς is used each time to make the comparison, except once when B03 reads the variant ὥσπερ: at Lk. 6.40, Jesus declares that a servant is like (ὡς) his master; at 18.11a+b, a Pharisee praying in the Temple thanks God that he is 'not like (ὡς) other men', nor 'like (ὡς [ὥσπερ B03]) this publican'.

b) Adjectival ὡσεί

There are three adjectival comparisons among the readings with ὡσεί by which one noun is compared with another: Lk. 24.11, the women's words appeared to the apostles like madness; Acts 2.3, tongues like fire appeared to the apostles on the day of Pentecost; 6.15, the Sanhedrin members saw Stephen's face like the face of an angel. On each occasion, it is a matter of one thing seeming like something else but not at the level of intrinsic qualities. The remaining occurrences of ὡσεί that have not yet been examined all introduce a number. These will be discussed in §III.3.v below.

c) Adjectival ὡς

The readings that compare one noun with another using ὡς in an adjectival manner are of a different nature from those that introduce the adjectival comparison with ὡσεί.

---

[18] This is as true of the other Gospels as of the Jewish Scriptures; cf. Read-Heimerdinger, *The Bezan Text*, 349–50.

The nature of the comparison presented by ὡς is such that it draws upon some intrinsic quality of the noun used as a point of comparison, and the similarity in consequence goes beyond appearances. Taking first the readings common to both texts:

Lk. 3.22: the sentence likening the coming of the Spirit on Jesus at baptism to a dove could be construed as meaning that 'the Spirit descended as a dove descends', in which case the function of ὡς is adverbial. However, the comparison with a dove is made carefully explicit by the phrase 'in bodily form' (σωματικῷ εἴδει), which suggests that it is the appearance and not the movement of the Spirit that is in focus. At the same time, the point of the comparison is rather more than simply to describe the appearance of the Spirit; it stresses the reality of what happened and gives the Spirit a visual identity.[19] It is this emphasis on the manifestation of the Spirit that warrants the use of ὡς rather than ὡσεί. It may be, furthermore, that the dove is an image evoking a sense that was recognized in contemporary Judaism. Although attempts to identify the significance of the dove in these terms have been inconclusive, it is worth noting that in the Rabbinic writings the dove is more a symbol than a metaphor, representing not only the Spirit of God but also Israel.[20]

Lk. 10.3: the metaphor employed by Jesus as he sends the 70 (72 D05) disciples ahead of him in Samaria compares them with lambs among wolves whose attacks would have meant certain death for them. Standing on its own, the comparison seems to make Jesus' action a somewhat senseless one. It takes on a poignant meaning, however, when considered in the context of a saying reported among the Rabbis: 'Hadrian said to R. Jehoshua: There is something great about the sheep (Israel) that can persist among 70 wolves (the nations). He replied: Great is the shepherd who delivers it and watches over it and destroys them (the wolves) before them (Israel)' (*Tanchuma Toledot* 32b).[21] By evoking the metaphor, therefore, Jesus' words evoke a familiar image that has more significance than a simple comparison.

Lk. 10.18: Jesus' description of the fall of Satan from heaven like lightning reflects the story of the 'Day Star, son of Dawn' (Isa. 14.12) being thrown down from heaven. The comparison draws a parallel not just between the appearance of Satan as a star and the flash of lightning, but with the fact of falling from the sky.

Lk. 17.6: the comparison of faith with a mustard seed is a complex one, referring not only to its small size but also to its ability to multiply abundantly.

Acts 11.5: this is the second of two references to Peter's vision of the clean and unclean animals (cf. on 10.11B03 below). In this instance, when Peter himself describes the object he saw in his vision, he says it was like a sheet being lowered by its four corners from the sky: εἶδον ἐν ἐκστάσει ὅραμα, καταβαῖνον σκεῦός τι ὡς ὀθόνην μεγάλην τέσσαρσιν ἀρχαῖς καθιεμένην. The description is quite specific and carefully observed, with even the detail that the sheet was held by each corner being noted. The

---

[19] See I. Howard Marshall, *The Gospel of Luke* (NIGTC; Exeter: Paternoster Press, 1978), 152–3.
[20] Louis Ginzberg, *The Legends of the Jews*, 7 vols, 11th edn, trans. Henrietta Szold and Paul Radin (1909–38; Baltimore: Johns Hopkins University Press, 1998), IV, 157, 365.
[21] G. Kittel and G. Friedrich (eds), *Theological Dictionary of the New Testament*, trans. G. W. Bromiley (Grand Rapids, Mich.: Eerdmans, 1964–76), I, 340.

comparison is deliberate, and gives the impression that Peter is struggling express to the brethren in Jerusalem what he had seen in his vision.

There are five more occurrences of ὡς used to introduce an adjectival comparison that are read by only one of the two texts in question. Twice D05 omits the particle whilst retaining the rest of the sentence:

Lk. 11.44B03: Jesus compares the Pharisees to graves that people walk over without knowing it in an image in which the resemblance of the Pharisees to graves obviously lies in their behaviour and attitudes, not their appearance. While D05 presents the comparison as a metaphor without any particle to introduce it, B03 uses a simile in which ὡς makes the figure of speech explicit.

Acts 10.11B03: at the first mention of Peter's vision by the narrator, the wording in the B03 text is identical to what Peter will later say (cf. on 11.5 above). The narrator in the Bezan text (of which only the Latin page is extant) is more direct, using a metaphor to describe the sheet rather than a simile, by omitting the comparative particle: *vidit... ex quattuor principiis ligatum vas quodam et linteum splendidum quod differebatur de caelo in terram* (retroversion: εἶδον ... ἐκ τέσσαρσιν ἀρχαῖς δεδεμένον σκεῦός τι καὶ ὀθόνην λαμπρὰν καθιέμενον ἐκ τοῦ οὐρανοῦ ἐπὶ τῆς γῆς); in other words, according to the Bezan narrator, it is only when Peter speaks that he resorts to using explicitly an image to explain what he saw, whereas the narrator implies the image with a metaphor.

For two instances of an adjectival comparison, ὡς is read by D05 where B03 omits either the verse or the phrase containing the particle:

Lk. 6.10D05: when Jesus restored the man's withered hand, he healed it not just so that it looked like his other hand but so that it was entirely like the other one.

Lk. 22.44D05: the description of Jesus' agony is considerably abbreviated in B03. D05, like many other MSS including ℵ01, contains the detail that his sweat became like drops of blood falling to the ground, though most witnesses read ὡσεί whereas D05 has ὡς.[22] The point of the simile has been much debated, with some commentators interpreting it as a reference to the appearance of the sweat which was the colour of blood,[23] or like the size and quantity of drops of blood,[24] for which ὡσεί would be appropriate (cf. §III.3.iv.b above). Others prefer the explanation that it is the falling of the sweat that is being compared with the falling of drops of blood. This adverbial force of the simile is more likely to be expressed with ὡς, according to findings of the analysis carried out here, and could account for the choice of ὡς by D. There is, however, rather more to the description of Jesus' sweat in terms of drops of blood than either its appearance or its manner of falling, for the comparison goes back to the Akedah legend (based on Gen. 22.1–19) according to which the sweat of Isaac as he lay on the sacrificial

---

[22] For details of the witnesses to the long reading at Lk. 22.44, see The American and British Committees of the International Greek New Testament Project (eds), *The Gospel According to St. Luke*. 2 vols (Oxford: Clarendon Press, 1984, 1987), Part 2. See also Claire Clivaz, *L'Ange Et la Sueur de Sang (Lc 22,43-44): Ou Comment On Pourrait Bien Encore Ecrire L'Histoire* (Biblical Tools and Studies 07; Leuven: Peeters, 2007), esp. 201–98.

[23] Marshall, *The Gospel of Luke*, 832–3.

[24] Craig A. Evans, *Luke* (New International Biblical Commentary; Peabody, Mass./Carlisle, UK: Hendrickson Publishers/Paternoster Press, 1995), 329.

altar was supposed to have become like drops of blood.[25] So, when applied to Jesus, the simile evokes the Isaac story and thereby serves as a kind of 'peg' to establish a comparison between Jesus and Isaac.

At one final place where ὡς introduces an adjectival comparison, the MS of D05 is defective:

Acts 9.18B03: when Saul recovered his sight in Damascus, it is said that, 'immediately there fell from his eyes like fishscales', καὶ εὐθέως ἀπέπεσαν αὐτοῦ ἀπὸ τῶν ὀφθαλμῶν ὡς λεπίδες. The comparison may be understood as indicating that something that looked like fishscales fell from Saul's eyes, for which ὡσεί would be the expected particle. ὡς on the other hand, as read by B03, would seem to point to the manner in which some kind of flaky substance fell from Saul's eyes, 'as fishscales fall'.[26] Another possibility is that ὡς activates an allusion to the use of the same image in the apocryphal book of Tobit (Tob. 11.7–13; cf. 2.10; 3.17) where the main character Tobit is a Jew of exceptional faithfulness and zeal for the Law (1.3–11). The choice of image suggests that it would be worth checking for any further evidence that Luke intended an assimilation between Tobit and Saul of Tarsus.

To conclude on the adjectival use for comparison of ὡς and ὡσεί: in all the instances of adjectival ὡς examined in this section, the comparison is more complex than a straightforward comparison of appearance. The adverbial use of ὡς is reflected to some extent in its adjectival use, in that the similarity between two nouns is often a matter of behaviour or actions, with the noun that stands as the object of reference sometimes being of special importance for the significance of the comparison. In such cases, the origin of the metaphor is underlined by ὡς to draw attention to its significance. The complexity of the simile or the allusion to its origin or earlier use seem to be factors that distinguish the significance of ὡς from that of ὡσεί.

III.3.v ὡς and ὡσεί before numbers

Comparing the presence of ὡς or ὡσεί before a number does not, of itself, reveal its force. It is only by analogy with the function of the two particles in other circumstances that their significance before numbers can be suggested. The occurrences of ὡς and ὡσεί to introduce numbers, together with a comparable instance of a distance measurement at Lk. 22.41, are given again in new tables for ease of reference. The procedure will be once more to examine the occurrences that are common to both texts as well as those that involve variant readings, taking the examples introduced with ὡσεί first.

a) Common readings of ὡσεί introducing a number

Table 7.9 lists seven readings found without variant in the texts of B03 and D05.

---

[25] F. García Martínez, 'Pseudo Jubilees fragment from Cave 4', in *The Sacrifice of Isaac: The Aqedah (Genesis 22) and its Interpretations*, ed. E. Noort and E. Tigchelaar (Themes in Biblical Narrative 4; Leiden: Brill, 2002).

[26] Charles Kingsley Barrett believes that this understanding of ὡς is the more natural one, see *A Critical and Exegetical Commentary on the Acts of the Apostles*, 2 vols (Edinburgh: T&T Clark, 1994, 1998), I, 458.

Table 7.9 Common readings of ὡσεί before a number

Ref.	Reading	Function
Lk.		
9.14b	make them sit in groups of about? 50	number
9.28	about? 8 days after this conversation...	number
22.41	he moved away from them about? a stone's throw	distance
22.59	about? an hour later someone else insisted	number
23.44	it was about? the 6th hour	number
Acts		
2.41	there were added on that day about? 3,000 persons	number
19.7	there were altogether about? 12 men	number

It has been seen that ὡσεί generally expresses the sense of 'something like', especially with reference to visible appearance. When applied to numbers, or a distance at Lk. 22.41, this sense is apparent as an indication of an approximate figure or measurement. So, at Lk. 9.14, the disciples were instructed by Jesus to sit the crowd down in groups of roughly 50 people. Likewise, when Jesus took his disciples to the Mount of Olives, he moved away from them to pray, leaving them at about a stone's throw away (Lk. 22.41).

Two points, however, should be noted: first, that elsewhere, Luke uses the preposition περί to express an approximate time (Acts 10.9, when Peter went to pray on the rooftop περὶ ὥραν ἕκτην; cf. 22.6B03 Ἐγένετο δέ μοι πορευομένῳ καὶ ἐγγίζοντι τῇ Δαμασκῷ περὶ [om. D05] μεσημβρίαν);[27] and secondly, that in most of the examples the number itself is not without significance. It is also worth pointing out that Luke is the only evangelist to use ὡσεί before a number. Consequently, consideration needs to be given to the possible metaphorical or symbolic meaning of the number to which, within the narrative context, the particle ὡσεί may be drawing attention. It must be borne in mind especially that Luke is a careful writer who pays close attention to detail, including all manner of information that is relevant as much, if not more, for its symbolic importance as for its literal meaning. Numbers are frequently used in Jewish writings to reveal the hidden meaning of an event, and by examining the way Luke uses numbers, it can be seen that he adopts this feature in his own work as a means to convey to his addressee an underlying, spiritual reality. In some of the cases in the above list, the number serves to connect an incident he is narrating to an event recorded in the Jewish Scriptures. The following observations may be made:

Lk. 9.28: The mention of 'about eight days' (μετὰ τοὺς λόγους τούτους ὡσεὶ ἡμέραι ὀκτώ) prefaces the transfiguration scene, separating it from a series of sayings pronounced by Jesus about the cost of following him, the prophecy of his future glory and the prediction that some among his listeners would see the kingdom of God before they died (9.23–27). The interval of eight days could be thought to refer to the time between this latter promise and its fulfilment as Peter, John and James witness the transfiguration of Jesus in glory on the mountain. If, however, the promise of seeing the

---

[27] Comparison can also be made with the anomalous reading of περί after ὡσεί at Acts 10.3B03, as discussed in §III.3.ii above.

kingdom of God is understood as a more general promise applying to those who accept to suffer for Jesus' sake, then the interval relates rather to the time between Jesus' mention of his glory and the scene in which his glory is seen by some of his chosen disciples. The mention of 'eight' days, which Luke has modified with respect to Mark's 'six' days (cf. Mk 9.2), is an indication that Luke has deliberately chosen the number. It may correspond to the first day after the Sabbath, the day of the resurrection and new life.[28]

Lk. 23.44: the time when Jesus was on the cross is specified as being from 'about' the sixth hour until the ninth, his actual death coinciding with the time of the afternoon sacrifice in the Temple (Josephus, *Ant.*, 14.65; cf. Acts 3.1; 10.3 [D05 *lac.*],30). The three-hour interval is recorded by all three of the Synoptics (cf. Mt. 27.45–46; Mk 15.33–34). The sixth hour, which corresponds to midday (μεσημβρία), may be an allusion to the time when, according to tradition, the Israelites were said to have worshipped the golden calf (cf. Exodus 32);[29] it was also thought of as the hour of destruction, perhaps because of the noontime heat (cf. Jer. 15.8). John specifies that it was the sixth hour on the Day of Preparation for the Passover when the Jews demanded of Pilate that Jesus be crucified (Jn 19.14, ὥρα ἦν ὡς [ὡσεί *vl*; D05 *lac.*] ἕκτη).[30] The importance of the sixth hour is thus underlined in all the Gospels, even if the precise meaning of the symbolism cannot be determined with certainty. Elsewhere in Luke's writings, midday is a time of divine revelation (to the Ethiopian eunuch, Acts 8.26;[31] Peter, 10.9; Paul, 22.6).

Acts 2.41: the number of souls added to the community of Jesus-believers in Jerusalem following Peter's preaching on the day of Pentecost is recorded as being ὡσεί τρισχίλιαι (3,000). The number three, and also its multiples, is a significant figure throughout Jewish tradition where it represents completeness.[32] By designating as 3,000 the number of those who believed on the first occasion of public testimony to Jesus, Luke is thus conferring a note of satisfaction and approval with the outcome on the day of Pentecost. The number may be compared to those recorded at 4.4 as later believing after the healing of the lame man, ὡς χιλιάδες πέντε (5,000; see §III.3.v.b below).

Acts 19.7: the disciples Paul found in Ephesus had been baptized with the baptism of John and had not received the Holy Spirit. They seem to have learnt about Jesus before Paul's visit from Apollo, a Jew from Alexandria who had been in Ephesus before

---

[28] 'Eight' is used again by Luke to provide a temporal context for the paralysis of Aeneas, a representative of the community in Lydda (Acts 9.31): it is after eight years of sickness that Peter brings healing to him. Cf. Lk. 24.1; Acts 20.7; Jn 20.1, 19, 26; *Barn.* 15, where the author reasons that the Sabbath that is acceptable to God is the eighth day 'which is the beginning of another world. Wherefore also we keep the eighth day for rejoicing in which Jesus also rose from the dead and having been manifested ascended into the heavens' (trans. J. B. Lightfoot, http://www.earlychristianwritings.com/text/barnabas-lightfoot.html (last accessed 30/09/21)).

[29] Ginzberg, *Legends*, III, 147–48. It is not clear how early was the tradition concerning the association of the sixth hour with the worship of the golden calf.

[30] The quaternion containing Jn 19.14 is missing from D05. A later hand has written ὡσεί + τρίτη, where other MSS read ὡς ἕκτη.

[31] μεσημβρία could also mean 'the south' at Acts 8.26.

[32] E. Frankel and B. P. Teutsch (eds), *The Encylopaedia of Jewish Symbols* (Northvale, N.J.: Jason Aronson, Inc., 1995).

Paul and had spoken in the synagogue there about Jesus but basing his instruction on the baptism of John (18.24-28). The belief in Jesus of these disciples was, in other words, gained within a Jewish context and their discipleship was based on a Jewish understanding of the matter. The limited Jewish perspective that existed within this community is indicated by the number '12' which, throughout Luke's work as indeed in Jewish writings, is used to symbolize the ancient institution of Israel by virtue of its association with the 12 tribes who make up the people of Israel. The particle ὡσεί which precedes should not, therefore, be thought as meaning an approximate number, but rather as acknowledging the restricted Jewish mentality of the men in Ephesus.

b) Common readings of ὡς introducing a number

In the text shared by B03 and D05, ὡς prefaces a number at four places in Acts, as shown in Table 7.10.

In the analysis of ὡς used to present a comparison (§III.3.iv.c) it was seen that the element of comparison was stronger than with ὡσεί, and also that the origin of the comparison was often rather more important than in the comparison introduced with ὡσεί. It may be expected, therefore, that when ὡς introduces a number, the number is not an approximate one without any importance in itself. It is more likely, rather, that the number has a special significance and that this significance may reside in another reference to which allusion is being made because it serves as a point of comparison. This seems to be what is happening on the four occasions in the above list, though determining a precise point of comparison is not always possible:

Acts 1.15: the number of people present in the upper room after Jesus' ascension, during the period when they were waiting for the arrival of the Holy Spirit, is recorded by Luke as 120, prefaced by ὡς in B03 and D05.[33] The number is cited in an emphatic clause, sandwiched between the words introducing Peter's speech and his opening address, when he stood up to propose to the gathering that a replacement for Judas be chosen. That the number has a symbolical rather than a literal purpose is indicated by the particle in both MSS, but the meaning of the symbol is most clearly apparent in the Bezan text:

Ref. D05	B03
1.15 ἀναστὰς ὁ Πέτρος ἐν μέσῳ τῶν μαθητῶν εἶπεν – ἦν γὰρ ὁ ὄχλος ὀνομάτων ἐπὶ τὸ αὐτὸ ὡς ·ρκ· (= ἑκατὸν εἴκοσι)	ἀναστὰς ↑ Πέτρος ἐν μέσῳ τῶν ἀδελφῶν εἶπεν – ἦν τε ↑ ὄχλος ὀνομάτων ἐπὶ τὸ αὐτὸ ὡς ἑκατὸν εἴκοσι

The narrator's parenthetical comment in D05 informs his addressee that the justification for Peter's standing up to speak (γάρ) was that there were 120 people present. This was the minimum number of people required for a formal, legal decision to be taken in Israel[34] and Peter's proposal will be precisely of this order, for it is nothing less than than to replace one of the 12 apostles, Judas, chosen by Jesus to represent Israel. ὡς

---

[33] ὡσεί in ℵ01.
[34] This requirement is found in a number of Jewish texts, e.g. m. Sanh. 1.6; b. Sanh. 17a; 1QS 6.3; 1QSa[b] 22.

Table 7.10 Common readings of ὡς before a number

Ref.	Reading	Function
Acts		
1.15 ℵ01 ὡσεί	the crowd numbered as? 120	number
4.4 om. ℵ01	the number of men became as? 5,000	number
5.7	as? a 3 hour interval	number
5.36	a number of men as? 400	number

underlines the correspondance between the number of people and the legal requirement, and further draws attention to a Scriptural paradigm cued by the words 'the crowd of names'. This unusual phrase (without the article in other MSS) takes up a motif repeated throughout the narrative of the first census of Israel in the book of Numbers (Num. 1.4–16). By evoking this paradigmatic event, Luke closely highlights how those present in the upper room in Jerusalem were considered, or considered themselves, to stand for Israel.

Acts 4.4: the second occasion on which a large number of people came to believe in Jesus as the Messiah (for the first, see Acts 2.41 above) is when Peter proclaims the gospel message to the Jews who gathered in the outer court of the Temple after the healing of the lame man at the Beautiful Gate (3.1–10). Having previously mentioned the metaphorical figure of 3,000 signifying completeness, Luke now notes that the number increased to 'ὡς 5,000'. The immediate point of reference to which this number alludes is the narrative of the feeding of the 5,000 recorded in Luke's Gospel (Lk. 9.14, see §III.3.v.c below). On that occasion, Jesus taught and healed the people (9.11), and the time of day was also the evening (9.12, cf. Acts 4.3). So a direct comparison is established between the activity of Jesus in drawing people to himself and his providing for their needs, on the one hand, and the activity of Peter and John after his death and resurrection, on the other. On the earlier occasion, the Twelve had wanted to send the people away whereas now they are active in attracting people to belief in Jesus. For possibilities of an earlier point of reference in Jewish tradition, see on Lk. 9.14 below.

Acts 5.7: when Ananias and Sapphira colluded to deceive the apostles about the amount of money for which they had sold their property, an interval of 'ὡς three hours' is said to elapse between the death of Ananias and the arrival of Sapphira in the gathering of the apostles when she herself dies. The symbolic value of three as representing completeness has already been noted (cf. on Acts 2.41, §III.3.v.a above), here signalling that Sapphira had all the time necessary to consider her action. Three hours also represents a complete segment of a day.[35] But the use of ὡς as opposed to ὡσεί would suggest that there is some specific allusion to a three-hour interval that is

---

[35] The 12-hour day was traditionally divided into four equal parts; cf. Ginzberg (*Legends*, V, 42) who refers to the Rabbinic writing describing the daily activities of God divided into periods of three hours each.

being used as a reference point. It may be that comparison is being drawn between the duration of the crucifixion (cf. Lk. 23.44–45) and the dying of the old order of Israel for which Ananias and Sapphira stand.[36] The community with its divided loyalties begins to die with the death of Ananias and is complete with that of Sapphira. Their deaths prepare the way for the 'younger' members (Acts 5.6) of the community, representing the new order of believers who are firmly committed to following Jesus, to take over as they wrap up the bodies and bury them (5.6, 10).

An alternative, or perhaps complementary, paradigm to be explored is the threefold denial of Jesus by Peter (Lk. 22.54–62), which has several features in common with the deception of Ananias and Sapphira interpreted in the way outlined above:[37] both, though knowing Jesus and having believed in him, do not accept the consequences of following him. In addition to various verbal tallies between the two passages (παραχρῆμα in Luke and Acts; συνειδυίης μὴ εἰδυῖα in Luke, οὐκ οἶδα x 2 in Acts; συνεφωνήθη in Luke, ἐφώνησεν in Acts), a chiastic correspondance exists between the two indications of an interval: καὶ διαστάσης ὡσεὶ ὥρας μιᾶς (between Peter's second and third denial, Lk. 22.59), and ἐγένετο δὲ ὡς ὡρῶν τριῶν διάστημα (between Ananias' death and Sapphira's arrival, Acts 5.7). ὡσεί before 'one hour' could signal the significance of a threefold denial within the space of single hour, whereas ὡς before 'three hours' would connect the two scenes, with the number three indicating the complete period of time Sapphira had to reflect on what she was about to do as well as confirming the link with Peter's denials.

Acts 5.36: in his defence of the apostles, Gamaliel reminds the Sanhedrin of earlier rebels who claimed to be the Messiah and who attracted popular support. He first cites Theudas who had a considerable following, said to consist of a number of men 'ὡς τετρακοσίων (400)'. Numbers based on multilples of four (40, 400) commonly occur in the Scriptures as a device to establish a connection with the early history of Israel where multiples of four abound. There are various instances recorded in Jewish tradition of leaders who were assisted in battle by 400 men: Esau (cf. Gen. 32.6; 33.1);[38] Manasseh;[39] David.[40] Gamaliel attaches some importance to the size of the following in mentioning the example of Theudas, not only prefacing the number 400 with ὡς but spelling out that this was their *number* (the word order of D05 highlights the word

---

[36] They represent a section of the Jewish believers in Jesus as Messiah who were unwilling to separate from the old system and accept the leadership of the apostles in place of the Temple authorities. See Rius-Camps & Read-Heimerdinger, *The Message of Acts*, I, 302–8; 311–14.

[37] Peter's denial will be echoed elsewhere in the narrative of Acts (his threefold refusal to eat unclean animals as food, 10.13–16; his three-fold attempt to get the door of Mary's house opened after his release from prison, 12.13–16). It should also be noted that while Peter denied in the presence of Jesus, the Lord, Ananias and Sapphira lie to the 'Spirit of the Lord' (Acts 5.9, the article in D05 making clear that Jesus is meant; see Read-Heimerdinger, *The Bezan Text*, 282–3).

[38] Ginzberg (*Legends*, V, 313) relates that the 400 men of Seir who accompanied Esau when he went to meet his brother Jacob deserted Esau out of respect for Jacob, an action that later resulted in 400 of their descendants being saved from David's attack on the Amalekites (another name for the people of Seir; see 1 Sam. 30.17).

[39] Ginzberg, *Legends*, II, 109, citing the tradition that Manasseh, son of Joseph, had '400 valiant heroes' among the army of Egyptians he gathered to withstand the attacks of Joseph's brothers.

[40] Ginzberg (*Legends*, IV, 119) refers to the 400 young men, who were the sons of women taken in battle, and who formed the vanguard of David's army.

ἀριθμός by placing it before ἀνδρῶν (see Chapter 4, §II.4.ii.b).[41] Given Theudas' nationalist aims and pretensions to be the redeemer of Israel, it would be fitting that Gamaliel should present him as in some way imitating ancient leaders of Israel. Since there are, however, problems in identifying Theudas with any certainty, it is not possible to be more specific about the source of the comparison.

c) Variant readings of ὡς/ ὡσεί introducing a number

On two occasions in the Gospel, D05 uses ὡς to introduce a number where B03, with the support of most MSS, reads ὡσεί. In contrast, on one occasion in Acts, B03 reads ὡς where D05 has καὶ ἕως in the midst of other variants (see Table 7.11).

Table 7.11 Variant readings of ὡς before a number

Ref.	Reading	Function	Variant Reading
Lk.			
3.23D05	Jesus began when he was as? 30 years	number	B03 ὡσεί
9.14aD05	there were as? 5,000 men	number	B03 ὡσεί
Acts			
13.20B03	as? 450 years	number	D05 καὶ ἕως

Taking the three references in turn:

Lk. 3.23: Jesus' age is given by Luke at the start of his ministry:

D05: ↑ [ἦν δὲ Ἰησοῦς ὡς ἐτῶν τριάκοντα ἀρχόμενος]
B03: Καὶ αὐτὸς [ἦν Ἰησοῦς ἀρχόμενος ὡσεὶ ἐτῶν τριάκοντα]

ὡσεί in B03 could mean that the age was approximate, though significance could be seen in the idea of completeness represented by the multiple of three, implying that Jesus was perfectly ready for his ministry. In addition, various parallels in the Scriptures illustrate that the age of 30 was viewed as appropriate for the start of public service: for example, 30 was the minimum age for Levites to enter into service in the Tabernacle, Num. 4.3 (LXX has 'over 25'); Joseph was 30 when he entered Pharaoh's service, Gen. 41.46; it was in the 30th year that Ezekiel received his prophecies, Ezek. 1.1. D05 with ὡς suggests a more specific parallel, that of David who was 30 years old when he began to reign (2 Sam. 5.4). In the opening chapter of Luke's Gospel, Jesus had already been presented as belonging to the line of David (Lk. 1.32: 'The Lord God will give to him the throne of his father David'; cf. 1.69: 'He has raised up for us a horn of salvation in the house of David', and now the point is restated in the Bezan text through the allusion

---

[41] D05 reads ᾧ καὶ προσεκλίθη [ἀριθμὸς ἀνδρῶν] ὡς τετρακοσίων, where καί before the verb further underlines the number of Theudas' followers (see Chapter 3 §II.2.i). B03, like most MSS, reads ᾧ ↑ προσεκλίθη [ἀνδρῶν ἀριθμὸς] ὡς τετρακοσίων.

to the onset of David's reign, to which ὡς serves as a cue to the significance of Jesus' age when 'he was beginning' ἦν ἀρχόμενος.

The construction of this sentence is noteworthy for several reasons. The verb ἄρχομαι in is used in the absolute, without any object, conferring on it an added importance as a marker of a new phase in the life of Jesus. Furthermore, it is set in a periphrastic construction, which has been identified as a means to underline the semantic content of the verb (and not the time, as in English). In D05, it is placed in a position of salience at the end of the sentence. The combination of these three features is surprisingly weighty simply to express the action of 'beginning', an observation that tends to confirm that Luke is making a significant point that goes beyond a straightforward narrative detail.

Lk. 9.14a: the story of Jesus' feeding of the 5,000 has a Scriptural parallel in Elisha's feeding of 100 men with 20 barley loaves and some fresh grain (2 Kgs 4.42–44). Here, though, the number of loaves is smaller, there being only five along with two fish, and the number of people who received food is greater. The number five frequently expresses an abundance in the Scriptures (e.g. Gen. 43.34) and the multiples of 1,000 designate an overwhelmingly large number. What happens, then, in Jesus' miraculous provision of food for the huge crowd of people listening to his teaching (Lk. 9.11) is that the few loaves represent an abundance and feed a multitude that corresponds in the ratio of 1:1,000. The idea of exact correspondance is conveyed by the particle ὡς; ὡσεί, while perhaps intended to signal the symbol of abundance represented by the figure five, could also express an approximate number (cf. Lk. 9.14b discussed in §III.3.v.a above).

Acts 13.20: B03 in common with many MSS has Paul, in his speech in Antioch of Pisidia, relate the period of 450 years to the time Israel occupied Canaan before the era of the judges, which contradicts the much shorter time of ten years generally assigned to this period. A frequently accepted way out of this difficulty is to suppose that Paul meant the figure to encompass the time of Israel in Egypt (400 years) plus the time spent in the wilderness (40 years) plus the time in Canaan before the judges (10 years). D05, in contrast, using ἕως[42] relates the 450 years to the time of the judges up to Samuel: 'God gave judges for up to 450 years until Samuel the prophet',[43] which is also too long. Whether ὡς or ἕως is what Luke intended, it is likely that the figure of 450 was not meant represent literal reality but was figurative in some way, possibly a number traditionally assigned to the period of the judges for a reason no longer understood.[44]

---

[42] ἕως may be being used for ὡς; see F. Blass and A. Debrunner, *Grammatik des neutestamentlichen Griechisch*, ed. F. Rehkopf, 18th edn (1896; Göttingen Vandenhoeck & Ruprecht, 2001), §455, n. 5. In the MS of D05, καὶ ἕως stands at the beginning of the first line at the top of a page and may have arisen by assimilation with the following time phrase at the beginning of the next line, ἕως Σαμουὴλ τοῦ προφήτου.

[43] Barrett works through the different ways that the MSS link 13.19 and 13.20 (*Commentary*, I, 633).

[44] Figures cited in Jewish historic reckonings often have a symbolic value. See e.g. the dating given in 1 Kgs 6.1 of the building of the Temple 480 years after the exodus, and the note in Adele Berlin and Marc Zvi Brettler (eds), *The Jewish Study Bible* (Oxford: Oxford University Press, 2004), 683.

d) Additional readings of ὡς introducing a number

It is interesting to note that there are no instances of ὡσεί being read by one text and omitted by the other. However, twice in Luke's Gospel, B03 prefaces a number with ὡς where D05 simply states the number. Table 7.12 presents the readings.

Table 7.12 Additional readings of ὡς before a number

Ref.	Reading	Function	Variant Reading
Lk.			
1.56B03	<u>as</u>? 3 months	number	D05 *om*. ὡς
8.42B03	<u>as</u>? 12 years old	number	D05 *om*. ὡς

These two occurrences of ὡς to introduce a number that has a strongly symbolic value need to be examined to understand why the particle is omitted by D05.

Lk. 1.56: After the angel Gabriel had announced to Mary the conception of her son, Mary went straight to the house of Elizabeth who was then six months pregnant (1.26, 36, 39), and she remained there for three months: she left at the time that the baby was due to be born (1.57). ὡς which prefaces 'three months' in B03 draws attention to the implied correspondance of dates, which D05 leaves without highlighting the coincidence of Mary's departure and the arrival of Elizabeth at term.

Lk. 8.42: Jairus, the leader of a synagogue in Galilee, asked Jesus to come to his house to help his dying daughter who was 12 years old. All Greek MSS except D05 preface her age with ὡς. In this context, the age has symbolic value, as confirmed by the incident which is inserted in the middle of the story in which a woman who had had a haemorrhage for twelve years, the lifetime of Jairus' daughter, seeks healing from Jesus. 12, as was seen before (§III.3.v.a), represents Israel on account of the 12 tribes of Israel. Jesus both heals the woman and restores Jairus' daughter to life, a sign that he is bringing healing and new life to the people of Israel. The number 12 will occur again immediately after these two stories when 'Jesus called the Twelve together' (9.1), the 12 disciples, also chosen to represent Israel (cf. 22.30).

The use of ὡς before the girl's age makes the correspondence between the two incidents clear, as well as highlighting the symbolic value of her age. The detail about her age is emphasized in B03:

8.42D05 [ἦν <u>γὰρ</u> θυγάτηρ αὐτῷ μονογενὴς] ↑ ἐτῶν δώδεκα καὶ αὐτὴ ἀπέθνησκεν
8.42B03 <u>ὅτι</u> [θυγάτηρ μονογενὴς ἦν αὐτῷ] <u>ὡς</u> ἐτῶν δώδεκα καὶ αὐτὴ ἀπέθνησκεν

In the D05 wording, the detail about the girl's age is given in passing, in an understated way. There is no doubt about the importance of the figure 12, but it would seem to be obvious enough to the narrator of D05 (as indeed it is in both MSS at 9.43) without drawing special attention to it.

To conclude on the use of ὡς and ὡσεί with a number: the findings presented at the end of §III.3.iv above relating to the analysis of Luke's use of ὡς and ὡσεί adjectivally are substantiated by the examination of the occurrence of the particles before numbers. While ὡσεί can indicate an approximate number, there is every reason to believe that ὡς never does. On the other hand, both serve to make a comparison by drawing attention to the figurative significance of a number, but ὡς makes a stronger point; it goes further than ὡσεί in using the number as a clue to point to a corresponding paradigm or parallel, which acts as a point of comparison to interpret the present incident.

III.4. General conclusions on the use of ὡς and ὡσεί

Overall, the results of the analysis carried out here indicate that Luke does indeed make a distinction between ὡς and ὡσεί, as was suspected at the outset. From a purely grammatical point of view, a formal difference is that only ὡς is used to introduce a clause, whereas both particles are found before a phrase or single word. Both are used to introduce comparisons including figures of speech (similes) but whereas the comparison prefaced with ὡσεί is a superficial one, often based on appearance, ὡς is based on resemblances at a deeper level. With ὡσεί, the accent is on the fact of comparison, whereas with ὡς the accent is on the nature of the entities being compared. More specifically, with ὡς, the comparison may be more of a 'correspondance' between two events or people than a comparison as such, with the earlier of the two serving as a point of reference or a paradigm. In some instances, Luke refers to a paradigm in the Jewish Scriptures or tradition, which he interprets as underlying an incident in the time of Jesus or the early Church; there are also times where he uses an incident recorded in his Gospel as a model for an incident described later in the book of Acts.

Differences between the MSS of Luke–Acts exist with respect to ὡς and ὡσεί, but they do not demonstrate any scribal preference. Although D05 tends to use ὡς more frequently than B03 does, the context of the individual variants suggests that this is because the comparison or correspondences operating at a deep level are more readily recognized. In some places, the particle ὡς is omitted altogether by D05 where the figurative meaning is sufficiently accessible without drawing attention to it.

8

The structure of Luke's books[1]

When Luke wrote to Theophilus, it is a moot point whether he would expect him to read the volumes silently or rather read them (or have them read to him) aloud.[2] Whatever the situation, the length of both the Gospel and of Acts makes the demand for some kind of indication of divisions inevitable, in order to give a shape to the books and thus facilitate the reading from beginning to end. Pointers that guided the reader through the development of the books would be needed to maintain their attention and keep their interest, without fear of them getting lost amid a string of incidents and a mass of characters. While readily recognizable devices can be detected in poetry that give it a framework – such as rhythm, rhyme, verses – the same is not so clearly true of ancient narrative. Indeed, in comparing the writings of the NT it emerges that, to some extent at least, different authors use devices to construct their narrative in different ways. Research in this field is relatively new, but some of the more detailed linguistic analysis that has been carried out for the NT relates to the book of Acts.[3] The present study of the structure of Luke's writings draws on that research to establish the divisions of Acts; it is then applied to an exploration of the structure the first volume, too, where it becomes apparent that there are further devices at work. Despite the uncertainties and tentative nature of some of the conclusions, it is nevertheless clear that Luke's entire work, from book level to individual sentence level, is built on an elegant arrangement of divisions, which are signalled by formal linguistic means. These divisions serve above all to communicate meaning, rather than to create aesthetic or rhetorical effect, although that is not to say that Luke was indifferent to those secondary purposes. It is in some respects the finely structured design of his work that led to identifying the literary genre of his writing to Theophilus as a 'demonstration' (ἐπίδειξις), in the sense that its purpose is to set out the truth about people and events, providing trustworthy information on the basis of careful research. The entire

---

[1] The material in this chapter was first published as Jenny Read-Heimerdinger, 'Discourse Analysis of the Book of Acts', in *Discourse Analysis of the New Testament Writings*, ed. Todd A. Scacewater (Dallas: Fontes Press, 2020), 159–92. Initial material on textual matters has been adapted and included in Chapter 1, §§II.1,2. The analysis of the structure of Acts has been expanded to include some consideration of the way Luke structured his Gospel.
[2] For discussion and further reading on the matter, see https://larryhurtado.wordpress.com/2018/11/28/silent-reading-in-roman-antiquity/ (last accessed 25/09/21).
[3] Particular note may be made of the work of Stephen H. Levinsohn, developed in *Discourse Features of New Testament Greek*, 2nd edn (1992; Dallas: Summer Institute of Linguistics, 2000).

structural arrangement can be seen in the edition of Luke's writings according to Codex Bezae, published by myself and my co-author, Josep Rius-Camps, and entitled *Luke's Demonstration to Theophilus,* where the Greek is accompanied by a parallel English translation.[4] As in the previous chapters of this current collection of linguistic studies, the full textual support and exegetical interpretation of passages referred to here can be consulted at the relevant places in our commentary on Acts.[5]

I. General considerations

I.1 The role of discourse analysis

An important contribution that discourse analysis makes to the study of language, one that is of particular relevance to ancient written texts, is the identification of structure on both a large and a small scale. This is because discourse analysis looks not only at the sentence and its components but also at the larger units which group sentences together in an organized structure from the smallest units and up to the level of the entire discourse. Discourse analysis examines how the boundaries between the various units are signalled. It is similarly concerned with the ways in which the units relate to each other, how they are ordered, and how they hold together to create a unified discourse.[6]

Because of the concern of discourse analysis with language above the level of the sentence, it opens up the way to consider how a writing is organized, specifically what are the inherent means available in a given language to group ideas or themes together, to create a framework that makes communication more intelligible and effective than would be a formless mass of utterances. All good speakers give shape to their discourse in a bid to get the audience's attention and keep them focused on what is being said. In the case of discourses intended to be read aloud rather than privately, communication is liable to be rendered ineffective if this condition is disregarded. The business of organizing discourse is generally a natural and instinctive operation for a native speaker in everyday speech, though in formal communication it may necessitate more careful effort and skill, and implies a more arduous task for a non-native speaker. For it is important to recognize that each language has its own way of building discourses; the similarities that may exist between languages are unpredictable and by no means regular, which means that ancient Greek has to be examined as a distinct language, independent of any apparent overlap with English, for example.

---

[4] Jenny Read-Heimerdinger and Josep Rius-Camps (eds), *Luke's Demonstration to Theophilus: The Gospel and Acts of the Apostles according to Codex Bezae* (English expanded edn; London: Bloomsbury, 2013).

[5] Josep Rius-Camps and Jenny Read-Heimerdinger, *The Message of Acts in Codex Bezae: A Comparison with the Alexandrian Tradition.* 4 vols (JSNTSup 257/LNTS 302, 365, 415; London: T&T Clark, 2004–09).

[6] Features of NT Greek that play a part in creating structure are discussed in Part VI of Levinsohn, *Discourse Features,* 271–84.

In modern writing, the structure of a text is greatly assisted by the use of visual devices. Books are divided into chapters, with paragraphs to mark the grouping and separation of topics. Punctuation, too, plays a critical role in conveying the speaker's intentions by the grouping of material into phrases, clauses, sentences. In ancient Greek writing, on the other hand, there was not only no visual system in regular use for dividing the material into smaller units, there was no punctuation either. Furthermore, the extant NT MSS of the first centuries are written exclusively in capital letters, and usually without separation between sentences or even between words. The familiar chapter divisions were introduced as late as the thirteenth century and verses only in the sixteenth century, and cannot be relied upon in order to identify the author's intended organization of a book. The problem with relying on other literary or rhetorical signposts – for example, changes in theme, location, time or protagonist, or the repetition of vocabulary or phrases – is that the high degree of subjectivity involved, associated with the expectations of readers in other times and other cultures, leads to not a little disagreement among exegetes as to where divisions occur.

Two principal features of Koine Greek identified by discourse analysis as key to the organization of narrative are. 1) connectives between sentences, and 2) word order at the start of the sentence. The way that Luke uses connectives has been considered in Chapter 3. General principles of word order have been discussed in Chapter 4, and the patterns of word order within the noun phrase have been examined in detail. In Section II of this chapter below, attention will be paid to the order of words at the start of sentences, for this is a factor that contributes to the structuring of a discourse. First, for the purposes of identifying the structure Luke gave to his work, the distinction between narrative and direct speech needs to be made clear.

I.2. Narrative

A primary consideration in thinking about the structure of Luke's writing is that it is presented as narrative discourse, as a story, with the typical features of a time frame, characters, locations, plot. As such, for discourse analysis purposes it is to be distinguished from writing which is overtly discursive, which presents an argument or seeks to persuade, for example. In describing the Gospel and Acts as narrative, however, that is not to say that the author was telling a story simply to entertain or to show off his literary skill. On the contrary, Luke said in the first volume of his work that his intention was to present his recipient, Theophilus, with a series of facts and to convince him of their truth (Luke 1.1–4; cf. Acts 1.1–2). Yet, whatever his purpose, he chose to express what he had to say as a narrative. It should be borne in mind that ancient conventions of recording factual reality allowed considerable licence with the organization and selection of material, without the present-day demands that the details of reported events and characters correspond to literal reality. In biblical narrative, the historian's freedom to re-arrange the sequence of incidents or to change details – for example, dates or names of people and places – reflects at least in part the notion that reality is first and foremost spiritual in nature, existing outside the confines of time and space of the physical world. This is the truth that the biblical historian must seek to communicate, and in so doing may need to modify literal details in the interests of expressing it more clearly.[7]

It is perhaps a consequence of not recognizing authorial licence in the composition of Luke's work, the second volume especially, that the work is often seen as a collection of sources, badly pieced together with gaps in the narrative thread, careless repetition and factual errors. In this case, no well-defined structure is looked for, except possibly some clumsy scaffolding erected to hold the thing together where it was in danger of falling apart.[8] Thus, it is relatively rare to find commentators discussing the narrative structure of the book of Acts – frequently, there is not thought to be one. Recognizing a structural framework depends on accepting the writing as the production of an author who knew what he was doing, and doing it deliberately. It is the contention of the analysis here that whatever sources Luke may have used for both of his volumes, he made them his own and crafted a highly complex narrative with a carefully planned and intricate structure that is not only a model of artistic skill but also a rhetorical tool that serves to convey his message.

1.3 Direct speech

Within Luke's narrative are passages of direct speech placed in the mouths of characters in the story. In some respects, the wording of these speeches is often closely tied to the wording of the surrounding narrative, so that on the basis of rhetorical or literary analysis there would be justification for considering their content as intertwined with the narrative content. From the point of view of discourse structure, in contrast, they are to be viewed as separate units that slot into the narrative structure as unified chunks. They have their own speaker and their own internal structure. In the presentation of the structure that follows, therefore, the internal structure of the speeches will not be analysed; rather, they will be viewed as blocks embedded within the overall narrative framework.

II. Word order to create structure

Word order plays a particularly important role in structuring narrative, where its impact is not so much on the relationship among constituents within a sentence as on the relationship between sentences themselves. It has been observed[9] that sentences in a Greek narrative typically start with the verb, followed by the subject if it is expressed,

---

[7] For Jewish historians, including the authors of records collected in the NT, there is the further notion that the whole of the history of Israel is contained within the Torah, subsequent events being re-enactments of the earlier, paradigmatic ones. This perspective is a factor that needs to be taken into account for its contribution to the reshaping of literal reality in Acts. For a discussion of the Jewish notion of history, see Bernard Barc, *Les arpenteurs du temps. Essai sur l'histoire de la Judée à la période héllenistique* (Histoire du texte biblique 5; Lausanne: Éditions du Zèbre, 2000).

[8] This is the position adopted by e.g. Charles K. Barrett in his *Acts of the Apostles*, 2 vols (T&T Clark, 1994, 1998), *passim*.

[9] Levinsohn, *Discourse Features*, 16–17.

then the object if there is one. This order, referred to as VSO, is as close to ordinary speech as can be determined in the NT (e.g. from the parables). The initial position of the verb in narrative reflects the fact that a story is about actions and events first of all – unlike hortatory discourse where people, a topic or a line of argument are more likely to be the prominent concern. Besides, in a continuous story in Greek, it is often unnecessary to specify the subject since this can be encoded in the verb ending and, furthermore, it can be understood to be the same as the subject of the previous main verb if no change is explicitly indicated; e.g. at Acts 12.1–2 the subject of successive main verbs is Herod.

12.1 … ἐπέβαλεν Ἡρῴδης ὁ βασιλεὺς τὰς χεῖρας κακῶσαί τινας τῶν ἀπὸ τῆς ἐκκλησίας
12.2 ἀνεῖλεν δὲ Ἰάκωβον …

It is usual to describe a typical pattern of word order of a language as the 'unmarked' or 'default' order, and to go from there to identify the effects of modifying that unmarked order to produce patterns that are described as 'marked'. With regard to the initial position of the verb in a narrative sentence, this means that the word order is marked if the verb is not at the head of the sentence, but rather some other constituent occupies that place.

Now, two reasons have been identified for word order to be marked in this way. First of all, when a constituent is moved to any position further to the left than it would occupy by default (i.e., it is 'fronted'), this is a means to underline it, to highlight it as being of particular importance at that point. For example, in a sentence where the subject is explicit, if the subject is placed before the verb, attention is being drawn to it for some reason such as contrast or surprise. For example, at 12.7 two new subjects, the angel of the Lord and a light, appear quite unexpectedly.

12.7 καὶ ἰδοὺ ἄγγελος κυρίου ἐπέστη καὶ φῶς ἔλαμψεν ἐν τῷ οἰκήματι

Placing any constituent before the verb at the start of a sentence in a narrative discourse ('fore-fronting') focuses special attention on it, because it disrupts the expected pattern. For example, at 16.3 Timothy is the object of the verb but the reference to him (with a demonstrative pronoun) is placed at the front of the sentence, which has the effect of highlighting the nature of the person just described and chosen by Paul to be his companion.

16.3 τοῦτον ἠθέλησεν ὁ Παῦλος σὺν αὐτῷ ἐξελθεῖν

In addition to focusing attention, there is another reason for placing a constituent before the verb at the start of a sentence, and it is this one that is relevant for the purpose of structure. A constituent may be fore-fronted in order to signal a new development in the narrative, one that forms a new basis for the next part of the story. This could be a change of place, time, protagonist, or topic, which acts a fresh 'point of departure' for the next part of the story.[10] Continuity is the norm in narrative, and so disrupting the expected order of words is a means to signal a change in direction of some kind. As such, these fore-fronted sentences serve as boundary markers, indications of structural breaks that the narrator intended for the narrative. A few examples will serve to illustrate the discontinuity signaled by this device. At 6.8, Stephen becomes the chief protagonist.

6.8 Στέφανος δὲ πλήρης χάριτος καὶ δυνάμεως ἐποίει τέρατα καὶ σημεῖα μεγάλα ἐν τῷ λαῷ.

At 10.23b, there is a change of time.

10.23b Τῇ δὲ ἐπαύριον ἀναστὰς ἐξῆλθεν σὺν αὐτοῖς

At 17.16, the change is one of place.

17.16 Ἐν δὲ ταῖς Ἀθήναις ἐκδεχομένου αὐτοὺς τοῦ Παύλου παρωξύνετο τὸ πνεῦμα αὐτοῦ ἐν αὐτῷ

It is important to distinguish between the purpose of fore-fronting for focus and the purpose for establishing a new point of departure, because only the latter instances contribute to the structure of the narrative. A general rule is that if the fore-fronted constituent is already present in the narrative, even if not explicitly stated, then the purpose should be understood as focus. In such cases, the directing of attention is also liable to be localized and short-term, without serving to develop the story on a larger scale. Thus, at 15.37–38, Barnabas and Paul are already active in the new time frame (cf. 15.36 Μετὰ δέ τινας ἡμέρας εἶπεν πρὸς Βαρναβᾶν Παῦλος ...), when the narrator directs attention first to one then the other by placing their names before the respective verbs, because of the disagreement between them.

15.37 Βαρναβᾶς δὲ ἐβούλετο συμπαραλαβεῖν καὶ τὸν Ἰωάννην τὸν καλούμενον Μᾶρκον· 38 Παῦλος δὲ ἠξίου

On some occasions, the two purposes may coalesce, as an already present participant is now brought into focus to become the main protagonist who moves the story forward – this is what happens at 6.8 cited above, for example.

Luke as narrator employs a further technique to mark a fresh point of departure, using the verb εἰμί (or γίνομαι in the aorist) to introduce a new factor into the narrative. In such sentences, the verb comes first, but by the very presentative nature of the verb the construction overall marks the importance of the new subject by setting it out in a separate sentence at the start of a new unit. The presentative technique is a kind of fore-fronting *par excellence*. Examples of presentative sentences with εἰμί are found in the

---

[10] Levinsohn, *Discourse Features*, 7–28.

firm text of Acts at 4.5; 9.10; 13.1 and with γίνομαι 5.7; 8.1b; 14.1; 16.16; 19.23. In the Gospel, ἐγένετο δέ is a frequent marker of a new section, being used with a high degree of regularity in the MS of Codex Bezae, D05, as will be seen in §VI below.

Conversely, if there is a change in time, or place, protagonist or topic, and it is not pre-posed, then continuity of situation is indicated. For example, in the introduction to the dispute over the circumcision of the Gentiles in Acts 15 a paragraph break is marked in the N-A text at 15.6, which most translations reproduce:

15.6 Συνήχθησάν τε οἱ ἀπόστολοι καὶ οἱ πρεσβύτεροι ἰδεῖν περὶ τοῦ λόγου τούτου

It may seem counter-intuitive not to start a new paragraph here, because there is a clear change of subject from the previous sentences (Paul and Barnabas 15.3-4; some of the Pharisees 15.5). However, despite the change to 'the apostles and elders', the first position in the sentence of the verb at 15.6 indicates that this sentence belongs closely with the preceding narrative. If a break is intended, it is in the following sentence at 15.7, where the dispute is fore-fronted:

15.7 Πολλῆς δὲ ζητήσεως γενομένης ἀναστὰς Πέτρος εἶπεν πρὸς αὐτούς

Using the criteria of word order to discern the divisions of the Acts narrative may, then, conflict with the divisions identified by noting thematic or other changes, which commentators typically look for in order to locate boundaries. However, taking account of word order, specifically fore-fronting, provides an objective basis for identifying the shifts or developments in the narrative that the narrator apparently intended. It reduces considerably the risk of anachronistically imposing on the text ways of understanding a story that derive from modern interpreters' expectations or preconceptions.

There arises, however, the difficulty of variation among the manuscripts, for there is a fair amount affecting word order at the start of sentences, which is by no means systematically noted by the critical edition of the Greek NT. Rather than assuming that word order variation arises from scribal preference for a different order of words, it would be more accurate, given the significance of word order as an indication of organisation of the text, to interpret it as arising from a different understanding of the structure of the narrative.

III. Connectives to create structure

It is time to bring the criterion of word order into contact with the choice of connectives, to see how these two factors work together to confer structure on a narrative. It has been noted that a point of discontinuity in the narrative is marked by a disruption of the default 'verb first' word order of a sentence, placing something before the verb that forms the basis for the next part of the narrative. Such instances serve as points of departure for the next part, and as such occur at the beginning of a structural unit. Thus, they can be used to determine the structural organization intended by the narrator. When they are examined systematically throughout the entire text of a book, it is possible to make observations about how the connectives are used at the various stages of the structural units, whether the beginning (in combination with fore-fronted word order), the end (just before the next fore-fronted word order), or somewhere between. Table 8.1 sets out the devices Luke uses to link sentences in Acts and classifies them according to their occurrence in a structural unit. The use and distribution of connectives in his Gospel is a matter that requires investigation (see §VI below).

Only two connectives are used to open a new unit, δέ on its own and μὲν οὖν in combination with δέ. This function of δέ is in keeping with the observation that δέ as a connective between sentences marks something as new or distinctive. As explained above, with μὲν οὖν the logical connection with the preceding unit is underscored, with two events being presented as resulting from it, of which the second (δέ) is seen as the one that carries the story forward. At the beginning of a structural unit, both δέ and μὲν οὖν ... δέ present a fresh point of departure in the development of the narrative. They are found at high level boundaries that mark major divisions in the narrative, as well as at lower levels of the structure.

There are, in addition, instances of asyndeton at the start of a new structural unit, but only as a variant reading: at 2.5D05 (ℵ01/B03 δέ), asyndeton underlines an important shift in register at the start of a new unit;[11] and at 18.1, ℵ01/B03 (D05 δέ) introduce Paul's departure from Athens simply with μετὰ ταῦτα, apparently viewing it as marking a break with the previous material rather than a development of it. It is worth noting that MS variation is a factor that only affects structural arrangement to a limited degree. However, care must be taken in referring to the Greek text of the current edition,[12] for it is an eclectic one that does not necessarily consider the relevance of connectives for identifying structural divisions. Some examples will be seen in the discussion that follows.

The remaining connectives used by Luke only link elements in the middle of a unit or bring the unit to a close.

Table 8.1 Distribution of connectives within structural units of Acts

Connective	Beginning	Middle	End
καί	√	√	√
μὲν οὖν ... δέ	√	×	×
asyndeton	√ (vll)	√	×
οὖν	×	√	×
καί	×	√	√
τότε	×	√	√
γάρ	×	√ (rare)	√ (rare)
rel. pro.	×	√ (rare)	√ (rare)
dem. pro.	×	√ (rare)	√ (once, vl)

---

[11] At 2.5D05, the register changes as the narrative moves from relating a historical account to presenting a figurative one, see Rius-Camps & Read-Heimerdinger, *The Message of Acts*, I, 154.

[12] N-A[28]. The same text is reproduced in UBS[5].

IV. Macrostructure of Acts

IV.1 Preliminary notes

Before presenting an analysis of the structure of Acts, words of caution are needed on several counts. The first concerns the Greek text used. As indicated earlier, an eclectic edition of Acts, such as the N-A text, does not take account of the significance of a) connectives, or b) word order for the narrator's organisation of the text, because the editorial committee did not apply principles of discourse analysis to their decisions about variants. The edited text is not necessarily, therefore, a reliable basis for analysing structure. Instead, individual manuscripts should be used, and in the following discussion the text of Codex Bezae, D05, is followed, noting variant readings in the principal MS adopted by the current edition, Codex Vaticanus, B03, where they impinge on matters of structure.

The second cautionary note concerns the overlapping nature of the structure of ancient narrative texts.[13] While linguistic features serve as formal markers of division at specific points, from a narrative point of view divisions are frequently accompanied by a series of carefully crafted sentences that link together two units, by anticipating at the end of one unit what will follow in the next, or by summarizing at the beginning of a unit what had gone before. As a result, the content itself cannot be appealed to in looking for a boundary at a single point. It may be, in fact, that the idea of single point boundaries is anachronistic, more in keeping with modern notions of structure. That said, in so far as the linguistic features described above allow new points of departure to be marked by the narrator, these can be used to identify specific points within overlapping passages as the start of a new unit.

A third issue concerns the levels of hierarchy. It is one thing to formally identify boundaries between units by observing the linguistic features of connectives and word order, but there is then the task of identifying how the narrator organizes these units into larger units. For that purpose, there do not appear to be clear linguistic clues; the markers in themselves do not allow different structural levels to be distinguished. In other words, the device of fore-fronted sentences in combination with the conjunction δέ is important for determining boundaries, for a division will not be expected without it, but this does not give information as to whether the sentence marks the start of a new unit at a high level (the equivalent of a modern section or chapter) or a lower level (e.g. a paragraph). So, at the point of seeking to understand the hierarchical organization of units, there enters a certain amount of interpretation that depends on the recipient's understanding of the narrator's purpose. Notably, at the higher levels of the hierarchy, thematic considerations play a dominant role in identifying the interplay of divisions.

Now, interpretation of Acts may seem to be a matter that does not elicit much contention in that, following the overwhelming majority of the manuscripts of Acts that are extant today, the work can be, and is, construed as presenting the leaders of the early Church as heroes who faithfully carried out God's plan for his people. The

---

[13] The rhetorical feature of overlap in ancient narrative is discussed by Jacques Dupont, *Nouvelles Études sur les Actes des Apôtres* (Lectio Divina 118; Paris: Éditions du Cerf, 1994), 27–36.

portrayal is somewhat more nuanced in copies such as D05, whose text was reproduced to a large extent by the earliest translations in Latin, Syriac, Middle Egyptian and even Aramaic,[14] dating from before the first standardized translations in the fourth century. In this text, the leaders are presented as fallible disciples who made mistakes as they slowly came to terms with the teaching of Jesus; by no means did either their actions or their speeches all make a positive contribution to the spread of the gospel. This is an important consideration in detecting the structure of the book because it means that, even though on the surface the narrative may appear to unfold in a sequence of time and place, logical connections of cause/effect or reason/consequence have to be anticipated. The way in which the separate units relate to each other is reflected in the way they fit into the wider organization of the book, and so the structure that can be identified inevitably differs from one form of text to another, according to their different messages. This factor adds a further complication to defining the structure of Acts, in addition to the problem posed by textual variation explained above. In the structural organization that is presented in the following discussion it is the text of Codex Bezae that is adopted, with comments made on variant readings where they do not involve lengthy exegetical expositions.

IV.2 Hierarchical levels

It is at the level of the overall plan of the book that work on analysing the structure of Acts has tended to be carried out. There is every reason, however, to expect in a work of the length of Acts that the author would provide a more detailed structure to aid his audience. By studying the successive sentences noted as signalling a division by their marked word order, the various levels of structure can be identified as set out in Table 8.2.

Table 8.2 Hierarchical arrangement of structural units

Halves
Parts
Sections
Sequences
Episodes
Scenes
Elements

In this arrangement, the smallest building blocks at the lowest level of the hierarchy are labelled 'elements', grammatical sentences that consist of a main verb and any associated clauses or phrases, introduced with some kind of connective, as discussed above. An element is the creation of the narrator – it reflects Luke's choice of how to express actions or facts, selecting one as the chief component and making any others

---

[14] The few extant fragments of Acts in Aramaic (10.28–29, 32–41) have readings that are otherwise only found in D05 or other early versions.

subordinate to it. That is not to say that the clauses (with verb forms such as participles, infinitives or subordinate verbs) or phrases (adjectival or adverbial expansions) that may cluster around a main finite verb are not important, but the narrator's choice to select one for the principal focus must be respected in analysing a sentence and seeing how the components have been fitted together to create a coherent and cohesive structure. Once again, the question of the Greek text is crucial for identifying the main finite verb of each sentence, for there is a great deal of variation affecting the verbal forms among the manuscripts.

Elements are organized into larger units, here labelled 'sequences' that often (though not always, indicated by the dotted lines) are made up of 'episodes' and 'scenes'. Sequences are grouped into 'sections', which combine to make 'parts' that fall into two 'halves'.

IV.2.i Halves

As far as the D05 text of Acts is concerned, at the highest level the book divides two 'halves', albeit of uneven length, for there is a clear separation between the chapters in which Peter is the main protagonist together with other leaders (Acts 1–12), and those where Paul takes over that role (Acts 13–28). The concern of the first half is to work through the story of Peter, from his imperfect grasp of Jesus' teaching in Acts 1 until his final realisation of the radical implications of it in Acts 12. Peter will make a brief appearance to speak at the Jerusalem meeting related in Acts 15 but from Acts 13 Paul takes over as the focus of the book. Paul, as Saul, had already been introduced in Acts 8–9, but it is only at Acts 13 that he replaces Peter as the main protagonist. The overlap between the two halves of the book reflects the tendency in ancient narrative to look forwards and backwards between sections as a means to tie them together closely, though in this case the anticipatory and retrospective references are some distance apart.

In the alternative text of Acts, where the characters are not, or not so clearly, presented as progressing over the course of the narrative in their understanding of the gospel, a boundary between two halves of the narrative at Acts 13 may not necessarily be identified at that point. If it is, no problems arise with the text from a linguistic point of view, for the divisions are the same whatever textual tradition is followed. Acts 13 begins with a presentative sentence, introducing a new set of characters in the Antioch church.

13.1 Ἦσαν δὲ ἐν Ἀντιοχείᾳ κατὰ τὴν οὖσαν ἐκκλησίαν προφῆται καὶ διδάσκαλοι

IV.2.ii Parts

The parts into which these two halves of Acts in turn fall are each characterized by their principal location. The first half is broadly divided between Jerusalem and Judaea, on the one hand, involving only the apostles (Part 1, Acts 1–5); and on the other, Samaria and other parts of Israel where the Hellenist leaders emerge as an identifiable group (Part 2, Acts 6–12). As for the second half of Acts, Acts 13–28 concerning Paul, the place where, or even if, a division occurs is open to dispute. When a division is recognized, it is generally taken to be located somewhere between the so-called missionary journeys to other countries outside of Israel (from Acts 13 to somewhere in Acts 19; 20; 21) and Paul's trial and journey to Rome (up to the end of the book at Acts 28), but even then, the exact point at which the missionary phase of Paul's activity ended is not at all clear, and different commentators fix it differently. This point will be returned to but meanwhile, Table 8.3 sets out the divisions so far.

Table 8.3 The four parts of Acts

Book of Acts			
First half		Second half	
Acts 1–12		Acts 13–28	
Peter and the other apostles		Paul	
Part 1	Part 2	Part 3	Part 4
Acts 1–5	Acts 6–12	Acts 13–?	Acts ?–28
Jerusalem and Judaea	Samaria and the rest of Israel	Gentile nations	Trial and Rome

Concerning the division in the first part, it is worth noting that there is a clear break at 6.1, with the typically fore-fronted formula Ἐν δὲ [ταύταις ταῖς ἡμέραις] D05 / [ταῖς ἡμέραις ταύταις] ℵ01/B03), 'In those days...', introducing the new section that develops the theme briefly hinted at in the earlier chapters, that of the disagreement between the Hellenists and the Hebrews.[15] There then follows a summary statement[16] in 6.7, which backtracks and brings the previous section concerning Jerusalem to a close.

6.7 Καὶ ὁ λόγος τοῦ θεοῦ (κυρίου, D05) ηὔξανεν καὶ ἐπληθύνετο ὁ ἀριθμὸς τῶν μαθητῶν ἐν Ἰερουσαλήμ...[17]

It is only after this summary statement that the theme of the Hellenists is taken any further, so that 6.1–7 constitutes a bridge between the two sections and creates a characteristic overlap.

As is often pointed out, the progression from Acts 1 to Acts 28 follows the order of the threefold command given by Jesus to the apostles just before he left them.

---

[15] The tension between Hellenists and Hebrews is implicit in the contrast between Barnabas, a Hellenistic Jew from Cyprus, who gave the proceeds of the sale of a field for the use of the believers (4.36–37), and Ananias and Sapphira, representative of the older Jews (cf. the young men at 5.6,10) who retained part of the proceeds of the sale of their property with disastrous consequences (5.1–11).

[16] There are five similar summary statements in Acts (6.7; 9.31; 12.24; 16.5; 19.20; 28.30–31), which D. L. Blood and D. E. Blood, in 'Overview of Acts', *Notes on Translation* 74 (1979): 2–36, take as marking out two sections, the first made up of 1.12–19.20 (1.1–11 are taken as an Introduction), and the rest of the book (19.21–28.31) forming a second section. Dividing the book up in this way depends on the text of 19.21 as read by the majority of MSS.

[17] The use of καί at 6.7 tells against the interpretation of this verse as marking a new section (*contra* David Wenham and Steve Walton, *Exploring the New Testament* I, *Introducing the Gospels and Acts* (London: SPCK, 2001), 272.

1.8 ἔσεσθέ μου μάρτυρες ἔν τε Ἰερουσαλὴμ καὶ [ἐν] πάσῃ τῇ Ἰουδαίᾳ καὶ Σαμαρείᾳ καὶ ἕως ἐσχάτου τῆς γῆς

It is in part because of the three-fold nature of the command that the chapters relating to Paul can be viewed as one block, with Acts 13–28 representing the third aspect of the command, the 'ends of the earth'. The narrative development reflects the gradual extension of the gospel, starting from the Jews in Jerusalem and then moving out geographically to other Jews and finally Gentiles. Most commentators, however, see at least one division in the section concerning Paul at the end of his missionary journeys, even though disagreement arises over where the end is intended: is it as he leaves Ephesus and sets off on his last journey to Jerusalem (19.20)?[18] After he has spoken with the Ephesian leaders at Miletus on his way to Jerusalem (20.38b)?[19] Or once he arrives in Jerusalem where he is confronted with the angry mob outside the Temple (21.26)?[20] The difficulty is first, that there is no definite break between Paul's mission in Ephesus and his journey to Jerusalem, and secondly, that the purpose of his journey to Jerusalem can be interpreted in various ways – was it a missionary journey, and if not, why did he go there? D05 has its own answers to these questions, seeing Paul's journey to Ephesus as the first stage on his journey to Rome, which was interrupted by his personal decision, against the guidance of the Holy Spirit, to go back to Jerusalem before finishing the journey to Rome (20.3D05; cf. 21.4). Additional references in D05 to the directions given to Paul by the Holy Spirit make it clear that Paul's work in Ephesus was at the prompting of the Holy Spirit, contrary to his own intention to stay in Jerusalem (19.1D05)[21] and, furthermore, that his return to Jerusalem was not how things were meant to be but came about because of the Jews' plot against him (20.3D05).[22]

---

[18] Blood & Blood, 'Overview', 9–11; F. F. Bruce, *Commentary on the Book of Acts. The English Text with Introduction, Exposition and Notes* (London: Marshall, Morgan and Scott, 1954), 325–92. From a linguistic point of view, however, the adverbial connection οὕτως at 19.20 looks back over the previous scene. It is the next sentence at 19.21, with the connective δέ and the subordinate clause Ὡς ἐπληρώθη ταῦτα, that moves the story forward as Paul takes the decision to go to Macedonia and Achaia.

[19] J. D. G. Dunn, *The Acts of the Apostles* (London: Epworth Press, 1996), 212–76; I. H. Marshall, *The Acts of the Apostles* (TNTC; Leicester, UK: IVP, 1980), 299–337. The initial position of the verb tells against 20.38b being intended as starting a new unit. The fore-fronted word order of 21.1, despite considerable variation between D05 (genitive absolute) and ℵ01/B03 (subordinate clause of time), indicates that this is where the new unit begins.

[20] Ben Witherington, *The Acts of the Apostles. A Socio-Rhetorical Commentary* (Carlisle: Paternoster, 1998), 562–641. Τότε at 21.26 in fact marks the conclusion of a unit, and it is the fore-fronted word order of 21.27, again with variation between D05 (genitive absolute) and ℵ01/B03 (subordinate clause of time), that introduces a new unit.

[21] 19.1D05 reads: Θέλοντος δὲ τοῦ Παύλου κατὰ τὴν ἰδίαν βουλὴν πορεύεσθαι εἰς Ἱεροσόλυμα εἶπεν αὐτῷ τὸ πνεῦμα ὑποστρέφειν εἰς τὴν Ἀσίαν ...

[22] While the ℵ01/B03 text has Paul's intention to sail to Syria thwarted by the plot of the Jews, in D05 it is the plot itself that prompts his decision to sail there. The Spirit directed him to Macedonia, from where he could have continued to Rome, but instead he turned eastward to fulfil his intention of going to Jerusalem. The reading is discussed in detail in J. Rius-Camps, 'The Gradual Awakening of Paul's Awareness of his Mission to the Gentiles', in *Apostelgeschichte als Kirchengeschichte. Text, Traditionen und antike Auslegungen*, ed. T. Nicklas and M. Tilly, 281–96 (BZNW 122; Berlin: De Gruyter, 2003).

In view of this portrayal of Paul's work and of his conflict with divine plan, it is not surprising that a top-level division in D05 can be understood between the end of the second phase of his missionary activity in the various nations outside Israel (13.1–18.23) and his circuitous travels to Rome (18.24–28.31), which take him via Ephesus and Jerusalem (18.24–28). The text leading up to 18.24 reads as follows, with little difference between the two forms of text:

Ref.	D05	B03
18.22	καὶ κατελθὼν εἰς Καισάρειαν, <u>καὶ</u> ἀναβὰς καὶ ἀσπασάμενος τὴν ἐκκλησίαν κατέβη εἰς Ἀντιόχειαν.	καὶ κατελθὼν εἰς Καισάρειαν, ↑ ἀναβὰς καὶ ἀσπασάμενος τὴν ἐκκλησίαν κατέβη εἰς Ἀντιόχειαν.
18.23	καὶ ποιήσας χρόνον τινὰ ἐξῆλθεν διερχόμενος καθεξῆς τὴν Γαλατικὴν χώραν καὶ Φρυγίαν, <u>καὶ</u> ἐπιστηρίζων πάντας τοὺς μαθητάς.	καὶ ποιήσας χρόνον τινὰ ἐξῆλθεν διερχόμενος καθεξῆς τὴν Γαλατικὴν χώραν καὶ Φρυγίαν, ↑ ἐπιστηρίζων πάντας τοὺς μαθητάς.
18.24	Ἰουδαῖος δέ τις [ὀνόματι <u>Ἀπολλώνιος</u>] [↑ γένει Ἀλεξανδρεὺς] ἀνὴρ λόγιος, κατήντησεν εἰς Ἔφεσον, δυνατὸς ὢν ἐν ταῖς γραφαῖς	Ἰουδαῖος δέ τις [<u>Ἀπολλῶς</u> ὀνόματι], [Ἀλεξανδρεὺς <u>τῷ</u> γένει] ἀνὴρ λόγιος, κατήντησεν εἰς Ἔφεσον, δυνατὸς ὢν ἐν ταῖς γραφαῖς

18.24 introduces a new character who is the basis on which the next part of the narrative is built. The narrator highlights his Jewish ethnicity by placing Ἰουδαῖος at the start of the sentence, and indeed, it is the fact that Apollo(nio)s is Jewish that is of particular significance for his activity in Ephesus and his relationship with Paul.

Whatever may be said of the text adopted by N-A, the resultant structure in D05 thus has a division in the second half as presented in Table 8.4.

Table 8.4 Parts 3 and 4 in Codex Bezae

Paul Acts 13–28	
Part 3	Part 4
13.1–18.23	18.24–28.31
Evangelization of the nations	Journey to Rome via Ephesus

IV.2.iii Sections

As explained above, each the four parts divides into a series of smaller sections, identified by their specific content. A change in the main topic marks the move from one section to the next, with various other features accompanying it to signal the move to a new section. A change in the principal character is frequently involved and, where this is the case, it is signalled by the name of the character being placed at the beginning of the sentence that opens the new section.[23] The change may also be marked by some

---

[23] Examples in Acts of the fronting of the names of new characters at the opening of a new section occur at 4.36 and 18.4.

reference to time, whether it be the same time as before (e.g. 'In those days') or a new time (e.g. 'After some days'), but it is noticeable that time markers at the start of a new section are more common in the Bezan text that in other manuscripts.[24] A change in place often occurs from one section to another, too. These features of boundaries between sections are criteria that are recognized by discourse analysis studies as typical signals pointing to a significant development in a narrative. Table 8.5 sets out the sections for each part of Acts that can be identified in D05. The identification of the exact boundary point between sections is determined by the linguistic criteria of word order and connectives, as will be illustrated with reference to Part 2 in the microstructure analysis that follows.

Table 8.5 Sections in Codex Bezae

		Part 1 Acts 1.1–5.42
Prolegomena	1.1–14	
Section I	1.15–26	Replacement of the twelfth apostle
Section II	2.1–47	Outpouring of the Holy Spirit
Section III	3.1–4.35	The sign of the lame man's healing
Section IV	4.36–5.42	The Jerusalem church
		Part 2 Acts 6.1–12.25
Section I	6.1–8.1a	The emergence of the Hellenists
Section II	8.1b–11.26	Removing the obstacles
Section III	11.27–30	The Antioch church
Section IV	12.1–25	Release of the Church from Israel
		Part 3 Acts 13.1–18.23
Section I	13.1–14.27	The first phase of the mission to the Gentiles
Section II	14.28–15.41	Judicial review in Jerusalem
Section III	16.1–18.23	The second phase of the mission to the Gentiles
		Part 4 Acts 18.24–28.31
Section I	18.24–19.40	The third phase of the mission to the Gentiles
Section II	20.1–21.14	The journey to Hierosoluma
Section III	21.15–27.1	Paul on trial
Section IV	27.2–28.31	Paul in Rome

V. Microstructures of Acts

In order to examine more closely the reasoning behind the structural divisions in Table 8.5, the rest of the discussion will focus on Part 2 (Acts 6–12), explaining how the

---

[24] Time indicators are given at the start of a new section at 6.1; 8.1; 11.27; 12.1; 14.28; 15.36; and additionally, in D05 at 1.15; 2.1; 3.1.

particular boundaries have been identified and pointing out where they are dependent on the readings of D05.

Within each of the four parts of the Book of Acts, the material is grouped according to theme and character following, as was pointed out earlier, a geographical path to bring about the progression of the gospel. After a preliminary account of Jesus' departure (1.1–14), Part 1 is concerned with the proclamation of the gospel in Jerusalem, where the first person to be freed from exclusion in full participation in the People of God, a Jewish lame man, is introduced.[25] In Part 2, the geographical area is expanded, as is the category of people now integrated fully into the People of God. Hellenistic Jews, Samaritans, a Jewish eunuch, sojourners among the Jews, and finally Gentiles. The expansion is reflected in the four divisions or 'sections' in Acts 6–12. The topic of the first section (6.1–8.1a) is the Hellenists, starting with their election and closing with the stoning of their leader, Stephen. The marked linguistic features of word order in the opening sentence of 6.1 have been discussed above. The second section (8.1b–11.26) consists of a series of incidents that contribute to the topic of the growth of the Church, culminating in the proclamation of the gospel to Gentiles. It opens with the presentative construction mentioned above in this study, ἐγένετο δὲ ἐν ἐκείνῃ τῇ ἡμέρᾳ διωγμὸς μέγας καὶ θλῖψις.[26] There follows a brief transitional third section (11.27–30),[27] introduced with ἐν δὲ ταῖς ἡμέραις ταύταις, just like the opening of Section I at 6.1; it establishes the relationship between the Antioch church (Jewish and Gentile) and the Jerusalem (Jewish) one. Finally, Section IV (12.1–25) begins with another fore-fronted time expression (κατ' ἐκεῖνον δὲ τὸν καιρόν ...) and brings the second part of Acts to a close with a critical presentation of the relationship of the Church with Israel.

V.1 Sequences

The sections themselves are subdivided into smaller units, 'sequences'. At this level of the structure, and at the lower level of episodes and scenes if a sequence is subdivided, an inner structure can be observed, created by the arrangement of the components within it. The arrangements follow recognizable and established literary patterns, for which the author would have drawn on rhetorical devices that were familiar to him, in part at least from the Jewish Scriptures.[28] Arrangements have been found in Acts that

---

[25] The lame man in Acts 3 had been prevented by Jewish law from entering the Temple because of his physical condition.
[26] καὶ θλῖψις is absent from most manuscripts, including ℵ01/B03.
[27] Given the exceptional brevity of this third section, it might be preferable to think of 11.27–30 as transitional, a bridging summary rather than a separate section. It is the opening time phrase, so characteristic of major breaks elsewhere in Acts, especially in D05, that suggests that the narrator views the material as a separate section.
[28] The narrator of the Bezan text of Acts is unmistakeably Jewish, shown by the sophisticated nature of the intricate allusions to Jewish oral tradition and ways of thinking that are found within it (see Chapter 1, §§I, II). Even if he were not, a first-century Gentile believer of the level of education displayed by the narrator of Acts can be expected to have been familiar with the literary structural devices that are an integral part of the Jewish Scriptures. See Robert Alter, *The Art of Biblical Narrative* (New York: Basic Books, 2011); Jerome T. Walsh, *Style and Structure in Biblical Hebrew Narrative* (Collegeville: The Liturgical Press, 2001).

Table 8.6 Section IV in Codex Bezae. 12.1–25

	Part 2, Section IV	
	Acts 12.1–25 Release of the Church from Israel	
Sequence [A]	12.1–4	Herod's persecution of the church in Judaea
Sequence [B]	12.5–17	Peter's escape from prison
Sequence [A']	12.18–23	The death of Herod
Colophon	12.24–25	Conclusion of Part 2

are concentric ([a b a'], organized around a single centre); symmetrical ([a b b' a'], two parts matching each other with a double centre); or linear (progressing in a single line [a b c d]). For example, Section IV of Part 2, the one dealing with the separation of the Church from Israel, displays a concentric pattern of three sequences [A] [B] [A'], with Herod the topic of the outer sequences and Peter that of the central one. The analysis of Section IV is set out in Table 8.6.

The first [A] and last sequences [A'] relate the treatment of the Church by Herod, as representative of the Jews opposed to the believers.[29] They form corresponding outer frames for the middle sequence [B] which focuses attention on Peter as the object of Herod's attack. All three sequences are complete units, without further divisions of episodes or scenes. A colophon summarizes the situation at the end of the three sequences to conclude both Section IV and Part 2, as well as preparing for the next section. The boundaries are justified as follows, citing from D05 though there are no variant readings in ℵ01/B03 that affect the analysis of the structure of this section.

[A] 12.1D05 Κατ' ἐκεῖνον δὲ τὸν καιρὸν ἐπέβαλεν τὰς χεῖρας Ἡρῴδης ὁ βασιλεὺς κακῶσαί τινας τῶν ἀπὸ τῆς ἐκκλησίας

The sequence is linked to the previous one with the conjunction δέ and is situated specifically within the time that Barnabas and Saul visited the brethren in Judaea (11.29-30). The relevance of the timing will be reinforced in the conclusion to the sequence (12.25), for it means that the persecution against the believers in Judaea coincided with the time when financial aid was brought to Jerusalem from the Gentiles in Antioch. The time is fore-fronted before the main verb ἐπέβαλεν to establish it as the basis of the new sequence and as a new point of departure. In D05, τὰς χεῖρας is also placed before the verb, anticipating the attack carried out by Herod. Herod is the topic of 12.1-4, being the subject of all the main verbs, apart from the parenthetical statement in 12.3b.

---

[29] Throughout Acts, the Bezan narrator, speaking from an internal Jewish perspective, highlights the conflict between the growing number of Jesus-believing Jews and those who rejected their claims that Jesus was the Messiah.

[B] 12.5D05 ὁ μὲν οὖν Πέτρος ἐτηρεῖτο ἐν τῇ φυλακῇ …

A new sequence is introduced with the connective μὲν οὖν at 12.5a, repeating the information of 12.4 but changing the topic so that Peter is now the focus of interest as the narrative develops. The connective μὲν οὖν makes this information secondary, anticipating the action (δέ) that carries the story forward in 12.5b. The prominence accorded to prayer by its fore-fronted position (πολλὴ δὲ προσευχὴ ἦν …) is crucial for the interpretation of the following part of the story, which D05 underscores by including the adjective πολλή, for it signifies that the church's prayer for Peter plays a key role in the events that unfold. It is by paying attention to the linguistic clues – the connective link with the previous sequence (μὲν οὖν … δέ) and the word order of the key development sentence (πολλὴ προσευχή at the front of the sentence) – that the narrator's intention can be seen.

[A'] 12.18D05 Γενομένης δὲ ἡμέρας ἦν τάραχος …

The third sequence returns to the day that was set for Peter's appearance before the people (cf. 12.4) and picks up the story of Herod who was the main character of the first sequence [A]. The time is highlighted by the presentative construction, fore-fronted as a genitive absolute before the finite verb ἦν. Attention moves away from Peter who has disappeared (12.17b, καὶ ἐξελθὼν ἐπορεύθη εἰς ἕτερον τόπον), to focus on his opponent, Herod, represented first by the guards before he himself takes centre stage in 12.19 where the switch of focus is indicated by the position of Herod's name at head of the sentence. The main verb of this sentence (ἐκέλευσεν) indicates the importance the narrator accords to it, other verbs being subordinate.

Colophon 12.24D05 Ὁ δὲ λόγος τοῦ θεοῦ ηὔξανεν καὶ ἐπληθύνετο

The section is brought to a close with two concluding statements that bring in new topics. The first concerns the growth of the word of God, which is positioned at the head of the sentence as a boundary marker. The justification for considering that the two main verbs, ηὔξανεν and ἐπληθύνετο, constitue a single element is that they represent two complementary aspects of the same action, conjoined with καί, rather than discrete actions. The other statement in the Colophon at 12.25 picks up the trail of Barnabas and Saul, whose presence in Judaea had provided the time-frame for Section IV (cf. 11.30 and comments above). The position of their names before the verb is for the purpose of focus; they have been implicitly present in the background of this section, for it was while they were in Judaea (cf. 11.30) that the events took place.

V.2 Elements

It is at the level of the smallest structural component, the element, that the structural patterns are at one and the same time the most visible and the most complex, as will be seen by taking the final sequence of Section IV [A'] for illustration.

Identifying an element is essentially a matter of noting the main verbs, as explained above. Once that has been done, the way the author has arranged the elements can be examined. Unless the events unfold in a strictly linear fashion, the centre of the arrangement is found by counting the main verbs. an equal number implies a symmetrical pattern, and an odd number a concentric one. Table 8.7 sets out the arrangement of elements in the Sequence [A′], including the final component of Sequence [B] and the initial component of the Colophon to show how the sequences are linked to one another. The main verb in the Greek text of each element is underlined

Table 8.7 Sequence [A′] in Codex Bezae, Acts 12.17–24

[B]	*Peter's Escape from Prison*	
a′	¹⁷ᵈ καὶ ἐξελθὼν <u>ἐπορεύθη</u> εἰς ἕτερον τόπον.	And he left and travelled to another place.
[A′]	*The Death of Herod*	
[a]	¹⁸ Γενομένης δὲ ἡμέρας <u>ἦν</u> τάραχος οὐκ ὀλίγος ἐν τοῖς στρατιώταις τί ἄρα ὁ Πέτρος ἐγένετο.	Now when day came, there was a disturbance among the soldiers over what had happened to Peter.
[b]	¹⁹ᵃ Ἡρῴδης δὲ ἐπιζητήσας αὐτὸν καὶ μὴ εὑρών, ἀνακρίνας τοὺς φύλακας <u>ἐκέλευσεν</u> ἀποκατθῆναι,	Herod searched for him and when he did not find him, he questioned the guards, and then ordered them to be killed;
[c]	¹⁹ᵇ καὶ κατελθὼν ἀπὸ τῆς Ἰουδαίας εἰς Καισάρειαν <u>διέτριβεν</u>.	and he went down from Judaea to Caesarea and stayed there
[d]	²⁰ᵃ <u>Ἦν</u> γὰρ θυμομαχῶν Τυρίοις καὶ Σιδωνίοις	(for he was embroiled in a dispute with the Tyrians and the Sidonians).
[e]	²⁰ᵇ οἱ δὲ ὁμοθυμαδὸν ἐξ ἀμφοτέρων τῶν πόλεων <u>παρῆσαν</u> πρὸς τὸν βασιλέα	Together, the people from both towns presented themselves together to the king
[f]	²⁰ᶜ καὶ πείσαντες Βλάστον, τὸν ἐπὶ τοῦ κοιτῶνος αὐτοῦ, <u>ᾐτοῦντο</u> εἰρήνην διὰ τὸ τρέφεσθαι τὰς χώρας αὐτῶν ἐκ τῆς βασιλικῆς.	and, having gained the favour of Blastus who was his chamberlain, they set about asking for peace, because their regions were provided for from the king's.
[e′]	²¹ᵃ τακτῇ δὲ ἡμέρᾳ ὁ Ἡρῴδης ἐνδυσάμενος ἐσθῆτα βασιλικὴν καὶ καθίσας ἐπὶ τοῦ βήματος <u>ἐδημηγόρει</u> πρὸς αὐτούς.	On an appointed day, Herod, clothed with a royal robe and seated upon the tribunal, addressed them.
[d′]	²¹ᵇ καταλλαγέντος δὲ αὐτοῦ τοῖς Τυρίοις.	(Note that he had been reconciled with the Tyrians.)
[c′]	²² ὁ δὲ δῆμος <u>ἐπεφώνει</u>· θεοῦ φωναὶ καὶ οὐκ ἀνθρώπου.	The crowd cried out, 'The proclamations of a god and not of a man!'
[b′]	²³ᵃ παραχρῆμα δὲ αὐτὸν <u>ἐπάταξεν</u> ἄγγελος κυρίου ἀνθ' ὧν οὐκ ἔδωκεν δόξαν τῷ θεῷ	Immediately, the angel of the Lord struck him because he did not give the glory to God;
[a′]	²³ᵇ καὶ καταβὰς ἀπὸ τοῦ βήματος γενόμενος σκωληκόβρωτος ἔτι ζῶν καὶ οὕτως <u>ἐξέψυξεν</u>.	and he came down from the tribunal, and was eaten by worms while still alive, and this is how he died.
Colophon	*Conclusion*	
[a]	²⁴ Ὁ δὲ λόγος τοῦ θεοῦ <u>ηὔξανεν</u> καὶ <u>ἐπληθύνετο</u>.	The word of God increased and continued to grow.

for clarity, though the English translation often requires more than one verb to be rendered with a finite verb to avoid an unnatural sentence form. It should be noted how the verse divisions do not serve to distinguish separate elements, since they often contain more than one.

All the standard components of a classical story are present in the sequence. an introduction setting the scene [a], initial action [b-c-d], steps that build the tension [e-f-e'], the climax [c'], resolution [b'] and the conclusion [a']. The structural centre [f] is located at 12.20c as the key step in the build up of tension that acts like a fulcrum, because it is the information that the Tyrians and Sidonians requested peace that is the turning point in the series of events and prepares for the acclamation of Herod as a god. The mention of Blastus at v. 20c could seem to be no more than a curious incidental detail were it not for its central position in the story, which suggests that it was meaningful to a contemporary audience.[30] Some striking correspondences between the two sides of the pattern can be observed.

[e]//[e'] at either side of the central element are placed references to the meeting of the people with the king
[d]//[d'] the dispute between the king and the people is stated and resolved
[b]//[b'] Herod orders Peter to be killed, and is himself struck dead by the angel of the Lord
[a]//[a'] the outcome of Peter who had escaped to another place (12.17d) contrasts with that of Herod who dies a dishonourable death.

The detail of Herod's death is spelt out in D05 with an adverbial (epexegetic) καί before the main verb (καὶ οὕτως ἐξέψυξεν), typical of the language of D05 (see Chapter 2, §II.1.ii), underlining the gruesome nature of it.

In other manuscripts including B03, the comment about the reconciliation with the Tyrians [d'] is absent (cf. 12.20b).[31] Consequently, the central point of the sequence is different, since the structure is symmetrical with a double centre of 12.20b–20c, and the parallels between the two sides of the sequence, noted above, are lost as a result.

Note that the aside in 12.21b in D05 is linked with δέ, for it looks forward to anticipate and justify the proclamation of the crowd. The unusual choice of a participle instead of a main verb in the Bezan clause serves to underline the information that it provides. The forward-looking function of the aside can be compared with that of 12.20a which, introduced with γάρ, looks back to explain that the reason for which

---

[30] Some commentators are all too ready to dismiss details such as the apparently irrelevant naming of Blastus as evidence of a story clumsily adapted from its source (see, e.g. Barrett, *Acts*, I, 589, citing Conzelman). Some humility is called for. It is much more probable that it is we today, so far removed in time and culture from the first-century context, who are poor listeners; unwilling to acknowledge our ignorance, we wrongfully set ourselves up as judges of ancient historians.

[31] In D05, the importance of the Tyrians is brought out by a series of details (see Barrett, *Acts*, I, 589), including the observation in 12.21bD05 that the king had been reconciled with the Tyrians. Such an emphasis in D05 brings out the parallel between Herod and the ancient prince of Tyre, whom the Jewish Scriptures present as a paradigm of hubris, proclaiming himself a god and not a man (Ezek. 28.2), echoed in the acclamation of the Roman client king by the Tyrians (cf. Acts 12.22).

Herod went to stay in the Roman capital of Caesarea was the need to resolve a problem with neighbouring provinces.

VI. Macrostructure of Luke's Gospel

As with the book of Acts, the starting point for identifying the structural framework of the Gospel was to list each and every sentence in the narrative (excluding sentences in direct speech, see §1.3 above) and to note both the connective and the word order at the start of the sentence. The texts of Codex Bezae, D05, and Codex Vaticanus, B03, were used and the readings without variant were noted as well as those where there is variation.

Preliminary study indicates that there are broad similarities in Luke's use of connectives in the Gospel and in Acts, in particular the distinction he makes between δέ, as a marker of discontinuity, and καί as a marker of continuity (see Chapter 2, §II). At the same time, there are also striking differences, notably in the use of καί as a development marker within episodes. The differences may perhaps be accounted for by the distinctive natures of Luke's two volumes, but closer analysis is needed to establish the way he uses connectives in the Gospel before drawing any firm conclusions (see Chapter 3, §I.1).[32] A factor contributing to the difficulty of identifying a detailed structural arrangement is the high proportion of variant readings that affect the synax of the writing above sentence level.

What can be established is that, just as in Acts, δέ signals something new and distinctive. The pattern is especially clear in D05 compared with B03: where καί is read as a variant reading for δέ in one text or the other, it is D05 more often than not that reads δέ (58 : 23). The force of δέ leads to noticing divisions that Luke makes that are not necessarily the ones that a modern reader would make. For example, Lk. 4.28 introduces the reaction of the people to Jesus' teaching in the synagogue. The next part of the story follows thus (each sentence is placed on a new line so that the connective and word order can be clearly seen):

Ref.	D05	B03
Lk. 4.28	οἱ δὲ ἐπλήσθησαν πάντες θυμοῦ ἐν τῇ συναγωγῇ ἀκούοντες ταῦτα	↑ καὶ ἐπλήσθησαν πάντες θυμοῦ ἐν τῇ συναγωγῇ ἀκούοντες ταῦτα
4.29	καὶ ἀναστάντες ἐξέβαλον αὐτὸν ἔξω τῆς πόλεως καὶ ἤγαγον αὐτὸν ἕως τῆς ὀφρύος τοῦ ὄρους ἐφ' οὗ ἡ πόλις οἰκοδόμηται αὐτῶν ὥστε κατακρημνίσαι αὐτόν	καὶ ἀναστάντες ἐξέβαλον αὐτὸν ἔξω τῆς πόλεως καὶ ἤγαγον αὐτὸν ἕως ↑ ὀφρύος τοῦ ὄρους ἐφ' οὗ ἡ πόλις ᾠκοδόμητο αὐτῶν ὥστε κατακρημνίσαι αὐτόν
4.30	αὐτὸς δὲ διελθὼν διὰ μέσου αὐτῶν ἐπορεύετο	αὐτὸς δὲ διελθὼν διὰ μέσου αὐτῶν ἐπορεύετο
4.31	καὶ κατῆλθεν εἰς Καφαρναοὺμ πόλιν τῆς Γαλιλαίας τὴν παραθαλάσσιον ἐν ὁρίοις Ζαβουλῶν καὶ Νεφθαλίμ καὶ ἦν διδάσκων αὐτοὺς ἐν τοῖς σάββασιν	καὶ κατῆλθεν εἰς Καφαρναοὺμ πόλιν τῆς Γαλιλαίας ↑ ↑ καὶ ἦν διδάσκων αὐτοὺς ἐν τοῖς σάββασιν

(continued)

---

[32] On Luke's usage of connectives in the Gospel, see Randall Buth, 'Evaluating Luke's Unnatural Greek: A Look at his Connectives', in *Discourse Studies and Biblical Interpretation: A Festschrift in Honor of Stephen H. Levinsohn*, ed. Steven E. Runge, 335–69 (Bellingham, Wash.: Lexham Press, 2011).

Ref.	D05	B03
4.32	καὶ ἐξεπλήσσοντο ἐπὶ τῇ διδαχῇ αὐτοῦ, ὅτι ἐν ἐξουσίᾳ ἦν ὁ λόγος αὐτοῦ	καὶ ἐξεπλήσσοντο ἐπὶ τῇ διδαχῇ αὐτοῦ, ὅτι ἐν ἐξουσίᾳ ἦν ὁ λόγος αὐτοῦ
4.33	[ἦν δὲ ἐν τῇ συναγωγῇ] ἄνθρωπος ἔχων πνεῦμα δαιμονίου ἀκαθάρτου καὶ ἀνέκραξεν φωνῇ μεγάλῃ...	[καὶ ἐν τῇ συναγωγῇ ἦν] ἄνθρωπος ἔχων πνεῦμα δαιμονίου ἀκαθάρτου καὶ ἀνέκραξεν φωνῇ μεγάλῃ...

At 4.28, the response of all the people of the synagogue and their attempt to kill Jesus is linked with δέ in D05, signalling a development in the episode, although B03 uses καί which downplays the development. In 4.30, Jesus manages to escape from the people and goes to Capernaum. Given the continuity of characters and place, it would be natural to attach the sentence of 4.30 to the preceding episode and start the new episode at 4.31a where there is a change of place; this division is adopted by most commentators, in accordance with the paragraph division of N-A[28]. However, taking account of the way Luke uses καί and δέ, it can be observed that as the narrator he considers Jesus' slipping away from his opponents to mark the beginning of a new episode rather than the conclusion of the previous one. The sentences that follow then continue to be linked with καί as the episode in Capernaum unfolds. According to D05, as a new character is introduced in the setting of the synagogue at 4.33a, another new development begins, with the word order focussing attention of the presence of the man by means of the initial presentative verb (see §II above); in the B03 text, the focus is on the new location of the synagogue (placed before the verb) and the incident there is connected to the preparatory sentences with καί.

In terms of the structural arrangement of Luke's Gospel, in B03 and consequently in the text of current edition, when this is considered linguistically rather than thematically it is somewhat obscure. In D05, a clearer pattern can be observed because of the recurring temporal expression, ἐγένετο δέ..., 'It happened that...'. It is found 15 times marking the start of a major new section, with all the material between each occurrence united by a distinct and common theme. The function of ἐγένετο δέ as a high-level boundary marker is established by its presence at the opening of the first section of the Gospel narrative at 1.5. There are only three places in the narrative where ἐγένετο δέ occurs in D05 without apparently indicating such a high-level division (Lk. 1.8; 17.14; 22.24). The expression καὶ ἐγένετο, in contrast, is found consistently as a lower-level boundary within a section (24 times in D05). Four further sections in D05 are signalled with an alternative device, making 19 sections in total as set out in Table 8.8.[33]

---

[33] In the edition of Luke's Gospel published in Read-Heimerdinger & Rius-Camps, *The Demonstration to Theophilus*, a section boundary was noted at Lk. 3.1, which begins ἐν ἔτει δὲ πεντεκαιδεκάτῳ... and continues through an extensive list of rulers and officials before the main verb at 3.2, ἐγένετο ῥῆμα θεοῦ.... The section was considered to last through to 3.1, where ἐγένετο δέ is found. On further reflection, however, it is felt that careful attention needs to be paid to the absence of ἐγένετο δέ at 3.21, given the presence of this temporal marker at the start of what can be seen as a structural division on every other occasion up to 22.1. On this basis, it seems that Luke intended the episode with John the Baptist to be viewed as integral to the section presentating of Jesus, beginning at 2.1.

Table 8.8 Section divisions in Luke's Gospel in Codex Bezae

Section	Reference	Theme
I	1.5	Presentation of John
II	2.1	Presentation of Jesus
III	3.21	The Messiah of Israel
IV	5.1	The Call to Discipleship
V	6.12	The Mission to Israel
VI	7.12 D05	The Reception of Jesus by Israel
VII	8.22	The Extreme Situation of the Gentiles
VIII	8.40 D05	The Extreme Situation of the Jews
IX	9.28	The Transfiguration
X	9.37	The Disciples' Lack of Power and Understanding
XI	9.51	Samaria
XII	10.38D05	Talking with God
XIII	11.27	The Credentials of the Messiah
XIV	18.35	From Jericho to Jerusalem
XV	20.1D05	The Temple
XVI	22.1	Passover
XVII	22.63	The Trial of Jesus
XVIII	23.26	The Crucifixion
XIX	24.1	The Resurrection

The four sections that are not introduced with ἐγένετο δέ are the final ones of the Gospel narrative, where there is a marked shift as the events all relate to the death and resurrection of Jesus. Luke's use of ἐγένετο δέ to signal section breaks in his narrative is in part accounted for by the function ascribed by Levinsohn to impersonal ἐγένετο in combination with a temporal expression[34] – he sees it as a transition marker, with the ἐγένετο sentence providing the link to the previous episode and the background information to the new one. The purpose of ἐγένετο to present background information could mean that its absence in the final sections of the narrative corresponds to the fact that the events of the final sections are more immediate for Luke, and of primary relevance to the account that he wants to give to Theophilus.

The summary of the study the structural divisions in Luke's Gospel is intended to present an initial analysis and to make some observations, starting from the more extensive analysis that has been carried out on the book of Acts (§§IV, V above). While some conclusions can be drawn, there remain points that require further consideration, for which detailed examination of the text and the variant readings will be necessary in order to reach a more complete understanding.

VII. Conclusion

Throughout this study of the structure of Luke's Gospel and Acts, it has been seen that an important contribution of discourse analysis is as a tool that provides a measure of

---
[34] Levinsohn, *Discourse Features*, 177–80.

objectivity for recognizing the way the writer constructs a text and intends it to be heard. It allows linguistic criteria to be identified that are not only generic to the particular language in question but also specific to the particular author of the text under scrutiny. Alongside a traditional grammatical understanding of the language, an approach based on discourse analysis reveals principles that operate under the surface, serving to give coherence and cohesiveness to a discourse. With regard to ancient Greek narrative in general, the main principles underlying the marking of divisions concern the choice of sentence connectives and sentence-initial word order. By analysing these aspects in Luke's work, some insight can be achieved into his organization of the narrative.

With regard to his second volume, at the lowest level of elements (a sentence composed of a main verb and any associated constituents), the structural arrangement can be ascertained with a high level of confidence, with the proviso that a single manuscript be used because of the extensive variation in sentence construction. Identifying the arrangement of elements into higher level divisions is also straightforward, by applying the division-marking criteria to locate the boundaries. Going on from there to detect a hierarchy of divisions, seeing how discrete episodes fit together to form larger sections at higher levels, is more problematic because at this point it is necessary to take account of the thematic development of the narrative, which in turn depends in large measure on what is understood to be the narrator's purpose in writing the account. Some indication of the variation in purpose among the varying forms of Acts has been given, and of the way in which the viewpoint and intention of the writer affects the higher-level divisions of the story.

As far as Luke's first volume is concerned, structural analysis using linguistic criteria is still a little explored area and is complicated by the extensive MS variation. Comparing the MSS for variant readings that affect the structure (notably connectives and word order) could provide interesting insights into the different ways successive editors and/or scribes viewed the arrangement of the episodes and the links between them.

9

Conclusion

I. Some general principles

The overall aim of the analyses in the articles gathered here has been to identify patterns of use in Luke's writing and to see how closely the Greek of two MSS representing different traditions of transmission correspond to the Greek in the text without variants. An exhaustive examination of data in the book of Acts, complemented by a consideration of some factors in the Gospel of Luke, indicates that by applying practical tools of discourse analysis characteristics of Luke's writing are brought to light that are not otherwise readily recognized. They are features that depend on principles operating on the level of the language above the sentence, ones that would be instinctively familiar to a Greek speaker at the time. Thus, connectives have been seen to give the narrative cohesion and show divisons, by the way they group the sentences together (Chapter 2); combined with word order at the start of the sentence, they allow Luke to construct a structure for his writing that corresponds to his purpose in creating his work (Chapter 8). Word order within the noun phrase (Chapter 4), like the use of the article before proper nouns (Chapter 3), are devices that serve to highlight sentence components such as adjectives or the names of people and places in order to draw attention to them for one reason or another. The same can be seen in the disruption of usual patterns that are used to keep track of participants by means of the personal pronoun (Chapter 6). Concerning the different expressions Luke uses throughout his work to make reference to the Holy Spirit, the variety allows the circumstances of the mentions to be distinguished (Chapter 5). In other words, his choices are not haphazard, and this is equally true of his use of parallel terms to convey nuances of meaning or intention (Chapter 7).

II. Further research

The implication of the absence of native speakers is that some of the conclusions proposed in the studies of the present book are tentative and invite ongoing research. Additional discourse features could be considered for the way that they contribute to the development of the story and the communication of meaning. A notable feature is the choice between expressing an action by means of a finite verb or by means of a participle. While the role of participles and their position in relation to the verb that they are subsidiary to has been the object of some investigation by scholars of NT Greek, consideration of the numerous variant readings involving participles may well enable findings to be refined. It would also be profitable to compare the features of Luke's writing with that of the other NT narratives, and even narrative texts outside the NT corpus, in order to isolate any characteristics that distinguish him from other writers of the period.

III. Luke as a writer

With respect to all the features that have been analysed, a certain flexibility in their use has been detected. This flexilibilty, on the one hand is true of the text without variant among the MSS that were selected for the studies and, on the other, shows up in the variation between the MSS. However, the most frequent forms that occurred were seen not to be a reliable indication of Luke's personal style, because reasons for alternative forms could be found. Instead, it is the patterns of alternation between forms that are neutral ('default') and those that depart from them ('marked') that are important; by taking account of the co-textual and contextual circumstances in which the dominant usage is not adopted, recurring patterns can be sought. The very variability in Luke's writing reflects his skill as a narrator to communicate his message effectively; its presence reflects his mastery of the principles of Greek at the level of grammar above the sentence. Thus, departure from usual patterns, or 'default' usage, is not a matter of style, as tends to be said, because it occurs for the purpose of conveying meaning rather than for aesthetic or literary effect.[1]

The availability of options in all the aspects of Greek considered reveal a kind of linguistic code that operates in such a way that enables the speaker to communicate a message with both clarity and subtlety. This is not a code that hides the meaning but one that, on the contrary, serves to open it up and communicate it to the recipient. It is a code that Luke is in control of and, it can be assumed, expects Theophilus to be sensitive to, otherwise it would be without purpose. While it is often pointed out that the language of Luke–Acts is that of a native speaker of Koine Greek, who writes with a literary and sophisticated style, the analysis of discourse features makes even more apparent just how masterful storyteller he was.

IV. The importance of using manuscripts

Because the approach adopted for these linguistic investigations has had as its subject 'language in use' (see Chapter I, §III.2), they have deliberately taken actual texts that existed and circulated as hand-written copies from among the earliest MSS that have

---

[1] Cf. Geer, Thomas, J. 'The Presence and Significance of Lukanisms in the "Western" Text of Acts', in *New Testament Text and Language*, ed. Stanley E. Porter and Craig A. Evans, 34–51 (The Biblical Seminar 54; Sheffield: SAP, 1997).

preserved Luke's writings over some length. Because they provide evidence for forms of Luke's writings that were used, these have been examined in preference to the current edited text (N-A^{28}/UBS^5), which has been reconstituted from mainly Alexandrian MSS without attention to matters of discourse analysis. Codex Vaticanus B03, usually alongside Codex Sinaiticus ℵ01, as representatives of the Alexandrian tradition favoured by the majority of textual critics, have been compared with the extant text of Codex Bezae D05, the only early Greek text which consistently displays differences from it throughout Luke's work. Taking his books in their entirety rather than as a string of variant readings has been essential to obtain a clear and objective picture of the variation. A further advantage of using variant MSS is that they enlarge the corpus of data available for investigation. The findings of several of the studies found numerous variant readings that are less due to scribal habit than different narratorial perspectives. As witnesses to texts adapted for different circumstances, they help to show how the external context of a MS, with the distinct perspectives of successive copyists or editors, can affect features of the language.

V. The relevance of context

In studying the occurrences of linguistic features in the books overall it emerges that the factors affecting both the flexiblity of Luke as a writer and the variation among the MSS are associated first, with what is happening in the story at any given point, the internal co-text: is there a development in the narrative or continuity with respect to the previous event? is the character a background or foreground one at this point? is a place of special significance to the unfolding narrative or has it already been established as the scene's location? These are the kinds of questions that can determine which pattern or form is used. Secondly, and at the same time, the variation may be dependent on the external context of the narrative, whether the real people and events of the story that are being related, or the situation of the writer and recipient at the time Luke was writing. Unlike the grammatical rules of morphology or syntax, for example, which operate independently of the circumstances of the writing, these factors are of a pragmatic nature. They involve the world outside the story; they call on the knowledge Luke and Theophilus share and rely for their effectiveness on Luke's constant internal monitoring of Theophilus' understanding of what he is seeking to communicate.

The difficulty in associating the language of Luke–Acts so closely with with the real-life situation of the writer and his addressee is, of course, that so little is known about them, since outside sources do not tell us who they were. As readers today, we are dependent on clues within the texts themselves. Here again, a comparison of MSS can be useful, looking at the content aside from the linguistic features. Close exegetical investigation of the content of Luke's writings transmitted by the two traditions, ℵ01/B03 and D05, indicates that, whoever they were, the writer and the recipient were not the same in each case. Whereas the Alexandrian text reads largely as a historical account albeit with an underlying theological message, the Bezan text reads primarily as a theological exposition with a different historical perspective than the one which is apparent in the more familiar text.[2] Drawing on research within the domain of Second Temple Judaism, analysis notably of D05 material absent from the Alexandrian text provides evidence of an author who was intimately familiar with Jewish written and oral traditions that he could manipulate in order to present his characters and the events of his narrative as anchored in the history of Israel.[3] This is a separate investigation from a discourse analysis of linguistic features, for it precedes the linguistic analysis and informs it.[4] Thus, while examination of the article with names of people or word order, for example, can demonstrate that the writer is drawing attention to someone or something, it is the independent study of the context of the narrative that reveals the nature of what is being highlighted.[5]

VI. Codex Bezae

A constant concern throughout the studies of this volume has been to consider the language of the variant readings against the language shared by the texts of both ℵ01/B03 and D05. It has been found consistently that, contrary to generalized evaluation of D05, the features of language analysed here display similar usage in the common text and in D05. The study of connectives (Chapter 2), use of the article (Chapter 3), word order (Chapter 4), tracking of participants (Chapter 6) and structure (Chapter 8) reveals a text with a cohesiveness that tells against it being the result of successive re-workings by a series of scribes. The links between events and episodes, like the highlighting of salient characters or actions, reflect a carefully constructed narrative with a single narrative purpose. The links in the text of ℵ01/B03, in comparison, are weaker and reflect a more straightforward telling of the story. The material peculiar to

---

[2] The results of the exegetical comparison of the textual traditions undergird the linguistic studies in this volume, as indicated in Chapter I, §2. They are published in Josep Rius-Camps and Jenny Read-Heimerdinger, *The Message of Acts in Codex Bezae: A Comparison with the Alexandrian Tradition*, 4 vols (JSNTSup 257/LNTS 302, 365, 415; London: T&T Clark, 2002–09).

[3] The finding tends to go against the frequently repeated notion that D05 was a rewriting in a Gentile context. Eldon J. Epp in *The Theological Tendency of Codex Bezae Cantabrigiensis in Acts*, SNTS 3 (Cambridge: CUP, 1966) identified a series of readings (several taken from witnesses other than D05) which, he maintained, intensified criticism of the Jews. My analysis of the Bezan readings leads me to a similar conclusion but I believe that close scrutiny of the context reveals that this criticism is made from a Jewish point of view, not a Gentile one. See, e.g Jenny Read-Heimerdinger, 'The Apostles in the Bezan Text of Acts', in *Apostelgeschichte als Kirchengeschichte*, ed. T. Nicklas and M. Tilly, 263–80 (BZNW 122; Walter de Gruyter, 2003).

[4] It is hoped to bring together studies of characters in Luke–Acts that bring to light an internal Jewish viewpoint as well as a critical evaluation of the leaders of early Church in a forthcoming volume, entitled *Being Theophilus*.

[5] In 'The Textual Traditions of Acts: What Has Discourse Analysis Contributed?', *Bib.* 100.4 (2019): 544–67, Zachary Dawson reviewed my approach to the text of Acts and claimed that I used 'discourse analysis as the method ... to demonstrate the priority and Jewish perspective of the Bezan text of Acts'. There is a serious misunderstanding underlying this claim. The tools of discourse analysis that I adopt are not capable of showing what the perspective of a text is. It is but one method among others that I apply to the task of evaluating the variant readings between D05 and ℵ01/B03. In particular, I identify the Bezan perspective as an inner Jewish one on the basis of the nature of the concerns that are highlighted by analysis of the vocabulary; intertextual studies; contextual studies; and historical studies, notably by Jewish historians.

D05 demonstrates that default and marked patterns are used in the same way as in the common text. No preference for one rather than the other can be observed in the references to the Holy Spirit (Chapter 5) any more than in the other features already mentioned above; likewise, the use of parallel terms (Chapter 7), which can be seen in the common text as a device to distinguish between nuances of meaning, is found more frequently in D05 than in ℵ01/B03 but always for the same reasons as those identified in the common text.

In short, on the basis on these aspects of discourse there is no justification for interpreting the variant readings of D05 as scribal fantasy or carelessness. Far from being alien to the Lukan language of the common text, the language of D05 is always in accordance with it; its use is controlled and the choices justifiable from the co-text and context.[6] It would be wrong to go so far as to affirm that the D05 text is definitely written by the same person as the author of the common text but it is, at the very least, a possibility.[7] As for the language of ℵ01/B03, it is not inconsistent either with that of the text without variant, but in comparison with that of D05 it is less subtle, less sophisticated in its use of marked patterns in the presentation of the characters and their actions, and in the articulation of the narrative. From that point of view, and looking at the situation objectively and without prejudgement, the text of ℵ01/B03 could be said to be more distant from the common text because it makes less use of the skilful play with the alternative forms and patterns.

In all of this, it is essential to remember that D05 is not the 'Western' text. It is a manuscript that stands alone, on the one hand because it is the only extant MS in Greek that has an alternative text to that of the Alexandrian tradition and, on the other, because it has readings that are not shared by any other MS. These studies have not drawn attention to these singular readings, but they are numerous. Indeed, textual critics appeal to the singular readings as an argument against the authenticity of Luke–Acts in D05, on the grounds that if they represented what Luke wrote they would have been more widely reproduced. It is interesting, then, that since the second half of the twentieth-century MSS have been discovered or newly examined that do attest some of the D05 readings hitherto without support, notably papyri including Papyrus 127 with several chapters of Acts, and early versions such as the Middle Egyptian with the first 15 chapters of Acts as well as Aramaic fragments of Acts.

In other words, if the bias in favour of the Alexandrian text is put to one side, the existence of singular readings could be interpreted as evidence for the priority of D05, dating from a time before the text began to be modified; they, too, deserve more focused study in order to circumscribe more precisely their linguistic features and narrative content. Meanwhile, their existence needs to be held in conjunction with the wide range of early attestation of the D05 text among all the pre-vulgate versions and the

---

[6] On their analysis of Lukan language, Boismard and Lamouille found that D05 is 'un texte abâtardi': M.-E. Boismard and A. Lamouille, *Le texte occidental des Actes des Apôtres: Reconstitution et réhabilitation*, 2 vols. (Paris: Éditions Recherche sur les Civilisations, 1984). Their evaluation is founded on the Lukan features that they identified on the basis of frequency.

[7] An early date for the language of D05 tallies with the high number of early forms of Greek among its readings, see Édouard Delebecque, *Les deux Actes des Apôtres*, EB n.s. 6 (Paris: Gabalda, 1986).

writings of the Church Fathers.[8] It was noted in the Introduction (Chapter 1, §II.1) that these are problematic facts for understanding the transmission history of Luke's writings,[9] and dealing with them has prompted various creative attempts, which usually have the starting presupposition that the text underlying the Alexandrian tradition is the earliest; everything else is derived from it, with D05 being the furthest from it.[10] My conviction is that the direction of travel is wrong, at least for Luke's writings. By changing the starting point to the text transmitted by D05 and observing the facts by travelling in time away from it instead of towards it, things begin to make sense: with its anchoring in Jewish tradition and its critical portrayal of the apostles, Luke's text would have been quickly, but gradually, modified as the Church became separated from its Jewish roots and the apostles became established as infallible leaders. Even while acquiring the form that would eventually be transmitted by ℵ01/B03, it was used for the first translations that were eventually brought into line with what became the standardized text in the West in the fourth century. It would also be referred to by early Church Fathers who had access to it in its changing form. Seeing the situation from this angle also explains why the language of Luke–Acts in D05 is the same as that found in the text shared with ℵ01/B03.

Certainly, reversing the direction of travel involves working against the long-held prejudice against D05. The linguistic studies gathered here do not prove that its text pre-dates the Alexandrian text or the one edited by N-A^{28}/UBS^5, but they do seek to provide factual information that challenges the notion that the current edition is as close to the original of Luke's writings as can be achieved. The hope is that readers will be open to hearing the challenge and recognize the contribution that an approach of discourse analysis can make to investigating the reasons for the variation that exists among the MSS of Luke–Acts and to identifying features of the Greek of Luke's work.

---

[8] In his review of K. and B. Aland, *The Text of the New Testament*, trans. Erroll Rhodes (Grand Rapids, Mass.: Eerdmans/Leiden: Brill, 1987), Daniel Wallace criticizes their dismissal of the versional and patristic evidence for the 'Western' text in favour of the early papyri that attest the Alexandrian text. He points out that they overlook at least 3 early papyri that do not have the Alexandrian text, and more could be added that have been discovered since Wallace wrote his review, 'The Text of the New Testament', *Grace Theological Journal* 9.2 (1988): 279–85.

[9] The terms 'enigmatic' and 'perplexing' are used by Thomas J. Geer, 'The Presence and Significance of Lukanisms in the "Western" Text of Acts', in *New Testament Text and Language*, ed. Stanley E. Porter and Craig A. Evans (The Biblical Seminar 54; Sheffield: SAP, 1997), 50, to refer to the presence of what he, and others, call many 'Lukanisms' in MSS that are traditionally disregarded. His survey takes account only of studies that determine Luke's language on the basis of frequency – how much more troubling, then, is the presence throughout D05 of Lukan language that can be established by acknowledging the flexibility of his usage and the reasons for it.

[10] This is the contention of Barbara Aland, 'Entstehung, Charakter und Herkunft des sog. westlichen Textes untersucht an der Apostelgeschichte', *ETL* 62 (1986): 5–65. She traces the development of the 'Western' text from a hypothetical base text, proposing that D05 was the culmination of the process of alteration.

Bibliography

Books and articles

Aland, B. 'Entstehung, Charakter und Herkunft des sog. westlichen Textes untersucht an der Apostelgeschichte'. *ETL* 62 (1986): 5–65.

Aland, B., K. Aland, J. Karavidopoulos, C. M. Martini and B.M. Metzger (eds). *Novum Testamentum Graece*. 28th edn. Stuttgart: Deutsche Bibelgesellschaft/United Bible Societies, 2013.

Aland, B., K. Aland, J. Karavidopoulos, C. M. Martini and B.M. Metzger (eds). *The Greek New Testament*. 5th edn. Stuttgart: Deutsche Bibelgesellschaft/United Bible Societies, 2014.

Aland, K., and B. Aland. *The Text of the New Testament*. Translated by Erroll Rhodes. Grand Rapids, Mass: Eerdmans/Leiden: Brill, 1987.

Alter, Robert. *The Art of Biblical Narrative*. New York: Basic Books, 2011.

The American and British Committees of the International Greek New Testament Project (eds). *The Gospel According to St. Luke*. 2 vols. Oxford: Clarendon Press, 1984, 1987.

Amphoux, Christian-Bernard, 'Le dernier repas de Jésus. Lc 22, 15–20 et par'. *ETR* 56 (1981): 449–54.

Amphoux, Christian-Bernard, 'Les manuscrits du Nouveau Testament: du Livre à la Parole. *ETR* 67 (1992): 345–57.

Amphoux, Christian-Bernard, 'L'édition savante ancienne des Evangiles'. *Résurrection. Revue de doctrine et d'actualité chrétiennes*, 40 (1992): 13–21.

Applebaum, A. *Judaea in Hellenistic and Roman Times*. Leiden: Brill, 1989.

Armstrong, Karl Leslie. *Dating Acts in its Jewish and Greco-Roman Contexts*. LNTS 637; London: T&T Clark, 2021.

Barc, Bernard. *Les Arpenteurs du Temps. Essais sur l'histoire religieuse de la Judée à la période hellénistique*. Histoire du texte biblique 5. Lausanne: Éditions du Zèbre, 2000.

Barr, James. 'Hebrew, Aramaic and Greek in the Hellenistic Age'. In *The Cambridge History of Judaism*, edited by W. D. Davies and L. Finkelstein, 79–114. Cambridge: Cambridge University Press, 1989.

Barrett, Charles K. *A Critical and Exegetical Commentary on the Acts of the Apostles*. 2 vols. Edinburgh: T&T Clark, 1994, 1998.

Bauer, W. *A Greek–English Lexicon of the New Testament and Other Early Christian Literature*, translated and edited by W. F. Arndt and F. W. Gingrich. Chicago: Chicago University Press, 1957.

Beatrice, P.-F. 'Apollos of Alexandria and the Origins of Jewish-Christian Baptist Encratism'. *ANRW* II 26/2, 1232–75. Berlin: W. de Gruyter, 1995.

Berlin, Adele, and Marc Zvi Brettler (eds). *The Jewish Study Bible*. Oxford: Oxford University Press, 2004.

Black, Matthew. *An Aramaic Approach to the Gospels and Acts*. Oxford: Clarendon Press, 1967.

Black, David Alan, and Benjamin L. Merkle (eds). *Linguistics and New Testament Greek*. Grand Rapids, MI: Baker Academic, 2020.

Blass, Friedrich W., Albert Debrunner and Friedrich Rehkopf. *Grammatik des neutestamentlichen Griechisch*. 18th edn. 1896. Göttingen: Vandenhoeck & Ruprecht, 2001.
Blood, D. L., and D. E. Blood. 'Overview of Acts'. *Notes on Translation* 74 (1979): 2–36.
Boismard, M.-E. and A. Lamouille, *Le texte occidental des Actes des Apôtres: Reconstitution et réhabilitation*. 2 vols. Paris: Éditions Recherche sur les Civilisations. 1984.
Botha, J. E. 'Style in the New Testament: The Need for Serious Reconsideration'. *JSNT* 43 (1991): 71–87.
Bruce, F. F. *Commentary on the Book of Acts. The English Text with Introduction, Exposition and Notes*. London: Marshall, Morgan and Scott, 1954.
Buth, Randall. 'Evaluating Luke's Unnatural Greek: A Look at his Connectives'. In *Discourse Studies and Biblical Interpretation: A Festschrift in Honor of Stephen H. Levinsohn*, edited by Steven E. Runge, 335–69. Bellingham WA: Lexham Press, 2011.
Caragounis, Chrys. *The Development of Greek and the New Testament. Morphology, Syntax, Phonology, and Textual Transmission*. Grand Rapids: Baker Academic, 2006.
Chilton, Bruce. *The Glory of Israel: The Theology and Provenience of the Isaiah Targum*. JSOT Supplement, 23; Sheffield: JSOT Press, 1982.
Chilton, Bruce. *A Galilean Rabbi and His Bible*. London: SPCK, 1984.
Chilton, Bruce (ed.). *The Isaiah Targum: Introduction, Translation, Apparatus, Notes*. The Aramaic Bible, II. Edinburgh: T&T Clark, 1987.
Clivaz, Claire. *L'Ange et la Sueur de Sang (Lc 22,43–44): Ou Comment On Pourrait Bien Encore Écrire l'Histoire*. Biblical Tools and Studies 07. Leuven: Peeters, 2007.
Clivaz, Claire, and G. V. Allen (eds). *Ancient Manuscripts and Virtual Research Environements*, Classics@ 18 (2021).
Comrie, B. 'Linguistic Typology'. In *Linguistics: The Cambridge Survey*. I, *Linguistic Theory: Foundations*, edited by F. J. Newmeyer, 447–61. Cambridge: Cambridge University Press, 1988.
Davison, M. E. 'New Testament Greek Word Order'. *Literary and Linguistic Computing* 4 (1989): 19–28.
Dawson, Zachary K. 'The Textual Traditions of Acts: What Has Discourse Analysis Contributed?' *Bib* 100.4 (2019): 544–67.
Delebecque, Édouard. *Les deux Actes des Apôtres* (EB n.s. 6. Paris: Gabalda, 1986).
Downing, P. and M. Noonan (eds), *Word Order in Discourse*. Typological Studies in Language, 30. Amsterdam/Philadelphia: John Benjamins, 1995.
Dunn, James D. G. *The Partings of the Ways Between Christianity and Judaism and their Significance for the Character of Christianity*. London: SCM Press, 1991.
Dunn, James D. G. *The Acts of the Apostles*. London: Epworth Press, 1996.
Dupont, Jacques. *Nouvelles Études sur les Actes des Apôtres*. Lectio Divina 118. Paris: Éditions du Cerf, 1994.
Elliott, J.K. 'Κηφᾶς: Σίμων Πέτρος: ὁ Πέτρος: An Examination of New Testament Usage'. *NovT* 14 (1972): 241–56.
Elliott, J.K. 'The Text of Acts in the Light of Two Recent Studies'. *NTS* 34 (1988): 250–8.
Elliott, J.K. *Essays and Studies in New Testament Textual Criticism*. Estudios de Filología Neotestamentaria 3. Cordoba: Ediciones El Almendro, 1992.
Elliott, J.K. 'The Position of the Verb in Mark with Special Reference to Chapter 13'. *NovT* 38 (1996): 136–44.
Epp, Eldon J. *The Theological Tendency of Codex Bezae Cantabrigiensis in Acts*. Cambridge: Cambridge University Press, 1966.
Evans, Craig A. *Luke*. New International Biblical Commentary. Peabody, Mass./Carlisle, UK: Hendrickson Publishers/Paternoster Press, 1995.

Frankel, E. and B.P. Teutsch (eds), *The Encylopaedia of Jewish Symbols*. Northvale, N.J.: Jason Aronson, 1995.
García Martínez, F. 'Pseudo Jubilees fragment from Cave 4'. In *The Sacrifice of Isaac: The Aqedah (Genesis 22) and its Interpretations*, edited by E. Noort and E. Tigchelaar. Themes in Biblical Narrative 4. Leiden: Brill, 2002.
Geer, Thomas, J. 'The Presence and Significance of Lukanisms in the "Western" Text of Acts'. In *New Testament Text and Language*, edited by Stanley E. Porter and Craig A. Evans, 34–51. The Biblical Seminar 54. Sheffield: SAP, 1997.
Gildersleeve, Basil L. 'On the Article with Proper Names'. *AJP* 11 (1890): 483–7.
Gildersleeve, Basil L. *Syntax of Classical Greek from Homer to Demosthenes*. 2 vols. New York: American Book Company, 1900–11.
Gildersleeve, Basil L. 'Problems in Greek Syntax: II. The Article'. *AJP* 23 (1902): 1–27.
Ginzberg, Louis. *The Legends of the Jews*, 7 vols. 11th edn. Translated by Henrietta Szold and Paul Radin. 1909–38. Baltimore: Johns Hopkins University Press, 1998.
Givón, T. *Syntax*. Amsterdam/Philadelphia: John Benjamins, 1984.
Givón, T. 'The Pragmatics of Word Order: Predictability, Importance and Attention'. In *Studies in Syntactic Typology*, edited by M. Hammonds, E.A. Moravcsik and J.R. Wirth, 243–84. Amsterdam/Philadelphia: John Benjamins, 1988.
Greenberg, J.H. 'Some Universals of Grammar with Particular Reference to the Order of Meaningful Elements'. In *Universals of Language*, edited by J.H. Greenberg, 73–113. 2nd edn. 1963. Cambridge, MA: MIT Press, 1966.
Gregory, Andrew. *The Reception of Luke and Acts in the Period Before Irenaeus: Looking for Luke in the Second Century*. WUNT II/169. Tübingen: Mohr Siebeck, 2003.
Grimes, J.E. *The Thread of Discourse*. Berlin: DeGruyter, 1975.
Harris, J. Rendel. *Codex Bezae: A Study of the So-called Western Text of the New Testament* Cambridge: Cambridge University Press, 1891.
Heimerdinger, Jenny (Read-), 'La foi de l'eunuque éthiopien: le problème textuel d'Actes 8/37'. *ETR* 63 (1988): 521–8.
Heimerdinger, Jenny (Read-), 'The Seven Steps of Codex Bezae: A Prophetic Interpretation of Acts 12'. In *Codex Bezae. Studies from the Lunel Colloquium June 1994*, edited by D. C. Parker and C.-B. Amphoux, 303–10. Leiden: Brill, 1996.
Hemer, Colin J. *The Book of Acts in the Setting of Hellenistic History*, edited by Conrad H. Gempf. Tübingen: J. C. B. Mohr, 1989.
Hengel, Martin. *The Hellenization of Judaea in the First Century*, translated by J. Bowden. London: SCM Press, 1989.
Hess, H. H. 'Dynamics of the Greek Noun Phrase in Mark'. *Optat* 4 (1990): 353–69.
Holtz, Louis. 'L'écriture latine du Codex Bezae'. In *Codex Bezae: Studies from the Lunel Colloquium, June 1994*, edited by David C. Parker and Christian-Bernard Amphoux, 14–55. Leiden: Brill, 1996.
Hull, J. H. E. *The Holy Spirit in the Acts of the Apostles*. London: Lutterworth Press, 1967.
Ilan, Tal. *Lexicon of Jewish Names in Late Antiquity: Part I: Palestine 330 BCE –200 CE*. TSAJ 91; Mohr Siebeck, 2002.
Johnson, Luke Timothy. *The Acts of the Apostles*. Sacra Pagina 5; Collegeville, Minnesota: The Liturgical Press, 1995.
King, Daniel. *The Article in Post-Classical Greek*. Dallas: SIL International, 2019.
Kirk, A. *Word Order and Information Structure in New Testament Greek*. Doctoral Thesis. LOT 311. 2012
Kittel, G. and G. Friedrich (eds), *Theological Dictionary of the New Testament*. Translated by G. W. Bromiley. Grand Rapids, MI: Eerdmans, 1964–76.

Kwong, Ivan Shing Chung. *The Word Order of the Gospel of Luke: Its Foregrounded Messages*. LNTS 298. London: T&T Clark, 2005.
Larsen, Iver. 'Word Order and Relative Prominence in New Testament Greek'. *Notes on Translation* 15, no. 2 (2001): 13–27.
Le Boulluec, A., and P. Sandevoir. 'L'Exode'. *La Bible d'Alexandrie*, II, edited by M. Harl. Paris: Éditions du Cerf, 1989.
Le Déaut, Roger. *The Message of the New Testament and the Aramaic Bible (Targum)*. Translated by S. F. Miletic. Rome: Biblical Institute Press, 1982.
Levinsohn, Stephen H. *Textual Connections in Acts*. Scholars Press, 1987.
Levinsohn, Stephen H. *Discourse Features of New Testament Greek: A Coursebook on the Information Structure of New Testament Greek*. 2nd edn. 1992. Dallas: Summer Institute of Linguistics, 2000.
Levison, John. *The Spirit in First Century Judaism*. Arbeiten Zur Geschichte Des Antiken Judentums und Des Urchristentums, 29. Leiden: Brill, 1997.
Lifschitz, B. 'L'héllenisation des juifs de la Palestine'. *Revue Biblique* 72 (1965): 520–38.
Louw, J. P. and E. A. Nida. *Greek–English Lexicon of the New Testament Based on Semantic Domains*. 2 vols. New York: United Bible Societies, 1988.
Lyons, Christopher. *Definiteness*. Cambridge: Cambridge University Press, 1999.
Marshall, I. Howard. *The Gospel of Luke*. NIGTC; Exeter: Paternoster Press, 1978.
Marshall, I. Howard. *The Acts of the Apostles*. TNTC. Leicester, UK: IVP, 1980.
Menzies, R. P. *The Development of Early Christian Pneumatology with Special Reference to Luke-Acts*. JSNT Supplement, 54. Sheffield: JSOT Press, 1991.
Merkle, Benjamin L. 'Where do we Go from Here?'. In *Linguistics and New Testament Greek,* edited by David Alan Black and Benjamin L. Merkle, 247–60. Grand Rapids, MI: Baker Academic, 2020.
Metzger, Bruce M. *A Textual Commentary on the Greek New Testament*. 2nd edn. 1975. London/New York: United Bible Societies, 1994.
Moule, C. F. D. *An Idiom Book of New Testament Greek*. 2nd edn. 1953. Reprint, Cambridge: Cambridge University Press, 1975.
Moulton, J. H. *A Grammar of New Testament Greek*. Vol. 2. Edinburgh: T&T Clark, 1929.
Nestle, E. *Novi Testamenti Graeci. Supplementum editionibus de Gerbhardt Tischendorfianis. Codicis Cantabrigiensis Collatio*. Leipzig: Tauchnitz, 1896.
Palmer, Micheál. 'How do We Know a Phrase is a Phrase? A Plea for Procedural Clarity in the Application of Linguistics to Biblical Greek'. In *Biblical Greek Language and Linguistics*, edited by Stanley E. Porter and D. A. Carson, 152–86. LNTS. London: Bloomsbury Publishing, 1993.
Parker, David C. *Codex Bezae: An Early Christian Manuscript and its Text*. Cambridge: Cambridge University Press, 1992.
Parker, David C. and Christian-Bernard Amphoux (eds). *Codex Bezae: Studies from the Lunel Colloquium, June 1994*. Leiden: Brill, 1996.
Parker, David C. 'Codex Bezae'. In *Cambridge University Library. The Great Collections*, edited by Peter Fox, 33–43. Cambridge: Cambridge University Press, 1998.
Payne, D. F. 'Semitisms in the Book of Acts'. In *Apostolic History and the Gospel*, edited by W. W. Gasque and R. P. Martin, 134–50. Exeter: Paternoster, 1970.
Pike, Kenneth L. *Language in Relation to a Unified Theory of the Structure of Human Behavior*. 1967. Reprint, The Hague: Mouton, 2015.
Pinchard, Laurent. 'The Greek Text of the Gospel of Matthew: A Renewed Text-Critical Approach with a Focus on the Issue of Harmonisations in Codex Bezae'. unpublished Ph.D. diss., University of Wales Trinity Saint David, Lampeter, 2015.

Porter, Stanley E. 'The Adjectival Attributive Genitive in the New Testament: A Grammatical Study'. *Trinity Journal* 4 (1987): 3–17.

Porter, Stanley E. *Idioms of New Testament Greek*. Biblical Languages: Greek 2. Sheffield: JSOT Press, 1992.

Porter, Stanley E. 'Word Order and Clause Structure in New Testament Greek: An Unexplored Area of Greek Linguistics, Using Philippians as a Test Case'. *FilNeo* 6 (1993): 177–206.

Read-Heimerdinger, Jenny. 'Acts 8:37: A Textual and Exegetical Study'. *The Bulletin of the Institute for Reformation Biblical Studies* 2 (1991): 8–13.

Read-Heimerdinger, Jenny. 'La tradition targumique et le Codex de Bèze: Ac 1:15–26'. In *La Bíblia i el Mediterrani*, edited by Agusti Borrell, Alfonso De la Fuente and Armand Puig. 2 vols. II, 171–80. Associació Bíblica de Catalunya: L'Abadia de Montserrat, 1997.

Read-Heimerdinger, Jenny. 'Barnabas in Acts: A Study of his Role in the Text of Codex Bezae'. JSNT 72 (1998): 23–66.

Read-Heimerdinger, Jenny. 'Where is Emmaus?'. In *The Early Text of the Gospels and Acts*, edited by D. J. Taylor, 229–44. Birmingham, Birmingham University Press, 1998.

Read-Heimerdinger, Jenny. *The Bezan Text of Acts: A Contribution of Discourse Analysis to Textual Criticism*. JSNTSup. 236; Sheffield: SAP, 2002.

Read-Heimerdinger, Jenny. 'The Apostles in the Bezan Text of Acts'. In *Apostelgeschichte als Kirchengeschichte*, edited by T. Nicklas and M. Tilly, 263–80. BZNW 122. Berlin/New York: Walter de Gruyter, 2003.

Read-Heimerdinger, Jenny. 'Luke's Use of ὡς and ὡσεί: Comparison and Correspondence as a Means to Convey his Message'. In *Grammatica Intellectio Scripturae: Saggi filologici di Greco biblico in onore di padre Lino Cignelli, OFM*, edited by R. Pierri, 251–74. Studium Biblicum Franciscanum, Analecta 68. Jerusalem: Franciscan Printing Press, 2006.

Read-Heimerdinger, Jenny. 'The Tracking of Participants with the Third Person Pronoun: A Study of the Text of Acts'. *Revista Catalana de Teologia* 31 (2006): 439–55.

Read-Heimerdinger, Jenny. 'Paul, a Fallible Apostle: Luke's Evaluation of Paul's Mission in the Manuscript Tradition of Acts'. Unpublished post-doctoral Licentiate in Divinity thesis, University of Wales, Lampeter, 2010.

Read-Heimerdinger, Jenny. 'The Use of the Article before Names of Places: Patterns of Use in the Book of Acts'. In *Discourse Studies and Biblical Interpretation: A Festschrift in Honor of Stephen H. Levinsohn*, edited by Steven E. Runge, 371–402. Bellingham WA: Lexham Press, 2011.

Read-Heimerdinger, Jenny. 'Eclecticism and the Book of Acts'. In *Texts and Traditions. Essays in Honour of J. K. Elliott*, edited by Peter Doble and J. Kloha, 71–92. Leiden: Brill, 2014.

Read-Heimerdinger, Jenny. 'The Interface between Rhetorical Analysis and Discourse Analysis'. In *Studi del Terzo Convegno RBS*, edited by R. Meynet and J. Oniszczuk, 325–46. Rome: GBPress, 2015.

Read-Heimerdinger, Jenny. 'L'analyse du discours au service de la critique textuelle: illustrations à partir du livre des Actes des Apôtres'. In *Actes du Colloque Philologie du Nouveau Testament 2014*, edited by Christian-Bernard Amphoux and Jacqueline Assaël, 261–82. Aix-en-Provence: Presses Universitaires de Provence, 2018.

Read-Heimerdinger, Jenny. 'The Function of the Article with Proper Names: The New Testament Book of Acts as a Case Study'. In *The Article in Post-Classical Greek*, edited by D. King, 153–85. Dallas: SIL International, 2019.

Read-Heimerdinger, Jenny. 'Discourse Analysis of the Book of Acts'. In *Discourse Analysis of the New Testament Writings*, edited by Todd A. Scacewater, 159–92. Dallas: Fontes Press, 2020.

(Read-)Heimerdinger, Jenny, and Stephen H. Levinsohn. 'The Use of the Definite Article before Names of People in the Greek Text of Acts with Particular Reference to Codex Bezae'. *FilNeo* 5 (1992):15–44.

Read-Heimerdinger, Jenny, and Josep Rius-Camps, 'Tracing the Readings of Codex Bezae in the Papyri of Acts'. In *Reading New Testament Papyri in Context. Lire les papyrus du Nouveau Testament dans leur context*, edited by Claire Clivaz and J. Zumstein, 307–38. Leuven: Peeters, 2011.

Read-Heimerdinger, Jenny, and Josep Rius-Camps, (eds). *Luke's Demonstration to Theophilus: The Gospel and Acts of the Apostles according to Codex Bezae*. English expanded edn. London: Bloomsbury, 2013.

Rius-Camps, Josep. 'The Gradual Awakening of Paul's Awareness of his Mission to the Gentiles'. In *Apostelgeschichte als Kirchengeschichte. Text, Traditionen und antike Auslegungen*, edited by T. Nicklas and M. Tilly. BZNW 122; Berlin: De Gruyter, 2003.

Rius-Camps, Josep, and Jenny Read-Heimerdinger. 'Emmaous or Oulammaous? Luke's Use of the Jewish Scriptures in the Text of Luke 24 in Codex Bezae'. *Revista Catalana de Teologia* 27 (2002): 23–42.

Rius-Camps, Josep, and Jenny Read-Heimerdinger. *The Message of Acts in Codex Bezae: A Comparison with the Alexandrian Tradition*. 4 vols. JSNTSup 257/LNTS 302, 365, 415. London: T&T Clark, 2004–9.

Robertson, A. T. *A Grammar of the Greek New Testament in the Light of Historical Research*, 4th edn. 1914. Nashville, Tenn.: Broadman, 1934.

Ropes, J. H. *The Text of Acts*, III. In *The Beginnings of Christianity*, Part I *The Acts of the Apostles*, edited by F.J. Foakes-Jackson and K. Lake. London: Macmillan, 1926.

Runge, Steven E. *Discourse Grammar of the Greek New Testament: A Practical Introduction for Teaching and Exegesis*. Lexham Bible Reference Series. Peabody, Mass.: Hendrickson Publishers, 2010.

Sacks, Jonathan. *Crisis and Covenant*. Manchester: Manchester University Press, 1992.

Sansone, David. 'Towards a New Doctrine of the Article: Some Observations on the Definite Article in Plato'. *CP* 88 (1993): 191–205.

Schürer, Emil. *The History of the Jewish People in the Age of Jesus-Christ 175 BC – AD 135*, translated, revised and edited by G. Vermes, F. Millar, M. Black. Edinburgh: T&T Clark, 1987.

Scrivener, F.H. *Bezae Codex Cantabrigiensis*, 1864. Reprinted, Pittsburgh, Penn.: Pickwick Press, 1978.

Silva, M. 'Bilingualism and the Character of Palestinian Greek'. *Bib.* 61 (1980): 198–219.

Smith, Catherine and Matthew Brook O'Donnell. 'Computer-Aided Linguistic Analysis for a Single Manuscript Witness: Preparing to Map the OpenText.org Annotation. In *The Language and Literature of the New Testament Essays in Honor of Stanley E. Porter's 60th Birthday*, edited by Lois K. Fuller Dow, Craig A. Evans, Andrew W. Pitts, 106–37. Leiden: Brill, 2017.

Strange, William A. *The Problem of the Text of Acts*. SNTS Monograph Series 71. Cambridge: Cambridge University Press, 1992.

Swanson, Reuben. *New Testament Greek Manuscripts: Variant Readings Arranged in Horizontal Lines Against Codex Vaticanus. Luke*. Carol Stream, IL: Tyndale House Publishers, 1995.

Swanson, Reuben. *New Testament Greek Manuscripts: Variant Readings Arranged in Horizontal Lines against Codex Vaticanus. The Acts of the Apostles.* Sheffield: SAP, 1998.

Turner, C. H. 'Notes on Marcan Usage'. *JTS* 29 (1928): 346–61. Reprinted in *The Language and Style of the Gospel of Mark: An Edition of C.H. Turner's 'Notes on Marcan Usage' Together with Comparable Studies,* edited by J.K. Elliott, 120–36. Leiden: Brill, 1993.

Turner, M. M. B. *Power from on High: The Spirit in Israel's Restoration and Witness in Luke-Acts.* Sheffield: SAP, 1996.

Turner, M. M. B. 'The Work of the Holy Spirit in Luke-Acts'. *Word & World* 23 (2003): 146–53.

Turner, Nigel. *A Grammar of New Testament Greek.* III, *Syntax,* edited by J. H. Moulton. Edinburgh: T&T Clark, 1963.

Wallace, Daniel B. 'The Text of the New Testament'. *Grace Theological Journal* 9.2 (1988): 279–85.

Wallace, Daniel B. *Greek Grammar beyond the Basics.* Grand Rapids, MI: Zondervan Publishing House, 1996.

Walsh, Jerome T. *Style and Structure in Biblical Hebrew Narrative.* Collegeville, MN: The Liturgical Press, 2001.

Wenham, David, and Steve Walton. *Exploring the New Testament* I, *Introducing the Gospels and Acts.* London: SPCK, 2001.

Wilcox, Max. *The Semitisms of Acts.* Oxford: Clarendon Press, 1965.

Wilcox, Max. 'Luke and the Bezan Text of Acts'. In *Les Actes des Apôtres: tradition, rédaction, théologie,* edited by J. Kremer, 447–55. Gembloux: Leuven University Press, 1979.

Winer, G. B. *A Treatise on the Grammar of New Testament Greek.* Translated by W. F. Moulton. 1882. Reprint, Eugene, OR: Wipf and Stock 2001.

Witherington, Ben. *The Acts of the Apostles. A Socio-Rhetorical Commentary* (Carlisle: Paternoster, 1998.

Yoder, James D. 'Semitisms in Codex Bezae'. *JBL* 78 (1959): 317–21.

Zerwick, M. *Biblical Greek.* Translated, revised and edited by J. Smith. Rome: Scripta Pontificii Instituti Biblici, 1963.

Websites

Barnabas, *Epistle*:
http://www.earlychristianwritings.com/text/barnabas-lightfoot.html

Codex Bezae:
https://cudl.lib.cam.ac.uk/view/MS-NN-00002-00041/1

Codex Vaticanus :
https://digi.vatlib.it/view/MSS_Vat.gr.1209
http://www.truebiblecode.com/codexvaticanus.html

Eusebius, *Historia Ecclesiae:*
https://www.newadvent.org/fathers/250105.htm.

Larry Hurtado:
https://larryhurtado.wordpress.com/2011/04/13/rethinking-the-text-of-acts/
https://larryhurtado.wordpress.com/2017/12/23/editio-ctitica-maior-acts-volumes/
https://larryhurtado.wordpress.com/2018/11/28/silent-reading-in-roman-antiquity/

Jewish Encyclopedia:
https://www.jewishencyclopedia.com/articles/7833-holy-spirit

Maurice A. Robinson:
New Testament Textual Criticism: The Case for Byzantine Priority
http://rosetta.reltech.org/TC/v06/Robinson2001.html

Steven E. Runge:
http://rblnewsletter.blogspot.com/2008/

Index of scriptural references

Hebrew Bible/Old Testament

Genesis
22.1–19	196
32.6	202
33.1	202
41.46	203
43.34	204

Exodus
32	199

Numbers
1.4–16	201
4.3	203

Deuteronomy
18.15	193, 194
18.18	193

1 Samuel
30.17	202 n.38

2 Samuel
5.4	203

1 Kings
6.1	204 n.44

2 Kings
4.42–44	204

Isaiah
14.12	195

Jeremiah
15.8	199

Ezekiel
1.1	203

Deutero-Canonical Books

1 Maccabees
5.29	192 n.14

Intertestamental Literature

Tobit
1.3–11	197
2.10	197
3.17	197
11.7–13	197

New Testament

Matthew
27.45–46	199

Mark
9.2	199
15.33–34	199

Luke
1.1–4	209
1.5	182
1.13	183
1.26	185, 205
1.27	182
1.31	183
1.32	183, 203
1.35	183
1.36	183, 205
1.39	205
1.56	189, 205
1.57	205
1.59	183
1.60	183
1.61	183
1.69	203
1.76	183
2.4	183
2.21	185
2.23	183
2.25	182
2.32	192 n.15
2.39	185
3.4	188, 191
3.22	188, 192, 195

Index of Scriptural References

Luke (continued)		20.4	183
13.23	188, 189, 190, 191, 203	21.35	188, 191
		21.37	183
4	180	22.3	183
4.3	180	22.25	183
4.4	180	22.26	188, 193
4.6	180	22.27	188, 189, 193
4.8	180	22.30	205
4.9	180	22.31	188, 191
4.12	180	22.41	190, 197, 198
5.27	185	22.44	189, 196, 196 n.22
6.10	189, 196	22.47	185
6.13	183, 185	22.52	188, 191
6.14	185	22.54–62	202
6.15	185	22.59	190, 198, 202
6.22	188, 193	22.61	186 n.12
6.40	188, 194	23.14	188, 193
6.46	183	23.33	183
7.11	183	23.44	190, 198, 199
8.2	183	23.44–45	202
8.41	182	23.50	182
8.42	189 205	24	185
9.1	205	24.1	199
9.10	185	24.11	190, 194
9.11	201, 204	24.13	184, 185
9.12	201	24.17	178, 179
9.14	189, 190, 198, 201, 203, 204	24.18	179, 184, 185
		24.19	179
9.23–27	198	24.44	189, 191
9.28	190, 198	24.47	189, 192, 192 n.14
9.43	205		
9.54	189, 191	John	
10.3	188, 195	19	199 n.28
10.18	188, 191, 192, 195	19.14	199, 199 n.30
10.27	188, 191, 192	20.1	199 n.28
10.38	182	20.19	199 n.28
10.39	183	20.26	199 n.28
11.2	189, 191, 192		
11.4	189, 191, 192	Acts	
11.36	189, 191, 192	1–5	217, 218
11.44	189, 196	1–12	217, 218
12.27	188, 191	1	217, 218
15.19	183, 188, 191, 192	1.1–2	209
15.21	183	1.1–11	218 n.16
16.20	182	1.1–14	221
17.6	188, 195	1.1–5.42	221
18.11	188, 189, 194	1.8	219
18.17	188, 191	1.10	186 n.12
19.2	185	1.12	183
19.29	183	1.12–19.20	219 n.16

Index of Scriptural References

1.15	221 n.24, 188, 200, 201	8.9	182
1.15–26	221	8.10	183
1.19	183	8.26	178, 199, 199 n.31
1.23	183, 184	8.32	188, 191
2.1	221 n.24	9.10	182, 213
2.1–47	221	9.11	182, 183
2.3	190, 194	9.12	182
2.5	214 n.11	9.18	189, 197
2.15	188, 191	9.31	218 n.16, 199 n.28
2.41	190, 198, 199, 201	9.33	182
3.1	199, 221 n.24	9.36	182
3.1–4.35	221	10.1	182, 183
3.1–10	201	10.3	190, 192, 193, 198 n.27, 199
3.11	183	10.5	184
3.12	188, 191	10.9	198, 199
3.22	188, 191, 192, 193, 194	10.11	189, 195, 196
		10.13–16	202 n.37
4.3	201	10.18	184
4.4	188, 199, 201	10.23	212
4.5	213	10.26	189, 193
4.36	184, 222 n.23	10.28–29	216 n.14
4.36–37	218 n.15	10.30	192 n.17, 193
4.36–5.42	221	10.32	184
5.1	182	10.32–41	216 n.14
5.1–11	218 n.15	10.47	189, 191
5.6	202, 218 n.15, 202	11.5	188, 195, 196
5.7	188, 201, 202, 213	11.12	179
5.9	202 n.37	11.13	184
5.10	218 n.15, 202	11.14	179
5.20	179	11.17	188, 191, 192
5.34	182	11.27	221 n.24
5.36	188, 201, 202	11.27–30	221
6–12	217, 218	11.28	182
6.1	218, 221 n.24	12	217
6.1–7	218	12.1	221 n.24
6.1–8.1	221	12.1–2	211
6.7	218, 218 n.16, 218 n.17	12.1–25	221
		12.7	211
6.8	212	12.8	179
6.15	190, 194	12.12	184
7.1	181	12.13	182
7.37	189, 190, 192, 193, 194	12.13–16	202 n.37
		12.14	180, 181
7.48	189, 191	12.15	180, 181
7.51	189, 191	12.24	218 n.16
7.58	183	12.25	184
8–9	217	13–28	217, 218, 219, 220
8.1–11.26	221	13	217, 218
8.1	213, 221 n.24	13.1	185, 213, 217

Acts (continued)

13.1–14.27	221
13.1–18.23	220, 221
13.6	184, 185
13.8	184
13.19	204 n.43
13.20	189, 203, 204, 204 n.43
13.33	189, 191
14.1	213
14.12	183
14.28	221 n.24
14.28–15.41	221
15	213, 217
15.3–4	213
15.5	213
15.6	213
15.7	213
15.22	183
15.36	212, 221 n.24
15.37	185
15.37–38	212
16.1	182
16.1–18.23	221
16.3	211
16.5	218 n.16
16.9	191, 193
16.14	182
16.16	213
16.38	181
17.14	192 n.14
17.15	189, 193
17.16	212
17.28	189, 191
17.34	185
18.1	214
18.2	182
18.4	220 n.23
18.7	182
18.14	178
18.22	220
18.23	220
18.24	182, 220
18.24	220
18.24–28	200, 220
18.24–19.40	221
18.24–28.31	220, 221
19	218
19.1	219, 219 n.21
19.7	190, 198, 199
19.20	218 n.16, 219
19.21	219 n.16
19.21–28.31	219 n.16
19.23	213
19.24	185
19.34	189, 190, 192
20	218
20.1–21.24	221
20.3	219
20.7	199 n.28
20.9	182
20.38	219, 219 n.19
21	218
21.1	219 n.19
21.4	219
21.10	182
21.15–27.1	221
21.26	219, 219 n.20
21.27	219 n.20
22.5	188, 191
22.6	198, 199
27.1	182
27.2–28.31	221
27.8	183
27.14	183
27.16	183
28	218
28.1	183
28.7	182
28.30–31	218 n.16

Josephus
Antiquities

14.65	199

Early Jewish and Christian Literature
Epistle of Barnabas

15	199 n.28

Rabbinic Writings

m. Sanh. 1.6	200 n.34
b. Sanh. 17a	200 n.34

Qumran

IQS 6.3	200 n.34
IQsa[b] 22	200 n.34

Printed in the USA
CPSIA information can be obtained
at www.ICGtesting.com
LVHW011626120724
785347LV00001B/53